THE NEUROPSYCHOLOGY
OF
MEMORY

Translated from the Russian by
Dr. Basil Haigh

THE NEUROPSYCHOLOGY

OF

MEMORY

ALEXANDER R. LURIA

PROFESSOR OF PSYCHOLOGY
MOSCOW UNIVERSITY

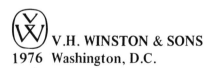

V.H. WINSTON & SONS
1976 Washington, D.C.

A HALSTED PRESS BOOK

JOHN WILEY & SONS
New York   Toronto   London   Sydney

V. H. Winston & Sons, a Division of Scripta Technica, Inc.,
Publishers
1511 K St. N.W., Washington, D.C. 20005

Distributed solely by Halsted Press, a Division of John Wiley
& Sons, Inc.

Library of Congress Cataloging in Publication Data

Luria, Alexander Romanovich, 1902–
    The neuropsychology of memory.

    An English-language translation of Нейропсихология
памяти comprising two volumes published by
Педагогика in the USSR, the first in 1974 and the
second in 1976.
    Includes bibliographical references and indexes.
    1. Memory, Disorders of.   2. Brain—Diseases.
3. Memory—Ability testing.   I. Title.
BF376.L8413   616.8'523   76–10186
ISBN 0-470-15107-2

Composition by Marie A. Maddalena, Scripta Technica, Inc.

Contents

Part Two

Introducing Neuropsychology of Memory

BY KARL H. PRIBRAM

This volume by Professor Alexander Romanovich Luria reporting his classical studies on brain function in the organization of memory is a most welcome addition to the existing Luriana. Luria's books, beginning with his studies on psychological conflict, through his earlier volumes on 'clinical neuropsychology to the most recent *Mind of a Mnemonist* and *Working Brain* have seriously influenced several generations of students. This latest addition gives every promise of continuing this influence.

What makes Luria's contributions so telling? First, of course, is the rich clinical material he describes. His data deal with man, with the human condition when brain illnesses strike. In this sense Luria's work is a direct extension of 19th Century neurology—a neurology which, in the space of scarcely a hundred years, brought intellect to brain and transferred emotion from viscus to nerve.

In another sense, Luria's studies are also an extension of 19th Century neurology. His observations are painstakingly detailed. Case after case is carefully reported and the import of his findings is clearly derived. But at the same time the examinations are simple, direct, and easy to repeat. Quantitative results, controls, experimental analyses of the behaviors used as indicators in the tests—these, as Luria once chided me when he observed my labors, take too long to make them clinically applicable and, in his opinion, confuse rather than enlighten. Luria's data must, therefore, be taken for what they are: the observations of a trained mind which has gathered wisdom from dedicated service to understanding the relationship between brain and mind—the neuropsychological process.

One of Luria's outstanding contributions is that he brings to these rather simple and direct clinical observations results obtained in relevant related disciplines. He was the first to use linguistic insights at the bedside; he has consistently applied the knowledge gained in primate experimental neuropsychology to his studies of the human brain. His observations are thus placed within the context of current knowledge, thereby providing the sophisticated reader with an unusual blend of 19th and 20th Century neuropsychology which is often refreshing, sometimes disconcerting.

This latest volume on brain and memory continues Luria's contributions in this tradition. One or more of a straightforward short battery of tests is given, where feasible, to a large number of subjects with a variety of brain lesions. The results are reported in terms of the locus of the lesion and its extent. Insights into the organization of memory are derived in part from these data and in part from the experimental literature on memory mechanisms.

Luria cautions the reader that his tests are for the most part verbal and thus tap largely conscious mnemonic processes. Still, there is remarkable convergence between his major finding and that obtained in my primate laboratory experiments using instrumental techniques. Two major categories of memory mechanisms can be discerned, and these are orthogonal to the more usual categorization along a short-term to long-term dimension. I have called these new categories (modality)-specific and contextual (Pribram, 1969); Luria also uses the term modality-specific and describes the contextual amnesias most often as showing "disintegration" of the memory process. In both nonhuman and human primates, the modality-specific memory disturbances are related to lesions of the brain's outer convexity, while the contextual amnesias result from damage to its frontolimbic core.

There are, of course, differences in disturbance within these major categories, differences which can be related to anatomical distinctions among brain structures. Here the laboratory analysis has the advantage because more precise and restricted resections can be made and verified. But Luria is not intimidated by the difficulties of localization which his clinical material poses. He separates patients with more or less restricted effects of lesions in a locus from those who show (by radiographic, neurological, and laboratory procedures) more massive effects, and proceeds with his analysis on the basis of this separation. A major contribution is this use of the more massively damaged patients, showing that a great deal about *local* pathology can be learned from them. Luria reasons that diaschesis dissects out the involved system and thus displays it to advantage while at the same time the more global impairment prevents the patient from using compensatory mechanisms to cover up his deficit.

Keeping such guideposts as these in mind, Luria's colleagues and students can, as heretofore, profit once again from his extensive experience in the neuropsychological clinic by perusing the detailed reports he has made in this volume on memory disturbances due to brain lesions.

For sheer wealth of material and insight, *The Neuropsychology of Memory* is unmatched and is likely to remain so for a long time.

Karl H. Pribram
Stanford University
February 1976

Preface to the Russian-Language Edition

This book describes the first results of research into the neuropsychology of memory undertaken by the author and his colleagues in the last seven years.

It seeks to describe the chief forms of memory disturbances associated with local brain lesions and to shed light on the psychophysiological bases of forgetting—the most common of all symptoms found in patients with brain lesions.

The author hopes that the detailed analysis of these two problems will help to improve the diagnosis of local brain lesions and also to solve some important problems concerned with the structure of human mnemonic activity and with the nature of forgetting. The general review of the mechanisms of memory disturbance is followed by descriptions of groups of patients with memory disturbances which contain an analysis of relationships between memory disorders and disturbances of consciousness.

Accordingly, this book can be regarded as a continuation of the analysis of neuropsychological symptoms developed in patients with local brain lesions presented by the author in his earlier books.[1]

The author takes this opportunity to express his sincere gratitude to the colleagues who have worked with him on the problem discussed in this book

[1] See *Higher Cortical Functions in Man* (1962, 1969; English translation, 1966), *The Human Brain and Psychological Processes* (Vol. I, 1963; English translation, 1966; Vol. II, 1970), *Traumatic Aphasia* (1947; English translation, 1970), and *Fundamentals of Neuropsychology* (1973).

and who prepared dissertations on certain aspects of the neuropsychology of memory. The work of N. A. Akbarova, N. K. Kiyashchenko, T. A. Karaseva, M. Klimkovskii, L. T. Popova, Pham Ming Hac, G. Chaltykyan, and M. A. Marzaganova, as well as joint investigations with A. N. Konovalov and A. Ya. Podgornaya (1970), have yielded valuable material for the analysis of memory disturbances in local brain lesions.

The author is also indebted to Dr. T. O. Faller, who rendered invaluable assistance in the clinical analysis of some patients with severe memory disturbances.

As ever, the author gratefully mentions the sustaining help received for many years from the staff of the N. N. Burdenko Institute of Neurosurgery of the Academy of Medical Sciences of the USSR, where he has worked for several decades.

A. R. LURIA

Preface to the English-Language Edition

During the course of recent decades, research in the psychology of memory became one of the most actively developing fields of modern science.

A part of the studies relating to this field deals with molecular and submolecular aspects of memory; a second, with problems of iconic, short-term, and long-term memory; the third, with coding processes in retention and retrieval of traces. The present volume could not be related to either of these fields.

During many years this author attempted to study the basic problems of the neuropsychology of memory—in other words, basic forms of derangements of memory in patients with local lesions of the brain.

The basic idea was that memorization, as well as retention and retrieval of traces, really comprise a very complex form of mental activity, possessing a complicated structure, and that in differently localized lesions of the brain this functional system of mnemonic activity can be broken down differently.

These specific differences of a breakdown of mnemonic processes can be seen especially clearly in verbal memory and its disturbances associated with different brain lesions. Here, the components of memory processes—the elements included in the data to be retained and retrieved, the general pattern to be preserved and reproduced—can be clearly analyzed; the strategies applied by the subject for memorizing can be analyzed with utmost success.

Consequently, the present volume deals with an analysis of memory defects in different local lesions of the brain both for neurological diagnostics of the lesion and for an approach to some basic theoretical aspects of the psychological structure of human memory.

The author hopes that such application of the methods of neuropsychology for a better understanding of the normal and deranged memory could really be of a help both to psychologists and neurologists who confront the problem in practice.

This book attempts to analyze several basic problems of human memory; the problem of inner mechanisms of forgetting, the problems of trace decay vs. interference theory of forgetting; those of modality specific vs. modality unspecific memory disturbances; the role of the levels of organization of memory processes; and last but not least, the problems of brain organization of mnemonic processes in man.

The author hopes that data presented in this volume will serve to stimulate further research in the field.

Professor Michael Cole and Dr. Ralph Norgren, both of the Rockefeller University, have been kind enough to spend a considerable amount of time in revising, editing, and checking with meticulous care, the English-language edition comprising the present volume. The author wishes to express his sincere appreciation to these two colleagues, to Dr. Karl Pribram for his thoughtful introduction, as well as to Dr. Basil Haigh for a superb translation.

October 1975   A. R. Luria
Moscow

CHAPTER I
Psychological and Neuropsychological Aspects of Memory

INTRODUCTION

In recent decades, the problem of memory has become one of the most actively researched fields of science. There are several reasons why this should be so.

Simulating memory processes with high-speed computer techniques has demonstrated their great complexity. A generation ago memory was regarded as a relatively simple process of imprinting, storing, and reproducing traces. These ideas have now been shown to be grossly inadequate, and scientists now have begun to interpret remembering and recalling as complex acts of information processing, taking place in consecutive stages and resembling cognitive activity in character.

This radical revision of our basic ideas of memory has of course brought with it the need to study its structure more carefully and to undertake the more detailed analysis of the mechanisms concerned with the imprinting ("recording"), the storage and recalling of traces, as well as the conditions causing them to be forgotten. Until recently, the number of investigations into problems of memory could be counted in tens, but during the last two decades thousands of such investigations are on record. The subject has attracted the attention of psychologists, physiologists, and physicians, who have tackled the problem from many different angles.

A second reason for this revival of interest in investigating memory has been progress in the biological analysis of the nature of trace processes.

1

Only a generation ago, an investigator wishing to explain the biological basis of memory to his students could fall back on no more than the very general propositions of Richard Semon and Karl Ewald Hering that memory is a general property of matter and that any action on living matter leaves traces in it which, under suitable conditions, can be recalled. In the last two decades this situation has changed radically.

Biological investigations at the molecular level have revealed that ribonucleic acid has a role in trace imprinting and storage. The most important results have been obtained, however, in probing at the neuronal level. Careful investigations have revealed interaction between the nerve cell and glia and they have provided new and valuable information on the mechanisms of trace retention. Other experiments have shown that the brain contains special neurons whose function is not so much to receive and analyze information but to compare new information with traces of past experience and to regulate the change in the state of excitability that arises if the new information does not coincide with the old—if there is "dissonance" between them. Research into the neuronal mechanisms of activation, attention, and memory has made new and valuable contributions to our understanding of the nervous processes lying at the basis of memory.

Finally, the third reason that has led to the revision of ideas of memory has been the development of psychological sciences. A generation ago it was customary to regard psychological phenomena as the "functions" or "properties" of the mind, and to permit their description without an adequate analysis of the structure and dynamics of the actual underlying processes. The situation has now changed radically.

In recent decades the view has developed that all psychological processes are based on complex forms of activity. Important evidence regarding its development in ontogeny has been obtained. The structure of cognitive processes has been described as active and selective forms of reflection of reality, controlled by appropriate motives, and based on hierarchical system of self-regulatory acts. To this picture must be added the many special investigations conducted by workers in the Soviet Union and elsewhere in order to analyze the basic forms and stages of mnemonic activity.

One section of the problem of memory, however, has not yet been adequately studied. I refer to the actual brain mechanisms of mnemonic activity and the analysis of brain systems which participate in the process of memorizing and recalling traces. A detailed study of this problem could fill the important gap that still exists in the analysis of the mechanisms of memory. Do parts of the brain play the same role in mnemonic activity or do they have different roles in the organization of memory? Can we distinguish structures in the human brain responsible for different aspects of mnemonic activity, and what is the function of these structures?

Answers to these questions would represent a great step forward in our knowledge of the biological basis of memory. The investigator would no longer be restricted to the notion that the imprinting of traces is a function of every nerve cell but he could set about describing the actual systems involved in concrete forms of memorizing, storing, and recalling of traces. Our ideas of memory processes would be greatly advanced and we would be able to distinguish the factors that underlie specific mnemonic processes.

There is another important aspect of the analysis of brain systems concerned with mnemonic activity. The chief method used in the neuropsychological analysis of brain systems responsible for actual mnemonic activity is the study of how memory is disturbed in local brain lesions. It is by the analysis of how the process of remembering is disturbed by lesions in different parts of the brain that we can draw fundamental conclusions about which brain structures are concerned with memory processes and for what aspects of complex mnemonic activity they are responsible.

Although complaints of memory disturbance are perhaps the commonest symptoms of brain diseases, the careful neuropsychological analysis of the role of individual brain systems in mnemonic activity is still only in the earliest stage. Fewer than 20 years have gone by since the role of the hippocampus in the processes of direct memorizing was first pointed out. Since that time, many special psychological investigations of the various forms of memory disturbances associated with local brain lesions have been undertaken.

Although this field is still relatively young, the work of such eminent investigators as Barbizet, Hecaen, Milner, Penfield, Talland, Teuber, Weiskrantz, and Zangwill has made a decisive contribution to this branch to psychology. As a result of their work, the outlines of the neuropsychology of memory began to emerge. and this sector of research began to contribute both to the development of the general psychological theory of memory and its various aspects, and so became of practical importance in the diagnosis of local brain lesions.

As a result of these investigations, previously unanswerable questions could be posed more clearly and fresh approaches to the analysis of some mechanisms of memory that had hitherto remained inaccessible became possible.

The first such question, to which special attention will be paid, is that of the general physiological mechanisms of forgetting—a symptom which may arise in any brain lesion and one which provides an approach to the analysis of the mechanisms of one of the most important aspects of mnestic activity.

This first question is inevitably followed by a second: Analysis of the role in memory played by different levels of organization of the material to be memorized, on the one hand, and its different spheres or modalities, on the other.

Analysis of these questions is naturally linked with the last of our tasks—description of the individual forms of memory disturbances arising in lesions of different parts of the brain, and hence with the vitally important problems of the cerebral organization of mnestic activity.

Modern Views of Remembering and Forgetting

Our purpose will be best served by giving a brief description of modern views on the processes of memory and its chief components—remembering and forgetting.

Remembering and Recalling

Investigations conducted in the recent decades by psychologists in several countries have shown that memory is a complex functional system, active in character, taking place as a consecutive series of events in time, and organized on several different levels (see Barbizet, 1970; Kintsch, 1970a; Norman, 1970; Pribram & Broadbent, 1970; Smirnov, 1948, 1966; Talland & Waugh, 1969; Zinchenko, 1961). This complex, systemic character is maintained in the fundamental processes of memory and it applies equally to the process of imprinting (or memorizing) and to the process of reproduction (or recall) of the imprinting traces.

According to many authorities, the first stages in the process of remembering are a direct continuation of the process of perception. It starts with the differentiation of a group of precise cues from the material imprinted—some of them elementary and sensory in character, others more complex. These first stages last for fractions of a second, and constitute the basis of ultrashort memory (Miller, 1969; Sperling, 1960; Wickelgren, 1970). Relatively simple sensory cues occupy the dominant place. The volume of material that can be remembered is very small. The next of the stages of memory is described by many writers as short-term, operative, or synthetic memory. Relatively fewer traces, selected by attention, can be maintained (Norman, 1969), and these traces are kept for a short time while they are included in some operation, and then disappear.

The combination of single impressions into complex forms, which takes place both in perception and in imprinting, is only the initial phase of the remembering process. It continues with the rapid change into "coding" of the imprinted material or, in other words, its incorporation into a system of conceptual connections. It is through this coding that the transition takes place from rapid, short-term memory with its restricted possibilities into long-term memory, with a wider scope, that must be understood psychologically as a complex cognitive process performed at a high level and comprising a series of logical operations.

The existence of this complex process of coding of material, which many workers regard as the basic characteristic of human memory, is particularly apparent during the investigation of the remembering of nonsense syllables or words. Remembering can be regarded as a gradual process resting on a multidimensional system of connections incorporating elementary (sensory) and more complex (perceptual) and, finally, the most complex (cognitive) components. The actual relations between these components of the multidimensional system of connections and the levels of organization to which the process of remembering of the material reaches will depend on the task facing the subject, on the character of the material to be remembered, and on how long a time the subject can take to imprint it.

The storage of the imprinted traces and the process of their reproduction or recall are no less complex than the process of imprinting itself. As investigations (unfortunately relatively few in number) have shown, the storage of traces in the memory has nothing in common with the storage of unchanging copies or prints. In the latent state, traces undergo further transformations and sometimes become more generalized and schematic. These changes naturally begin to distinguish old traces substantially from those recently imprinted (Solov'ev, 1959).

Recalling likewise is no longer understood as a simple outpouring of previously imprinted forms, but rather as a complex process of active searching. It is thus seen as a special form of cognitive activity. A person who has to recall a series of words read out to him must first choose the necessary connection or necessary component from among a large number of possible alternatives, inhibit the outpouring of random, irrelevant components, and pick out the essential ones.

This process of active selection of the required trace is similar in its structure to the process of "decoding" of a complex text and it consists of a conflict between different (sensory, figurative, and conceptual) connections and cues incorporated into the multidimensional system, from which only the one essential connection must be chosen. It assumes some degree of searching, the success of which depends both on the complexity of the coding systems used and on the strategy used by the subject attempting to reproduce the imprinted material. Finally, the process of active recalling must inevitably include comparison of the results of the search with the original material. Only by such a comparison can the subject stop all further searching, in some cases, and accept the reproduced material as correct; or in other cases reject the traces produced as inadequate and continue his search until he finds the correct solution. Clearly, this notion of the psychological nature of the recall process, shared by many authorities (Feigenbaum, 1970; Kintsch, 1970; Morton, 1970; Norman, 1969, 1970; Reitman, 1970; Shiffrin, 1970), demonstrates the whole complexity of the process of recalling and contrasts this complex concept of active memory sharply with the simplified views of recalling as a simple outpouring of forms.

Two chief forms of reproduction of traces are well known in psychology: The recognition of previously imprinted information, on the one hand, and its active recall, on the other.

Compared to active recall, the recognition of a newly presented cue has a much simpler structure. The subject has no need to seek actively for the necessary connections, to compose hypotheses, or to carry out active selection. His task is simply to pick out the necessary cues and to compare the newly presented object with what was imprinted previously. Naturally, the large number of complex operations characteristic of active remembering are eliminated in this case although, as before, the last part of this complex process still remains—the critical comparison of the cues thus identified with those possessed by the object presented previously. If the newly presented object disagrees with the previous object, the conclusion from this operation is that they are not identical, but if they do agree the old object is "recognized" and further searching is discontinued. We shall see again later that this apparently simple process is really not so simple and that under certain conditions it may not be completed or may not have the necessary results.

The characteristics of memory as a complex and multidimensional activity discussed above apply equally well to the remembering and recalling of visual objects, movements, or words. The process is seen particularly clearly, however, in the remembering of verbal material. We must, therefore, examine verbal memory (used as a fundamental material for the investigation of mnestic processes) in rather greater detail.

* * *

Comparatively recently, memory for words was regarded as being in the same system of concepts as any other mnestic process. A word heard by a person was considered to evoke a certain object, which was then imprinted (recorded) and stored in the memory and reproduced ("read out") under the necessary conditions. Nothing can be more mistaken than this simplified impression of verbal memory.

A word itself is a multidimensional system embracing a whole network of connections distinguishable by different cues. They include: Acoustic cues (the word "koshka"—cat can evoke words of similar sound, such as "kroshka"—crumbs, "okoshko"—small window, and so on); morphological connections (by which the word "teacher" may evoke the word "nurse," or the word "ink-stand" may evoke the words "sugar basin," "pepper pot," and so on); figurative connections (by which the word "apple-tree" may evoke an apple, a garden, a stool, and so on); finally, semantic connections, on the basis of which the word may be incorporated into a complete hierarchic system of categories (the word "dog" may evoke the words "cat" or "animal" and the word "rye" may evoke the words "oats," "millet," "plant," and so on).

The perception of a word (and its remembering, even more so) is invariably a complex process of incorporating it into a system of known codes, in which the leading cues are dominant and the secondary, unimportant cues are relegated into the background. This means that during the imprinting of a word there is always a process of selection of the dominant system of connections and inhibition of the rest. It is unlikely that in a normal person the word "skripka" (violin) would evoke, not the image of a musical instrument (a cello, a guitar, and so on), but the image of "skrepka" (a clip) with a similar sound.

Methods are now available which can objectively demonstrate the presence of these multidimensional connections embodied in a word, and analyze their "semantic fields." It is only in certain pathological states (for example, in mentally retarded persons) that connections evoked by a word lose their selectivity: in response to the test word "koshka," words of similar acoustic structure, such as "kroshka," "kryshka," or "okoshko" begin to evoke the same involuntary response (e.g., vasoconstriction) as the principal word, thereby becoming equal with the semantic connections (Luria & Vinogradova, 1959). This shows that the word potentially conceals many connections evokable on different bases, and that only under normal conditions can the semantic system of codes, in which the word is incorporated, dispel all the other, more elementary connections. If this fact of the multidimensional connections inherent in the word is of decisive importance for its imprinting, or "coding," it remains just as important for its recalling.

Under normal conditions the choice of a word to denote a certain object from many possible alternatives is made easily and almost automatically. Only if unfamiliar or rare words have to be recalled do difficulties arise that have been called the "tip of the tongue phenomenon": The person seeking the word is overwhelmed by a flood of random words similar to the one he seeks in their acoustic, morphological, or situational connections (Brown & McNeil, 1966). We shall see below that similar phenomena, in an even more conspicuous form, may arise in special pathological conditions leading to a disturbance of the selectivity of audioverbal memory.

All this shows that memory for words is by no means a simple process of imprinting and reproducing a ready-made image and that the concept of remembering as coding and of recalling as a complex process of choosing from a series of alternatives is manifested particularly clearly in the phenomena of verbal memory.

Forgetting

I have discussed the profound changes introduced by modern psychology into our views of the processes of remembering and reproducing (recalling) material imprinted previously. Equally radical changes have occurred in our views of forgetting. At the earliest stages of research focused on memory, associated with the work of Ebbinghaus (1885), forgetting was understood to be the spontaneous extinction of traces, increasing gradually in intensity as time goes on. Ebbinghaus drew his well-known curve of forgetting on the basis of precisely those views, and this concept of the cuases of forgetting remained virtually unchanged for a very long time. Doubts about the validity of the hypothesis that forgetting is a passive process resulting from the gradual decaying of the trace caused by excitation arose from two sources: The data of modern physiology, and observations made in psychoanalysis.

In the writings of Pavlov and his pupils it is already apparent that the usual understanding of inhibition as the simple decay of excitation has been complicated by the idea that inhibition is active in character. Even the simplest forms of inhibition came to be understood as the result of "conflict between two excitations," or as the influence of random, irrelevant foci of excitation on the course of the nervous processes and on the stability of their traces (Anokhin, 1958). More complex forms of inhibition and, in particular, those described by the Vvedenskii–Ukhtomskii school as limiting or parabiotic inhibition, and those categorized by Pavlov's school as "internal inhibition," came to be regarded as the active process of blocking of stimuli that are too powerful and that must be inhibited in order to protect the organism against excessive, destructive influences. Closely similar views were expressed by Freud in his theory of "repression," defined as the protective inhibition of excessively strong excitation.

These observations suggested that, besides a passive weakening of traces, increasing as time went on, an active inhibition must also be distinguished; in some cases this is the blocking of traces by irrelevant foci of excitation but in others it can be regarded as an active, protective reaction of the organism to excessive excitation.

A similar change in the basic concepts has also taken place recently in psychology. The process of forgetting (the psychological expression of decay or inhibition) has ceased to be regarded as a process of gradual, passive, weakening of traces. Psychologists now distinguish two completely different processes, differing both in their structure and in their neurodynamic nature.

The first of these processes was the previous idea of forgetting as trace decay. This process was linked with the usual observation that with an increase in the time elapsing after the onset of excitation the traces of that excitation gradually weaken or decay, and eventually disappear altogether. Those writers who have regarded this process of passive decay as the main, or even the only cause of forgetting, approached forgetting as a passive process, a simple function of time, and they "localized" forgetting in the "recording" or "storing" of information.

These views on forgetting as a passive process of trace decay soon ceased to satisfy investigators. Even had they been suitable to explain the processes taking place in the circle of events more recently called "short-term" or "operative" memory, they proved quite unsuitable to explain some of the phenomena of forgetting in the sphere of "long-term" memory.

Observations have shown that the traces of this "long-term" memory can be preserved for very long periods of time (perhaps throughout life), and that those which have apparently been forgotten may under certain conditions be revived and be manifested quite clearly. An example is the familiar observation that in a state of hypnosis traces of earlier, childhood experiences may arise; although apparently completely forgotten, they were in fact simply blocked and inhibited.

Facts such as these compelled psychologists to recognize a completely different class of forgetting, a class not explicable as trace decay, but only as active inhibition of traces, and the "localization" of the forgetting process had to be moved from the "imprinting" and "storing" of traces to the process of their reproduction.

The classical investigations of Müller and Pilzecker (1900) revealed that the forgetting of imprinted elements may be the result of the inhibitory influence from preceding and succeeding excitation. This theory of the role of proactive and retroactive inhibition as the essential source of forgetting (reflected in the well-known phenomenon of the better retention of the extreme, and the worse retention of the middle elements of a series) laid the foundations of the theory of forgetting as the temporary, dynamic inhibition of traces.

In recent decades, this understanding of forgetting as the result of inhibition of traces by irrelevant, interfering excitation has been confirmed by many additional facts. Forgetting is increasingly regarded as the distraction of attention by irrelevant stimuli, and the "interference" theory of forgetting has been supported by the work of many investigators (Marston, 1964; Melton & Irwin, 1940; Norman, 1969; Postman, 1965, 1969; Smirnov, 1948; Underwood, 1945, 1957; Waugh & Norman, 1965, 1968; etc.).

The supporters of this theory considered that the facts of "forgetting" traces of long-term memory can be explained by the influence of irrelevant, interfering impressions or of irrelevant, interfering forms of activity. The fact that the subject also received irrelevant, interfering impressions continuously caused them to question the basis of the classical "trace forgetting curve" obtained by Ebbinghaus. It may result not from trace decay, but from inhibitory irrelevant stimuli or interfering reminiscences which are almost impossible to take account of in special experiments, and which can only be characterized by the term "irrelevant" (extra-experimental) inteference (Postman, 1961, 1969).

Further investigations showed that the inhibitory action of interfering agents assumes different forms at different stages and different levels of the remembering process. At the stage of sensory, ultrashort memory, at which traces of actions taking place are not yet "coded" and incorporated into definite systems, any external action, distracting the subject's attention, and any irrelevant activity inevitably have an inhibitory effect and block the basic activity and the traces left by it. Conversely, in the late stages of the memorizing process, when the traces have now been incorporated into a certain system of "codes," the inhibitory effect of interfering impressions or interfering activity is much more differentiated. At this stage of long-term memory, only actions similar to the basic action coded by the system of traces or types of activity incorporated into a corresponding system can block the appearance of the imprinted traces, whereas more distant actions have no such inhibitory effect. The organization of traces into a definite semantic system becomes a factor limiting the inhibitory effect of irrelevant stimuli and, as Broadbent (1970) rightly points out, learning a series of words in Russian can block the recalling of Greek words, but has no effect on a distant system (for example, on remembering a telephone number). Consequently, at the stage of consolidation of traces and their incorporation into a complex system of codes, the process of inhibitory effect of interfering agents acquires new features and becomes much more selective.

It is therefore perfectly natural that completely new—systemic—factors of forgetting can be formed in the sphere of "long-term" memory, with its complex organization. Often the nonincorporation of a certain trace into a corresponding system of codes may give rise to its forgetting, whereas incorporation into the appropriate system gives it much greater stability.

The concepts of the complex, multistaged, and multidimensional structure of memorizing and recalling introduced into psychology by recent research inevitably make our ideas of the process of forgetting more complex. When we go on to analyze it, this complexity must under no circumstances be forgotten.

The Neurological Basis of Mnemonic Activity

We have examined the basic facts of memorizing, recalling, and forgetting material as they appear in the psychology of today. Let us now turn to the chief topic of this book and briefly examine some fundamental aspects of the neurological organization of memory.

Very little was known about the cerebral mechanisms of memory before the end of the 1950s. It was not until the 1880s that Korsakov (1890, 1892) described the severe disturbance of memory arising as a result of alcoholic poisoning of the cortex, and at the beginning of this century Bekhterev (1907) published the first observations to show that structures in the medial zones of the temporal region, especially the nuclei of the hippocampus, most probably participate in the mechanisms of direct memory.

Soon thereafter, several observations indicating the importance of structures connecting the medial zones of the temporal region (the hippocampus), the hypothalamus, and the thalamic nuclei (the so-called circle of Papez) in the imprinting and reproduction of traces were published. A special role in this process was ascribed to the mammillary bodies (now regarded as relay nuclei for the flow of excitation arising in the hippocampal region). Based on observations that seemed paradoxical, these investigations led to the view that memory is not a process connected equally with all regions of the brain, and that systems of particular and special importance for the storage and reproduction of traces of direct experience can be distinguished in it. Scoville and Milner (1957) published the first observations to show that bilateral resection of the hippocampus leads to gross disturbances of the direct imprinting and reproduction of current information (in other words, makes it impossible for new traces to be transferred into long-term memory), although it leaves the old traces of long-term memory intact.

The patient described by these workers could retain traces from stimuli which acted on him for a long period of time (for several seconds or even minutes) if no irrelevant, distracting stimuli acted during that period. He could form motor skills and retain them for a short time, but a fact of decisive importance was that all impressions that succeeded in reaching him disappeared quickly from his memory, and after a few minutes (or after slight distraction) the patient could not even remember that the corresponding material had been presented to him, that he had taken part in a conversation or that he had carried out certain actions, and he did not recognize the physician who had worked with him a few minutes before. Characteristically, this patient showed no changes in personality, he retained complete lucidity of consciousness, he did not give confabulations, and his intellectual operations (sometimes even quite difficult) remained completely unaffected. Another characteristic fact was that this patient's memory of previous and well consolidated events was preserved. A lesion of organic areas of the brain gave rise to only limited disturbances of the transfer of current impressions into long-term memory, without affecting preconsolidated traces of previous experience.

This phenomenon was observed only in bilateral lesions of the hippocampus, but also appeared as a result of the injection of sodium amytal into the carotid artery of a patient with a unilateral lesion of the hippocampus, as a result of temporary blocking of the function of the opposite hippocampus. Unilateral lesions of the hippocampus evoked only subclinical disturbances of memory, a lesion of the left hippocampus affected verbal memory particularly clearly while a lesion of the right hippocampus affected the retention of nonverbalized, visual material in the memory and its reproduction (Corkin, 1965; Kimura, 1963; Milner, 1958, 1965, 1968, 1970; Prisco, 1963).

Many investigations carried out at the same time on monkeys showed that the inferior and medial zones of the temporal region are absolutely essential for trace retention. Extirpation of these zones of the brain makes the animals unable to form elementary skills (Bagshaw & Pribram, 1953; Mishkin & Pribram, 1955-1956; Pribram, 1969; Pribram & Weiskrantz, 1957). The intimate mechanisms of this defect became clear after a series of investigations at the neuronal level (Adey, 1962; Andersen & Lomo, 1967; Kandel & Spencer, 1961; Vinogradova, 1965, 1969; Vinogradova, Semyonova, & Konovalov, 1970) had shown that a high proportion of hippocampal neurons belonged to a special class of nerve cells that do not respond selectively to stimuli of a given modality, but respond actively to any change in a stimulus; or, in other words, they have the function of comparing new stimuli with traces of stimuli that acted in the past. This fact explains why destruction of these formations or of their tracts inactivates a vital apparatus essential for direct memory and leads to such unusual consequences—a disturbance of the retention of traces of previous experience.

* * *

The brain systems I have discussed are essential for the normal imprinting of traces, but do not by any means exhaust the list of brain systems that participate in mnemonic activity. As mentioned above, it is only in the most elementary cases that the process of memorizing is limited to the simple imprinting of impressions directly reaching the subject. As a rule, recalling comprises a process of direct impressions and the channelling of incoming information into a particular perceptual system.

This perceptual system may be based on different modalities (visual, auditory, tactile) and nearly always has, as one of its components, a verbal organization. In some cases, this verbal organization is reduced to the naming of the perceived object (this occurs almost invariably in all perceptual processes), but in other (more complex) cases it depends on a complex process of placing the perceived material in a certain category or incorporating it into a certain logical system. It was this fact which led several investigators, among those cited above, to equate the processes of memory with perceptual processes and to assert that memory, in its pure form, is practically never found in man.

If this is true, other brain systems different from those mentioned above must also play a role in the processes of memory. The perception of external information, reaching the brain through the sense organs, is based on the work of the posterior, gnostic zones of the cerebral cortex. Its course in man lies through the modality-specific zones of the cortex—occipital (visual), temporal (auditory), and parietal (tactile-kinesthetic). We also know that each of these parts of the cortex has a complex, hierarchic structure. The primary zones of each of these regions are concerned with the reception and analysis of incoming information, whereas the secondary zones, superposed above the primary, convert the "somatotopic projection" of the receptor surfaces into their functional organization, thereby carrying out the "mobile syntheses" of information reaching the human brain (Luria, 1962).

Consequently, the processes of material memory (memorizing material reaching the human brain) must inevitably require the activity of these posterior, gnostic zones of the cortex that have brought to the brain material which will later be memorized. Only when it has reached the gnostic zones of the cortex and become incorporated into certain perceptual systems can this material be imprinted. As already stated, this imprinting takes place with the participation of special comparing systems of the brain, but it could not take place had the material to be imprinted not been received and processed in the gnostic zones of the cortex.

Whether the gnostic zones of the cortex participate not only in perception, but also in memory processes remains an unsolved problem. The classical authors of the theory of cerebral localization regarded all the complex parts of the gnostic zones of the cortex as an apparatus for specific sensory forms (in other words, an apparatus for sensory memory). Other neurologists considered them as an apparatus of perceptual activity, which must inevitably include the preservation of traces from previous actions directed at the same sensory sphere.

Whatever the answer, the contribution of the gnostic zones of the cortex to memory processes is naturally connected with their function of organizing sensory experience and the mnemonic functions of these cortical zones are inseparably linked with their gnostic functions; consequently, these cortical zones are directly concerned with special, modality-specific forms of memory. A lesion of the corresponding gnostic zones of the cortex can lead to disturbances of memory confined to one particular modality, leaving intact all other types of memory linked with other modalities (Klimkovskii, 1966; Luria & Karaseva, 1968; Luria & Rapoport, 1962; Milner, 1970; Pham Ming Hac, 1971).

The brain systems participating in memorizing processes are not confined to the systems just described for comparing traces of previous experience with the actual agents, or the systems of the modality-specific, gnostic zones of the cortex. The fact that in man every step in the analysis of incoming information takes place with the close participation of speech—a fact already referred to above—implies that the speech areas of the cortex of the left hemisphere must play an important role in the system of cortical zones in the organization of memory traces.

The numerous observations published in the world literature, commencing with the classical work of Goldstein and his collaborators, Head, Isserlin, and others, and including my own investigations (Luria, 1947, 1962, 1970), suggest that the process of coding incoming information into certain logical-grammatical and semantic systems, without which it would be difficult to imagine how traces of short-term memory can be converted into long-term, requires the participation of the parietal-temporal (speech) areas of the cortex in memory processes. Naturally, their role in the organization of mnemonic processes is quite different from the role of the hippocampus and the modality-specific, gnostic zones of the cortex.

The cortical speech areas, through which speech participates in the processing of information, make an important contribution to the organization of individual special impressions into whole, differentiated systems or, in other words, they participate directly in the conversion of isolated, fractional actions into enlarged, organized structure. A lesion of the cortical speech zones is bound to be reflected on the ability to retain discrete material. For that reason, just as Ombrédane (1951) and other workers correctly pointed out some time age, a lesion of the speech zones and a disturbance of the organization of incoming information with the aid of the semantic system of language must inevitably lead to substantial disturbances of memory. In this case, however, the disturbances are system-specific and not modality-specific in character; they are reflected in all processes requiring the participation of speech and are not reflected in sensory processes taking place without the aid of speech. This fact has been noted by many investigators (recently by Milner and her collaborators). Later, I shall make a special examination of the distinctive disturbances of memory associated with a lesion of the cortical speech zones.

* * *

I must now consider the last of the brain systems which seems to be important in mnemonic processes—the frontal lobes. After destruction of the prefrontal zones of the brain, animals were unable to carry out delayed responses, whereas immediate responses to stimuli were performed successfully (Jacobsen, 1935; and many others). Later observations showed these facts still told us nothing about disturbances of memory: Extirpation of the prefrontal zones of the brain sharply reduced the process of inhibition of responses to irrelevant stimuli and increased the distractability of the animal. It was this factor that led to the difficulty in the delayed responses (Konorski, 1969; Malmo, 1942; Pribram, 1961, 1963; Weiskrantz, 1966). As soon as these workers excluded the effects of irrelevant stimuli (for example, by carrying out the experiments in darkness, or by lowering the state of excitability of the cortex), animals with destruction of the prefrontal cortex were perfectly capable of performing the delayed responses.

Nevertheless, the frontal lobes (especially the frontal lobes of the human brain) undoubtedly play an important, but very special role in memory processes.

As stated earlier, human memory must be understood as an active process. This is manifested in the fact that man actively processes incoming information and does not simply imprint traces of stimuli received by him, but codes this information, chooses its essential features and incorporates it into a definite system, into a certain "subjective organization" (Feigenbaum, 1970; Reitman, 1970; Shiffrin, 1970). In some cases, moreover, man makes a special task of remembering or recalling the corresponding material, which converts the process of unpremeditated passive imprinting into an active form (Leont'ev, 1959; Smirnov, 1948, 1966; and others) and it confers on memory its selective and specifically human character.

It is well known in neuropsychology that the following of plans and programming of activity in accordance with those plans, as well as the active comparison of the effect of activity with the intended purpose, are the principal functions of the frontal lobes. This fact has been confirmed by many observations on the disturbance of psychological processes in patients with massive lesions of the frontal lobes. These patients can still perform simple reactions but the complex, selective forms of behavior, conforming to certain programs, are disturbed and replaced either by primitive, echopraxic actions or by pathologically inert stereotypes (Anokhin, 1949; Luria, 1962, 1963, 1970; Luria & Khomskaya, 1966).

Lesions of the frontal lobes, destroying active, goal-directed activity, must thus also have some effect on mnemonic processes. These lesions do not necessarily impair the direct imprinting of traces or even their coding into complex systems (including those of speech). It is quite clear, however, that they must radically disturb active, selective mnemonic activity, by replacing the process of active memorizing or recalling with the passive retention of traces, leading to the uncontrolled outpouring of irrelevant traces or to inert stereotypes. We shall discuss the extensive facts on which these arguments are based in one of the following chapters.

* * *

The following conclusions can be drawn from the material discussed above.

Analysis of the evidence obtained in recent decades has shown conclusively that although the process of imprinting and retention of traces is a general function of the nerve cell, this does not mean that mnemonic activity, with its complex structure, involves all parts of the brain uniformly and is a function of the entire cerebral cortex, regarded as an indivisible whole. The facts at the disposal of modern physiology and neuropsychology offer convincing proof that mnemonic activity is undertaken by a complex system of different parts of the brain, working together and each making its own contribution to the activity as a whole.

Those facts suggest that the hippocampal structures are responsible for the elementary comparison of actual stimuli with traces of previous experience. The gnostic and speech areas of the cortex are concerned with the analysis and coding of incoming information and establishing the essential conditions for the organization of the material to be memorized. The anterior (frontal) areas of the cortex perform completely different roles in this system, since they provide for maintenance of the plan, the programing of behavior, and the performance of active, selective mnestic activity.

With such a conception of this complex cerebral organization of human memory, we can make a fresh approach to the analysis of its mechanisms, and the forms of memory disturbances that arise in local brain lesions.

Neurodynamic Conditions for Mnemonic Activity

Integrity of the brain systems described above is the principal, but not the only, condition for successful memorizing and recalling of material perceived. A second and equally important condition is an optimal state of cortical neurodynamics. These fundamental laws of neurodynamics may be seriously disrupted in pathological states of the brain.

The first condition characterizing the waking state of the cortex is integrity of the normal tone or strength of the active processes. This is manifested in the phenomena which Pavlov called the "law of strength": Strong (or biologically essential) stimuli become dominant in character and evoke strong responses, whereas weak (or unimportant) stimuli are easily inhibited and evoke only weak responses, or sometimes they remain subliminal and evoke no response at all.

Maintenance of the "law of strength," whereby certain systems of excitation can be distinguished as dominant, gives the psychological processes their necessary selectivity. Systems of strictly selective connections can be activated and, at the same time, irrelevant connections not corresponding to the subject's immediate task, can be inhibited. If the waking state of the cortex is altered and its tone becomes lowered, and if the inhibitory or "phasic" state of the cortex characterized by its lowered tone develops, the "law of strength" is seriously disturbed. In the initial phases, weak (or unimportant) stimuli become equal to strong (or essential) stimuli (Pavlov described this state originally as the "balanced phase"). In deeper "phasic" states of the cortex, weak (or unimportant) stimuli evoke distinct responses as before, but strong (or essential) stimuli lead to a state of limiting inhibition of the cortex so that no response is evoked.

Lowering the cortical tone removes the most important condition for selective psychological processes. In addition to essential (corresponding to the immediate purpose) stimuli and essential connections, irrelevant and unimportant connections spring up involuntarily. It will suffice to recall the drowsy or oneiroid state which we all experience just when going to sleep, during light sleep, or immediately before waking in order to understand the unusual place that these irrelevant associations or connections begin to occupy when tone is lowered.

In *War and Peace*, Tolstoy provides an example of associations disturbed in an oneiroid state by an uncontrollable outpouring of irrelevant connections and images in the mind of Nikolai Rostov.

> On this hill there was a white patch which Rostov could not make out at all: Was it a clearing in the forest lit up by the moon, a patch of unmelted snow, or white houses? ... "It must be snow, this patch; patch- *une tache*, -thought Rostov, first in Russian, then in French. No, of course, not *tache* ...." Natasha, sister, brown eyes. Na ... tashka ... (diminutive), Na ... tashku (accusative). Take my *tashku* (sabretache) ....

The easy change from images to words, from words to their acoustic elements and to other closely sounding words (patch–*tache* in French–Na-tashka, dimunitive of Natasha–*tashka*, Russian for sabretache, or cavalry officer's satchel, etc.) completely untypical of the waking state, begins to predominate in a state of drowsiness, interfering with the organized course of thought and with the selective reproduction of the necessary system of connections.

Consequently, selectivity is the first and most important result of the normal state of cortical neurodynamics. The second result, closely linked with the first, is ability to maintain the waking state for a long time and to inhibit the effects of excitation when they arise. In an optimal state irrelevant stimuli not only do not inhibit dominant connections, but under certain conditions they may actually strengthen them. This has been shown conclusively by the work of A. A. Ukhtomskii's school.

The situation is totally different when the cortical tone is lowered and the "phasic" state described above develops. In such cases, weak (or irrelevant) stimuli not only become equal in strength to strong (or important) stimuli, but they invariably begin to inhibit traces of these important, basic stimuli. This will be clear if the phenomenon of increasing forgetfulness characteristic of memory in old age is recalled. This condition ought to be described as increased inhibitability of established traces by irrelevant, interfering effects rather than a primary weakening of the traces themselves.

Optimal cortical tone is maintained by the normal state of the brain stem and reticular formation (Jasper, 1954, 1957; Lindsley, 1955, 1960: Moruzzi & Magoun, 1949). A lesion of diencephalic structures located near the walls of the third ventricle can give rise to a marked decrease in cortical tone which is manifested equally in all modalities: it is thus modality-nonspecific in character.

I have still to describe one last neurodynamic condition essential for the normal recall. This is the optimal mobility of nervous processes. Normally, man retains and reproduces many traces that as a rule are resorted to in a certain order of time, one after the other. Naturally, to recall the necessary traces, man must inhibit the traces of the previous connections and switch from some traces to others. This requires considerable mobility of the nervous processes. If the cerebral cortex is in its normal state, the mobility of its nervous processes is perfectly adequate to ensure that preceding traces do not interfere with the recall of new traces and the switch from one system of connections to another presents no particular difficulty.

It is a different matter if the cortex is in a pathological state. Classical and modern investigations have shown that pathological states of the brain may often severely disturb the mobility of nervous processes and, in some cases (for example, in lesions of the frontal lobes), the disturbances may be very severe, so that any trace, one it has been formed in the cortex, becomes so pathologically inert that the normal switching from an established system of connections to another is virtually impossible. As stated above, this fact has been studied in relation to conditioned-reflex activity of animals with lesions of the frontal lobes (Anokhin, 1949; Shumilina, 1966), to pathological changes in the higher nervous processes of mentally retarded children (Luria, 1956, 1958, 1960) and, finally, in the behavior of patients with massive lesions of the frontal lobes (Luria, 1962, 1963, 1969; Luria & Khomskaya, 1966). There is every reason to suppose that this pathological inertia of higher nervous processes, as it arises in certain types of brain lesions and is manifested particularly clearly in lesions of the anterior zones, must inevitably affect mnemonic processes and may sometimes create conditions stimulating severe memory disturbances.

I have mentioned the neurodynamic conditions essential for normal mnemonic processes because they are just as important for the memorizing and recalling of material as the structural-morphological conditions described above. Analysis of the conditions governing the course of mnemonic activity will also serve as the basis for our neuropsychological analysis of mnemonic processes and their disturbances in local brain lesions.

Clinical Forms of Memory Disturbance

After this examination of the facts concerning the neurological basis of mnemonic processes and the neurodynamic conditions of memory, we can turn to the analysis of the clinical pictures arising in patients with brain lesions and to the description of the principal forms of memory disturbances found in clinical practice.

Korsakov (1887), in his classical paper "on alcoholic paralysis" first described a picture of gross disturbances of memory arising after alcoholic poisoning. He returned to this description in 1887-1890, and "Korsakov's syndrome" has become the point of departure for many investigations. In such cases, he wrote (Koraskov, 1887):

Memory of recent events is disturbed almost exclusively, recent impressions apparently disappear soonest, whereas impressions of long ago are recalled properly, so that the patient's ingenuity, his sharpness of wit, and his resourcefulness remain largely unaffected.

The description of the syndrome which Korsakov observed in alcoholic poisoning at once distinguished it from diffuse dementia. It was the first description of a special disturbance of mnemonic processes. Later it was discovered (and as often happens with massive lesions) that the phenomenon described initially is much more complex and wider in its implications than Korsakov himself supposed.

The massive disturbances of memory arising in Korsakov's syndrome usually formed part of a wider symptom-complex which, as a rule, included a general diminution of the patient's activity, confusion in his assessment of his surroundings, and sometimes confabulations in the early (or acute) stages of development of the disease. Disturbances of memory, always manifested more clearly with respect to current events, in the most serious cases also spread to relatively distant events. In the mildest cases the disturbances may be only partial, so that the patient can still retain traces even of current experience in his memory. Clinical observations have shown that the defect in patients with severe disturbances of memory is manifested unequally at different levels. The most elementary (conditioned-reflex) levels of trace imprinting may remain intact, but the voluntary recalling of events that have just taken place is severely disturbed.

Claparède (1911) first showed this fact when he published an experiment in which a patient with Korsakov's syndrome, having been pricked by a needle when shaking hands, would never again offer his hand to the experimenter although he remembered nothing about the previous prick nor about the experimenter himself. Similar observations were later made by Leont'ev (1930). Kohnstamm (1917) described a pianist with an amnestic syndrome who was quite capable of accompanying a singer, but later could recall nothing about it. Other cases are described by Williams and Smith (1954), Talland (1965), Talland and Waugh (1969), and Milner (1958, 1965, 1966, 1967, 1968, 1969, 1970). Milner showed that a patient with a bilateral lesion of the hippocampus, who was unable to retain traces of an impression for more than a few minutes, could nevertheless develop sufficiently stable motor skills so that traces could be detected even after an interval of three years (Milner, 1970).

Although the memory defect in a massive Korsakov's syndrome cannot be explained in terms either of defects of perception (Bonhoeffer, 1901, 1904) or of intellect (Kraepelin, 1900) gross disturbances of the organization of impressions of events and their sequence in time can always be observed in such patients. The precise organization of their traces in time ("the recording of the sequence of events," noted by Bernard, 1951; Conrad & Ule, 1951; Grünbaum, 1930; Van der Horst, 1932; Williams & Zangwill, 1950) always remains severely disturbed. As a result, these patients lose their integral experience of time and begin to live in a world of isolated impressions.

The evidence obtained by later investigations complicated still further the picture described in the first reports of cases identified as Korsakov's syndrome. It was found that traces of direct impressions do not disappear inevitably in patients with that syndrome. The direct retention of memory traces for a relatively short period by these patients does not differ all that greatly from normal (Brion, 1969; Milner, 1969, 1970; and many others). Under favorable conditions, these patients have reasonably good retention both of meaningful material (Gregor, 1909) and of meaningless syllables, words or pictures (the facts are surveyed by Talland, 1965). These findings shifted the attention of investigators from the process of imprinting ("recording") of traces to the process of their reproduction ("reading"), and induced a search for factors which, without upsetting the processes of trace recording, could affect their reproduction. Workers began to seek the causes of the memory disturbance in the "distraction of attention" (Gregor, 1909; Gregor & Römer, 1907), in the "situation" (Van der Horst, 1932), and also in the inhibitory effect of some traces on others or the interfering action of irrelevant impressions (Brodmann, 1909). The description of Korsakov's syndrome brought to light phenomena far more complex than mere "defects of trace imprinting" and raised fundamental questions of the psychological nature of forgetting that were not answered until much later.

The development of clinical observations showed a second (this time neurological) complication of the syndrome first described by Korsakov. Very severe defects of memory may arise not only as the result of general poisoning, as was the case in the patient first observed by Korsakov, but also from very local brain lesions. As a rule, these lesions are located not in the cortex, but in the deeper parts of the brain.

As long ago as in 1896, Gudden showed that alcoholic poisoning, producing very severe memory disorders, causes degeneration predominantly of the two mammillary bodies. It was later found that a similar general (not limited to one particular modality) disturbance of memory can arise in patients with lesions of the mesencephalic nuclei, which depress the autonomic functions and disturb the state of wakefulness (Gamper, 1928, 1929) and in lesions of the hippocampus (Conrad & Ule, 1951; Ule, 1958). Similar defects can arise in lesions of the medial thalamic nuclei (Delay, Brion, & Ellisade, 1958; Collins, Victor, & Adams, 1961; Ule, 1958) and in lesions of the walls of the third ventricle (Victor & Yakovlev, 1955; Williams & Pennybacker, 1954). The severest disturbances of general (modality-nonspecific) memory may be the result of a hippocampal lesion, especially if the lesion is bilateral in character (Milner, 1970; Penfield & Milner, 1958; Scoville & Milner, 1957).

Another significant fact is that alcoholic (or other) poisoning of the brain is by no means the only etiological factor causing massive disturbances of memory. Similar disturbances can be produced by tumors, by surgical operations, or even experimentally if (as in the brilliant experiments of Milner, 1966) sodium amytal was injected into the carotid artery supplying the opposite hemisphere of a patient with a unilateral lesion of the hippocampus, inactivating the opposite hippocampus for a short time, and giving rise to short-term but severe disturbances of general memory.

These facts suggested that the basic neurological condition for the preservation of general (modality-nonspecific) memory is the integrity of the deep brain structures mentioned above, grouped together under the familiar term of the "hippocampal circle" or "circle of Papez," consisting of the hippocampus, mammillary bodies, the thalamus, the mammillo-thalamic tract, and the anterior zones of the limbic region. Evidently the integrity of this system is essential for memory traces not only to be imprinted, but also to be reproduced in an organized manner. Early indications of the decisive role of such small structures as the mammillary bodies in mnestic processes can be explained only by the fact that these bodies are the principal relay connecting the hippocampus with all the other elements of the system described above.

The lesions described above give rise to general, modality-nonspecific disturbances of memory manifested as inability to retain and reproduce traces of current stimuli, in whatever sphere they were presented. Other forms of memory disturbances found in clinical practice are confined to defects of the retention and reproduction of traces belonging to a particular sphere of experience (visual, auditory, tactile).

Korsakov (1954) drew a sharp distinction between these forms of memory disturbance which he linked with lesions of particular parts of the cortex, and the general type.

Special memory is evidently localized in certain parts of the cortex and, depending on their degree of development and fineness of structure . . . affections of special memory—partial amnesia—are quite common, chiefly in patients with focal brain lesions.

It is well known in clinical practice that focal lesions of the lateral, convex surface of the cortex never lead to general disturbances of memory accompanied by disorientation in space and time, disintegration of traces of past experience, and confabulations, the components of Korsakov's syndrome.

Local lesions of these parts of the cortex can give rise to disturbance of gnosis or praxis, speech and intellectual operations, and the performance of complex action programs. These disturbances have served for a long time as the basis for the topical diagnosis of local brain lesions but they are not accompanied by any general diminution of wakefulness or by any appreciable disturbances of general (modality-nonspecific) memory.

In the first stages of development of the neurology of cortical processes, the disturbances evoked by local lesions were often interpreted as partial disturbances of memory. Broca, for instance, spoke of the disturbance of the motor image of words (motor speech memory) arising in patients with a lesion of the posterior third of the first frontal gyrus of the left hemisphere. The authors who first described the phenomena of visual agnosia arising in lesions of the occipital lobes were inclined to regard it as the partial loss of visual memory images. Those who described the disturbances of spatial orientation accompanying lesions of the inferior parietal region interpreted this syndrome as a disturbance of spatial memory.

With the development of clinical neurology, and the influence exerted on it by new movements in psychological science, this interpretation gave way to another. Disturbances such as aphasia and alexia, agnosia and acalculia, began to be interpreted not so much as disturbances of memory and associations but rather as forms of disturbance of analytical and integrative activity (Luria, 1947, 1962, 1969, 1970). The basic proposition that all these disturbances are special in character, that defects of optical gnosis as a rule are unaccompanied by any disturbances of acoustic gnosis, and that speech defects are not necessarily accompanied by any appreciable defects of processes other than speech, remained securely established, and this partial character of the defects continued to be the basic feature distinguishing local lesions of the cortex from lesions of the deeper brain structures.

Are the phenomena of optic and acoustic agnosia and of spatial apraxia accompanied by corresponding disturbances of mnemonic processes? If so, what clinical symptoms are manifested, and what physiological mechanisms lie at their basis? These questions have not received a precise answer. The mnemonic defects associated with local cortical lesions have never undergone detailed analysis.

Aims and Methods of Investigation

The Plan of Investigation

Investigations of memory disturbances in local brain lesions have rarely been sufficiently broad or differentiated in character. Usually they consist of nothing more than a general clinical description of the memory disorder, or of a carefully established narrowing of the range of traces that the patient can retain by comparison with the normal subject (classical investigations conducted in Kraepelin's school are an example of this type of analysis). Only the few investigations conducted, for example, by Milner and his co-workers from 1958 to 1970, by Weiskrantz (1964, 1966, 1968), Barbizet (1963) or Talland (1965), constitute exceptions to this general rule.

I have investigated memory disturbances arising from local brain lesions with both broad and differentiated neuropsychological tests to delineate the syndromes involved and analyze the mechanisms forming the basis of these disturbances. The facts described on the preceding pages considerably clarified the aim of my investigation and enabled groups of special problems to be distinguished in the general plan.

First it was necessary to describe the types of memory disturbance observed in brain lesions in different areas. The classical neurologists were inclined to regard memory disturbances as partial defects accompanying lesions of particular zones of the cerebral hemispheres contiguous with the corresponding receptor or motor area.[2] With the first description of Korsakov and the later discovery of the functions of the "hippocampal circles" and limbic region, interest of investigators switched to the description of general memory disturbances resembling disturbances of consciousness.

My problem was to distinguish clearly the localization of brain lesions leading, on the one hand, to general, modality-nonspecific disturbances and, on the other, to special, modality-specific disturbances of memory.

The essence of my hypothesis was that lesions of the higher levels of the brain stem, inducing dysfunction of both cerebral hemispheres, as well as lesions of the limbic region and hippocampus give rise to general disturbances of memory affecting all modalities equally. Local lesions of the lateral, convex surface of the cortex, on the other hand, lead either to special, modality-specific disturbances, or to localized system-specific disturbances of memory that never assume the form of general disturbances of consciousness. This problem required both a careful clinical description of the syndrome accompanying the memory disturbances, as well as special tests for comparing disturbances of memory affecting different modalities.

The second problem, directly contiguous with the first, is whether a given local brain lesion leads to the disturbance of mnemonic activity itself, or produces only a defect in activities required for performance of the mnestic task.

The character of the memory disturbance is profoundly different in these two cases. If he can still imprint traces but loses the task of memorizing material presented to him, the patient will naturally be unable to distinguish between the traces he must reproduce and irrelevant traces springing up uncontrollably, so that the organized goal-directed brain activity is converted into a cycle of arbitrary associations or a series of inertly reproduced traces of past experience. Conversely, when mnestic activity remains intact, but the operative links of the process are affected, the patient's attitude toward the memorizing process remains adequate, and the disturbance of the mnemonic processes assumes a completely different character.

[2] Such opinion was expressed quite clearly in the early 1900s by the eminent neurologist Ramon-y-Cajal (1909-1911) in the concluding chapter of his well-known classic entitled "Histology of the Nervous System of Man and Vertebrates."

The two forms of memory disturbance just referred to in fact are found in patients with brain lesions in different areas. For instance, in patients with lesions confined to the gnostic zones of cortex or to the hippocampus, conscious activity remains intact although the performance on mnemonic tasks may run into serious difficulties. The patients of this group show defects in memorizing modality-specific material, or in the retention of material of any modality. They are, however, well aware of their defects and try to compensate them. As a rule, when reproducing material they do not recall irrelevant traces.

A completely different syndrome is apparent in the nonspecific memory disturbances accompanying toxic states, acute trauma, the acute period after rupture of an aneurysm, in some cases of deep brain tumors located in the mid-line and, in particular, in massive lesions of the frontal lobes. In such cases the goal-directed mnemonic activity itself disintegrates, the patient cannot retain the plan of memorizing, and he therefore no longer has a critical attitude toward his defects. He demonstrates acute disorientation in space and time; he confabulates; he is not really aware that his memory is seriously disturbed. As a rule, these symptoms accompany a syndrome of general aspontaneity, so that the memory disorders come to resemble general disorders of consciousness.

The essence of my hypothesis was that the first form of memory disturbance results from a lesion of the deep zones of the brain unaccompanied by any marked general cerebral reactions, and does not involve the frontal lobes. The second form of memory disturbance is accompanied by a general cerebral reaction and is always linked with dysfunction of the frontal lobes (in particular, with a disturbance of the function of the medial and basal zones). I shall examine such cases very closely and describe patients with deep lesions of the anterior zones of the brain, paying particular attention to patients in whom spasm of the anterior cerebral arteries leads to a definite disturbance of the functions of the medial zones of both frontal lobes (Luria, Konovalov, & Podgornaya, 1970).

The third problem investigated involved describing the level of these disturbances. Under normal conditions, the amount of material retained can be considerably extended by coding. Bühler (1907, 1908) postulated that the "memory of ideas" has a capacity far greater than the "memory of isolated elements." This problem was carefully studied by Vygotskii and his collaborators (Leont'ev, 1930; Zankov, 1944) and has been explained in light of information theory by Miller (1969), Broadbent (1958, 1969), and others. This work has clearly shown that the transfer of mnemonic processes to a higher level of semantic organization significantly enlarges capacity, and makes traces incomparably more stable.

There is every reason to suppose that the disturbances arising in patients with lesions in different parts of the brain may involve different levels of mnemonic organization. In some cases the disturbances of memory are elementary in character, and semantic organization for retention is still possible, but in other cases the disturbance is at a higher level, and any attempt at semantic organization will be largely unsuccessful.

Local lesions deep in the brain, like those located in the posterior (temporal, parietal and occipital) zones of the hemispheres, give rise only to elementary disturbances of memory that can be compensated by a transfer to a higher lèvel of semantic organization. When the lesions are accompanied by a massive general cerebral reaction, or when they lie in the anterior zones of the brain, the situation is quite different. Facts which I shall discuss more fully below indicate that in these cases the entire structure of mnemonic activity is profoundly disturbed, and that transferring the memorizing process to a higher level of semantic organization does not give the result observed in the normal subject. Among the patients of this group there are presumably some in whom the transfer of memorizing to a higher level of semantic organization is quite impossible. The algorhythm for memorizing complex semantic structures is disturbed even more than the process of memorizing the individual elements.

Special methods must be used to determine if lesions in different parts of the brain disturb different levels of mnemonic processes. First, the process of memorizing of discrete material, not organized into semantic systems, must be compared with the memorizing of material organized into semantic (grammatically and logical) structures. Second, we must analyze the modification of mnemonic activity resulting from a change from direct retention to memorizing with the use of specific aids and supporting cues (the transition to "indirect" memorizing). Perhaps the most important problem is the last one: What is the physiological nature of the memory disturbances observed?

I gave two possible answers to that question. Some writers have attempted to explain memory disturbances in brain lesions as defects of recording, consisting of weakness of the imprinted traces and their rapid disappearance. Others, on no less firm grounds, regard the cause of the memory disturbances in brain lesions as the pathologically increased inhibitability of traces by irrelevant, interfering factors. In other words, they regard the basic pathology of mnemonic processes not as disturbances of trace imprinting, but as a disturbance of trace reproduction (ecphoria).

This alternative interpretation was apparent from the very first moments of the study of memory disturbances. In many patients direct retention remained intact, but reminiscence of apparently unimprinted traces could be observed after a period. Following the first steps of this study, the processes of forgetting in normal and pathological states of the brain came to be interpreted as the result of proactive and retroactive inhibition rather than primary disappearance (Talland, 1965; Talland & Waugh, 1969).

As the study of the dynamics of higher nervous processes made further progress, these observations received more support. The imprinting and reproduction of traces came to be regarded more and more as a neurodynamic process in which the traces may be exposed both to the inhibitory effect of irrelevant (interfering) factors and to the influence of mutual inhibition arising from the action of some components of the imprinted traces on others. Evidence of the inhibitory effect of interfering factors, previously described for the normal subject, assumed particular prominence with progress in the study of the pathophysiology of higher nervous activity. The description of phasic states of the cortex, in which newly formed traces start by becoming equal in strength and later are inhibited abnormally quickly (the strongest traces may sometimes pass into an inhibitory state faster than weaker traces), suggested that in local brain lesions, which induce an inhibitory state of the cortex, the pathologically increased inhibitability of traces may be the chief cause of memory disorders.

In both normal and pathological states the methods for studying memory disturbances were based on the assumption that the analysis must concentrate on the process of imprinting and retention irrespective of the factors to which these traces are exposed. The techniques most commonly used in clinical practice were investigating the retention of an increasingly long series (the method described in the classical German literature as the study of "Merkfähigkeit"), and rote learning a series of elements while recording the gradual increase in the number of elements retained. Neither of these methods is adequate for the investigation of the forgetting process, although this, in my opinion, is the main task in the study of mnemonic disturbances resulting from local brain lesions.

To obtain material adequate for the study of this problem, I had first to re-examine existing methods and use techniques that would permit study of the effect of interfering factors on trace retention. The methods I chose compare, first, how trace reproduction is affected by "empty" (unoccupied with irrelevant activity) pauses, and by pauses occupied with interfering activity, and second, how recall is affected by acitivity that differed sharply from the mnemonic activity (heterogeneous interference), on the one hand, and by activity similar in character and content to the mnemonic activity (homogeneous interference), on the other.

These methods provided the most information because irrelevant forms of activity (heterogeneous interference) have an incomparably weaker inhibitory effect than homogeneous forms of interference, which present the subject with a new and particularly difficult task—choosing the required series of traces from many possible alternatives.

Finally, I had to plan the investigation in such a way that the material obtained could be analyzed qualitatively. The inhibitory effect of an irrelevant activity must be distinguishable from its other effects, such as the leveling of excitability of different traces, or increased inertia of the nervous processes, making the switch from some traces to others impossible. All these forms of inhibition could be the result of completely different factors, and they could be manifested in totally different forms in patients with lesions in different parts of the brain. As presented below, I substantially modified the usual method of studying memory disturbances precisely in order to solve the problem I have just described. Clinical investigations, as a rule, have been directed toward the study of changes affecting voluntary mnemonic activity. Voluntary (premeditated) memorizing, however, is only a small part of the phenomena of memory observed in man. It is equally important to study the course of unpremeditated memorizing in man, which, in fact, is the source of the predominant mass of man's experience. The process of involuntary (unpremeditated) memorizing has become a subject of study only very recently, and Soviet workers (Smirnov, 1948, 1966; Zinchenko, 1961) have taken a leading part in the development of this field. The question naturally arises: To what extent do the memory disturbances observed in pathological states of the brain extend to involuntary (unpremeditated) memorizing, and to what degree does the inhibitory effect of interfering activity extend to the sphere of unpremeditated memorizing?

In one of his most important books devoted to the relationship between matter and memory, Bergson (1896) pointed out the profound differences that exist between involuntary reproduction of traces, such as occurs during the performance of habitual movements, and the voluntary recalling of traces imprinted without any premeditated attempt at consolidation, that arises whenever man attempts to recall isolated events from his past life. The same writer showed that the two forms of reproduction of involuntarily imprinted traces can appear separately. In many pathological cases, involuntarily formed habits (Bergson calls them "body memory") remain intact, but the ability to recall involuntarily imprinted traces of the past (Bergson calls them "mind memory") voluntarily is badly affected. He felt this was the essential feature of many forms of memory disturbance in organic brain lesions. Dissociation of this type was also described by Monakow, Janet, and other writers.

To what extent do local brain lesions give rise to significant defects not only in voluntary memorizing, but also in those two types of unpremeditated memorizing and voluntary recalling of involuntarily formed traces that I have just described? Unlike all the problems examined earlier, each of which is the subject of a pathopsychological and neuropsychological literature of considerable length, the problem of changes in traces of unpremeditated memorizing in pathological states of the brain has not been the subject of psychological investigation. The facts relating to it are limited purely to the changes observed in direct orientation in space and time and general phenomena of amnesia taken from clinical psychiatry.

In order to answer this question, it is first necessary to devise a completely new technique of investigation, capable of comparing the process of memorizing material learned voluntarily with the process of memorizing traces arising involuntarily. In addition a study must be made both of the process of involuntary habit formation, as well as the possibility of recalling past events in cases when the traces of this past experience were not formed voluntarily. No one has yet succeeded in devising an adequate technique for all these requirements, and I was compelled to make do with existing methods (such as the unpremeditated formation of traces in a test of set formation and Lewin's tests on the recalling of completed and uncompleted actions). The problem I have just enunciated is thus not reflected as faithfully as it should be in the facts described below, and its proper study is a task for future research.

Principles of Neurodynamic Investigation of Memory

The plan of the investigation described above determines the system of methods that must be used to study memory disturbances in local brain lesions. In each case, my investigation had to begin with a careful analysis of the syndrome in which the memory disorders arise, and of the general clinical situation of which they are a part. Isolated defects of memory in patients with normal consciousness and adequate orientation to themselves and their surroundings contrast sharply with the massive disturbances of memory associated with general disorders of consciousness, defects of orientation in space and time, and sometimes confabulations relative to the present and the immediate past, which are frequently found in patients with an advanced Korsakov's syndrome.

The group of problems I have just formulated also implies that no single method could meet our purpose. We must have recourse to a system of methods, compare their results, and, on that basis, make the necessary assessment of the character of the disturbances arising in patients with lesions in different parts of the brain.

The scheme of investigation devised for this purpose was similar to that described by Petersen and Petersen (1962). Each test of memorizing appropriate material was carried out under the following conditions:

(1) *Reproduction of the material immediately after its presentation.*

(2) *Reproduction of this material after a relatively short pause* (30 sec–1.5 min) not filled with any interfering activity (an "empty" pause). This test could show the strength of the traces formed by the patient and whether they disappear or not within a short time, despite the absence of controllable interfering actions.

(3) *Reproduction of this material after the same pause, but filled with interfering activity*. For instance, if the patient was required to memorize cards, words, sentences, or stories, after the presentation of the corresponding series he was instructed to do mental arithmetic for one minute (adding or subtracting double figures or counting backward from 100 in sevens), after which he had to reproduce the series presented previously. This test, which I have described as the heterogeneous interfering inhibition test, reveals the effect

of interfering activity on trace preservation. Of course, this series of tests was carried out within limits that under normal conditions did not give rise to any marked inhibitory effect.

(4) *A test of the inhibitory effect of homogeneous interfering activity.* The method developed for these purposes was as follows. The patient was instructed to memorize certain material (pictures, words, sentences, stories) and was warned that he had to retain the material in his memory and he would have to recall it later. The patient was then presented with another similar series (pictures, words, sentences, stories), which he had to repeat. After repeating the second series, he was asked to recall the first series. The inhibitory effect of the second series retained by the patient was such that (a) he could either not recall the first series after repeating the second or reproduce the first series incorrectly, or (b) instead of repeating the first series he inertly repeated elements of the second series, or finally (c) he confused elements of the first and second series. This effect showed clearly that forgetting previously imprinted traces could be the result of the inhibitory effect of homogeneous interfering activity.

If a patient was found to be unable to recall the first series of traces after reproducing a second, similar series, the test was repeated several times until he was able to reproduce the required series. In that case, the degree of the inhibitory effect of the second (interfering) series was measured by the number of repetitions necessary before recall became possible. It could also be measured in another way if a patient was able to reproduce the traces of the first series after reproducing the second. He was instructed several times in succession to answer the question: How many elements were in the first, and how many in the second series? Stability was manifested when the subject could recall both of the imprinted series of traces selectively and repeatedly. Instability was manifested by loss of the ability to recall them selectively, so that after several attempts he began either to forget one of the series or to exhibit contamination of one with the other.

The test I have just described has another important advantage: It can be used to study important neurodynamic features during changes in selective retention trace preservation. Three types of abnormalities have been observed in this test. In some cases the reproduction of the second series is sufficient to "obliterate" the traces of the first, similar series. The subject declares that he has "forgotten" which series he has just repeated. Results of this type indicate the ready inhibitability of the nervous system by interfering homogeneous traces. They resemble retroactive inhibition.

In other cases, the patient has difficulty in reproducing the second series but inertly repeats the first series. This phenomenon of severe "proactive" inhibition indicates pathological inertia of the earlier traces, and constitutes evidence that the memory disturbances are based on a disturbance of mobility of the nervous processes. I have made such observations frequently when examining patients with massive lesions of the frontal lobes, and a disturbance of the mobility of nervous processes is known to be a particularly characteristic feature of frontal lobe pathology.

The third type of defect observed in this series of tests is particularly interesting. In these cases, when the patient tries to recall the first series he has memorized after reproducing a second, similar series, he loses his selectivity with respect to each series and begins to exhibit contamination of one series by the other, frequently unaware that he has made any mistakes. These phenomena may arise equally in patients with a general lowering of cortical tone accompanying deep brain lesions and in frontal and temporal lesions. In the latter case, the lesions are usually partial and affect only audioverbal memory. The patient's inadequate critical attitude toward this contamination may be of particular diagnostic significance. In some cases it correlates with signs of general disorientation and with confabulations, but in others (if it is modality-nonspecific and manifested equally in different types of mnemonic activity) it may appear as an early symptom, before general disorders of consciousness, or as a late symptom, indicating residual phenomena of the disturbance of selectivity that, at the height of the disease, led to similar disturbances of consciousness. The contamination of two separate systems of traces can, therefore, serve as appropriate experimental models of more extensive disturbances of consciousness.

In some cases, increased inhibitability by interfering factors may be manifested uniformly in all modalities (during the memorizing of visual, motor, and audioverbal series). In others, it is confined to only one modality. This fact is of decisive importance, for it shows that the neurodynamic basis of the memory pathology may be either general or modality-specific. As I shall show below, the first type is characteristic of deep brain lesions (especially disturbances of the "hippocampal circle" and the limbic region) and also, in a rather special form, of lesions of the frontal lobes. The second type, in which increased inhibitability of traces is limited to one particular sphere, is characteristic of local lesions of the posterior (temporal, parietal, and occipital) zones of the hemispheres. These symptoms sensitively suggest strictly circumscribed, local brain lesions.

In another dimension, the increased inhibitability by interfering factors sometime appeared only at a lower level (during the memorizing and recalling of discrete, meaningless material) and was abolished with the change to tests of the memorizing and recalling of material organized into meaningful systems (for example, the recalling of sentences and stories). In other cases, the situation was different; the increased inhibitability applied equally to the recalling of discrete, meaningless material and of material organized into semantic systems. Characteristically, the first case is seen in patients with local lesions of the brain stem or the posterior (gnostic) zones of the cortex. The second form of memory disorders is particularly conspicuous in patients with massive brain lesions affecting both hemispheres, and in certain types of lesion of the frontal lobes. The neurodynamic analysis of retention and recall not only represents a great step forward for the investigation of the general physiological mechanisms of memory disturbance, but it is also of special importance for the analysis of their local significance.

Methods of Investigation of Memory Disturbances in Local Brain Lesions

As stated above, my objective was to determine whether the memory disturbances are modality-specific or general (nonspecific) in character, to discover the levels of psychological processes which they affect, and to obtain data on the neurodynamic mechanisms lying at their basis. I shall briefly describe this series of tests but delay detailed description for subsequent presentation together with the results obtained.

(1) *Experiments on learning series of words.* To determine the general characteristics of the memorizing process, I began my investigation with a test involving the learning of a series of 10 isolated words, repeating the test many times (up to 10) and plotting a "learning curve." The results of this test can show the level of the patient's mnemonic activity, whether or not he can retain the problem presented to him, whether he exhibits any form of strategy of learning, the character of the "learning curve," and the extent to which the results obtained differ from normal.

(2) *Experiments on retention of traces of a fixed set.* This method, developed in the school of Academician D. N. Uznadze (1958), aims at determining whether the simplest sensorimotor traces are preserved in the patient. The experiments test whether the patient develops an ordinary illusion of contrast, whether it persists after a pause of 1 to 2 minutes unoccupied by interfering activity, and whether it is preserved after similar pauses when occupied by interfering activity (by mental arithmetic or by motor exercises). These tests determine whether the memory disturbances affect the most elementary level of unpremeditated retention of an established sensorimotor illusion, and under what conditions (a long pause or the inhibitory effect of interference) traces formed earlier disappear.

(3) *Tests on the tension of perceived shapes (after Konorski).* This series of tests has an objective similar to the previous one. It attempts to discover whether the patient preserves the image of a presented previously shape (a triangle or rhombus of arbitrary color and size), and whether he can decide if it is identical with, or different from, another figure of different shape, color, or size. As in the previous case, the second figure was presented either immediately after the first or after a pause of 30, 60, 90, or 120 sec

unoccupied by interfering activity, or after a similar pause but occupied by interfering activity (mental arithmetic, examination of picture cards).

The results of this test, like those of the preceding test, show whether the disturbance is at the elementary level of retention of perceived shapes (not learned by heart) as well as what conditions (a long pause or the inhibitory effect of interference) are necessary to manifest disturbances of simple perceptual memory.

(4) *Tests on retention of a series of visual forms or movements.* Unlike the previous series, this (and also the next) test is aimed at studying voluntary memorizing or, in other words, mnemonic activity. Its purpose is to test how firmly the patient can retain several visually perceived objects (two or three geometric shapes or pictures of objects); and whether he can reproduce them (by naming or drawing them) at once or after a pause of 1 to 2 min unoccupied or occupied by interfering activity (counting, examination of pictures). As a special form of this test, the inhibitory role of homogeneous interfering activity is examined by presenting a first series of 1, 2, or (less frequently) 3 drawings, and then presenting a similar second series. The patient has to recall the pictures forming the first series and then those forming the second series. These tests show whether memory defects are connected mainly with the visual sphere and identify the physiological nature of these defects if they exist. Tests on the retention of movements (a series of one, two, or occasionally, of three movements) are carried out similarly. This series will show whether the defect of memory extends to the motor sphere.

In the tests described above, the patient has to retain visual images or movements presented to him as simple stimuli. To determine the patient's ability to retain conditioned connections, tests were carried out in which he had to perform a certain conditional action (for example, in response to one tap he must raise his right hand; in response to two taps, his left hand). If he performed this test correctly, a test was carried out to discover if he retained this connection after a pause of 1, 1.5, or 2 min, unoccupied or occupied by interfering activity (for example, mental arithmetic). The results of this test can show whether the retention of all traces (even direct) is disturbed or whether the patient's conditioned codes only are disturbed, or vice versa.

(5) *Tests of retention of word series.* Unlike tests (1)-(4), with which I began my investigation, these tests assumed the direct retention of a short series of 2, 3, or 4 isolated words and their reproduction in the order in which they were presented. In this sense, they can be classified as typical tests of short-term memory. Like the previous tests, these were carried out under the conditions of direct recall, reproduction after a pause of 1, 1.5, or 2 min unoccupied by interfering acticity and also under the inhibitory influence of interference. In the last case, the pause separating reproduction of the word series from its presentation was occupied by interfering activity (mental arithmetic) or, after the first series, the patient was instructed to memorize a

second, similar series, after which he had to recall the words of the first series and those of the second. If the patient could not do this, the test was repeated from 3 to 10 times (depending on his performance).

(6) *Tests of sentence retention.* To study the changes in word retention resulting from semantic organization, the patient was instructed to repeat a simple sentence, at first immediately but later after a pause of 1, 1.5, or 2 min unoccupied with interfering activity, and finally, the same test was repeated after a pause occupied by interfering activity (mental arithmetic). If the disturbances of mnemonic activity extended to the higher levels of intellectual organization, it could be expected that this test would give results similar to the previous test; if, on the other hand, the defect was limited to the more elementary levels, semantic organization of the elements into a sentence could be expected to abolish the primary instability of the traces.

(7) *Tests of retention of meaningful fragments.* These tests were aimed at studying forms of memory for which analytico-synthetic activity is essential (in other words, requiring coding). The patient was not required to reproduce the material presented word for word but he had to relate the meaning of the material by picking out its most important components and creating a semantic scheme of the text. A story (or meaningful fragment) with a particular construction was read to the patient. He had to reproduce this fragment immediately, after a short pause (1.5 to 2 min) without interfering activity, or after the same pause occupied with interfering activity (for example, mental arithmetic). Particular attention was paid to tests of homogeneous interference in which one fragment was read to the patient who had to repeat it immediately; then a second similar fragment was read (usually including certain components common to it and the first fragment) which he also had to repeat; he was then instructed to recall the content of the first fragment and later of the second as well. The examiner paid particular attention to the existence of contamination between the two fragments. If the test was not performed satisfactorily, it was repeated several times.

In my investigation, I attempted to adhere to the program just described but, since the work was clinical as well as psychological in character, and the tests had to be carried out on patients in different states, the program could not always be followed exactly. Thus, at times certain items had to be omitted.

CHAPTER II
Disturbances of Basic Mnemonic Processes in Local Brain Lesions

This chapter gives a general account of a study performed during the course of several years and involving many patients with tumors of various parts of the brain, local vascular lesions of the brain (surgically verified cases of aneurysm of the cerebral arteries and arterio-venous aneurysms in various situations), and brain injuries (Table 1). I have also included the results of investigations of mnemonic disturbances in patients with aneurysms of the anterior communicating artery (Luria, Konovalov, & Podgornaya, 1970). The investigations were carried out by the author as well as his colleagues Akbarova (1971), Chaltykyan (1968), Kiyashchenko (1969), Klimkovskii (1966), Marzaganova (1971), Pham Minh Hac (1971), Popova (1964), and others.

The clinical character of the neuropsychological investigation permitted extensive syndrome analysis of psychological disturbances in individual patients (Luria & Artem'eva, 1970). Before describing the syndromes, let us study how mnemonic processes are disturbed by lesions of different parts of the brain. Such analysis will enable us to draw distinction between the general and special forms of memory disturbances. Only after a careful examination of these results can we integrate and describe the complex syndromes of memory disturbances arising in local brain lesions. I shall examine the data obtained by the use of methods described above in the order in which they were given; each time I shall describe more fully the actual technique, and indicate the results obtained.

TABLE 1

DESCRIPTION OF 317 PATIENTS

Types of brain lesions					
		Tumors			
Aneurysms	Injuries	Deep	Frontal lobes	Left temporal region	Left occipito-parietal region
40	120	59	36	45	17

Rote Learning of Word Lists

This test is well known in both general and clinical psychology. A series of discrete (unconnected) words is read out to the patient. He must memorize them, and repeat them in any order. Since the memorizing of a series containing the maximum number of words (as a rule, 10) did not give the desired results at once, the test was repeated several times in succession (usually 6 to 10 times) and not only the number of elements retained, but also the order in which the subject reproduced the words was recorded. The increasing number of items recalled over trials was shown as a "learning curve." In those relatively rare cases in which such a test was completely impossible (for example, patients with sensory aphasia), the series was reduced to 4 or 5 words.

As a rule, normal subjects set about the task of learning the word series without hesitation and displayed mnemonic activity with clearly defined features. The subjects use strategy for memorizing. They group the material to be learned and, having learned a certain number of words, concentrate their attention on words not at first recalled, so that, when they reproduce the series a second time, they begin to recall words that were omitted in the first attempt. The order of recall varies, reflecting the strategy of the subject's active mnemonic operations. This strategy is clearly visible in the change in recall order over trials of a typical normal subject (Table 2).

As a rule, this process reveals the serial position effect (reproduction of the first and last members of the series first), well-known in the literature, and itself an indication of the influence of proactive and retroactive inhibition. During successive trials, however, the serial position effect ceases to apply and is replaced by the active, selective strategy.

Another important feature of normal serial learning is the gradual increase in the number of items recalled, manifested under normal conditions in learning curves. It will be clear from Figure 1 that such a curve steadily rises without

TABLE 2

RECALL ORDER OF A 10-WORD SERIES BY A NORMAL SUBJECT

Order of word presentation	dom (house)	les (forest)	kot (cat)	stol (table)	noch' (night)	igla (needle)	pirog (pie)	zvon (ringing)	most (bridge)	krest (cross)
					Successive trials					
I	1	2	3	4					5	6
II	4	5	6	7	8		9	1	2	3
III	4	5	6	7		8		1	2	3
IV	3	4	5	6	2	1	7	8	9	10

Note. – The arabic numbers in Tables 2–5 indicate the recall order of the words.

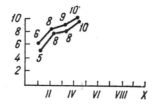

FIG. 1. Learning curves for 10-word series for a normal subject: Abscissa, trials; ordinate, correct responses.

appreciable fluctuation or decrease in the number of words recalled. These learning curves may assume a different character in patients with local brain lesions.

For patients with lesions of the frontal lobes, the process of memorizing a series of words is significantly changed. As a rule, these patients (especially those with a massive, usually bilateral lesion of the frontal lobes associated with general aspontaneity) make no effort to memorize the series. Usually, they repeat echolalically four or five words of the series—usually the first (the primacy effect) or the last (the recency effect) words of the series—and they continue to repeat them in all subsequent trials, making no attempt to add other items in the series.

If these patients make a mistake of any sort (for example, if they include a word with a similar sound or one connected by association) during the first recall trial, this word will be repeated uncontrollably during subsequent trials. The process of memorizing will be converted into the repetition of inert stereotypes. Often the pathological inertia of trace processes, characteristic of patients with a frontal lobe lesion, will cause the patient to begin to repeat the same word twice. In such cases, he makes no attempt to correct a mistake. For instance, when recalling a series of 10 words (dom—les—kot—noch'—zvon—most, etc.), he reproduces part of the series (dom—kot—les—zvon—kot), repeating one of the words twice, but does not notice his mistake or correct it even after his attention has been drawn to it. Once a mistake has been made, it is converted into an inert stereotype and can be repeated indefinitely.

Perhaps the most characteristic feature of patients with a lesion of the frontal lobes and the collapse of active mnemonic activity is that no rearrangement of the words is ever made in successive trials. This is reflected, first, in the fixed order of the words recalled (Table 3) and, second, in the number of words recalled which does not increase over trials. As a result, instead of the normal learning curve, we obtain a typical plateau phenomenon for the patient with a frontal lobe lesion. The basic feature of these patients is

TABLE 3

RECALL ORDER OF 10-WORD SERIES BY A PATIENT WITH THE FRONTAL SYNDROME

Order of word presentation	Successive trials									
	dom (house)	les (forest)	kot (cat)	stol (table)	noch' (night)	igla (needle)	pirog (pie)	zvon (ringing)	most (bridge)	krest (cross)
I	1	2	3					4		
II	1	2	3					4		
III	1	2	3					4		
IV	1	2	3					4		
V	1	2	3					4		
VI	1	2	3					4		

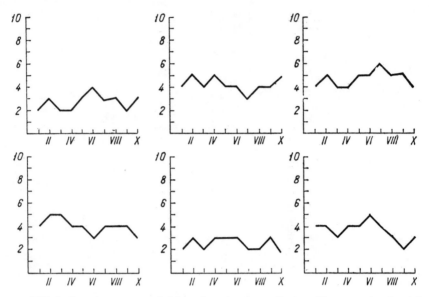

FIG. 2. Learning curves of 10-word series for patients with a massive frontal syndrome: Abscissa, trial number; ordinate, correct responses.

replacement of active mnemonic function by the stereotyped repetition of initially imprinted group of traces (Figure 2).

Tests for recall of audioverbal material by patients with lesions of the left temporal cortex provide a different picture. As we know from the literature, patients with lesions in this region have unimpaired kinesthetic and visuo-spatial gnosis, but display audioverbal disorders in the form of acoustico-gnostic or acoustico-mnemonic defects, most frequently exhibited as the corresponding forms of sensory or acoustico-mnemonic aphasia (Luria, 1947, 1966, 1969, 1970, 1973). Patients with the severest manifestation of this syndrome are unable to differentiate the sounds of speech (although their musical hearing and retention of melodies may remain relatively intact). They are unable to carry out tests of audioverbal memory.

Patients with less severe acoustico-gnostic disorders (most commonly with lesions of the middle temporal zones or with deep intracerebral temporal tumors or abscesses) do not always show gross disorders or difficulty in discriminating between similar phonemes. In these cases, the phenomenon of "alienation of word meaning" (Luria, 1947, 1970) is found in relatively milder forms, although there is no doubt about their difficulty in retaining series of sounds or words. Patients in this group have no difficulty in repeating one sound or one simple word, or of retaining it indefinitely, provided that the interval between its presentation and recall is not filled with interfering activity.

Frequently, even a group of two sounds or two words can be retained and reproduced by these patients without much difficulty.

A definite disturbance is found in such patients when they recall a series of three or four items. It then becomes quite clear that the traces of some items start to inhibit the traces of others. The patient is unable to recall the series in the order in which it was presented. As a rule, recall of the first or last item of the series is easier, in such cases, than recall of the middle items. If the patient finds a way of memorizing the first item, retention of the remaining items vanishes; if he does not find such a way, he recalls the last (the most recent) item, and is unable to reproduce any of the previous elements. Examples of such cases, illustrating three possible types of disturbances, are given in Figure 3.

The tendency to reproduce the last words of a series led to a unique form of inversion, in which a series of two words was recalled in the opposite order, i.e., the last word first, and the first word last. This tendency is also seen with a series of three words or more, the only difference being that as the series lengthens the patient recalls the last word first, then the first word, but fails on the middle words.

An example is given below of the recall of word lists by patient Blokh. (a 35-year-old male with a wound of the left temporal region), who was instructed to maintain the order of the words in the series.

Reproduction of one word: no difficulty.
Reproduction of a series of two words[3]

Shkaf—les	*Stol—svet*	*Zhuk—dym*
Les . . . shkaf	Svet—stol	Dym. . . zhuk

Did you reproduce them properly? "I don't know. . . I'm not sure."

Reproduction of a series of three words

Klyuch—grib—mokh	*Ten'—glaz—nozh*	*Dom—les—okno*
. . . Mokh . . .	Nozh. . . glaz	Okno. . . dom

Reproduction of a series of four words

Krest—most—luch—stol	*Myach—zvon—noch'—krest*
Stol. . . luch. . .	Krest. . . noch'. . . krest. . .

This tendency to recall the last word of the series, as well as the retroactive inhibition of the previous elements, is a persistent characteristic in this group of patients. Characteristically, this pathological inhibition is confined purely to audioverbal memory. With a change to lists of letters or written words, recency effect disappeared immediately. Although the subject always began to reproduce an acoustic series with the last item, he now recalled the first item

---

[3]The words in the order presented are given in the numerator; the words in the order recalled are given in the denominator. (This applies also to all subsequent examples.)

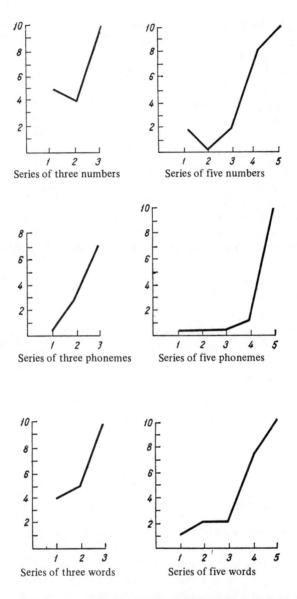

FIG. 3. The recency effect (predominance of the last word) during recall by a patient with a lesion of the left temporal region: Abscissa, serial/position (phoneme, word, number); ordinate, recall frequency in 10 trials.

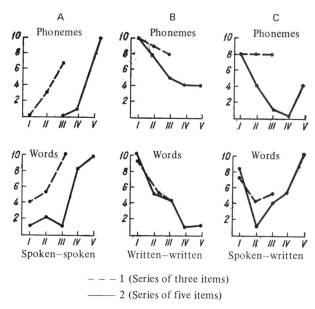

A   B   C

Phonemes   Phonemes   Phonemes

Words   Words   Words

Spoken—spoken   Written—written   Spoken—written

– – – 1 (Series of three items)
——— 2 (Series of five items)

FIG. 4. Recall order of phonemes and words by a patient with a lesion of the left temporal region, as a function of the method of presentation and recall. A) Spoken presentation–spoken recall. B) Written presentation–written recall. C) Spoken presentation–written recall (abscissa, serial position; ordinate, recall frequency in ten trials.

first and produced a learning curve similar to a normal subject. Given the opportunity, these patients would recode the acoustic series into a visual series, and retroactive inhibition did not appear. When the patient was instructed to listen to a series of words and then reproduce them in writing, the phenomenon of inversion was no longer exhibited and the series was recalled normally (Figure 4).

Finally, many observations demonstrate that number series (even when spoken) give better results with these patients than spoken word series. Evidently, numbers are more easily visualized than spoken words.

The increased mutual inhibitability of audioverbal traces explains the narrowing of the range of audioverbal memory observed in patients with lesions of the left temporal lobe. A typical example of this phenomenon follows.

Patient Blokh. (wound of the left temporal region) was asked to learn a series of five spoken words. Even repeated presentation of the same series did not abolish the mutual inhibition significantly.

Sneg (snow) – shkaf (cupboard) – les (forest) – most (bridge) – dom (house)[4]
(1) Les–shkaf. . . most. . . nos (nose). . . zvon (ringing). . .
(2) Les–shkaf. . . les. . . most. . . stol (table). . .
(3) Sneg. . . shkaf. . . most. . . stol. . . zvon. . .
(4) Sneg. . . shkaf. . . most. . . stol. . . zvon. . . No, the words "stol" and "zvon" were not there!
(5) Sneg. . . les. . . stol. . . No, "sneg". . . I am all mixed up!
(6) Sneg. . . shkaf. . . most. . . stol. . . zvon
(7) Sneg. . . shkaf. . . les. . . stol. . . zvon
(8) Les. . . shkaf. . . stol. . . zvon. . . and one more
(9) Sneg. . . les. . . shkaf. . . No, we have had "les" already. . . no, I can't.

Okno (window) – luna (moon) – pila (saw) – stakan (tumbler) – noga (leg)
(1) Steklo (glass). . . no, okno. . . luna. . . stol. . .
(2) Steklo. . . luna. . . stakan. . . pila. . .
(3) Okno. . . luna. . . stakan. . . pila
(4) Pila. . . stakan. . . noga. . . okno. . . luna. . .
(5) Okno. . . luna. . . pila. . . stakan. . . steklo. . . "No, something else."
(6) Steklo. . . luna. . . pila. . . noga. . . stakan. . .
(7) Steklo. . . luna. . . stakan. . . pila. . . steklo. . .
(8) Okno. . . luna. . . stakan. . . pila. . . luna. . .
(9) Okno. . . luna. . . pila. . . luna. . . no, pila. . . stakan
(10) Okno. . . luna. . . pila. . . noga. . . no. . . stakan. . . and steklo. . .

Similar findings were observed when *patient Bel.* (injury to the left temporal region) was tested.

Patients with a lesion of the left temporal lobe cannot reproduce a limited series of words presented verbally. The number of words recalled does not exceed three or four, and they are not recalled in the correct order. The patient frequently repeats the same words several times, or replaces them with other words. Usually, however, he retains the general "melody" of the presented series and repeats the required number of items (five), but substitutes inappropriate words or the same word twice or three times.

The role of increased mutual inhibition was confirmed by L. S. Tsvetkova's (1972) observations. If the intervals between the individual items of the series are increased (for instance, if the separate words are presented at intervals of 10 to 15 sec), the patients can reproduce a longer series of words. If such a patient were permitted to repeat every separate word, the stability of the traces increased still further. Following is an example of such a test.

Patient Kr., 46 years of age (after-effects of a penetrating gun-shot wound of the left parieto-temporal region), could repeat single sounds without difficulty, but repetition of two or three sounds was accompanied by appreciable acoustico-mnemonic difficulties.

[4] Arabic numbers indicate consecutive trials.

k–g	t–d	l–n	v–f	k–a–n	r–sh–s
I didn't	d. . .	no	d. . . and	I forget. . .	r. . . and
grasp the			something	l. . . and	something else
second			else	something else	

The patient could reproduce separate simple words without difficulty, but he found repeating complicated words very difficult. He retained only one or two syllables and forgot the rest:

Korablekrushenie (shipwreck)
(1) Kora. . . no, I can't remember.
(2) Korobko. . . no, I can't.

Gromkogovoritel' (loudspeaker)
Gromko. . . and something. . . I
don't know.

Kilimanjaro
(1) Kilo. . . kili. . .
(2) Kili. . . yes I remember

Arachnoidendothelioma
Oh. . . what did you say, no. . . I can't.
a. . . arach. . . no. . .

The patient was completely unable to reproduce a series of words:

Stol–zvon–klyuch (key)
(1) Stol. . . no. . . I can't. . .
(2) Stol. . . and something else.

Stuk (tap)– dub (oak)–steklo
Steklo. . . no, I don't know.
Steklo. . . stuk. . . no. . .

Repetition of sentences gave the patient great difficulty:

At the edge of the forest a hunter killed a wolf.
In the forest. . . no, I have forgotten. . . they shot something
like. . . about a hunter.

These difficulties can be overcome if the elements of a complex system are given separately, with long pauses between them:

k. . . g	k. . . g	u. . . t	u–t	k. . . l. . . n
k. . . g	k. . . g	u. . . t	u. . .t	k. . . l. . . n

Magnoliya (magnolia) mag no li ya *Magnoliya*
    Gives up.   mag no li ya Magnoliya. I know, it is the
flower the magnolia.

Stol	*Dom*	*Klyuch*	(Experiment repeated	*Stol–dom–klyuch*
Stol	Dom	Klyuch	3 times)	Stol–dom–klyuch

Stuk	*Dub*	*Steklo*	(Experiment repeated	*Stuk–dub–steklo*
Stuk	Dub	Steklo	3 times)	Stuk–dub–steklo

Patient Leb., a 40-year-old female (after clipping of an aneurysm of the middle cerebral artery), had no difficulty repeating isolated sounds and syllables. Repetition of a series of three sounds gives rise to great difficulty:

d–t–l	k–l–m	s–zh–s
t–d. . .	kl. . . l	s. . . no. . . r. . . s

Repetition of simple words was easy; but repetition of long words, very difficult:

Dobrozhelatel' (wellwisher)
dobro. . . I know this much, but
I have forgotten what comes next.

Gromkogovoritel (loudspeaker)
Grom. . . grom. . . radio

Kilimanjaro
Kilim. . . no, I can't remember.

Arachnoidendothelioma
(1) Ara. . . no
(2) Arach. . . no
(3) Arano. . . no

Noch' (night)	Igla (needle)	Pirog (pie)	(Experiment repeated	Noch –Igla –pirog
Noch	Igla	Pirog	3 times)	Noch –Igla –Pirog

Stuk	Voda	Krest (cross)	(Experiment repeated	Stuk –Voda –Krest
Stuk	Voda	Krest	3 times)	Stuk –Voda –Krest

Repetition of a sentence also gave rise to great difficulties:

Behind the window blossomed a white fragrant lilac
(1) Behind the window. . . grew. . . lilac. . . something else I don't know.
(2) Behind the window. . . something else. . . lilac. . .

These difficulties could be overcome by presenting the elements consecutively and with long pauses between them:

Ki	Li	Man	Ja	Ro	(Experiment repeated	Kilimanjaro
Ki	Li	Man	Ja	Ro	3 times)	Kilimanjaro. Yest I know, it is in Africa.

Behind the window	Blossoms	A white	Fragrant	Lilac
Behind the window	Blossoms	A white	Fragrant	Lilac

(Experiments repeated 3 times, after which the sentence was reproduced intact.)

A second observation confirmed that the chief factor preventing recall of an audioverbal series is the inhibitory effect of interfering factors rather than weakness of the traces (Klimkovskii, 1966). First, he increased the interval between presentation of the word series and their recall (10, 20, 30, or 60 sec), without filling this interval with any interfering stimulation. Second, he filled the relatively short pause between the end of the series and its recall (10 to 15 sec) with interfering conversation (for example, asking the subject whether he can remember a series easily, or how he feels, and receiving the appropriate reply).

If not filled with any interfering activity, increasing the interval to 10-15 or even to 30-60 sec did not limit recall when the series did not exceed two elements. When the series consisted of three items or more, the results varied: In 15 to 37 subjects, an interval not filled with interfering activity did not disturb recall of the series, but actually improved it. In the remaining 22 of the 37 patients, lengthening the interval did not improve recall, and lengthening the pause to 30-60 sec actually reduced it. When interfering activity (conversation) was introduced into a short interval (10 to 15 sec) recall was severely disturbed, and in some cases completely impossible. A short pause, filled with interfering activity, had a greater effect on recall than a long "empty" pause in all subjects tested. Inhibition by external interfering factors plays a large role in the pathology of audioverbal memory in patients with a lesion of the left temporal region. Examples of these tests are given below.

Patient Blokh. (injury to the left temporal region).

Tests with an "empty" pause

Retention of 3 words

Dom—kot (cat)—stol	*Noch'—zvon—khleb (bread)*
Dom. . . kot, stol	Zvonok, khleb

(After the second presentation, the words are retained.)

After a pause of 15 sec:

Kot. . . stol. . . dom	Khleb. . . zvon

After a pause of 30 sec:

Stol. . . khleb. . . now I have forgotten.	Zvon. . . khleb. . . I have forgotten one.

After a pause of 1 min:

Kot. . . and stol	Zvon. . . and also khleb

Tests with interference by irrelevant conversation

Retention of one word

Dozhdik (shower)	*Pricheska (hair style)*	*Provozka (cart)*
Dozhdik	Pricheska	Provozka

This is not difficult, is it? "No." Did you remember them well? "Yes." Was it difficult to remember? "No, dozhdik, volosy, arba. . . no, I have forgotten, no I can't think." Did you remember them exactly? "Yes. . . golova (head)."

Retention of series of 2 words

Telega (waggon)—arbuz (watermelon)	*Noch'—khleb*	*Divan (sofa)—butylka (bottle)*
Telega—arbuz	Noch'—khleb	Divan—butylka

After interfering questions:

Arby. . . and arbuz, no, I have forgotten.	Noch', I have forgotten.	Divan. . . no, I can't. . . they have beaten me.

In some cases with severe left temporal syndrome, recall of even a single word may be unstable and easily replaced by a word of similar meaning [pricheska (hair style)—volosy (hair), povozka (cart)—arba (a cart of oriental type)]. A series of two words leads either to complete inhibition of one item or to replacement by a word of similar meaning [okno (window)—steklo (glass)]. Recall of three words is completely impossible. Although the patient retains the general semantic meaning of the words, he cannot reproduce even one correctly. In these patients, interfering activity leads to inhibition of audioverbal traces so that the accurate recall is replaced by words of similar meaning ("verbal paraphasia"). The instability of audioverbal traces and their replacement by semantic equivalents are revealed by tests of word recognition (Klimkovskii, 1966). Patients with left temporal lesions are given a series of five isolated words and are instructed not to recall the words, but to identify them by picking them from ten suggested words. These patients have great difficulty in recognizing test words among those suggested, and sometimes either choose at random or substitute words of similar meaning. A typical example follows.

Patient Fed. (wound of the left temporal region). After the series svet–doroga (road)–reka–shlyapa–dym (smoke) is read to him, he correctly picks out only one word (svet) from a series of 10 words, and follows this by two confabulations (ozero and pole).

Not only the active reproduction, but also the recognition of words read previously is disturbed. Traces of previous words can be replaced by similar words (sometimes semantically equivalent).

All the phenomena described above are confined to the audioverbal sphere. They are not found in tests using visual material. If a patient with a left temporal lesion is asked to recall a series of four or even five written words, their recall after a delay can be carried out successfully. Even the interfering effect of distracting activity (such as questions and answers) no longer has any effect.

Patient Mikh. (tumor of the left temporal region) is given a series of five spoken (A) and written (B) words. The record shows the profound differences in reproduction of the series in these two cases:

A. Spoken words

*Igla–klyuch–okno–dozhd' (rain)
–dver' (door)*

(1) Igla. . . dozhd'. . . khleb. . . okno

(2) Igla. . . khleb. . . kot. . . dver. . . and
I have missed something in the middle

(3) Igla. . . dozhd'. . . khleb. . . and another

(4) Igla. . . dozhd'. . . khleb. . . dver. . . dozhd'

After a pause of 15 sec:

(5) Igla. . . okno. . . dver. . . khleb. . . and
something else. . .

After distraction:

(6) Igla. . . no. . . I can't remember anything.

B. Written words

*Klyuch–dym–nozh (knife)–luk
(onion)–ten' (shadow)*

(1) Klyuch–dym–nozh–ten'

After a pause of 15 sec:

(2) Klyuch–dym–nozh–luk–ten'

After a pause of 30 sec:

(3) Klyuch–dym–nozh–luk–ten'

After a pause of 1 min:

(4) Klyuch–dym–nozh–luk–ten'

After distraction:

(5) Klyuch–dym–nozh–ten'

Phenomena of this type could be observed only in patients with a pathological focus confined to the left temporal region. If the focus was in the posterior zones of the temporal region and involved the occipital region, the differences in recall of spoken and written series of words disappeared. This is illustrated by the following case.

Patient Van., a 41-year-old male with a tumor of the left parieto-occipital region.

A. **Spoken words**	B. **Written words**
Noch'—zvon—klyuch—dym—grib	*Glaz—dom—stol—nozh—myach*
(mushroom)	*(ball)*
(1) Noch'. . . zvon. . . grib	(1) Glaz. . . dom. . . stol. . . myach
(2) Noch'. . . klyuch. . . grib. . . zvon	(2) Glaz. . . dom. . . stol. . . myach
(3) Noch'. . . zvon. . . klyuch. . . grib	(3) Glaz, dom, nozh. . . stol
(4) Noch'. . . zvon. . . dym, grib	
(5) Noch'—zvon—klyuch—dym—grib	

After a pause of 15 sec:	After a pause of 15 sec:
Noch'—zvon—klyuch—dym—grib	Glaz—dom—nozh—stol. . .

After a pause of 30 sec:	After a pause of 30 sec:
Klyuch. . . no. . . zvon. . . dym. . . grib	Glaz—dom. . . nozh—stol

After distraction with conversation:	After distraction with conversation:
Noch. . . klyuch. . . zvon. . . grib	Glaz—dom. . . nozh. . . stol

* * *

The modality-specific disturbance of recall and recognition of acoustic series in patients with left temporal lesions and the relatively better preservation of visual series was further tested in my laboratory by E. N. Bulgakova, N. K. Kiyashchenko, and V. P. Fominykh. The material used in these tests consisted of meaningless figures (such as Japanese characters) and syllables (such as vag, rup, tsev), presented in the spoken form.

After presentation of four items, the subject was instructed to identify them from 10 possible alternatives (characters or syllables). In the first series, identification was tested immediately after presentation; in the second series, 1.0 to 1.5 min elapsed after presentation (this interval was not filled by distracting activity); and in the third series, the same interval was filled with interfering activity (mental arithmetic).

The results demonstrate that patients with left temporal lesions were significantly less able to identify spoken syllables than written characters. The opposite was observed in patients with left occipital lesions.

These results are summarized in Figure 5.

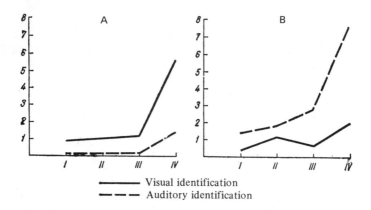

FIG. 5. Identification of auditory (syllables) and visual (meaningless figures) material by patients with lesions of (A) the left occipito-parietal and (B) the left temporal region (averaged data for three patients in each group). Ordinate, trials I–IV; abscissa, correct responses.

Similarly these patients recalled a series of spoken words less successfully than they recalled visually perceived pictures, and the converse was true with patients with parieto-occipital lesions. Patients with left parietal lesions differ considerably from those just described in recalling word series. The active mnemonic activity of these patients as a rule remains largely intact. Like normal subjects, they actively try to recall a series of words, attempting to group the words and changing from one strategy of recall to another. They may start to recall the series from either the beginning or the end. None of these patients reproduced inert stereotypes as observed in patients with frontal lesions. They showed no clear evidence of word searching or the phenomena of "alienation of word meaning" manifested in patients with left temporal lesions.

Only if the patients had distinct amnesic-aphasia were the features of word seeking observed during recall and the naming of objects. As a rule, the symptoms were less marked and accompanied only by verbal paraphasia, replacing a word by another of similar meaning or morphological structure [the word "Bol'nitsa" (hospital) was replaced by the words "militsiya" (police), "shkola" (school), and so on].

An investigation by Pham Minh Hac (1971) demonstrated these patients can retain many fewer items than normal subjects. Even after repeating a 10-word series eight to ten times, they could not recall the whole series. Characteristically, when attempting to recall the whole series they turned first to one, then to another group of words, but every time forgot the words they had just recalled. For this reason, the word recall order was significantly different from normal (Table 4). These findings suggest that the difficulty of

TABLE 4

RECALL ORDER OF A 10-WORD SERIES BY A PATIENT WITH A LEFT PARIETAL LESION

Order of word presentation	Successive trials									
	dom (house)	les (forest)	stol (table)	kot (cat)	noch' (night)	igla (needle)	pirog (pie)	zvon (ringing)	most (bridge)	krest (cross)
I	1	2	3	3	4				2	3
II	1	2	6	5		5		1	6	6
III	4	2	3							
IV	1	2		3	4	5				
VI	5	6		7	4	5	4	1	2	3

TABLE 5

RECALL ORDER OF A 10-WORD SERIES BY A PATIENT WITH A TUMOR OF THE THIRD VENTRICLE

Order of word presentation	Successive trials									
	dom (house)	les (forest)	stol (table)	kot (cat)	noch' (night)	igla (needle)	priog (pie)	zvon (ringing)	most (bridge)	krest (cross)
I		1					3		2	4
II									1	3
III		1			2	2	4	3		
IV		1			2	3	4	3		
V		1			3	5	4	1		
VI	2					5				
VII	1			2		4	3			
VIII	1			3	2		4	5		

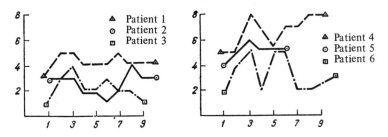

FIG. 6. Learning curves for 10-word series by six patients with tumors of the upper levels of the brain stem and marked Korsakov's syndrome: Abscissa, trials; ordinate, correct responses.

recall manifested by patients with left parietal lesions is based not so much on a disorder of active mnemonic activity, as on a reduction in the maximum number of retained items, associated with increased mutual inhibition of individual traces.

Patients with lesions affecting the upper levels of the brain stem and the medial zones of the cerebral hemispheres, accompanied by a clearly defined Korsakov's syndrome, have characteristic disturbances when recalling a limited series (for example, 10 isolated words). As a rule, they reproduced a series of four or five words completely, but showed signs of difficulty when attempting to recall a series of ten. They could still make active attempts to learn the series by grouping the material and trying to recall sometimes from the beginning, sometimes from the end. After repeating the series many times, they manage to remember six or seven words, but only very rarely could they retain the recalled words with any stability. The recall order was unstable and dispersed, and as the example demonstrates, the patient often "forgot" a word as soon as he had recalled it (Table 5).

The word learning curves of these patients (Figure 6) show some superficial similarity to learning curves obtained from frontal syndrome patients, but in fact they have nothing in common. Pathological inertia of previously imprinted traces was not evident in these cases. The flattened curves resulted from increased instability and mutual inhibition of traces rather than from inactivity or stereotyped responses. This is demonstrated by the serial position effect which was evident in the responses of most of these patients. In other patients, however, the decrease in recall was so sharp that it was difficult to speak of a serial position effect.

Unexpectedly the aggregated learning curves do not in the least reflect the severity of the clinical picture of memory disorders. There are some patients with a distinct Korsakov's syndrome for whom learning a 10-word series sometimes differed comparatively little from normal. Similar observations have also been reported in the literature (Brion, 1969; Milner, 1969, 1970). This suggests that the learning of a series of ten words, however informative, cannot be regarded as a sufficient test of the memory disorders arising from local brain lesions. Other analytical methods are required to delineate the pathophysiological features of memory disorders. These considerations prompted development of the methods for investigating memory described below.

Retention of a Fixed Set

I began my investigation with tests designed to determine how firmly traces of relatively simple events are retained, and what conditions lead to their disappearance.

The fixed set test, developed by Uznadze (1966) and his school, consists of instructing a subject to feel two balls of different sizes, actively 12 to 15 times, compare their sizes, and report what he finds. Next, without opportunity for visual inspection, he is given two balls of the same size, and again asked to compare the sizes. The illusion of contrast leads the subject to estimate that the smaller ball is in the hand which previously held the larger ball. The illusion is often present after even 8 to 12 trials.

I used three variations of the test. First, I gave the control (equal) balls immediately after formation of the fixed set. Next, I introduced an "empty" interval of 1 to 2 min between presentations of the contrasting sets of balls and the tests involving the formation of a set. Finally, I filled the pause with distracting activity (usual mental arithmetic), or introduced this distracting activity so that it separated the first contrast test from subsequent assessments.

The data yielded valuable information about disturbances of memory for elementary forms of sensomotor activity. In normal subjects, a fixed set is easily preserved after empty pauses of 1 to 2 min, and often remains intact even if the pauses are filled with distracting activity as long as it does not include movements. Patients with relatively mild mnemonic disturbances (for example, from pituitary tumors disturbing the normal energy balance of the cortex) or local lesions of the posterior, gnostic zones of the hemispheres behaved similarly. In patients with severe mnemonic disorders (Korsakov's syndrome), however, a fixed set appeared after the usual preliminary tests, but even a short pause destroyed the contrast (unpublished investigation by N. A. Filippycheva and Yu. V. Konovalov). More frequently, an "empty" pause of 1 to 1.5 min had no effect, but a pause filled with interfering activity destroyed the illusion of contrast. Data obtained in my laboratory using this test on patients with distinct amnesic syndromes associated with massive deep midline tumors are given in Table 6.

The chief variable affecting performance is not a delay of 1 to 2 min, but the interfering activity during that interval, even if the interference was unrelated to the original sensomotor activity.

TABLE 6

PRESERVATION OF A HAPTIC FIXED SET AFTER "EMPTY" AND "FILLED"
PAUSES IN SEVEN PATIENTS WITH DEEP BRAIN LESIONS

Type of pause	Duration of pause			
	–	30 sec	1 min	2 min
Immediate testing	100	0	0	0
"Empty" pause	0	100	100	72.2
Pause with interfering activity (mental arithmetic)	0	48	22	0

Note. – In this and the subsequent tables, performance (reproduction, recognition, or preservation of the set) is assessed by the ratio, in percent, between successes and the total number of tests carried out, averaged for all the subjects.

Retention of Simple Visual Stimuli (Konorski's Method)

The stimulus is arbitrary and unconnected with the mnemonic task. The method of recall, identification, is among the simplest forms of mnemonic activity.

In Konorski's test, the patient is shown a geometrical shape (triangle, square, rhombus), in one of three colors (red, blue, green), for a short time (10 sec). He is then shown the same or a different shape or color figure and requested to answer whether or not the second figure is identical with the first. As in the previous series, the test was carried out under three conditions: (a) the second figure was presented immediately following the first; (b) after an "empty" interval of 1, 1.5, or 2 min; (c) after an interval filled with interfering activity (mental arithmetic or the examination of irrelevant cards).

The results of these tests were similar to those described above. Normal subjects had no particular difficulty with these tests: Neither an "empty" nor a "filled" pause significantly disturbed the ability to assess whether the two figures were identical or different. Patients with relatively mild mnemonic disorders resulting from upper brain stem tumors (pituitary) differed from normal only slightly.

Patients with severe amnesic syndromes associated with massive deep midline tumors affecting the activity of both hemispheres could assess the difference between the two shapes even after empty pauses of 30· sec or 1 min. After pauses of 2 min, one-quarter of the patients began to give hesitant and, sometimes, mistaken answers.

TABLE 7

RECOGNITION OF VISUAL STIMULI IN KONORSKI'S TESTS AFTER "EMPTY"
AND "FILLED" PAUSES BY 13 PATIENTS WITH DEEP BRAIN LESIONS

Type of pause	Length of pause			
	–	30 sec	1 min	2 min
Patients with pituitary tumors and mild amnesic syndrome				
Direct comparison	100	0	0	0
Comparison after an "empty" pause	0	100	100	100
Comparison after a "filled" pause	0	100	96.7	96.6
Patients with massive deep midline tumors and severe amnesic syndrome				
Direct comparison	100	0	0	0
Comparison after an "empty" pause	0	100	100	76.8
Comparison after a "filled" pause	0	48	22	0

Note.—Numbers are the percentage of patients responding correctly.

The situation changed radically if the pause between presentation of the first and second figures was filled by interfering activity. Many patients were unable to give the correct answers, stating that they "could not remember which figure had been shown first." In the extremes cases, they could not remember having had the first figure presented, and insisted they were seeing it for the first time. This type of response increased as the pause was lengthened, and after a 2-min pause filled with interfering activity, not a single patient performed satisfactorily. Both heterogeneous (mental arithmetic) and homogeneous (examination of cards) interfering activity had the same effect (Table 7).

In a similar investigation (Popova, 1964), patients with upper brain stem and medial cortex lesions, accompanied by Korsakov's syndrome, made relatively few mistakes when the second item (figure or sound) was presented directly after the first. As a rule, the mistakes occurred only during repetition of the same item. Mistakes were made inconstantly, when the interval between presentation of the items increased to 15 to 20 sec. When the interval was increased to 40 to 60 sec, mistakes occurred constantly. In a severe Korsakov's syndrome, a delay of 10 to 12 sec was sufficient to cause mistakes. In less severe cases, mistakes occurred only if the interval was lengthened to 60 to 90 sec (Popova, 1964).

While the data do not rule out primary decay of memory, they are consistent with increased inhibition by interfering activity.

In both experiments, a short pause between presentation of the first and second figures did not obliterate memory of the first figure, and the patient could make correct comparisons. The introduction of interfering activity, however, rapidly made correct comparisons impossible. These effects could only be observed in patients with massive deep tumors affecting both hemispheres.

Preliminary data suggest interfering activity does not inhibit simple sensory memory in patients with local lesions of the posterior (gnostic) zones of the hemispheres, but some effect can be found in patients with lesions of the visual (occipito-parietal) zones.

Patients with massive frontal lobe lesions produce results similar to those obtained from deep tumor patients with a severe amnesic syndrome. In the frontal lobe patients, however, the process of comparison was itself deeply disturbed. They often abandoned the task and inertly repeated "I don't know" or "the same," whatever figures had been presented.

Retention of Learned Motor Responses

This technique was used with most of the patients studied, and has been previously applied to the investigation of normal and abnormal children (Luria, 1956, 1958, 1961), and patients with local brain lesions (Luria, 1963, 1966, 1969; Luria & Khomskaya, 1966).

In the simplest test, the patient is instructed to raise his right hand in response to one tap and his left hand in response to two taps, or to raise his hand in response to one tap and not to respond to two taps.

In another, more complex test, the patient had to show his fist when shown a finger, and show a finger in response to a fist. Alternatively he had to respond to two taps with one tap and to one tap with two taps. In a still more complicated test, the patient had to respond to a loud tap with a small hand movement and to a weak tap with a powerful movement, or respond to a short acoustic stimulus with a slow movement and to a long acoustic stimulus with a rapid movement (Marushevskii, 1966). These latter tasks test conflicting responses. Obeying the instruction forces the subject to inhibit the direct echopraxic motor response.

After instructions and two or three trials of a learned motor response, an "empty" pause of 1, 1.5, or 2 min was introduced. Without repeating the instructions, the patient was then tested to determine if the signal evoked the required motor response. The same test was also used with interfering activity during the pause. The most complex form of this task involved homogeneous interference by a second similar task. This test was carried out as follows: As soon as the first task was mastered (for example, showing a finger in response to the examiner's fist, or a fist in response to the examiner's finger), a second task was instituted (for example, responding with two taps to one tap, or with one tap to two taps). Without repeating the instructions, the patient was then given the signals for the first task, and the evoked motor responses observed. Finally (also without warning), he was shown the signals of the second task and his responses recorded a second time. Although sufficient statistics are not yet available, preliminary analysis indicates these tests give results similar to those already described.

Normal subjects have no difficulty with the most complex tests in which two or sometimes three different tasks were compounded (Khomskaya, 1959, 1960; Tsao Ping, 1960).

Patients with lesions restricted to the gnostic zones of neocortex showed no evidence of specific performance deficits during these motor task tests. Neither empty nor filled pauses significantly disrupted retention provided the number of tasks was not large. The only exceptions were patients with occipital lobe lesions tested with visual stimuli (figures and colors) or patients with temporal lobe lesions tested with auditory stimuli (Khomskaya & Sorkina, 1960; Lubovskii & Klimkovskii, 1966, unpublished investigation).

Patients with upper brain stem lesions or pituitary tumors had no distinct difficulties with the learned motor responses even when tested after pauses filled with interfering activity. Only the last type of tests—confounding two similar tasks—occasionally disrupted retention.

More serious defects were found in patients with massive midline tumors. Learned motor responses were formed with considerable difficulty, often accompanied by long periods of mistakes, and were relatively unstable. An empty pause did not add to the difficulty, introduced no appreciable changes into the formed traces; but a filled pause often led to total collapse of performance. Sometimes presentation of a previously conditioned stimulus either evoked a response of "what am I to do? . . . . I have forgotten," or revealed that the patient had completely "forgotten" that the stimulus now presented was the cue for a motor response. The patient asked, in a puzzled way, "And now what?"—sometimes accompanying the question by the echopraxic imitation of a movement performed by the examiner.

Patients with massive bilateral frontal lobe trauma or tumors, or a ruptured aneurysm of the anterior communicating artery, accompanied by spasm of both anterior cerebral arteries, exhibited still more severe disturbances of the learned motor responses. These disturbances were often apparent both during training and testing, even after empty pauses. These phenomena were described in detail elsewhere (Luria, 1969).

One particularly interesting phenomenon I seen in several patients with hemorhage into the medial zones of the hemispheres, or cysts or tumors near the third ventricle, involves a dissociation between virtually complete retention of a learned motor response and the inability of the patient to answer verbally about the response. This dissociation can sometimes be found in patients with distinct Korsakov's syndrome, and clearly demonstrates that the memory disturbances accompanying this syndrome affect primarily spoken recall. A typical example is given below.

Patient Gavr., a 38-year-old male, recovered from clipping an aneurysm of the anterior communicating artery; cyst deep in the left frontal region (severe amnestic syndrome).

The patient is instructed to raise his right hand to one tap and his left land to two taps. He does this without difficulty and continues to perform satisfactorily even after a 2 to 3 min pause filled with interfering activity (mental arithmetic). Shortly after test, however, the patient was asked what he had done immediately before. He was completely unable to answer and said, "Before this I was at the aerodrome, taking measurements of a certain area . . . . " and so on.

This dissociation between the ability to learn an action and an inability to recall that action unaided or express it in words was observed in other patients of this group. A second example follows.

Patient Iv., a 35-year-old male, recovered after an operation on an aneurysm of the anterior communicating artery accompanied by spasm of both anterior cerebral arteries (definite amnesic syndrome with general inactivity).

The patient was asked to raise his fist in response to the sound "u" and to raise his palm in response to the sound "b." He learned the response well, and performed correctly, even after a pause of 1 to 2 min. When asked to say what he had just done, however, he was unable to do so and said, "I didn't understand, I was lifting something, squeezing something. . ." When were you lifting, when were you squeezing? "When I ran. . .; when I fell. . ." When did you raise your fist? "I did not raise my fist . . . ." And when did you raise your hand? "I raised my hand to the sound b." And your fist? "Fist—to the sound k." And when I said "b" what did you do? "I did nothing!" And when I said "u"? "Again I did nothing. . . " When the patient was unable to express his action in words, the previously well learned response disintegrated under the influence of interfering conversation. When the sounds "u" and "b" were again presented, he remained completely confused and did nothing.

After further testing with both responses, the patient continued to perform even after a long pause (5 to 10 min), but was still unable to give a verbal account of his task.

This dissociation between a learned motor response and its verbal recall, described originally in the classical literature, has proved to be one of the functional phenomena accompanying anterior lesions associated with a deep-seated pathology of the upper brain stem.

*   *   *

The results described above were obtained with tests devised to study retention of simple stimuli or motor tasks. The next series of tests requires special mnemonic activity or voluntary memorizing. As before, these tests involve different modalities, and are arranged in order of increasing semantic organization, beginning with motor and visual tasks and ending with audioverbal tasks.

Retention of Nonverbal Visual Forms and Movements

The patient was instructed to memorize a picture card or a series of two or three cards, each shown for à short period (2 to 3 sec), after which the cards were placed face downward in front of him. The patient had to recall the cards shown to him, and then identify them from among several others. The test was carried out in the now familiar alternative forms—immediate recall, recall after an empty pause of 1, 1.5, or 2 min, and again after a filled pause (addition or subtraction of two-figure numbers or counting backward from 100 by sevens). If the subject failed at any point, the test was repeated several times. Finally, to analyze the effect of homogeneous interfering activity, the subject was instructed to memorize a picture card or two (rarely three), then asked to memorize a second similar set of cards and immediately asked to separately name the cards in both series.

The test for memory of movements was similar. The patient was instructed to make one, two, or, less frequently, three movements. He was then asked to state what movements he had performed and to reproduce them. This test was also carried out in the four alternative forms just described. These tests also provide data relevant to the two primary questions which concern us: Do memory defects extend to different modalities (visual and motor), and does time and/or interference contribute to the decay.

The tests described above were carried out on normal subjects, and no difficulty was experienced.

Patients with upper brain stem lesions (pituitary tumors) and mild mnemonic disorders had no difficulty in recalling one or two cards (or movements). They could retain them after an empty pause. Filled pauses occasionally produced difficulties for some patients, but they could be overcome by repeating the test two or three times. If the test consisted of recalling two sets of two or three pictures (or movements), then returning to the first group gave rise to considerable difficulty. The most frequent mistakes consisted of confusing stimuli of one group with the other. Repetition abolished the mistakes very slowly, if at all. No significant differences occurred between recall of pictures or movements. Partial results from these tests are presented in Tables 8 and 9.

As Table 9 shows, recall of an initial set of visual forms or movements after reproducing a second similar group (series 2) was clearly difficult. These results support the interference hypothesis of forgetting, and suggest that upper brain stem lesions do not give rise to modality-specific memory disturbances. Much more serious disturbances are observed in patients with massive deep midline brain tumors, associated with a severe amnesic syndrome.

Characteristically, a series up to five pictures (or the same number of movements) was not difficult even after an empty pause of 1 to 1.5 min. Ocassionally, some difficulty was experienced after an "empty" pause lasting two minutes. If the pauses were filled by interfering activity, however, many

TABLE 8

RECALL OF PICTURES AND MOVEMENTS AFTER "EMPTY" AND
"FILLED" PAUSES BY 30 PATIENTS WITH PITUITARY TUMORS

Stimuli	Conditions of recall		
	Immediate	"Empty" pause	Homogeneous interference
Patients with mild amnesic syndrome			
Pictures	100	100	92.7
Movements	100	100	94.4
Patients with severe amnesic syndrome			
Pictures	100	100	80.0
Movements	100	100	83.3

TABLE 9

CONSECUTIVE RECALL OF TWO SERIES OF STIMULI BY 30 PATIENTS
WITH PITUITARY TUMORS

Stimuli	Conditions of recall			
	Immediate		Recall series 1 after series 2	Recall series 2 after series 1
	Series 1	Series 2		
Patients with mild amnesic syndrome				
Pictures	100	100	77.7	57.1
Movements	100	100	86.5	84.2
Patients with severe amnesic syndrome				
Pictures	100	100	55.7	27.5
Movements	100	100	66.7	70.9

patients were unable to recall series of pictures or movements correctly. These patients showed particularly severe defects when tested with homogeneous interference. In the severest cases, the patients declared that they were totally unable to remember memorizing the first group of pictures (or movements). An example of one such test is given below.

Patient Rakch., a 40-year-old female with a tumor of the posterior corpus callosum affecting the hippocampal region (severe amnesic syndrome). Although this patient easily recalled single dissimilar pictures, she had great difficulty in recalling similar pictures, and was completely unable to recall pairs of such pictures.

Recall of dissimilar cards

[Kot = cat, arbuz = watermelon, vedro = bucket, poleno = log]

I. *(Kot)*[5]	II. *(Arbuz)*	*?/I*	*?/II*	*?/I*	*?/II*
Kot	Arbuz	Kot	Arbuz	Kot	Arbuz
I. *(Vedro)*	II. *(Poleno)*	*?/I*	*?/II*	*?/I*	*?/II*
Vedro	Poleno	Vedro	Poleno	Vedro	Poleno

Recall of similar cards

[Petukh = cock, gus' = goose, utka = duck, kuritsa = hen, plat'e = dress]

I. *(Petukh)*	II. *(Gus')*	*?/I*	*?/II*	*?/I*	*?/II*
(1) Petukh	Gus'	Utka	Utka	I have fot-gotten	I have for-gotten
(2) Petukh	Gus'	Utka, I think	Kuritsa, for sure	Utka	Kuritsa
(3) Petukh	Gus'	Gus'	Utka	Gus'	Utka
(4) Petukh	Gus'	Now a large utka	A small utka or gus'	I have for-gotten	I have for-gotten

Again, recall of dissimilar cards

I. *(Vedro)*	II. *(Plat'e)*	*?/I*	*?/II*	*?/I*	*?/II*
Vedro	Plat'e	Vedro	Plat'e	Vedro	Plat'e

Recall of paired pictures

[Samolet = airplane, yabloko = apple, tufli = slippers, limon = lemon, botinki = boots]

I. *(Samolet –yabloko)*	II. *(Tufli –limon)*	*?/I*	*?/II*	*?/I*	*?/II*
(1) Samolet –yabloko	Tufli –limon	Botinki. . . and arbuz	Tufli. . . and something be-sides, I have forgotten	I have for-gotten	I have for-gotten
(2) Samolet –yabloko	Tufli –limon	Tufli and limon	Men's tufli and fruit	I have for-gotten	I have for-gotten
(3) Samolet –yabloko	Tufli –limon	Polu- (half) botinki and limon	Limon and tufli	I have for-gotten	I have for-gotten
(4) Samolet –yabloko	Tufli –limon	Samolet and men's botinki	Limon and la-dies' botinki	Lemon peel	I have for-gotten
(5) Samolet –yabloko	Tufli –limon	Of course, a large limon and tufli	Tufli and something be-sides	Tufli. . . I have for-gotten	I have for-gotten

[5] The name of the object shown on the card is given in parentheses; the patient's reply is given below. In the reports of these tests, the original Russian words are given in transcription, accompanied by their translation, so that the reader can appreciate both the morphological and the semantic qualities of the tests. (Translator's note)

Attempts to recall the first pair of cards (even if heterogeneous) after presentation of a second, similar pair was completely impossible. The patient began either to describe irrelevant objects (boots—watermelon, airplane—boots) or to repeat the second group inertly (slippers—lemon, lemon—slippers). The results of these observations are summarized in Table 10.

The tumors in these patients disturbed the "circle of Papez" but did not affect the frontal lobes. In patients with frontal lobe damage or in the acute period after rupture of an aneurysm of the anterior communicating arteries, accompanied by spasm of the anterior cerebral arteries, the phenomena just described were even more severe. Some of these patients were able to retain a series of two (or sometimes even three) cards (or movements) after an empty pause of 1 or even 2 min, but any interfering activity completely disrupted recall. Sometimes they refused to accept that they had even been shown any cards. Performance on any of the more complex tasks was negligible. Two examples follow.

Patient Bit., a 26-year-old male with a tumor of the left frontal lobe spreading into the right (severe "frontal syndrome" with marked disturbances of memory) was asked to perform first one, and then a second action and then was immediately asked to state what action he had performed the first and second time. The first action performed disappeared completely from his memory, although his ability to recall the second action remained relatively stable.

(1) The patient was asked to take an apple and hide it under the blanket. He did so. Have you forgotten what you did? "No, truly, I have not forgotten." After a pause of one minute: What did you do? "I hid an applie under the blanket . . . in my things . . . by my head."

(2) The patient was asked to take a comb and to comb his hair. He did this without difficulty.

What were you combing? And what were you doing before that? "I was combing my hair . . . with a comb." And just before that you were doing something else. What was it? "Before I combed my hair? . . . . I was shaving . . . or wasn't I?" No, you just did something else at my request! "I will tell you now . . . we left separately and went in different ways . . ." Did you take an apple? "No." Look what there is under your blanket. He looks. "Some one has put an apple there." But who? "You, of course . . . . it did not occur to me that this apple was under the blanket! . . . ."

The test was repeated with the same result. Two days later, the test was repeated a third time.

(1) Hide the apple under your blanket. "Like yesterday!" (The fact was recalled, as a reminiscence.) Yes. He takes the apple and hides it under his blanket. Where have you put the apple? "In the old hiding place of the other day." Remember, this was the first action. "Very well. If they ask I shall say I hid it in the old hiding place."

(2) Comb your hair with the comb. The patient takes the comb, combs his hair, and returns the comb. What have you just done? "I have combed my hair." And what did you do before that? "I combed as well. . ." And before you combed your hair, just before that, what did you do? "Before that I went to the toilet . . ." No, I asked you to do something, and to remember what you had done. "I went to the toilet . . . upstairs . . ." Did you hide something? "No, I hid nothing . . ." Did you do something with an apple? "With an apple? . . . in the toilet, where I was? Or wasn't I? . . . No, I can't remember." The blanket

TABLE 10

RECALL UNDER SEVERAL TEST CONDITIONS BY 13 PATIENTS WITH DEEP BRAIN TUMORS

| Material | Recall conditions | | | | | | |
| | Immediate | After "empty" pause | | | After pause of 2 min filled with: | | |
		30 sec	1 min	2 min	Conver-sation	Counting	Homogen-eous activity
Five cards	100	100	100	95.4	53.0	43.4	31.7
Five movements	100	100	100	80.0	65.6	39.2	35.1

is lifted and the patient shown the hidden apple. "Where did it come from? Who can have put it there?" The patient was confused.

In this test, the retroactive inhibition of the second action obliterated the traces of the first action. A similar effect could also be induced by any other type of interfering activity.

Patient Ban., a 46-year-old female with a large pituitary adenoma extending beyond the sella turcica and pressing on the upper parts of the brain stem and the frontal region (marked diencephalo-frontal syndrome with severe amnesia and aspontaneity).
Firstly, the patient was instructed to take a comb and put it in her pocket. She did so. She was then asked to place a card under an exercise book.
What did you do first? "I put a comb in my pocket." And what did you do then? "I put a card under the exercise book." Remember these two actions. "Very well, I will try." Count 1, 2, 3, 4. The patient does so.
What did you do first? "I counted . . . ." No, I asked you to do something? "I don't know . . ." And what did you do then? "Nothing, except I hid a paper." And what did you do before that? "I don't know." And what then? "All I know is about the paper and the numbers." Look what you have in your pocket. "I don't understand . . . here is my piece of paper." Takes out a comb. "Oh. . . this is your comb. I took it by mistake. . ." The test was repeated. Again, to begin with, she put the comb in her pocket and then in response to the second instruction she hid the card beneath the exercise book.
What did you do first? "I hid a card and comb under the exercise book. . ." And the second time? "I hid a piece of paper . . ." After a pause of 30 sec: Once again, what did you do first? The patient's glance fell on a spoon. "The spoon was in my pocket. . ." And the second time? "I drank from the spoon . . ." Are you sure about this? "I don't know." What was your first action? "The first time there was a carrot" (reminiscence of an onion drawn on the card). And the second action? "Carrot!" What did you hide in your pocket? "One or two tablets . . . . tablets . . . .I have forgotten . . ." And the second time? "I have forgotten . . . Here you are, under the exercise book . . . tablets." The results were no better when the test was continued.

The observations just described are very similar to the observations made on the previous patients. The only difference is that recalling the first action in this case was possible prior to interfering activity (counting). Recalling the first action then disappeared completely, and only confused ideas of the second action remained. In addition, the recalling of the action previously performed began to be inhibited by inert expressions (a carrot) or by actions associated with hospitals (tablets). In these cases, the retention of real actions was affected more severely than visual impressions, again emphasizing the role of the frontal lobes in the organization of actions.
Patients with temporal lesions showed no significant retention disturbances for either visual stimuli (picture cards) or their own movements in sharp contrast to the defects of audioverbal memory (Klimkovskii, 1966). Patients with parieto-occipital lesions, associated with symptoms of simultaneous agnosia and semantic aphasia, had no difficulty in reproducing two or three picture

TABLE 11

RECALL BY PATIENTS WITH LESIONS OF THE LEFT PARIETO-OCCIPITAL
REGION (10 PATIENTS)

Material	Recall conditions			
	Immediately	After empty pause	After interfering activity (counting)	After homogeneous interference
2 picture cards	100	100	80	67
3 picture cards	100	100	90	62

TABLE 12

RECALL OF GEOMETRICAL SHAPES BY PATIENTS WITH LEFT
PARIETAL LESIONS (10 PATIENTS)

Number	Task requirements	
	Memorizing shapes in no particular order	Memorizing shapes arranged in a particular order
4	100	100
6	100	70
8	100	50

cards, or two or three movements. They could retain them well after empty pauses, but if the pauses were filled with interfering activity retention was definitely disturbed (Table 11).

These patients found it much more difficult to retain pictures and movements that involved spatial relationships than those which did not. Interference prevented satisfactory results even after frequent repetition (Table 12).

* * *

So far we have considered the data obtained by testing nonverbal (visual and motor) memory. Let us now turn to the principal part of the investigation—disturbances of verbal memory.

I set out to study the hierarchical organization of verbal memory, starting with discrete elements, at the lowest level of organization, and ending with the memorizing of complex verbal stimuli organized into semantic systems.

Retention of Series of Isolated Words

The patient was given a series of isolated words (as a rule, simple and monosyllabic, less frequently bisyllabic) which he had to memorize and repeat in the order in which they were given. Usually, I began by repeating one or two words, then moved on to three or, less frequently, four words. If the patient was unable to reproduce the words, the test was repeated (usually 6 to 8 times). It ended if the words were repeated correctly, or if it became clear that performance was not improving. The words were unrelated and the presentation speed (one sec between the words) did not permit semantic organization. The words usually used were dom (house)—kot (cat); noch' (night)—igla (needle); pirog (pie)—zvon (ringing)—kot; and so on. This test was carried out in the familiar alternative forms. After the first series, the subject was asked to learn another series, after which he had to repeat both in order. To investigate whether a patient who could not reproduce the corresponding series of words could still identify the words presented, in some cases I used an additional test. Words were presented separately to the patient and he was asked whether they formed part of the previous series. This series of tests made it possible to study the stability of direct retention of an audioverbal series, and to identify the factor—the presence of an empty pause or inhibitory interfering factors—which played the principal role in forgetting.

Normal subjects could easily repeat a series of three or four words and retain them during a pause of two minutes filled with interfering activity. The test with homogeneous interference (recalling the first series memorized after recalling a second, similar series), as a rule, revealed only very slight difficulty. In a few cases, it was necessary to repeat the test twice in order to stabilize the subject's recall. The results of the tests carried out on a group of normal adult subject, ages 30 to 55 years, are given in Table 13. On the basis of these results, the method described can be confidently used to study patients with local brain lesions.

A completely different picture is obtained when patients with pituitary tumors are studied. I investigated 30 patients with this type of lesion, divided into two groups. In one group (22 patients), the pituitary tumors did not spread outside the sella turcica (endosellar) and were not accompanied by noticeable signs of brain stem involvement or of increased intracranial pressure. In this group, complaints of memory defects were relatively mild, amounting to nothing more than the statement that "my memory is not as good as it was," or "they tell me a word and I forget it." Some did not even voice these

TABLE 13

RECALL OF WORDS BY NORMAL SUBJECTS (AVERAGE DATA FOR 25 SUBJECTS)

Material	Immedi-ately	Recall conditions							
		After empty pause				After heterogeneous interference		After homogen-eous interference
		30 sec	1 min	1.5 min	2 min	Conver-sation	Mental arith-metic	
Five words	100	100	100	100	100	100	99	0
Two series of three words each	0	0	0	0	0	0	0	93.1
Two series of four words each	0	0	0	0	0	0	0	91.5

complaints. The curve of learning ten words differed only slightly from normal. The second group consisted of eight patients with endosellar, suprasellar and parasellar tumors, or sometimes with retrosellar pituitary tumors, accompanied by evidence of brain stem involvement and circulatory disturbances of the cerebrospinal fluid or blood. These patients complained of memory disorders and their learning curves were grossly abnormal. Usually it was plateau-shaped, i.e., performance did not improve after two to four repetitions.

The recall of even five words after an empty pause posed no difficulty for these patients. The same series, after a pause filled with interfering activity, resulted in some disruption of performance, which was more severe in the second group. The results are summarized in Table 14.

The following example illustrates the inhibitory effect of interfering activity.

Patient Ban., a woman 46 years of age, with a pituitary adenoma spreading beyond the sella turcica and involving both the brain stem and the frontal lobes (severe amnesic syndrome with perseveration).

The patient was asked to repeat a series of 1, 2, 3, and 4 words after both empty and filled pauses of 30 sec to 1 min. The empty pause caused no difficulty, but after a pause occupied by interfering activity recall was impossible, or replaced by fragments of the intervening mental arithmetic.

Recall of words after a pause filled with interfering activity (mental arithmetic).

Single words

Dom
Dom

After interference by mental arithmetic (2 + 1 = "7"; 5 + 4 = "9"):
"I have forgotten, I don't know."

Series of two words

Noch'–igla
Noch'–igla

After interference by mental arithmetic (2 + 7 = "9"; 14 − 3 = "21...8"): "Twenty eight. ..." No, try to remember what the words were. "I have forgotten ..." The test was repeated many times, but without success.

Although this was a particularly severe case, a similar inhibitory effect of interfering activity was evident in patients with milder mnemonic defects.

The inhibitory effect of homogeneous interfering activity was more distinctly manifested when the first series (A) was recalled after repetition of a second similar series (B). The results of these tests are given in Table 15.

Quantitative analysis shows that homogeneous activity causes the patients to fail to recall the first series (they declared they had forgotten them), to recall only partially, or to exhibit disturbances of selectivity, reproducing words sometimes from the first series, sometimes from the second.

TABLE 14

RECALL OF FIVE WORDS BY 30 PATIENTS WITH PITUITARY TUMORS

Type of tumor	Recall conditions							
	Immedi-ately	After empty pause				After heterogeneous interference		After homogen-eous interference
		30 sec	1 min	1.5 min	2 min	Conver-sation	Mental arith-metic	
Endosellar, no brain stem involvement or increased intracranial pressure (22 cases)	100	100	100	100	100	95	95	88
Endo-, supra- and parasellar tumors involving the brain stem and disturbing circu-lation of CSF and blood (8 patients)	100	100	100	100	100	92	80	70

TABLE 15

RECALL OF TWO SERIES OF THREE WORDS BY 30 PATIENTS WITH
PITUITARY TUMORS

Experiment No.	Recall conditions			
	Immediately		Return to series 1 after recall of series 2	Return to series 2 after recall of series 1
	Series 1	Series 2		
I	100	100	66.6	42.8
II	100	100	66.6	63.2
III	100	100	50.0	48.4
IV	100	100	76.1	66.6

These results show convincingly that forgetting in patients with very mild disturbances of memory still results largely from the inhibitory effect of interfering activity.

These phenomena are manifested much more severely in patients with massive deep midline tumors, involving both hemispheres and disturbing the function of the "circle of Papez." This material was obtained as the result of many observations by myself and my colleagues Popova (1964) and Kiyashchenko (1969).

The memory disturbances of these patients were shown to be nonspecific and to be present despite retention of relatively simple sensomotor traces. Rapid forgetting is based not so much on the weakness of established traces as on the increased inhibitability of the traces by interfering factors. This same phenomenon appears in a more severe form when tests required a series of isolated words. These patients were by no means always unable to recall a series of 2, 3, 4, or even 5 words immediately. As a rule, they did so, maintaining the required word order, and many could still retain a series after an empty pause of 1.5 to 2 min. This indicates there are no adequate grounds for assuming any significant weakness of traces. Unlike the cases described above, however, as soon as interfering activity (conversation or mental arithmetic) was introduced the patients were either unable to recall the series, or they did so partially, retaining only one or two words (usually words at the beginning or end of the series). The data for one such group of patients obtained by Kiyashchenko are given in Table 16.

In tests including homogeneous interference, the patient was quite unable to recall the first series, and either reproduced isolated elements or exhibited contamination of the words of one series with those of the other. In the severest cases, inhibition of the first group by the second group was so great

TABLE 16

RECALL OF 5-WORD SERIES BY 25 NORMAL SUBJECTS AND 13 PATIENTS WITH
DEEP BRAIN TUMORS

Type of subject	Recall conditions				
	Immedi-ately	After empty pause of 2 min	After hetero-geneous inter-ference		After homo-geneous interference
			Conver-sation	Mental arith-metic	
Normal subjects	100.0	100.0	100.0	96.0	94.4
Patients with massive deep brain tumors and severe disturbances of memory	100.0	91.6	46.6	39.7	25.0

TABLE 17

RECALL OF TWO SERIES OF THREE WORDS BY PATIENTS WITH DEEP BRAIN TUMORS
AND AN AMNESIC SYNDROME (MEANS FOR 13 PATIENTS)

Trials	Immediately		Recall conditions			
			First return		Second return	
	Series 1	Series 2	To series 1 after reproducing series 2	To series 2 after repeating series 1	To series 1 after reproducing series 2	To series 2 after repeating series 1
I	100	100	52.3	39.7	14.3	4.8
II	100	100	83.3	42.8	9.5	4.8
III	100	100	66.6	33.3	23.8	4.8
IV	100	100	76.1	42.8	23.8	19.0

that, having repeated the second group of two or three words, the patient declared he had completely forgotten the words of the first group, even after many repetitions significantly improved recall of the first series. These results are summaried in Table 17.

The inhibitory effect of the second group on the first did not lead to inert repetition of the second group (this is what happens, as a rule, in patients with a massive frontal syndrome), but produced a combination of lost elements from each group and contamination of one group by another. The inhibitory effect of homogeneous interfering activity reduces selective recall. These results are summarized in Table 18.

As Table 18 shows, errors in the first series resulted more often from contamination by the second series than from omissions (inhibition). During reproduction of the second series, however, the number of elements lost equalled the number incorrectly reproduced (as a result of the increasing mutually inhibitory effect of the two groups of words). Frequent repetition is necessary for this influence to be partly overcome. Finally, repetition of the test four times produced only slight improvement in recall.

One example clearly illustrating these facts is given below.

Patient Pet., female, with a tumor of the anterior portion of the corpus callosum and a severe amnesic syndrome.

I. *Okno–krug–shapka*	II. *Den' (day)–sosna–kniga*	*?/I*	*?/II*
(1) Okno–krug–shapka	Den'–sosna–kniga	Okno... shapka ... kniga	... Den'... okno... and something else
(2) Okno–krug–shapka	Den'–sosna–kniga	Kniga... den'	... Den'... okno and something else
(3) Okno–krug–shapka	Den'–sosna–kniga	Okno... sosna...	... Den'... okno

Disturbances in recalling word series assumed another form when a lesion of the frontal lobes was involved in the amnesic syndrome. These observations include patients with massive bilateral deep frontal lobe tumors, injuries of the frontal lobes associated with well-marked general cerebral symptoms, or rupture of the anterior communicating artery leading to spasm of both anterior cerebral arteries.

Patients of this group could retain a group of two (or sometimes of three) words, even after an empty pause. After interfering activity such as mental arithmetic, however, the patients, as a rule, could not reproduce a group of words presented previously. At best, they could reproduce only one word of the group, and at worst they were quite unable to recall any of them. In patients with the most massive lesions and the severest frontal syndrome, distraction was sufficient to cause the patient to forget that words had been

TABLE 18

MISTAKES DURING RECALL OF TWO MUTUALLY INTERFERING 3-WORD SERIES BY PATIENTS
WITH DEEP BRAIN LESIONS AND AN AMNESIC SYNDROME
(MEANS FOR 13 PATIENTS)

Trials	With immediate recall	Number and character of mistakes					
		Return to series 1 after reproducing series 2			Return to series 2 after reproducing series 1		
		Total number of mistakes	Loss of words	Substitu- tion of words	Total number of mistakes	Loss of words	Substitu- tion of words
I	0	47.7	9.5	38.2	81.0	42.8	38.2
II	0	38.9	27.3	11.6	57.7	31.0	26.7
III	0	33.4	9.4	24.0	66.7	28.3	38.4
IV	0	23.9	9.5	14.4	57.3	9.8	47.5

presented to him at all. In reply to the question of what words he recalled, he either said that no words had been given to him in that day's test, or began to reproduce the numbers with which he had just carried out mental arithmetical operations. A most characteristic example illustrating disturbances of this type is given below.

Patient Ban., a 46-year-old female with a large pituitary adenoma extending beyond the sella turcica and exerting pressure on the brain stem and frontal lobes, was asked to repeat isolated words; after repeating one word correctly and then a second, she was asked to recall both of them. This she did without any difficulty. She found it just as easy to recall each word even after an empty pause of 1 to 1.5 min. After 30 sec of simple mental arithmetic, however, the words she had learned either disappeared completely from her memory (she declared that she had not just learned any words), or, instead of the words imprinted previously, she reproduced the numbers she had just used in her calculations. The record of a typical experiment is as follows.

[Stol = table, zima = winter]

I. Stol	II. Zima	?/I	?/II	(Empty pause of 1 min)	?/I	?/II
Stol	Zima	Stol	Zima		Stol	Zima

After interference with mental arithmetic for 30 sec (2 + 3 = "5"; 7 – 4 = . . . "3"):

?/I	?/II
Number 3	3 + 4

I have just repeated some words with you.
"No, I don't remember . . . I remember '3' but nothing else . . ." Did I say "stol?" "No, you did not say it . . ." And did I say "zima?" "I remember! You did say 'zima'." In response to prompting, this patient recalled only the second of the two words.

Repetition of the test

I. Stol	II. Zima	?/I	?/II
Stol	Zima	Stol	Zima

(Interference with mental arithmetic for 30 sec: 2 + 9 = . . . "2 + 3. . . 4. . . 3. . . 4. . . 2. . . 9. . . 8. . . 7. . . of course, 7") What was the first word? "94." No, the first word? "2 + zima." And the second word? "Zima. . ." And the first word? "A pair, I should say. . . 2 + zima."
The test was repeated five times in succession with detailed explanations and external aids (the words to be recalled were associated with external supporting aids, such as pieces of paper lying in various places on the table), but the effect was still as before.

In this case, the pathologically increased influence of interfering activity, acquiring the form of pathological inertia and blocking, was apparent in a test of recalling single words. In the other patients of this group, similar phenomena were observed in tests of recalling series of words.

Homogeneous interfering activity produced an even greater deficit in these patients. They were completely unable to recall one group consisting of only two or three words, after recalling a second similar group. As a rule, having just repeated the second group of words, when asked what words they repeated previously, these patients either declared they did not know, repeated the words of the second group which became inertly "frozen," or contaminated inertly frozen traces of the second group with fragments from the first. It is interesting to note that all the phenomena described above were very rare in tests of a single word, after which the patient had to recall a second word, but as a rule they always occurred after the change to the memorizing of groups of words. This suggests that pathological inertia inhibiting preceding traces retroactively arises only at the level of whole groups (or systems).

The phenomenon described above is so stable that even many repetitions were not generally followed by any substantial improvement. The example below illustrates this.

Patient Krup., a 41-year-old male with a large tumor (meningioma) of the basal portions of the left frontal lobe (a clear adynamic syndrome with evidence of pathological inertia), was asked to remember single words and to recall them after memorizing a second word. No defects were found in this case. Next he was given two separate words, which he easily repeated, followed by another pair. He was then asked to recall the first pair of words, followed by the second pair of words. This test was more difficult; he perseverated the elements of the second pair.

[Dom = house, zvon = ringing, kot = cat, noch' = night]

I. *Dom–zvon*	II. *Kot–noch'*	*?/I*	*?/II*
(1) Dom–zvon	Kot–noch'	Kot–zvon	Kot–noch'
(2) Dom–zvon	Kot–noch'	Kot–dom	Kot–noch'
(3) Dom–zvon	Kot–noch'	Kot–dom	Kot–noch'

Persistent pathological inertia began to appear on the change to a test involving reproduction of two series, each of three words, under the same conditions. In this case, contaminations appeared, making selective recall of the two series impossible. On the first repetition, the patient reproduced series that differed from each other. But on repeating the test, the correct recalling of the two series was replaced by a consistent and stable inert stereotype.

[Kholod = cold, rama = frame, knigi = books, golod = hunger, znoi = heat, luch = ray]

I. *Kholod–rama–knigi*	II. *Golod–znoi–luch*	*?/I*	*?/II*
(1) Kholod–rama–knigi	Golod–znoi–luch	Kholod–znoi–dom	I have forgotten
(2) Kholod–rama–knigi	Golod–znoi–luch	Kholod–znoi–rama	Golod–znoi–rama
(3) Kholod–rama–knigi	Golod–znoi–luch	Kholod–znoi–rama	Kholod–znoi–luch
(4) Kholod–rama–knigi	Golod–znoi–luch	Kholod–znoi–rama	Kholod–znoi–luch
(5) Kholod–rama–knigi	Golod–znoi–luch	Kholod–znoi–rama	Kholod–znoi–luch
(6) Kholod–rama–knigi	Golod–znoi–luch	Kholod–znoi–rama	Kholod–znoi–luch

Perhaps the most typical feature is that, after inertly repeating the same stereotype many times over, the patient is unaware it does not match the groups presented to him, and makes no attempt to correct his mistakes. This inactive attitude toward the inert stereotype is one of the most distinguishing features of the mnemonic disturbance in the frontal syndrome.

The facts described above are sufficiently illustrative. Although the patient has no appreciable difficulty returning to single words, returning to a word series after recalling a second similar system frequently encounters insuperable obstacles.

Repetition of the test may lead to successful reproduction of two pairs of memorized words but, as a rule, this is ineffective in tests involving three words. The syndrome involving severe pathological inertia of traces is the typical result of a lesion of the anterior zones of the brain.

The memory disturbance in patients with local lesions of the lateral zones of the cerebral hemispheres differs radically from the forms just described. Localized lateral lesions never give rise to general disturbances of memory, but often produce a severe disturbance of consciousness with defective orientation in place and time. Disturbances of audioverbal memory encountered in these cases are always limited. They never occur in patients with lesions of the right (nondominant) hemisphere. In patients with lesions of the dominant (left) hemisphere, they assume completely different forms depending on the location of the lesion.

Patients with lesions of the posterior frontal zones of the left hemisphere (usually from intracerebral tumors) often exhibit disturbances of spontaneous speech, frequently referred to as "transcortical motor aphasia" and interpreted more recently as "dynamic" aphasia (Luria, 1962, 1969). This defect was characterized as a disturbance of internal speech (Luria & Svetkova, 1966), and the verbal memory of these patients remains intact. This interpretation has been modified recently with the discovery that, in some cases, these disturbances may be based on a unique pathological inertia of verbal traces once they have been formed (a condition similar to the one just described), but limited to verbal memory (Luria, 1940 unpublished investigation).

The patients of this group can readily repeat individual words or sentences. Patients with the severest form of this disturbance, however, cannot repeat series of words. They inertly reproduce individual fragments, and cannot switch from some words to others. Patients with a less severe syndrome have no difficulty in repeating a short series of words, retaining them in the correct order and after an empty pause. Nevertheless, after homogeneous interference, they have extreme difficulty switching back to a previous group of words.

Two examples illustrating the principles just described are cited below. In the first, severe pathological inertia of speech prevents even the direct reproduction of word series. In the second, it is manifested only in tests involving homogeneous interference.

Patient Ob., a 30-year-old male, was admitted to the Institute of Neurosurgery complaining of difficulty in spontaneous, narrative speech. The signs of increased intracranial pressure and choked discs suggested a brain tumor. Left-sided carotid angiography revealed a large intracerebral tumor in the posterior zones of the left frontal lobe and anterior zones of the left temporal lobe. A tumor (15 x 10 x 10 cm) attached to the lesser wing of the sphenoid bone and extending from the posterior part of the anterior cranial fossa into the middle cranial fossa was removed. The medial wall of the tumor was on the medial surface of the left frontal lobe. Histologically, the tumor was a meningioma of mixed structure.

Patient Ob. showed no visible signs of a disturbance of praxis and only occasionally showed features of pathological inertia of his movements. He easily repeated individual sounds and words (even quite complicated ones), but had great difficulty with two or three word series, usually repeating the last word first and the rest with difficulty. Frequent repetition of the test did not improve the result. The repetition of single words was intact.

[Dom = house, les = forest, noch' = night, kot = cat, zima = winter, pirog = pie, most = bridge, stol = table, dub = oak]

Repetition of series of two words

Dom–les	Noch'–kot	Zima–pirog	Most–noch'
Dom–les	Kot. . . No	Zima–pirog	Noch'. . . and noch'

Repetition of series of three words

Dom–les–kot	Stol–noch'–dub
(1) Kot. . . les. . . no. . .	(1) Stol–dub–kot. . .
(2) Kot. . . les. . . no. . .	(2) Stol–dub. . . no, I don't know. . .
(3) Kot. . . les. . .	(3) Stol. . . dub. . . ah. . .
(4) . . . no. . . I can't. . .	(4) Stol. . . no. . .
(5) Kot. . . les. . . no. . .	(5) Stol. . . something like it. . . oak. . . no

This record shows that the disturbance was associated with pathological inertia, manifested both within the series and also as contamination by a previously established series, rather than with primary defects of memory.

The second case demonstrates this phenomenon not less clearly.

Patient Evch., a 40-year-old male, was admitted to the Institute of Neurosurgery complaining of severe disturbances of spontaneous speech and of "forgetting words." The illness began when the patient (a teacher by occupation) suddenly found himself unable to lecture. Soon after, he developed paresis of the right limbs and choked discs; he began to have headaches and attacks of unconsciousness. Clinical examination revealed a tumor in the anterior parts of the left hemisphere; electroencephalography and left-sided carotid angiography showed that the tumor lay in the posterior zones of the left frontal region. A large intracerebral tumor (6 x 6 x 6 cm) was removed. It extended anteriorly into the frontal and posteriorly toward the anterior zones of the temporal region. Histologically, the tumor was an oligoastrocytoma.

The patient showed no clear disturbances of praxis (tested in the left upper limb); but because of the development of perseveration he had difficulty, after reproducing two pairs of movements, if he were asked to repeat the first movement first, followed by the second. He had no difficulty repeating individual sounds and words, or even pairs of words. If asked to recall two pairs of words in succession, however, he could not do so; the second pair of words was so inert, it was impossible for him to switch to the previous pair. The record of this test follows.

[Okno = window, ochki = spectacles, dom = house, zvuk = sound, most = bridge, stol = table]

Repetition of single words

I. *Okno*	II. *Ochki*	*?/I*	*?/II*	*?/I*	*?/II*	
Okno	Ochki	Okno	Ochki	Okno	Ochki	and so on.

Repetition of series of two words

I. *Dom−zvuk*	II. *Most−stol*	*?/I*	*?/II*
(1) Dom−zvuk	Most−stol	Most. . . stol	Dom. . . I am confused
(2) Dom−zvuk	Most−stol	Most−stol	Most. . . I don't know. . .
(3) Dom−zvuk	Most−stol	Most−stol	Most−stol
(4) Dom−zvuk	Most−stol	Most. . . stol	Mo. . . something like it. . . what a memory. . . I don't remember at all. . .
(5) Dom−zvuk	Most−stol	I mean. . . dom−stol. . .	Most. . . stol
(6) Dom−zvuk	Most−stol	M. . . most. . . stol. . .	Most. . . stol. . . I can't. . .
(7) Dom−zvuk	Most−stol	M. . . most. . . stol	No. . . I can't
(8) Dom−zvuk	Most−stol	Most−stol. . .	I can't. . .

Disturbances of verbal memory in patients with lesions of the inferior parietal and parieto-occipital regions of the left hemisphere, long associated with the so-called amnesic or semantic aphasia, are quite different in character. Pathological inertia of verbal stereotypes is either not observed or obviously a secondary defect.

The primary symptom in these cases is an inability to find the right word when naming an object or seeking a particular word. These attempts are often accompanied by the unexpected production of words acoustically, morphologically, or semantically similar to the one required. For instance, instead of the word "uchitel'nitsa" (teacher), the patient may unexpectedly burst out with "fel'dsheritsa" (nurse), "rodstvennitsa" (a female relative), or expressions such as "now let me see, someone who works in a school." The attempt to find the word "resnitsa" (eyelash) may result in words such as "brovi" (beard), "nozhnitsy" (scissors), or "volosnitsy" (a hair style) and so on. I have observed a patient in this group whose unsuccessful attempts to say that he was now "v bol'nitsu" (in hospital) led consecutively to expressions such as "in this school," followed by corrections "no. . . in this. . . Red Army (instead of 'Red Cross Hospital'). . . no. . . 'v militsiyu' (in the police; morphological similarity). . . no, not the police, but the place where people are taken when they are ill."

These phenomena in which random words with some acoustic, morphological, or semantic features of the word sought are unexpectedly produced can be explained most easily on the assumption that the damaged parieto-occipital (or parieto-temporo-occipital) cortex is in a pathological (phasic) state in which strong and weak past traces become equalized in strength. As a result, recall of dominant (required) traces becomes very difficult and the organized character of the ecphoria of required semantic traces is lost.

In some cases, this disturbance of verbal memory is also manifested during the repetition of presented words. Similar words can be substituted both during the repetition of isolated words and, more clearly still, during the repetition of pairs of words, giving rise to the complex syndrome described inadequately in classical neurology as "conduction asphasia." Under these conditions, the disturbance of selective retention of verbal traces is so marked that tests of words repetition after pauses are no longer necessary. Once the patient has experienced difficulty in repeating the required word immediately, he will most frequently occupy any pause with attempts to find the required word, and this sometimes may be successful. In these cases, therefore, the specific defects of verbal memory are based not so much on increased inhibitability by interference or pathological inertia of previously established traces, as on a mechanism described by Sokolov as the equalized excitability of traces of different strengths (Luria, Sokolov, & Klimkovskii, 1967).

It will be most helpful if this type of disturbance of verbal memory is illustrated by a suitable example:

Patient Bich., a 36-year-old male, was admitted to the Institute of Neurosurgery complaining of sudden onset headache with raised temperature and disturbances of speech. Left-sided carotid angiography revealed an aneurysm of the posterior zones of the Sylvian fissure. An arteriovenous aneurysm of the left temporo-parieto-occipital region was removed, after which the patient's condition began to greatly improve.

He was able to speak actively, but when doing so showed the basic phenomenon of amnesic aphasia—difficulty in choosing the necessary words. He intermingled irrelevant words morphologically or semantically similar to the one he sought. For instance, when describing the onset of his illness, he said: "Well now. . . as I. . . zabyl (forgot). . . zabyl. . . zabolel (fell ill). . . I was at work. . . and this. . . upal (happened). . . did not happen, more exactly. . . quite. . . golos upal (I lost my voice) and I could not speak. . . no. . . I knew nothing. . . and so I joined the army. . . no, . . . the police. . . no. . . the red. . . where they take people when they are ill. . ." To hospital? "Why yes, to hospital. . . we don't need the police. . . they did a good job and I started to work. . . they sent me to another polycli. . . no. . . to another job. . . and then of course, after a month. . . no, a week, exactly. . . my head ached. . . my head became very bad. . . I could not see letters. . ." Your head or your eyes? "Why of course, my eyes! When I look I can see nothing. . . later I became very bad. . . my head (golova) (he means glaza, eyes) could see nothing. . . and they sent me to Kostroma, I think that that was where I go this (he points). . . . they cut my head. . . what is it for?" A tumor (opukhol')? ". . .yes, this. . . opolzat'. . . and. . . vypolzat'. . . opisat'. . . opuskat'. . . (all words resembling opukhol' in form but not in meaning). . . I cannot say. . . they kept me a long time in Kostroma. . . then they realized that what I had was. . . what do you call it?" Hemorrhage (krovoizliyanie)? "Yes. . . krovo. . . provisanie. . . koro. . . kono. . . kroo. . . krosv. . . komo. . . provisanie. . . Two months later I came to Moscow. . . what do you call it. . . to the sr. . . to your place, what is it?. . . I don't know. . ."

Similar difficulties arose during the naming of objects and the repetition of words. When trying to say March, he would say: "this. . . Thursday. . . no. . . what do you say. . ."

Attempting to say the month October (Oktyabr'), he would say: "What do you say. . . devyatyr'?" When trying to say trolleybus (trolleibus), he would say: "samolet (airplane). . . no. . . avtobus (bus). . . no. . . okrobulyus'. . . revolyutsiya. . ."

This patient experienced still greater difficulties when repeating pairs of words. Appropriate examples are given below:

[Dom = house, les = forest, shkaf = cupboard, truba = pipe, shofer = driver; other words are meaningless.]

Dom—les	Pause of 30 sec	*Shkaf—truba*
Les. . . well, it is. . .	Dom, les	(1) Shaf. . . no. . . it. . . it
dom		goes on top. . . there
		(2) Trub. . . and shafen. . .
		shumaren. . . shofer. . .
		shofar

[Noch' = night, igla = needle, kot = cat, sneg = snow, chasy = clock, pila = a saw]

Noch'—igla	*Sneg—chasy*	
Noch'. . . and les. . .	(1) Chasy. . . no. . . sneg	
kot. . . no. . . igla	. . . and pila. . . no. . .	(3) Sushat. . . I
	(2) Chasy. . . sneg and	think. . . . it will
	sneg. . .	not come. . .

[Volk = wolf, ovechka = ewe lamb, derevo = tree, pilka = a filling]

Volk—pila	*Volk*	*Volk—pila*
Who? it will not	Volka. . . ovechka. . .	Volk. . . and. . . pila. . . no, derevo
come out.		. . . you write with it. . . pilka

The record shows clearly that the main defect of verbal memory in this case was that the patient could not restrain traces of other connected words. Selection based on dominance of required meaning became very difficult. Characteristically, these disturbances of verbal memory are strictly specific, and manifested neither in the patient's general orientation nor in his memory for visual forms and movements.

Less severe defects of this type become evident when the patients of this group are required to repeat a series of words after a filled pause. The percentage of words recalled falls sharply and there is a corresponding increase in the frequency of uncontrollable outpouring of morphologically or semantically similar words.

The results of tests showing increased difficulty in recalling words by the patients of this group, especially if homogeneous interference is included, are given in Table 19.

I shall not dwell on disturbances of audioverbal memory in patients with lesions of the left temporal region, because the disturbances of verbal memory are so overlapped by defects of acoustic gnosis that it is impossible to distinguish any pure mnemonic defects. What is essential is that patients who can neither name nor repeat even isolated words can still reproduce series of visually presented shapes or movements, a clear indication of the specific audioverbal nature of the disorder.

TABLE 19

WORD RECALL BY PATIENTS WITH LESIONS OF THE LEFT PARIETO-
OCCIPITAL REGION

Material	Recall conditions			
	Immedi-ately	After empty pause	After heterogeneous interference	After homogeneous interference
2 words	100	100	80	60
3 words	100	100	40	10

Patients with left temporal lesions which do not affect the caudodorsal zones (i.e., the audioverbal areas in the narrow meaning of the term) have a syndrome of acoustico-mnemonic aphasia (Luria, 1957, 1962) rather than acoustico-gnostic aphasia, and are extremely interesting for our purpose. Although these patients show no definite disturbances of phonemic hearing or "alienation of word meaning," they exhibit severe defects in remembering words. They have been studied in detail by a number of investigators (Klimkovskii, 1966; Luria, 1947, 1955, unpublished work; Luria & Karaseva, 1968; Luria & Rapoport, 1962; Luria, Sokolov, & Klimkovskii, 1967; Popova, 1964) and I will briefly summarize the results obtained.

In none of the many patients studied (42 by Popova, 37 by Klimkovskii) were any general disturbances observed—no disorientation in place and time or inability to retain traces of current events, as occurred in patients with deep brain lesions. As a rule, memory for visual and motor series remained intact. Only their retention of word series was severely disturbed. As pointed out above, nonsequential recall of up to ten words was only partially defective in these patients. This was reflected in a comparatively slow and fluctuating increase in the number of words recalled per trial. Attempts to recall words in their exact order, however, gave rise to such severe disturbances that this symptom served as the basis for distinguishing the syndrome of "acoustico-mnemonic aphasia." The patients of this group easily retained one word and reproduced it both immediately and after a pause of 30 sec to 2 min. Many could repeat pairs of words, retaining their traces after an empty pause. A few with particularly severe disturbances of audioverbal memory had great difficulty in reproducing pairs of words: Either they reproduced only the last word of the pair, or they rearranged the words to give the last one first (Klimkovskii, 1967; Luria & Karaseva, 1968; Luria, Sokolov, & Klimkovskii, 1967).

The phenomenon became more apparent when the series was lengthened to three or four words. Immediate reproduction of a series was affected by retroactive inhibition, traces of the most recent word inhibiting those preceding it. This is one of the causes preventing reproduction of the series in the correct order. It is interesting to note that this phenomenon occurred only during verbal recall of a series of words presented verbally. It was not present when the patient recalled words presented in writing, or even when he wrote down words presented verbally (see Figure 3). Examples are given below.

Patient Blokh., a 35-year-old male with a traumatic injury to the left temporal lobe.

Repetition of single words

[Koshka = cat, noch' = night, koster = bonfire, raduga = rainbow]

Koshka	*Noch'*	*Koster*	*Raduga*
Koshka	Noch'	Koster	Raduga

Repetition of series of words

[Shkaf = cupboard, les = forest, stol = table, svet = light, zhuk = beetle, dym = smoke, dom = house, chasy = clock]

Shkaf-les	*Stol-svet*	*Zhuk-dym*
Les. . . shkaf	Svet. . . stol	Dym. . . zhuk

Dom-noch'	*Stol-chasy*	*Shkaf-les*
(1) Noch'. . . no	Chasy. . . no	Les. . . shkaf. . .
(2) Noch'. . . no	Chasy. . . no	Les. . . no. . . les. . . shkaf
(3) Noch'. . . no	Chasy. . . no	

[Ten' = shadow, glaz = eye, nozh = knife, klyuch = key, grib = mushroom, mokh = moss, kon' = mare, brat = brother, shag = step, stuk = tap, mol' = moth, mel' = chalk]

Ten'-glaz-nozh	*Klyuch-grib-mokh*	*Kon'-brat-shag*
Nozh. . . glaz. . .	Mokh. . .	Nozh. . . mokh. . . kon'. . .

Stuk-nozh-mol'
Mel'. . .

Reproduction in writing of words presented in writing

[Luk = onion, mysh' = mouse, kot = cat, zvon = ringing, pol = floor, gus' = goose, tsvet = flower, nos = nose, flag = flag]

Zhuk-shkaf	*Luk-mysh'*	*Brat-sneg*	
Zhuk-shkaf	Luk-mysh'	Brat-sneg	etc.

Kot-svon-pol	*Gas'-zhuk-shkaf*	*Sneg-svet-stol*
Kot. . . svon. . .	Shkaf. . . grib	Sneg. . . brat

Nos-flag-stol
Nos-flag-stol

Reproduction in writing of words presented by ear

[Divan = sofa, dver' = door, rot = mouth]

Shkaf-les	*Stol-svet*	*Brat-dom*	
Shkaf-les	Stol. . . divan. . .	Brat-dom	etc.

Klyuch-grib-mokh	*Kon'-brat-shag*	*Kot-dver'-rot*
Klyuch-grib-mokh	Kon'. . . brat. . .	Kot. . .

Lengthening the audioverbal series not only maintained inverted word order, but also caused the first elements of a series to disappear altogether. A series of words could not be retained as a single melody.

Patient Fil., a 38-year-old male with a hematoma in the floor of the middle temporal gyrus of the left hemisphere.

Repetition of series of five words

[Reka = river, derevo = tree, sumka = bag, shlyapa = hat, nozh = knife, voda = water]

Reka–derevo–sumka–shlyapa–nozh
(1) Reka. . . sumka. . . pila. . . sumka. . . reka. . .
(2) Reka. . . sumka. . . reka. . . sumka. . . voda?. . . no. . .
(3) Reka. . . sumka. . . derevo. . . voda. . . no, not voda. . .
(4) Reka. . . sumka. . . derevo. . . verevka (fan), I said. . . reka. . .
(5) Reka. . . sumka. . . shiyapa. . . shlyapa. . . nozh. . .
(6) Reka. . . sumka. . . pole (field). . . derevo. . . voda. . . derevo. . .
(7) Reka. . . sumka. . . voda. . . derevo. . . reka. . .
(8) Reka. . . voda. . . reka. . . derevo. . . we have had voda already. . .

[Pila = saw, bryuki = trousers, maslo = oil, pole = field, stakan = tumbler]

Pila–bryuki–maslo–pole–stakan
(1) Pila. . . stakan. . . maslo. . . bryuki. . .
(2) Pila. . . maslo. . . pole. . . stakan. . .
(3) Pila. . . bryuki. . . maslo. . . stakan. . .
(4) Pila. . . bryuki. . . pole. . . stakan. . .
(5) Pila. . . bryuki. . . pila. . . bryuki. . . stakan. . . pole. . .
(6) Pila. . . bryuki. . . pole. . . pila. . .

This phenomenon, described some time ago by Lashley (1937) as a disturbance of seriality, is a fundamental feature of left temporal lesions. The physiological analysis of its basic mechanisms has only recently begun (Luria, Sokolov, & Klimkovskii, 1967), and requires further research.

When patients of this narrow group were permitted to reproduce a pair of words after an empty pause of 10 sec, the retroactive inhibition was abolished and in some cases, they were able to recall the words in the proper order. Patients whose defects were less severe were able to reproduce series of two words in the proper order without difficulty, even after pauses of 15 or 30 sec and 1 min. If the series was increased to three, however, not only did the order difficulties reappear but when recall was possible, even a short pause led to complete failure. This shows that left temporal lesions not only produce increased inhibitability of audioverbal traces by interfering factors, but also direct weakness of audioverbal traces when formed. An example illustrating this defect is given below.

Patient Van., a 41-year-old male with a tumor of the middle zones of the left temporal region.

Repetition of series of words immediately and after an empty pause

[Zvonok = bell, baraban = drum, reka = river, plotina = dam]

Zvonok–baraban	*Reka–plotina*
Zvonok–baraban	Reka–plotina

After a pause of 15 sec:	After a pause of 30 sec:
Zvonok–baraban	Reka–plotina

After a pause of 30 sec:	After a pause of 1 min:
Zvonok–baraban	Reka–plotina

[Dom = house, les = forest, stol = table, noch' = night, zvon = ringing, khleb = bread]

Dom–les–stol	*Noch'–zvon–khleb*	*Stol–khleb–les*
Dom–les–stol	Noch'–zvon–khleb	Stol–khleb–les

After a pause of 15 sec:

Kot–stol–dom	Noch'. . . khleb. . . zvon	Kot. . . khleb. . . and all

After a pause of 30 sec:

Stol. . . kot. . . there	Zvon. . . khleb. . . and one I have forgotten.	Kot. . . no, now I can't remember.

After a pause of 1 min:

Kot. . . and stol	Zvon. . . and again, khleb. . .	

As the length of the series increased, perseveration begins to be significantly impaired and rearrangements or complete loss of words arise. Naturally, the defects are still more severe when the pause is occupied by interfering activity. In the patient with a left temporal lesion, conversation on random subjects lasting for 30 sec was sufficient to cause considerable difficulty. The difficulty sometimes occurred with single words and, of course, was more severe with groups of two or three words. This familiar fact clearly shows that the inhibitory effect of an interfering factor contributed to the destruction of audioverbal traces which were already in a state of relative weakness.

Patient Van., a 41-year-old male (diagnosis as above).

Repetition of single words

[Pricheska = hairstyle, povozka = wagon, volosy = hair, arba = cart of oriental type, golova = head, telega = carriage, arbuz = watermellon, divan = sofa, butylka = bottle]

Pricheska	*Povozka*
Pricheska	Povozka

Did you remember them well?	After a pause with interference:
Yes. . . volosy	Arba. . . no. . . I have forgotten.

Did you remember it exactly?	*Did you remember?*
. . . golova!	Now. . . it seems, I got it. . . no, I didn't. . .

Repetition of series of two words

Telega—arbuz	*Noch'—khleb*	*Divan—butylka*
Telega—arbuz	Noch'—khleb	Divan—butylka

After a pause of 15 sec with interference:

Arba. . . and arbuz	Noch'. . . I have forgotten	Try to remember! No. . . I can't. .
		I was interrupted. . . and I have
		forgotten.

Is that right?
Arba. . . and arbuz

Patient Ved., a 42-year-old male with a tumor of the middle zones of the temporal lobe.

Repetition of single words

[Maslo = oil, sapogi = slippers, tsvetok = flower, pole = field]

Kukla	*Maslo*	*Sapogi*
Kukla	Maslo	Sapogi

After a pause of 1 min:

Kukla	Malso	Sapogi

After a pause of 15 sec with interference:

Kukl?
Something on the
feet. . . to walk?
No.

Repetition of pairs of words

Okno—pila	*Tsvetok—pole*	*Khleb—les*
Okno—pila	Tsvetok—pole	Khleb—les

After a pause of 15 sec:

Okno—pila	Tsvetok—pole	Khleb—les

After a pause with interfering conversation:

Pole. . . pole. . . and
one other. . .
And now. . . pole and
leto. . . no, I don't
know

Similar phenomena were observed in patients with a less severe disturbance of audioverbal memory, but this time they were manifested in tests of the retention of series of three words.

Patient Mor., a 35-year-old male with a deep tumor of the left temporal region.

Repetition of series of three words

Dom–kot–stol	Zvon–noch'	Zhuk–shkaf–glaz
Dom–kot–stol	Zvon–noch'	Zhuk–shkaf–glaz

After a pause of 30 sec:

Dom–kot–stol	Zvon–noch'	Zhuk–shkaf–glaz

After a pause of 1 min:

Dom–kot–stol	Zvon–noch'	Zhuk–shkaf–glaz

After a pause with interference by conversation:

Stol... dom... and kot	Noch'... kot... noch'...	Zhuk... glaz... noch'
	zvon and khleb	

The relative weakness of audioverbal traces, and their increased inhibitability by interfering factors, naturally suggested that the inhibitory effect of homogeneous interfering speech activity would be manifested strongly. This was confirmed by tests. Recalling even a pair of words, after a second similar pair has been repeated, is quite beyond the capacity of these patients. They either completely forget the first series of words, which they could easily retain after an empty pause or even a short distraction, or they retain only one word, belonging sometimes to the first and sometimes to the second series.

Patient Van., a 41-year-old male (diagnosis as above).

Recalling of pairs of words

[Luna = moon, brat = brother, dym = smoke, koshka = kitten, luk = onion, pol = floor, klyuch = key, flag = flag, glaz = eye, ten' = shadow]

I. *Myach–zhuk*	II. *Stol–noch'*	?/I	?/II
Myach–zhuk	Stol–noch'	Zhuk?...	Luna?...
I. *Dom–brat*	II. *Zvon–kot*	?/I	?/II
Dom–brat	Zvon–kot	...dym...	Koshka?
I. *Luk–pol*	II. *Noch'–khleb*	?/I	?/II
Luk–pol	Nozh–khleb	Luk... now I have forgotten...	Khleb... nozh?
I. *Klyuch–flag*	II. *Glaz–ten'*	?/I	?/II
Klyuch–flag	Glaz–ten'	Klyuch... flag?	No... I have forgotten.

Patient Fil., a 38-year-old male (diagnosis as above).

[Lampa = lamp, mukha = fly, yabloko = apple, ruka = arm, chasy = clock, lisa = fox]

I. *Pila–sneg*	II. *Kot–les*	?/I	?/II
Pila–sneg	Kot–les	...pila...	I have forgotten.. sneg! Pila!...

I. *Lampa—shkaf*	II. *Voda—chainik*	*?/I*	*?/II*
Lampa—shkaf	Voda—chainik	Lampa. . . shkaf	I have forgotten. . .
I. *Yaitso—mukha*	II. *Yabloko—ruka*	*?/I*	*?/II*
Yaitso. . . mukha	Yabloko—ruka	Yaitso. . . mukha	. . . I have forgotten. . .
I. *Noga—chasy*	II. *Lisa—pole*	*?/I*	*?/II*
Noga—chasy	Lisa—pole	. . . noga. . . pole	. . . I have forgotten

All the disturbances are exhibited by these patients only with respect to audioverbal memory, only some with respect to auditory memory, and absolutely none in tests of visual and motor memory. In other words, they are strictly modality-specific.

The results of tests (carried out on 37 patients with lesions of the left temporal region) are summarized in Table 20.

Retention of Sentences

So far, we have dealt entirely with memory for isolated elements (picture cards, movements, words). It is extremely important, however, to know to what extent semantic organization helps in memorizing, and to what extent this factor is preserved in patients with lesions of different parts of the brain.

In the first of these tests, the patient was instructed to memorize simple sentences. Some were completely different in meaning, but others were similar in structure or phonetic and semantic content.

The first group included sentences such as "Apple trees grew in the garden behind the high fence," and "A hunter killed a wolf on the edge of the forest." The second group included the sentences: "In Tashkent, there was a severe earthquake and many houses were destroyed," and "In Tushino there was an air display and parachute jumps." If these sentences were too difficult for the patient (as in some special cases of nonspeech disorders), they were replaced by simpler

TABLE 20

WORD SERIES RECALL BY PATIENTS WITH LESIONS OF THE LEFT
TEMPORAL REGION

Material	Recall conditions			
	Immediately	After short empty pause	After short heterogeneous inteference	After short homogeneous interference
3 words	100	28	0	0
5 words	0	0	0	0

TABLE 21

SENTENCE RECALL BY PATIENTS WITH PITUITARY TUMORS

Quality of recall	Recall conditions				
	Immediately	After empty pause	After heterogeneous interference	After homogeneous interference (recalling a second similar sentence)	
				Return to sentence 1 after reproducing sentence 2	Return to sentence 2 after reproducing sentence 1
Complete	100	100	100	90.2	100
Partial	0	0	0	9.8	0
Schematic	0	0	0	0	0

ones, such as: "The boy is cold," "The girl is asleep," or "The boy hit the dog," "The girl drinks tea," etc. As in the previous series, tests of sentence memorizing were carried out in the following alternative forms: Immediate recall after presentation; recall after an empty pause of 1, 1.5, or 2 min; recall after a similar pause but filled with interfering activity (mental arithmetic); or recall after homogeneous interfering activity. In this last test, the patient had to repeat one sentence first and then another, after which he was asked which sentence had been given to him first and which second. To test the stability of trace retention, this last test can be repeated several times in succession without reiterating the original sentence (the examiner asked the patient several times: "Which was the first sentence? And the second? And the first? And the second?"). If the patient was unable to reproduce the sentence correctly, the whole test was repeated several times in succession; this showed whether the patient was able to learn or not.

The tests with normal subjects (as is well known from the literature) gave completely uniform results. Whereas a group of 7 to 10 isolated words could not as a rule be memorized at once, the same 7 to 10 words organized into a sentence, forming a single semantic entity, could be reproduced after the first reading without the slightest difficulty. Neither an empty pause nor a pause occupied by interfering activity had any effect whatsoever on the recalling of sentences. The test of recalling the first sentence after a normal subject had repeated another similar sentence also gave no difficulty. This is shown by control tests carried out with a group of 25 healthy adult subjects (Kiyashchenko). Different results (highly heterogeneous) were obtained in tests on patients with lesions of various parts of the brain.

Patients with lesions of the upper parts of the brain stem and with pituitary tumors with a relatively mild syndrome of mnemonic disorders showed no appreciable disturbances in these tests. All these patients easily repeated a sentence, even after a pause (whether empty or occupied by interfering activity). The overwhelming majority (including those with relatively more severe mnemonic defects) easily retained traces of the first sentence after repeating a second sentence. They had no difficulty in recalling the content of either sentence. Only in a few cases was recall incomplete: The patient either repeated part of a sentence or gave the general meaning correctly although the text was not followed exactly.

The results, averaged for 30 subjects, are summarized in Table 21.

An example in which the patient reproduced each of the two sentences incompletely or only schematically when recalled under conditions of mutual inhibition is given below.

Patient Rom., a 29-year-old male with a pituitary tumor (marked disturbances of memory).

I. *In Tashkent there was a severe earthquake and many houses were destroyed.*
In Tashkent there was a severe earthquake and many houses were destroyed.

II. *In Tushino there was an air display with parachute jumps.*
In Tushino there was an air display with parachute jumps.

?/I
In Tashkent there was an earthquake. . . and something was destroyed there. . .

?/II
In Tushino there was an
. . . air. . . display. . .

These results indicate that in patients with a relatively mild lesion of the upper parts of the brain stem, with the cerebral cortex intact, the semantic organization of verbal material readily compensates defects that were clearly visible during the recall of unconnected words.

The compensatory effect of semantic organization on trace retention may be absent in patients with massive brain tumors located in the midline. The cases to which I have referred showed a much more severe amnesic syndrome than in the preceding group of patients. It often bordered on Korsakov's syndrome, and was frequently accompanied by confusion about orientation and immediate past. As we have already seen, these patients could reproduce short series of material immediately (pictures, movements, words), or after relatively short and empty pauses, but not if interference with homogeneous activity was introduced.

Essentially, similar results were observed in tests of recall of verbal sentences. The patients could easily repeat sentences read to them immediately and could retain them after short empty or filled pauses of 1 to 2 min. Only if the pause was occupied, not by mnemonic but by speech activity (repetition of rapid speech), was there some increase in the number of unsuccessfully recalled sentences (Table 22).

The results were quite different when the patient, having repeated one sentence followed by a second similar sentence, was then asked to recall both in the order presented. They either completely lost both the sentences, distorted them severely, mixing the elements of one sentence with those of the other, or stated they had completely forgotten the first sentence. Recall of the second sentence met with the same fate. Mutual inhibition of two organized semantic systems made the selective reproduction of their traces impossible. The defects of recalling previously imprinted sentences remained unchanged even after several consecutive repetitions of the test. The corresponding results (averaged data for 13 patients) are given in Table 23; these results are extremely instructive. Clearly, the immediate reproduction of each of the two sentences separately presented no difficulty. No sooner had the patient repeated the second sentence, however, than he could no longer return to the first. Even

TABLE 22

SENTENCE RECALL BY PATIENTS WITH DEEP BRAIN TUMORS AND
AN AMNESIC SYNDROME (AVERAGED DATA FOR 13 PATIENTS)

Quality of recall	Recall conditions		
	After empty pause of 1–1.5 min	After heterogeneous interference (mental arithmetic)	After homogeneous interference (rapid speech)
Complete	100	100	86.7
Incomplete or inaccurate	0	0	13.3
Severe defects	0	0	0
Complete forgetting	0	0	0

if the test were continued, in fewer than half of the cases was he able to recall the second sentence successfully.

The patients began to contaminate the two sentences. This loss of selectivity and contamination of the two semantic systems not only persisted, but actually increased as the test was prolonged. Complete forgetting of the first sentence, which initially occurred in half of the cases, decreased gradually. Subsequent instructions to recall the second sentence also produced severe disturbances, but of a different character. The first attempts to recall the second sentence after an attempt had already been made to recall the first resulted in the successful reproduction of this sentence in nearly half of the cases (42.8%). Nevertheless, the majority of patients (57.2%) repeated the second sentence with contamination. Further prolongation of the test introduced interesting changes into the responses. Recall of the second sentence declined sharply, and the number of sentences completely forgotten increased considerably. The repetition of the test, which might be expected to strengthen the traces, not only did not have that effect, but led to increased mutual inhibition of the two semantic systems.

This pathological increase in the mutual inhibition of two homogeneous acts of mnemonic activity resulting in loss of semantic selectivity is a particularly important phenomenon. In some degree, it can be regarded as an experimental model of the confused state of consciousness manifested in patients with massive, deep brain tumors affecting both hemispheres and leading to a marked amnesic syndrome.

Examples to illustrate the facts just discussed are given below.

TABLE 23

CONSECUTIVE RECALL OF TWO SENTENCES BY 13 PATIENTS WITH DEEP BRAIN LESIONS
AND A MARKED AMNESIC SYNDROME

No. of repetitions	Conditions and quality of recall								
	Immediately		Return to sentence 2 after reproducing sentence 1			Return to sentence 1 after reproducing sentence 2		
	Sentence 1	Sentence 2	Complete reproduction	Contamina-tion	Complete forgetting	Complete reproduction	Contamina-tion	Complete forgetting
I	100	100	0	57.2	42.8	45.8	54.2	0
II	100	100	0	85.7	14.3	14.4	42.8	42.8
III	100	100	0	65.7	14.3	14.3	14.3	71.4

Patient Rakch., a 40-year-old female with a deep intracerebral brain tumor growing from the septum pellucidum (severe amnesic syndrome)

I. *Apple trees grew in the garden behind the high fence.*	II. *A hunter killed a wolf on the edge of the forest.*	?/I	?/II
(1) Apple trees grew in the garden behind the high fence.	A hunter killed a wolf on the edge of the forest.	We saw something... on the edge of the forest... a wolf.	Now... the second... we saw... a wolf, we saw a wolf on the edge of the forest.
(2) Apple trees grew in the garden behind the high fence.	A hunter killed a wolf on the edge of the forest.	On the edge of the forest... where did you see?...	And the second... what did we see?...
(3) Apple trees grew in the garden behind the high fence.	A hunter killed a wolf on the edge of the forest.	In the garden... wait a moment... they saw a wolf on the edge of the forest.	And the second... they killed it.
(4) Apple trees grew in the garden behind the high fence.	A hunter killed a wolf on the edge of the forest.	Well now... they saw ... wait a moment.... somehow the brains don't work.	I don't remember the second one at all... once I didn't remember the first, now I don't remember the second.
(5) Apple trees grew in the garden behind the high fence.	A hunter killed a wolf on the edge of the forest.	The first was that on the edge of the forest...	And the second... that they killed a wolf... let me see, they saw it and began to kill...
(6) Apple trees grew in the garden behind the high fence.	A hunter killed a wolf on the edge of the forest.	Well now, they saw something on the edge of the forest... what did they see?	I've forgotten it all.

Similar results were obtained in tests 7 through 10. Continuation of the experiment a week later gave the following results:

| (11) Apple trees grew in the garden behind the high fence. | A hunter killed a wolf on the edge of the forest. | The forest one— it wasn't that a hunter killed a wolf on the edge of a forest | On something or other... also on the edge of the forest... no, not the forest... it must be... |
| (12) Apple trees grew in the garden behind the high fence. | A hunter killed a wolf on the edge of the forest. | On the edge of the forest... not a hunter there... well of course... a hunter killed a wolf... | On the edge of the forest... a hunter ... killed a wolf ... but there they simply killed... |

(13) Apple trees grew in the garden behind the high fence.	A hunter killed a wolf on the edge of the forest.	Apple trees!... how could they be there? ... easy... and difficult...	No, I have forgotten.
(14) Apple trees grew in the garden behind the high fence.	A hunter killed a wolf on the edge of the forest.	Red apples on the edge of the forest	A hunter killed a wolf on the edge of the forest.

Similar defects appeared during the repetition of a second series of two sentences (in this case longer and more complex in structure):

I. *In Tashkent there was a severe earthquake and many houses were destroyed.*	II. *In Tushino there was an air display with parachute jumps.*	*?/I*	*?/II*
(1) In Tashkent there was a severe earthquake and many houses were destroyed.	In Tushino there was an air display with parachute jumps.	The first—an earthquake began there.	Well of course, when the earthquake began 15 parachutists had jumped.
(2) In Tashkent there was a severe earthquake and many houses were destroyed.	There was a display in Tushino but an earthquake began.	The first—I simply took them and made presents.	The second—I simply made presents.
(3) In Tashkent there was a severe earthquake and many houses were destroyed.	In Tushino there was an air display and, of course, everything was destroyed.	The first—either they eat or they don't eat, I don't know.	The second, counting the girls and boys, what they had to take...
(4) In Tashkent there was a severe earthquake and many houses were destroyed.	In Tushino there was an air display with parachute jumps.	The first was that ... there was an air display with parachute jumps.	The second—the girls were drawing ... not drawing but painting... is it true? I think it is true.
(5) In Tashkent... in Tushino there was a severe earthquake and many houses were destroyed.	In Tushino there was an air display with parachute jumps.	"The first... now... there was an air display... 9 boys took part... and girls... and for these boys"... Was there really such a sentence? "No, certainly there wasn't, certainly I guessed it ..."	"Nine boys won something... and there was a victory..." Is that true? "True..." Was there really such a sentence? "Why yes, 9 boys won something and as a reward ..."
(6) In Tashkent there was a severe earthquake and many houses were destroyed.	In Tashkent there was a display and many houses destroyed.	About an air display	The second—about some woman or other

During repetition of the first group of sentences, the predominant feature was persistence of the second sentence, indicating severe pathological inertia. During repetition of a second group of two sentences, not only was contamination a conspicuous feature, but the sentences were mingled with elementary irrelevant associations which sprang up when the test was prolonged. The patient was unable to distinguish these words from the true substance of the sentences she had reproduced earlier. Mingling irrelevant connections during the recall process was particularly characteristic of patients with deep brain tumors located in the midline and giving rise to an oneiroid state. The possibility of producing this phenomenon experimentally by conflict between two homogeneous mnemonic activities is particularly important.

The disturbance of recalling organized verbal structures (sentences) assumes still more severe forms in patients with massive lesions of the frontal lobes. If these lesions involve mainly the medial zones of the frontal lobes (medial tumors of the frontal lobes, or rupture of anterior communicating artery, complicated by spasm of the anterior cerebral arteries), the patient developed typical features of confusion and disturbance of the mnemonic selectivity. In the test described above, these disturbances are manifested chiefly as contamination during the reproduction of sentences presented previously. If these lesions involve the prefrontal zones of the hemispheres, and are also accompanied by a massive amnesic syndrome, the dominant feature is pathological inertia of established stereotypes, sometimes making a return to the first sentence after repetition of the second sentence completely impossible. In the severest cases, irrelevant associations are mingled even with immediate recall. In other cases, immediate recall is possible, but interference (especially by homogeneous activity) leads to complete inhibition of the sentences. No form of compensation by transferring the sentences to higher levels of organization, or converting them into a single semantic structure, was evident. Examples illustrating these facts are given below.

Patient Vas., a 35-year-old male with a bilateral tumor of the medial zones of the frontal lobes.

Repeat the sentence "Apple trees grew in the garden behind the high fence."

(1) "Well, let me see. . . in Moscow. . . behind a high fence. . . grew. . . I mean didn't grow. . . or else. . ."
(2) "In Moscow. . . behind a high fence (yawns, is distracted). . ."
(3) "Apple trees grew in the garden behind the high fence."

After a pause of 20 sec occupied by distracting conversation:

Repeat the sentence you have just given me. "I have to repeat. . . that. . . that in Moscow. . ." Go on. "In Moscow. . . behind a high fence. . ." Yes? "There lived. . . well now, who lived. . . the parents. . ."

In this case, repetition of even a single sentence was impossible because of the patient's general aspontaneity and the uncontrollable springing up of irrelevant associations. In the following cases, the same phenomenon came to light in tests involving the return to a sentence after repetition of a similar sentence.

Patient Iv., a 35-year-old male with rupture of an aneurysm of the anterior communicating artery and spasm of both anterior cerebral arteries.

Recalling two separate sentences

I. *In Tashkent there was a severe earthquake and many houses were destroyed.*	II. *In Tushino there was an air display with parachute jumps.*	?/I	?/II
(1) In Tashkent there was a severe earthquake and many houses were destroyed.	In Tushino there was an air display with parachute jumps.	I don't know.... something about air exhibitions. . .	I don't know, I have forgotten. . .
(2) In Tashkent there was a severe earthquake and many houses were destroyed.	In Tushino there was an air display with parachute jumps.	"Now I remember (scratches his ear) . . . something to do with the ear . . ." Not with Tashkent? "An accident. . . many people were crushed. . . it seems like. . ."	Now. . . about an earthquake. . . somewhere in the south. . .
(3) In Tashkent there was a severe earthquake and many houses were destroyed.	In Tushino there was an air display with parachute jumps.	"Now I remember . . . Tashkent, there was an air display. . ."	No, I don't remember. . .

Sometimes these phenomena appeared only if the recalling of short sentences was separated by a pause of 1.5 to 2 min and took place "from traces."

I. *The old man drank sweet tea.*	II. *The dvornik swept the wet street.*	?/I	?/II
The old man drank sweet tea.	The dvornik swept the wet street.	The old man drank sweet tea.	The dvornik swept the wet street.

?/I	?/I	?/II	?/I
The old man drank sweet tea.	The old man drew something.	What did I tell you? He drank tea.	He also drank tea. . .

Patient Mal., a 42-year-old female with rupture of an aneurysm of the anterior communicating artery (severe amnesic syndrome).

I. *Apple trees grew in the garden behind the high fence.*	II. *A hunter killed a wolf on the edge of the forest.*	*?/I*	*?/II*	*?/I*	*?/II*
(1) Apple trees grew in the garden behind the high fence.	A hunter killed a wolf on the edge of the forest.	There were many apples on the edge.	A hunter killed a wolf on the edge of the forest.	There were splendid apples on the edge . . .	A hunter killed a wolf, not a bear, on the edge of the forest.
(2) Apple trees grew in the garden behind the high fence.	A hunter killed a wolf behind the high fence on the edge of forest.	I have forgotten.	I have forgotten.		
(3) Apple trees grew in the garden behind the high fence.	A hunter killed a wolf on the edge of the forest.	Apples grew on the edge of the forest.	Apple trees grew on the edge. . . on the border. . . behind the high fence.	On that edge of the forest, no fence. . . a hunter killed a wolf.	

I. *In Tashkent there was a severe earthquake and many houses were destroyed.*	II. *In Tushino there was an air display with parachute jumps.*	*?/I*	*?/II*
(1) In Tashkent there was a severe earthquake and many houses were destroyed.	In Tushino there was an air display with parachute jumps.	In Africa there was a severe earthquake and many houses were smashed.	In Tushino there was an air display and many airplanes.
(2) In Tashkent there was a severe earthquake and many houses were destroyed	In Tushino there was a visit. . . no. . . in Tushino there was an air display attended by. . .	In Tashkent there was a severe earthquake and many houses were destroyed.	In Tushino there was an air display and many airplanes came. . . I don't know. . .

Patient Kalimk., a 38-year-old male with rupture of an aneurysm of the anterior communicating artery (severe amnesic syndrome).

I. *Apple trees grew in the garden behind the high fence.*	II. *A hunter killed a wolf on the edge of the forest.*	?/I	?/II
(1) Apple trees grew in the garden behind the high fence.	A hunter killed a a wolf on the edge of the forest.	A hunter killed a wolf. . . somewhere . . . on the edge of the forest.	What was the second? . . . on the edge of the forest. . . and something else. . .
(2) Apple trees grew in the garden behind the high fence.	A hunter killed a wolf on the edge of the forest.	But I have forgotten the first,. . . a hunter killed a wolf on the edge of the forest.	I have forgotten it already. . .
(3) Apple trees grew in the garden behind the high fence.	A hunter killed a a wolf on the edge of the forest.	A hunter killed a wolf. . . in the forest behind the fence. . .	I have forgotten it already. . .
(4) Apple trees grew in the garden behind the high fence.	A hunter killed a wolf on the edge of the forest.	The wolves were. . . grazing. . . in the forest behind the fence.. . .	I don't remember at all. . .

Among the patients with a circulatory disturbance of the anterior communicating and anterior cerebral arteries, a test involving separate recall of two sentences invariably revealed severe defects, including complete forgetting or partial recall of one sentence together with marked contamination. These phenomena increase greatly in severity during the acute period of the disease, but they are also demonstrable in patients in a stabilized condition. The results (averaged for 30 patients) are summarized in Table 24.

The fact that half of these patients were able to recall both the first and the second sentences merely shows that this group also included patients with a relatively mild syndrome of the circulatory disturbance in these arteries. However, the following feature was characteristic: Both incomplete recall of the first of the two sentences and contamination occurred in about equal proportions, but "forgetting" the second sentence was much less common than recall with contamination. Another characteristic feature was that the number of cases of imperfect recall and contamination did not decrease with repetition. This demonstrates once again that the disturbance in memorizing organized verbal structures is not simple extinction, but rather the interfering effect of the two semantic groups with their mutual inhibition and loss of recall selectivity.

The most interesting results are obtained in tests on patients with massive lesions of the frontal lobes accompanied by a general reaction of the brain as a

TABLE 24

CONSECUTIVE RECALL OF TWO SENTENCES BY 30 PATIENTS WITH DISTURBANCE OF THE CIRCULATION IN THE ANTERIOR COMMUNICATING AND ANTERIOR CEREBRAL ARTERIES

No. of repetitions	Conditions and quality of recall							
	Immediately		Return to sentence 1 after reproducing sentence 2			Return to sentence 2 after reproducing sentence 1		
	Sentence 1	Sentence 2	Complete reproduction	Partial reproduction	Contamination	Complete reproduction	Partial reproduction	Contamination
I	100	100	53.3	20.6	26.1	53.3	20.1	26.6
II	100	100	53.3	23.4	23.3	65.6	7.8	26.6
III	100	100	60.0	13.4	26.6	60.0	10.0	30.0
IV	100	100	53.3	20.1	26.6	60.0	13.4	26.6
V	100	100	56.6	20.1	23.3	56.6	10.1	33.3

whole, leading to a marked amnesic syndrome. In these patients, the predominant factor disturbing normal recall is the pathological inertia of pre-existing stereotypes. This same factor also persists during the recall of organized verbal structures (sentences), preventing the switching from one series to another and making it impossible for the patient to recall a new sentence (and sometimes even a sentence repeated previously). For example:

Patient Kork., a 24-year-old male with massive bilateral trauma of the frontal lobes and a well-marked amnesic syndrome.

Recalling sentences

I. *Apple trees grew in the garden behind the high fence.*	II. *A hunter killed a wolf on the edge of the forest.*	*?/I*	*?/II*
(1) Apple trees grew in the garden behind the high fence.	A hunter killed a wolf on the edge of the forest.	A hunter killed a wolf on the edge of the forest.	A hunter killed a wolf on the edge of the forest.

Do you know that both sentences are the same? "No, they are different." How are they different? "The pronunciation was different. . . the stress does not go where it should. . ."

(2) Apple trees grew in the garden behind the high fence.	A hunter killed a wolf on the edge of the forest.	A hunter killed a wolf on the edge of the forest.	A hunter killed a wolf on the edge of the forest.

Do you know that the sentences were still the same? "Not quite. . ." What was the difference? "To begin with, the stress. . . second, the arrangement of the question. . ." What question? "The final question of course. . ." And so on.

Continuation of the experiment four days later

I. *In Tashkent there was a severe earthquake and many houses were destroyed.*	II. *In Tushino there was an air display with parachute jumps.*	*?/I*	*?/II*
(1) In Tashkent there was a severe earthquake and many houses were destroyed.	In Tushino there was an air display with jumps from airplanes.	In Tushino there was an air display with parachute jumps.	The second? In Tushino there was an air display and jumps from airplanes.

You mean these sentences are the same? Surely I gave you different sentences! The patient is silent.

| (2) In Tashkent there was a severe earth- quake and many houses were destroyed. | In Tushino there was an air display with parachute jumps. | In Tushino there was an air display and jumps from airplanes. | In Tushino there was an air display and jumps from airplanes. |

Were the sentences I gave you the same? "No, different." How were they different? "Because they said different things." What was the first sentence? "In Tushino there was an air display and jumps from airplanes." And the second? "In Tushino there was an air display and jumps from airplanes." Surely these are the same? "Not quite. . . the difference is. . ." Well what is it? "In pronunciation. . ."

| (3) In Tashkent there was a severe earth- quake and many houses were destroyed. | In Tushino there was an air display with parachute jumps. | In Tushino there was an air display and jumps from airplanes. | In Tushino there was an air display and jumps from airplanes. |

Are you sure that you have said them properly? "Quite sure." Surely the sentences were the same? "No, not quite, but nearly. . . "

Depending on the size of the lesion, the phenomena described above occurred with different degrees of severity, but the basic structure of the mnemonic disorders, inert persistence of the most recent system, and the almost total inability to recall the first sentence, continued unchanged.

The results of tests on 14 patients with massive lesions of the frontal lobes are summarized in Table 25.

When massive deep midline lesions or bilateral frontal lobe lesions are accompanied by a marked amnesic syndrome, they lead to disorders of audioverbal memory which are not mitigated by semantic organization.

With deep midline lesions, the memory disturbance consists of contamination or forgetting, but with frontal defects it is mainly due to pathological inertia of pre-existing stereotypes.

Patients with lesions on the postero-lateral surface of the hemispheres, on the other hand, demonstrate memory disturbances which are modality-specific, unrelated to general disturbances of consciousness or orientation in the immediate part, and compensated for by imposing semantic organization on the material to be memorized. Admittedly, these patients differ in their ability to compensate for memory defects (depending on the site of the lesions), and the memory defects are based on different factors. Nevertheless, attempts to reproduce a whole semantic structure and the active search for adequate trace systems are characteristic features of all patients with local lesions of the posterior zones of the cortex (and in particular, lesions of the left, dominant hemisphere).

Most similar to the defects characteristic of massive frontal lesions are the disturbances of sentence repetitions exhibited by patients with lesions of the

TABLE 25

CONSECUTIVE RECALL OF TWO SENTENCES BY PATIENTS WITH MASSIVE LESIONS OF
THE FRONTAL LOBES

Quality of recall	Recall conditions			
	Immediately		Return to sentence 1 after reproducing sentence 2	Return to sentence 2 after reproducing sentence 1
	Sentence 1	Sentence 2		
Complete	100	100	10	70
Partial	0	0	35	25
Grossly incorrect	0	0	55	5

posterior frontal zones of the left hemisphere. In the severest of these cases, a patient who could easily repeat an entire sentence had great difficulty in switching to another sentence. When instructed to repeat it, he inertly reproduced the first sentence or contaminated elements of the second sentence with inertly perseverating components of the first. In less severe cases, direct repetition of two sentences remained intact, but attempts to return to the first sentence after successfully repeating the second elicited mistakes characterized by pathological inertia of pre-existing traces. Two corresponding examples are given below.

Patient Ob., a 30-year-old male with an intracerebral tumor of the left posterior frontal and temporal regions.

Repetition of sentences

The girl cries.	*The boy sleeps.*	*The cow moos.*	*The dog barks.*
The girl cries.	The boy sleeps.	The cow. . . moos.	The dog barks.
The house burns.	*The snow falls.*	*The cow moos.*	*Spring has come.*
Burns. . . no. . . what is it. . . dog. . . no. . .	The snow falls.	The cow moos.	(1) What is it. . . the cow moos.
			(2) What is it. . .
			(3) What is it. . .
			(4) No. . . I can't.

The phenomenon becomes more evident during repetition of more complex sentences.

The boy hit the dog.	*The girl drinks tea.*	*The boy hit the dog.*
(1) Dog. . . dog. . . was hit. . . dog	The girl. . . drinks. . . tea.	The girl. . . no
(2) The boy. . . dog. . .	Once again. The girl. . . dog. . .	The girl. . . no. . . the dog . . .
(3) The dog. . . was hit. . . the dog. . .	The girl drinks tea.	I can't. . .

The patient exhibits the familiar tendency to repeat the most recent word first (the "recency" factor), as a result of which the word order is upset. Another phenomenon is worthy of note, although it has so far received little study. This is the tendency toward simplification of the structure of the sentence. Instead of "mal'chik (subject; the boy) udaril (predicate; hit) sobaku (object, the dog, accusative case)" the patient may repeat: "mal'chik (subject) udarilsya (predicate; was hit, passive form of the verb)," or sometimes he simply inertly repeats one word: "sobaku. . . udarilsya. . . sobaku. . .". Note that the general structure of the sentence remains intact. The patient continues to search actively for the lost sentence while changing its elements.

Similar phenomena are seen in patients with a mild form of this syndrome, but in these cases they are manifested only under more sensitive conditions—either after a pause, or when the patient must return the first sentence after having repeated the second.

Patient Evch., a 35-year-old male with an intracerebral tumor of the left posterior frontal and temporal region.

After memorizing a series of words (cat–bridge–night–needle), the patient's ability to repeat simple sentences was tested. At the beginning, the results were good. Later, he began to change the word order. Later still, the repetition was interrupted by interjection of isolated words learned previously. Finally, after a pause of one minute, recall of two sentences gave way to the inert repetition of only one of the two.

I. *The house burns.*	II. *The moon shines.*	*?/I*	*?/II*
(1) The house burns.	The moon shines.	The moon shines.	The moon shines.
(2) The house burns.	The moon shines.	The moon shines.	The moon shines.

The same test is carried out when the patient is rather tired.

I. *The boy sleeps.*	II. *The dog barks.*	*?/I*	*?/II*
(1) The boy sleeps.	The dog barks.	Night–needle	The dog barks.
(2) The boy sleeps.	The dog barks.	Night–needle	The dog barks.
(3) The boy sleeps.	The dog barks.	Night–needle, no . . . the dog barks.	The dog barks.
(4) The boy sleeps.	The dog barks.	The dog barks.	The boy sleeps.

After a pause of 1 min (the original sentences are not given again):

?/I	*?/I*	*?/II*
The dog barks.	The dog barks.	The dog barks.

As in the preceding case, these phenomena were more severe when the patient was required to repeat more difficult sentences.

I. *Snow is falling on the street.*	II. *The boy has learned his lesson.*	*?/I*	*?/II*	*?/I*	*?/II*
(1) Snow is falling on the street.	The boy has learned his lesson.	The sun. . . on the street. . .	Winter. . . on the street. . . I'm not sure.	Gives up.	Gives up.
(2) Snow is falling on the street.	On the street . . . no. . .	Gives up.	Gives up.	Gives up.	Gives up.
(3) Snow is falling on the street.	The boy is learning the lesson.	The lesson is falling. . . on the street. . .	Winter on the street.	Gives up.	Gives up.

The patient was able to reproduce the two sentences correctly only after six repetitions.

When the material is made a little more difficult (or if the patient is a little tired), repetition of the test does not necessarily result in improvement, but often aggravates the defective recall despite the patient's critical awareness of his mistakes and attempts to correct them.

In patients with lesions of the posterior parieto-temporo-occipital zones of the left hemisphere, perseveration (often less clear and less persistent than in the cases just described) is joined by word searching, resulting from the equalization in excitability of different traces. In attempts to repeat a sentence, it is not so much the patient's ability to reproduce an organized structure that is disturbed, as the possibility of correctly recalling its components. Appropriate examples are given below.

Patient Bich., a 36-year-old male with an arterio-venous aneurysm of the left parieto-temporo-occipital region.

Repetition of simple sentences

The boy sleeps.	*The girl is ill.*	*The dog barks.*	*The cat mews*
The boy sleeps.	(1) The boy. . . is ill.	The dog. . . (meaningless word)	(1) The hen. . . no, I don't know, . .
	(2) The girl. . . was ill.	The dog. . . barks.	(2) The fish. . . I have forgotten ca. . . then. . .
			(3) Cares. . . cares

The boy (mal'chik) caught a fish.
(1) The little boy (mal'chishka). . . caught a fish.
(2) Ibid.

The cat caught a mouse (mysh').
(1) (Mysha. . . mysha. . .) fish. . . what is it. . . ate this. . . bear (mishku). . .
(2) Myshka. . . ate chicken. . . eagle. . .

One month later the patient could again reproduce sentences immediately, but all the phenomena described above returned as soon as the conditions of the test were made more difficult.

1. *The girl drinks tea.*	II. *The boy hit the dog.*	*?/I*	*?/II*
The girl drinks tea.	The boy hit the dog.	The girl drinks tea.	The boy fell. . . (upal). . . the dog. . . hit (udaril) the dog

?/I	*?/II*	*?/II*	*?/II*
The girl drinks tea.	The girl hit the dog.	The boy drinks tea.	The girl poured the tea.

I. *Apple trees grew in the garden behind the high fence (zaboram).*	II. *A hunter killed a (ubil) a wolf at the edge (na opushke) of the forest.*	*?/I*	*?/II*
(1) In the garden. . . under (pod ra. . . rabodom—meaningless) lived. . . long words.	A hunter. . . a hunter. . . killed (ubila—feminine under the vegetable garden (ogorodom). . .	On. . . near the house . . . under the fence. . . . . . in general, some sort of apple trees. . . what apple trees. . . near the house. . . in the garden	"This hunter killed a horse. . ." Killed what? "A dog. . . no. . . a wolf? Both together? In the forest. . . a hunter killed a dog! Oh. . . a wolf!"
(2) Under the fence there lived. . . flowers. . .	A hunter. . . hid (ukryl). . . killed (ubil) something	*?/I* Near the house. . . in the forest. . . in the forest. . . in the (yablo. . . yabloki . . .) apples on the tree. . .	*?/II* Wolf! Dog! He killed. . . a dog. . . I have mixed them all up.
(3) Under the apple tree. . . there lived. . . flowers. . . no. . . apple trees			

Similar results were obtained from tests on patients with left temporal lesions. As a rule, these patients also had difficulty in finding the components rather than in repeating whole sentences. The difficulties of both groups consisted of: Replacement of the required word by another, verbal paraphasias (in patients with lesions located outside Wernicke's area, and acoustico-mnemonic aphasia), or literal paraphasias (characteristic of patients with acoustico-gnostic speech disorders). Examples of audioverbal memory defects arising from tests of sentence repetition are given below.

Patient Van., a 41-year-old male with a deep tumor in the left temporal region.

Repetition of sentences

I studied on a course.
I. . . am working on a course.

At school I was an excellent pupil.
At school I studied. . . for 5 rubles.

In the evening it snowed heavily.
In the evening. . . at night. . . snow. . . rain

The clock points to midday.
"In the street it was midday."
Repeat more accurately! "I have forgotten it all. . . all was left was midday. . . the first part I have forgotten. . ."

A hunter killed a wolf on the edge of the forest.
(1) On the edge of the forest. . . wolves were fighting. . . no. . .
(2) On the edge of the forest a hunter killed. . .a bear. . .no, the last word is not quite right. . .

On the wet sidewalk there stood a policeman.
In the rain. . . walks. . . a policeman. . . no, it isn't right. . .he isn't walking. . .he isn't moving
. . . something different. . .

Similar phenomena were seen in patients with milder forms of acoustico-mnemonic aphasia, although they were only manifested under more complex conditions. I shall not describe the tests of sentence repetition by patients with the acoustico-gnostic form of temporal aphasia, because this would go beyond the main theme of this investigation, the analysis of mnemonic disturbances resulting from local brain lesions.

In all these cases, there was no evidence of pathological inertia preventing the patient from recalling the sentence reproduced first. Under all conditions, patients with left temporal lesions had difficulty with precise recall of verbal structures, but showed no "freezing" or inert repetition of the most recent sentence (typical of patients with massive lesions of the frontal lobes). The corresponding data (mean values for nine subjects) in Table 26 should be compared to that given in Table 25 for patients with frontal lobe lesions.

To summarize, lesions of the upper zones of the brain stem (and pituitary tumors), which leave the cerebral cortex intact, give rise to defects of audioverbal memory which can be compensated for by changing to organized speech structures (sentences). In patients with massive deep midline brain

TABLE 26

ORDER OF RECALL OF TWO SENTENCES BY PATIENTS WITH LESIONS OF
THE LEFT TEMPORAL LOBE

Quality of recall	Recall conditions		
	Immediately	Return to sentence 1 after repeating sentence 2	Return to sentence 2 after repeating sentence 1
Complete	70	15	25
Partial	30	60	70
Grossly inaccurate	0	25	5

tumors affecting both hemispheres and accompanied by a marked amnesic syndrome and, in particular, in patients with massive bilateral lesions of the frontal lobes, this compensatory effects of organized speech structures is absent. Finally, in patients with lesions of the lateral convexity of the hemispheres, the mnemonic defects primarily involve individual components (words) of the sentence, and organized sentences do not reduce mistakes.

Retention and Reproduction of Semantic Fragments

Sentence recall is merely the first step in the investigation of memorizing and reproducing organized speech structures. The next step involves testing retention of semantic fragments or stories. Unlike a small group of words or sentences, story recall is never exactly word for word. As a rule, semantic fragments are composed of many more separate elements than can be directly retained in memory, but they can be organized into a single semantic system. When required to reproduce the meaning of a story, as Bartlett (1932) showed originally, the subject is faced with the problem of decoding this meaning, selecting the most important and informative elements, combining them into an integral semantic structure, and then relating (reconstructing) not the exact textual series of words in that structure, but the meaning of the fragment.

In a simple narrative fragment, a "communication of events," distinguishing the basic meaning presents no appreciable difficulty. In a fragment with a double meaning (a fable or proverb), decoding the meaning is more complex. In fragments of complex structure, incorporating several semantic groups, decoding the basic meaning is a task of considerable difficulty (Luria, 1962, 1969).

I began to test recall of semantic fragments not so much to study elementary memory as to analyze the degree to which our patients could decode complex semantic structures, pick out the most informative scheme (or program), and retain it. I used semantic fragments which had a second meaning. They were arranged in order of increasing complexity. The first fragments had a relatively simple semantic structure. One example is L. N. Tolstoy's short story, "The Hen and the Golden Eggs."

> A man had a hen which laid golden eggs. He wanted to get more of the eggs at once, and so he killed the hen. But inside he found nothing; it was just a hen like any other.

To decode (and memorize) this story it was necessary to distinguish the basic fact (the hen laying the golden eggs), the man's motive (greed), the basic action (the man killed the hen), and the result with which the action concluded ("but he found nothing inside it"). The fact that the basic meaning of the story was grasped is established by questioning its moral ("What does this story teach?") after the story had been retold.

The second, more complex fragment included an extended event that could be broken up into two semantic entities. The second semantic entity (necessary for grasping the meaning of the fragment) was given only in the shortest form. A characteristic example of this type is Tolstoy's "The Jackdaw and the Pigeons."

> A jackdaw heard that some pigeons had plenty of food. She painted herself white and flew into the pigeon house. The pigeons thought she was a pigeon, and took her in. However, she forgot herself and cried like a jackdaw. The pigeons then realized that she was a jackdaw and sent her away. She went back to her family, but they did not recognize her, and would not have her either.

This fragment is structurally much more complex. Two groups of active characters are represented here (jackdaws and pigeons), belonging to one class (birds). One of the characters concerned in the story (the jackdaw) changes (by changing color) into another active character (into a pigeon); she then blunders by revealing her deception ("forgot herself and cried like a jackdaw"), and the deception came to light ("they saw that she was a jackdaw"), with the consequences ("and they sent her away"). To all these elements, included in one situation, is added a simple sentence ("she went back to her family, but they did not recognize her and would not have her either"), transferring the action to another situation and acting as the key to the whole subsidiary meaning of the story ("do not paint yourself the wrong color").

The decoding of the meaning of this story is much more difficult, not only because two different groups of active characters belong to the same category, and exist in complex relationships ("painted herself white"—changed herself into a pigeon), but also because later the narration includes the opposite change ("cried like a jackdaw"..."the pigeons saw that she was a jackdaw"). The last complex feature of this fragment is that the sentence with which it ends transfers the narration into a new situation and binds together the whole semantic context.

The third and last degree of structural complexity is represented by fragments including two extended semantic contexts which must be compared in order to deduce the ultimate meaning. An example is Tolstoy's "The Ant and the Pigeon."

> An ant went down to the stream to drink. A wave swamped him and he began to drown. A pigeon flew past him and threw him a twig. He climbed on the twig and was saved.
> Next day, a hunter set a net and caught the pigeon. When he took it from the net, however, the ant crept up stealthily and bit the hunter on his hand. The hunter cried out and the pigeon flew away.

The additional difficulties introduced by this semantic fragment are obvious. First, it incorporates a whole chain of events ("the ant began to drown," "the pigeon threw a twig," "the ant was saved," etc.). Second, a third person is introduced in the middle of the narrative (a hunter) and a second part of the story, equally complete, is brought in ("the hunter caught the pigeon"; "the ant bit the hunter on his hand"; "the pigeon flew away"). Finally, the ultimate meaning of the story can be deduced only by comparing the two complete semantic contexts.

The above stories also have another feature. In each one there are active characters belonging to the same category ("hen," "jackdaw," "pigeon"), although appearing in different contexts. This deliberately chosen complication was used to examine the extent to which retention and recall remained selective across the semantic structures presented, or became contaminated by mixing the common elements in context.

For this purpose I also introduced a pair of stories with the same performers, but in different situations.

(1) "The Lion and the Mouse." A lion was asleep and a mouse ran over his body. The lion awoke and caught the mouse. The mouse begged him to let her go. The lion laughed and let her go. Next day a hunter caught the lion and tied him with a rope to a tree. The mouse came up stealthily, gnawed through the rope, and set the lion free.

(2) "The Lion and the Fox." A lion grew old and could no longer hunt animals. So the lion had to consider how to live by cunning. He lay in his den and pretended to be ill. The animals came up to him and he ate them. One day a fox came but would not go into his den. The lion asked her: "Why don't you come in?" The fox replied: "I can see tracks going into your den but none coming out."

The object of testing recall with these stories is to analyze whether the subject retains the whole semantic program of the story as well as its details, retells the basic story but substitutes details, or deforms even the theme of the story into disconnected fragments. Can the patient return to the original line of narration after distraction, or does he substitute random associations? And finally, when relating the subject of two isolated stories, does the patient lose the selectivity and contaminate the material of one story with another?

As in all previous cases, tests of story recall were carried out first immediately after presentation, then after pauses both with and without interfering activity. The interfering activity varied from simple distracting conversation to special speech activity, but did not include mnemonic activity (mental arithmetic, problem solving, etc.). If the patient was unable to reproduce the semantic fragment immediately after it had been read (as a result of a memory disturbance or a disruption of his activity), a control test was given in which the content of the fragment was broken up into separate elements and the patient had to respond to questions concerning each element separately.

In some cases, when long-term retention was to be tested, the patient was instructed to recall the content of stories read to him several hours or days beforehand. If he could not perform this task, he was asked whether stories of particular scenes had been read to him. Some of the promptings were false ("Did you have a story read about a horse? About a cat?"), and some were correct ("Was there a story about a hen? About a jackdaw?" and so on). Prompting could determine whether the patient retained latent traces of stories read to him.

The last—and possibly the most important—variant of the test involved homogenous interference. The patient was first instructed to reproduce one story and then immediately after that to reproduce a second story. Later he was asked to recall the first story first, and the second story last.

In cases when the recalling of the first story after presentation of the second was impossible, the test could be repeated. In cases in which recalling in this way was possible after the first presentation, the test could be made more difficult: Three stories were read in succession to the patient and he had to reproduce each of them immediately. Later he had to recall all three stories in the same order.

* * *

Normal subjects showed no difficulty in the reproduction of semantic fragments. The semantic structure of the fragment was reproduced satisfactorily both immediately and after an empty pause. As a rule, these subjects could recall the fragments after an interval of several hours (or days). They had no appreciable difficulty in giving the substance of the first fragment after a second, similar fragment had been read to them. No contamination of the meanings of different fragments occurred in this group.

As shown originally by the classical work of Bartlett (1932) and later by Smirnov (1948, 1966), the reproduction of a complex semantic fragment usually starts with its analysis into definite semantic groups, which are recalled in the proper order (often not word for word). This suggests we are concerned with the retention and reproduction of whole decoded bits of communication (Miller, 1969), that the whole process of semantic coding is fully preserved. The law of "recollection of thoughts" formulated many years ago by K. Bühler (1907) applies here, with its full force, and we were thus able to assess the abnormalities that occurred in our patients as a result of pathological conditions.

The results of tests on patients with local brain lesions were varied, and as a whole, repeated the facts I have already described. Nevertheless, these results produced far more information than those described in previous sections.

Patients with tumors of the upper parts of the brain stem (and, in particular, of the pituitary), who showed marked signs of generalized mnemonic defects when recalling isolated elements (e.g., words), showed no such defects when asked to memorize stories. Neither an empty pause nor one filled with interfering activity disturbed 'the patient's ability to recall a semantic fragment. Recall of two different fragments presented in succession was also largely unimpaired. The quality of content recall was somewhat lower than the quality of sentence recall, but in no case was the preceding semantic fragment completely forgotten or contaminated with elements from the other fragments. The inhibitory effect of homogeneous interference was relatively mild, and the compensatory role of logical structures remained fully intact.

This will be clear from the data given in Table 27.

Patients with lesions (tumors, aneurysms, injuries, toxic lesions) accompanied by a well-marked Korsakov's syndrome were completely different. These lesions affected the deep parts of the brain, spreading as a rule to the walls of the ventricles and the medial zones of the hemispheres.

It might be presumed that the patients of this group would be unable to recall any form of complex semantic fragments. The facts obtained by experimental investigation, however, show a much more complex picture. Most of the patients are able to repeat a simple thematic fragment immediately after it is read to them. Very often they retell it completely, and only occasionally is their narration inaccurate and fragmentary. Only patients with the severest form of Korsakov's syndrome retell the story as follows: "Well, there was something about a hen. . . it laid eggs. . . and there was something else. . . but what it is I have forgotten. . ."

When such a patient is asked to retell a story consisting of two narrative units, such as "the ant and the pigeon," they tell the first part of the story as follows: "An ant began to drown in a stream. . . and then. . . a pigeon flew past and threw it a twig. . . and it was saved. . ." But they completely omit the second part. No less frequently, they reproduce the second part alone: "Now a hunter. . . caught a pigeon. . . and an ant crept up and bit the hunter on his arm. . . and then. . . why, the pigeon flew away. . . ," but were completely unable to recall the first part. This is a clear example of the retroactive inhibition exerted by the last part of a story, consisting of two semantic units, on the whole of the first part—a phenomenon not found if the patient is instructed to recall a simple semantic structure in which two equally complete semantic units cannot be distinguished. This can be illustrated by appropriate examples.

Patient Bond., a 43-year-old female with a deep brain tumor.

"The Lion and the Mouse" story was read to the patient and she was asked to reproduce it immediately. She started: "Of course, mutual aid. . . one helped the other. . . they were hunted, they caught the lion and tied it to a tree. . . it was saved by the mouse. . . she gnawed through the rope and set the lion free. . ."

The patient was informed that she had not retold the whole story and it was read to her a second time. She said: "The lion found he was free. And the mouse found that she

TABLE 27

RECALL OF SEMANTIC FRAGMENTS UNDER DIFFERENT CONDITIONS BY PATIENTS WITH PITUITARY TUMORS (MEAN RESULTS FOR 30 PATIENTS)

Quality of recall	Recall conditions				
	Immediately	After an empty pause	After heterogeneous interference	After homogeneous interference by a second similar fragment	
				Return to the first fragment after reproducing the second	Return to the second fragment after reproducing the first
Complete	100	100	100	76.6	86.7
Partial	0	0	0	12.0	8.7
Schematic	0	0	0	14.4	4.6

was free. . . mutual aid. . ." In reply to the suggestion that she tell the story completely, the patient, although fully grasping its semantic scheme, once again retold only the last part. The patient could narrate each part separately with ease, but she was unable to tell the whole story.

The complete story was read to her a third time. This time she said: "A lion was asleep. . . and he was tied to a tree with a rope. . . around this tree ran a mouse. . . the lion stood up and wanted to be set free. . . but the rope would not give. . . the mouse then came to help. . . chewed through the rope. . . and he wanted to hang a bell. . . wanted to hang it around his neck and to go. . ." The patient was distracted.

The story was read a fourth time and the patient again asked to tell it completely. She said: "The lion was asleep. . . a mouse ran around him. . . the trees wanted to bind him and to leave him standing on the rope. . . a mouse ran around him. . . the trees decided to bind the lion and they did so. . . and then the mouse decided to set him free. . . jumped up to the rope and gnawed it. The lion slipped out of the rope and run away. . ." What does the story mean? "A drowning man will clutch at a straw. . ."

In the case of a semantic fragment with a complex structure, with two narrative units, the second part retroactively inhibits the first. The patient has correctly grasped the meaning ("mutual aid") from the beginning, but when retelling the story, simple repeats the second part and forgets the first. Only after the fourth repetition of the complex story did she at last begin to produce traces of the first part, but they disappeared at once. After frequent repetition of the story, the semantic structure of the second part of the story began to disintegrate ("the trees wanted to bind him. . . the trees decided to bind him"), the first part of the story could not be recalled, and the general semantic scheme of the story was deformed.

The same thing happened during the attempt to retell a second story with a similar complex structure. "The Ant and the Pigeon" story was read to the same patient. She again started to retell the story be reproducing its end: "The pigeon flew away and was saved. . . and the ant was saved. . . no one knew why it was. . ."

Tell the whole story again from the very beginning. "An ant went about its business. . . just then a pigeon was flying. . . she was holding something in her beak and let it fall. . . the ant ran further. The pigeon ate it. . . the ant approached stealthily from behind and grabbed hold. . . and soon they flew away together." What is the meaning of the story? "The little can help the big. The ant helped the pigeon and the pigeon helped the man. . ."

The story was read a second time. "The ant bit the hunter and the pigeon flew away. . ." And what happened before? "Before the man caught the pigeon. The ant saw this but could not help at all. And then he waited until the man took the pigeon in his hand and bit him. . . And the pigeon flew away. . ." And what happened before this? "The pigeon flew where there was a water barrier. She saw the ant. He was saved and swam across. And later, when it was necessary, the ant showed himself. . . and the pigeon fell into the hands of a hawk. . . of the hunter. . . and the ant bit him and the pigeon got away. . ."

What is the meaning of the story, then? "Helping one another."

Similar observations were made on the other patients of this group.

Patient Gund., a 41-year-old male with a tumor of the third ventricle (slight amnesic syndrome).

"The Lion and the Mouse" story was read to this patient and he was asked to retell it. At first, he told only the last part of the story: "The lion was asleep... a mouse ran into his tangled place, gnawed everything, and the lion escaped..."

After the story had been read a second time the patient began to narrate only the first part: "A lion was asleep. A mouse ran beside him. The lion seized her but granted... next day the lion was asleep... and the mouse ran away..."

Patient Vor., a 32-year-old female with a deep tumor in the midline (amnesic syndrome).

The same story was read to this patient. She repeated it as follows: "The mouse gnawed through the net and released the lion... I can't remember anymore..." No, recollect, there was something else. The story was read again. The patient retold it: "A lion was asleep... the mouse realized that the lion had fallen into the net and set the lion free... and something else... but I don't remember..."

In both cases the patient retained only the second part of the story.

Patient Ar., a 34-year-old female with a tumor of the third ventricle and an amnesic syndrome.

The same story was read to the patient. She tried to reproduce it but could recall only the first part: "A lion was asleep. The mouse ran over his body... and something else... there was something after... the lion caught the mouse?..."

The story was repeated. The patient reproduced it: "The lion was asleep... the mouse ran over his body and seized the mouse... no... not like that..."

The story was read a third time. The patient tried to reproduce it: "The lion was asleep. The mouse ran over his body and awakened the lion... the lion awoke... and caught the mouse... no, I have forgotten..."

In all three cases the patient retained only the first part of the story in her memory.

Patient Bobr., a 40-year-old male with a deep brain tumor in the midline (amnesic syndrome).

"The Ant and the Pigeon" story was read to the patient. He retold it as follows: "... there... I have forgotten the beginning... a hunter wanted to catch a pigeon, but the ant bit him on his hand so that he could not catch..." Only the last part of the story was reproduced.

"The Jackdaw and the Pigeons" story was read to this patient. He retold it as follows: "The jackdaw began to cry like a jackdaw... the pigeons recognized her and sent her away. And the jackdaws sent her away. She was painted white..." In this case only the second part of the story was retained and the first was forgotten.

The general sense of the story was well retained by the patient, indicating that the processes for distinguishing the general semantic structure of the story were intact. Coherent narration of details, however, met with considerable difficulty due to the primary mnemonic disorders and the mutual inhibition of the separate "chunks" of the story.

The immediate reproduction of the semantic fragment was often incomplete, but a delay of 5 to 10 min always introduced substantial defects. In this situation, the basic scheme of the story was usually retained, but important alterations in the content were inserted into the story. Examples of this type of deformation after a pause follow.

Patient Vak., a 20-year-old male with residual sequelae after a severe head injury with damage to both temporal lobes; Korsakov's syndrome (observations by L. T. Popova).

"The Jackdaw and the Pigeons" story was read to this patient.

Immediate reproduction of the story: "A jackdaw heard that the pigeons had plenty of food. She painted herself white and flew to the pigeons. They took her in, but the jackdaw gave herself away because she cried like a jackdaw and the pigeons turned her out. She then flew back to the jackdaws, but they also would not have her. . ."

Reproduction of the same story after 5 min: "So. . . the jackdaw and the pigeon. . . the jackdaw heard that the pigeons had plenty of food. . . she painted herself white, lived with them. Once, however,. . . the jackdaw was caught in the rain and the paint was washed off so that the pigeons could see and they turned her out. . . the meaning of the story. . ." And is this how it ended? "No. . . she flew to the jackdaws and they turned her out, and the jackdaw could not go to one or the other."

Reproduction of the story after 5 min: Certain important details disappeared and were replaced by compensatory guesses.

"The Hen and the Golden Eggs" story was read to the patient.

Immediate retelling of the story: "A man had a hen and she laid golden eggs. . . he was greedy and wanted to have more gold. He killed the hen, but found nothing inside her."

Reproduction of the story after 10 min: What was the story about? "What about?. . . I don't remember. . . animals. . . no, give me a clue. . ." A man and a hen. "Yes, yes, I have remembered! A hen laid eggs, every day an egg. . . he ate them and was satisfied. . . suddenly she stopped laying eggs, he cut her up, and found a golden egg inside. . . he. . . what did he do with it? He smashed the golden egg. . . and then what? Surely he did not cook it. . . something fell from it. . . something good, but what?"

In this case, after a pause of 10 min the patient was no longer able to reproduce the complete scheme of the story.

After a rest (45 min), a short fragment was read to the patient: "It was raining in the street; looking through the window I saw puddles lying on the street and decided to take an umbrella; however, I remembered that I had left my umbrella with a friend; I telephoned him and he brought my umbrella."

Immediately after presentation of the fragment, it was reproduced by the patient almost exactly as it was presented. After a pause of 20 min not filled with any special activity, however, the patient, who was already a little tired, could no longer reproduce the story or even recall that it had ever been read to him.

Tell me about the story I read to you. "Story? What story?. . . I can't remember. . . something about a girl and a wolf (this was not in the story at all). . . a story about a hen. . . but that wasn't today. . ." It was raining. . . "someone was caught in the rain. . . then shook himself. . . no, I can remember nothing. . . my brain won't work. . ." Umbrella. "The girl and the umbrella. . . no. . . I can't remember. . ." Rain—umbrella—telephone. "Somebody telephoned somebody else to bring an umbrella. . . but who. . . telephoned whom? No. . . I can't remember. . ."

The examples I have just given involved relatively simple semantic fragments. Recall of more complex fragments may give rise to appreciable disturbances even in the course of immediate reproduction which cannot be overcome even by frequent repetition. In these cases, despite the obvious fragmentation, the patient never went beyond the context of the fragment read to him or slipped into irrelevant associations (a typical feature, as we shall see below, of patients with a lesion involving the frontal lobes).

Patient Vak. (details of this patient are given on p. 115). "The Ant and the Pigeon" story was read to him, but because of his failure to repeat the story completely, it was read to him several times in succession. Every time his narration became fragmented immediately after the story was read to him.[6]

(1) "The ant saved the pigeon. . . the pigeon saved the ant. . . he fell into the river. . . she threw him a twig and he was saved. The pigeon fell into misfortune. . . but how she was saved. . . I can't remember. . ."

(2) "Ah. . . the ant bit. . . once an ant fell into the water, the pigeon threw him a twig. . . once a hunter set a net. . . the ant climbed up and disentangled the net. . ."

(3) ". . . the ant fell into the water, the pigeon threw him a twig. . . a hunter caught the pigeon and the ant disentangled the net. . . no, I don't know, tell me again. . ."

(4) ". . . the ant crawled along the twig and fell into the water. A pigeon flew past and threw him a twig. The hunter set a net and pigeon flew into it. . . when the ant saw this he disentangled the net. . . no, tell me again. . ."

(5) ". . . Ah. . . he bit! How did I forget. . . why, they have bitten me as well!. . . The ant crawled along a twig and fell into the water, the pigeon threw him a twig. . . he was saved. . . the hunter set a net and caught the pigeon. . . the ant bit the hunter on his hand and the pigeon flew away. . ."

The difficulties arising here are purely mnemonic. The patient retains the problem of recalling the story as instructed, his attitude toward his poor performance is critical, and he attempts to fill in the gaps. He retains the general scheme of the narrative and never steps beyond it. Characteristically, the semantic scheme of the narrative remains undisturbed even after long intervals, although some of the details of the story lapse.

The results of tests with the same patient are:

(1) *Reproduction of a story after 2 min:* "They set one another free—the ant the pigeon and the pigeon the ant. The ant set the pigeon free, he loosened the rope and the pigeon set the ant free by throwing him a stick." Who helped the other first? "The ant. . . he was the man and must have been well-mannered. . ."

(2) *Reproduction of a story after 5 min:* "About an ant, and something else. . . someone saved him. . . the ant climbed on a twig. . . who would save him?. . . He fell into the water and someone saved him. . . broke off a branch and he climbed on. . . who broke it? Any normal person. . . Animals themselves could have set him free. . . What animal is more favorably disposed to the ant?. . . The jackdaw or the crow (reminiscences from stories read previously). . . and what came after. . . I have forgotten. . ."

(3) *Reproduction of a story after 20 min:* "Once upon a time a pigeon fell into a net. . . an ant set her free. . . he was able to disentangle the net. . . but where the ant fell I can't remember. . . ah, I have remembered, he fell into the water, the pigeon threw him a stick, and he was able to climb out. . ."

(4) *Reproduction of a story after 24 hours:* What was the story you had read to you yesterday? "Four stories. . . a girl and a wolf. . . and something else. . ." The ant and the pigeon. "Ah, the pigeon helped each other. The ant fell into the water and the pigeon saved him. . . the ant bit the man who had caught the pigeon. . ."

[6] Here and later in the book the numbers in parentheses denote reproduction of the text by patients after successive repetitions of having the story read to him.

The record of these tests is very instructive. The patient who (after many repetitions) could reproduce a complex story correctly after a short pause of 2 min started to lose its details after a pause of 5 min. Reminiscences of previous stories ("The Jackdaw and the Crow") began to intrude and some of the details were replaced by guessing. After 20 min, the main parts of the theme were reversed so that the last part was retained better than the first. Only when the test was repeated after 24 hours was the story forgotten, although a little prompting was sufficient to restore the semantic scheme. In the case described above, despite very severe amnesic defects, the general law of the preservation of thought (formulated by Bühler) remained unaffected and no departure from the bounds implicit in the story was observed.

It is clear (from the records given above) that if the fragment is reproduced after a delay of 5 to 10 min, irrelevant associations begin to creep in. Recall starts to lose its selective character. This effect is manifested particularly clearly in tests incorporating "homogeneous interference," or in other words, when the patient has to listen to a second story just prior to recounting the first (particularly if the stories contain certain details in common). In these cases, reproduction of the story read to the patient first is completely inhibited or the two semantic systems begin to contaminate one another. A few examples of both types of deformation, as seen during attempts to recall the preceding story, are cited:

Patient Vak. "The Hen and the Golden Eggs" story was read to him. He reproduced it immediately after hearing it: "A man had a hen; she laid golden eggs. He wanted to get more gold without waiting for it; he killed the hen but inside her there was nothing, she was just like any other hen."

"The Jackdaw and the Pigeons" story was read to him. He reproduced it immediately after hearing it: "A jackdaw heard that the pigeons had plenty of food, she painted herself white and flew to the pigeons, who welcomed her. However, she cried like a jackdaw and the pigeons sent her away. She flew back to her own kind, but they also sent her away."

What was the first story? "The patient's face became blank. "The first?. . . what?.·. . I told you about the jackdaw. . . and now you want the first. . . no, you did not tell me anything else. . ." About the man and the hen? "Ah, yes. . . you did tell me that story. . . a hen laid golden eggs. . . the man was glad. . . and began to pay great attention to the hen. . ."

After 15 min the patient was again asked about the first story. This time, however, he contaminated the two stories: "A pigeon laid a golden egg. . . and someone carried it away. . . a hen or not. . .? Who carried it away. . .? The hen, wasn't it?. . ."

Patient An., a 34-year-old male with a circulatory disorder in the system of the vertebro-basilar artery; severe Korsakov's syndrome (L. T. Popova's observations).

"The Jackdaw and the Pigeons" story was read to this patient. He retold the story satisfactorily.

He also quite satisfactorily repeated immediately "The Hen and the Golden Eggs" story.

What was the first story? "The first. . . I have forgotten. . . about somebody. . . no. . . I have forgotten. . ." About a jackdaw and some pigeons. "Oh, no. . . I cannot say anything. . . how many jackdaws and how many pigeons. . ." What happened there? "I can't say. Perhaps they quarrelled, perhaps they fought. . . no. . . they settled everything peacefully, and they all went to one master. . ." How did the story end? "The master carried out some tests. . . only I don't know what tests. . ."

Patient Bel., a 43-year-old female with a tumor of the septum pellucidum, destruction of the mammillary bodies, and invasion of the right hippocampus; marked Korsakov's syndrome (N. K. Kiyashchenko's observations).

"The Jackdaw and the Pigeons" story was read to the patient. When asked to reproduce it immediately, she did so satisfactorily.

"The Ant and the Pigeon" story was read to her. When she retold it, elements of contamination with the first story appeared: "An ant was drowning in the river. . . was drowning, and cried out. . . a pigeon began to save him but she herself began to drown. . . she was saved by a crow. . . no, a jackdaw. . . and fell into a hunter's net. . . on the hunter there was an ant. . . she chased the ant away and she herself was left with the hunter. . ."

What was the first story? "About a chicken. . . and. . . (looks at the bedside table) and about a lump of sugar. . ." Really? "How the ant found a lump of sugar. . ."

And what was the second story? "A jackdaw flew to a hunter. . . and he caught her. . . and she began to cry: 'Let me go. . .,' but he did not let her go. . . she escaped and the hunter was left with nothing. . ."

In this case, reproduction of the first story was perfect, but during reproduction of the second story elements of the first (the jackdaws) began to be mixed up with it and the meaning began to disintegrate. On return to the first story, she began to mix in elements of immediate impressions. Finally, in an attempt to reveal the traces of the second story, the theme became completely disrupted and, by way of reminiscence, she began to introduce elements of the "The Lion and the Mouse" story that had been read to her a few days beforehand.

The picture of the mutually inhibtory influence of discrete semantic structures is seen still more clearly in patient Snyatk., who had no difficulty in reproducing the substance of each of two stories read to her immediately, but when she returned to the story read first her selective reproduction was severely disturbed.

Patient Snyatk., a 42-year-old female with a tumor of the third ventricle. "The Hen and the Golden Eggs" story was read to her. She retold it without much difficulty.

The second story, "The Intelligent Crow,"[7] was read to her. She also reproduced this story without difficulty.

She was asked to recall the first story. She replied: "No, I have forgotten it. . . about a jug, I think. . . and something else. . ."

The patient was asked to recall the second story. She began hesitatingly to recall it: ". . . the sun was shining. . . and fell on a jug in which there were golden eggs. . . the crow knew that there were golden eggs in this jug. She placed the jug so that the sun made it hot and the eggs rose up. Then she could take them. . ."

What was the first story? "That was also about golden eggs. . . and about a jug. . . the sun shone on the jug and warmed the golden eggs. . ." Are you sure that both stories were about golden eggs? "Yes, both. . ."

---

[7] A crow wanted to drink, but there was only water at the bottom of the jug and she could not reach it. The crow threw pebbles into the jug, the water level rose, and the crow was able to drink.

Although both stories could be repeated immediately after presentation, subsequent recall produced a composite of both stories with the addition of some extraneous material which was, nevertheless, consistent with the type of action in one of the stories. Similar phenomena could be observed in many patients of this group.

Patient Bobr., a 38-year-old male with a closed head injury and hemorrhage into the upper parts of the brain stem.
"The Hen and the Golden Eggs" story was read to the patient and he reproduced it without difficulty.
A second story—"The Stupid Dog"[8]—was then read. He reproduced it as follows: "A hen was walking along the road over a bridge. She saw the reflection of the moon. She thought she could eat it, but there was nothing in the water... then the hen began to be crushed until everything was pressed out... but again there was nothing."
Even more striking situations of those contaminations between three stories at once can also occur.
The same patient, having heard the stories—"The Ant and the Pigeon," "The Lion and the Mouse," and "The Hen and the Golden Eggs,"—reproduced the last story as follows: "A hen wanted to fly up high, but it was heavy (contamination from the first story) with golden eggs. She flew and stopped in some places. Everything flew out... the ant helped... he was about to eat her (contamination from the second story)... the master was content."

The above material demonstrates that although the immediate reproduction of a complex semantic structure can take place relatively normally in patients with deep brain lesions and a general lowering of cortical tone, the selective reproduction of semantic systems from memory, in complicated situations, or in the presence of other recently memorized material, may be grossly disturbed. Besides mutual inhibition of traces, there may also be signs of contamination. Characteristically, a second presentation of the material is not followed by improvement, but only by aggravation of the contamination. Short empty pauses generally have no appreciable effect on the recall of a semantic structure already imprinted. The presence of interfering activity has the opposite effect. In contrast to patients with parahypophyseal tumors and a mild amnesic syndrome, on the other hand, interfering activity led to definite disintegration of meaningful speech structures only recently imprinted and to a clear disturbance of the selective reproduction of semantic systems.
There are three characteristic features which clearly distinguish patients of this group from patients in whom the pathological process affects the frontal systems. First, mnemonic activity is always preserved. The patients can retain the problem of reproducing and recalling a theme presented to them and they do not replace this activity by irrelevant activity. Second, as a rule, all these patients can retain

---

[8] A dog was walking over a bridge at night and saw the reflection of the moon in the water. The dog decided that it was cheese and jumped into the water. But of course she found nothing and only got wet.

the scheme of stories narrated to them, although their reproduction is often incomplete and fragmentary. Finally, all the patients of this group retain some degree of critical attitude toward their mnemonic defects. The overwhelming majority, should they reproduce semantic fragments incorrectly, remain unsure whether or not they have correctly solved the problem given to them, and sometimes they state directly that they cannot recall the essential meaning, that "they are confused," that they have "said too much," etc.

Table 28 summarizes the results obtained by testing the recall of complex semantic fragments by the patients of this group.

The features described are only evident in relatively mild forms in the first stages of the test, but become more marked as it goes on. When the patient becomes tired, they are seen in all their richness, reflecting the features of the "oneiroid state of consciousness" characteristic of patients with lesions of the deep systems of the brain affecting the normal functioning of the medial zones of both hemispheres.

* * *

Patients with lesions involving the frontal lobes, particularly their medial and basal aspect, present a different clinical picture of memory disturbance. This pathology arises from craniopharyngiomas spreading anteriorly, tumors located deep in the fronto-temporal regions or growing from the septum pellucidum, and from circulatory disturbances in the anterior cerebral artery system (Luria, Podgornaya, & Konovalov, 1969).

The basic syndrome of the memory disturbances arising in these cases may be similar to that just described. The most important difference is simply that, although general cerebral factors (hypertension, dislocation, a general lowering of cortical tone, an oneiroid state) may be exhibited to a lesser degree, the involvement of the frontal lobes results in the memory disorders described above being manifested against the background of general disturbances of goal-directed activity. When the frontal lobes are only partly involved in the pathological process, this loss of goal-directed activity may be seen in the fact that, although the general scheme of the semantic fragment remains intact, the patients can be easily distracted and irrelevant associations begin to intrude.

When a lesion of the frontal lobes becomes more massive, however, the patient entirely replaces the substance of the story by these unrestrained associations. To illustrate this important situation better, let us first consider an example of the partial disturbance of semantic fragment recall in such patients, after which we can go on to analyze its complete disintegration in patients with more massive lesions of the frontal lobes.

Patient Avot., a 34-year-old male with a craniopharyngioma and cyst spreading to the chiasmal region; well-marked amnesic syndrome with confusion and disturbance of consciousness.

TABLE 28

CONSECUTIVE REPRODUCTION OF TWO COMPLEX SEMANTIC FRAGMENTS BY 30 PATIENTS WITH DEEP BRAIN TUMORS AFFECTING MIDLINE STRUCTURES AND ACCOMPANIED BY KORSAKOV'S SYNDROME

Patients	Conditions and quality of reproduction											
	Immediate				Return to fragment 1 after reproducing fragment 2				Return to fragment 2 after reproducing fragment 1			
	Fragment 1		Fragment 2									
	Complete repro-duction	Partial repro-duction	Complete repro-duction	Partial repro-duction	Complete repro-duction	Schematic repro-duction	Partial repro-duction	Complete forgetting	Complete repro-duction	Schematic repro-duction	Partial repro-duction	Complete forgetting
With mild memory defects	100.0	0.0	100.0	0.0	76.6	11.4	12	0.0	86.7	4.6	8.7	0.0
With a severe amnesic syndrome	75.4	24.6	84.6	15.4	7.6	13.6	23	55.8	14.6	30.8	23	31.6

In the acute period, when the amnesic syndrome was associated with marked disinhibition of the patient, the uncontrolled outpouring of irrelevant associations made semantic fragment recall impossible. In the residual period, when the pathological changes in the mediobasal zones of the frontal lobes had receded, the irrelevant associations appeared only within a properly narrated story, taking the form of digressions, after which the patient invariably returned to the original semantic theme.

Some appropriate findings are given below.

"The Ant and the Pigeon" story was read to the patient and he was asked to relate it.

He did so as follows: "Once upon a time there was a pigeon. . . and an ant in the forest. They both felt friendly toward each other: The ant toward the pigeon and vice versa. One day an impudent hunter with fascist views came into the forest and caught the pigeon. When he took the pigeon the ant became angry, bit the hunter on his hand, and set his dear friend and pigeon free. . . no, I haven't told it all. . . I can't remember the first part. . ."

Besides the retroactive inhibition (the second part of the semantic fragment was related first), the patient could not control irrelevant "additions" to the story ("the ant and pigeon felt friendly toward each other," "an impudent hunter with fascist views"), interpolated into the narration without, however, disturbing its semantic structure. Later these additions began to appear more distinctly and interfered considerably with the correct reproduction of the story.

"The Lion and the Mouse" story was read to the patient and he was asked to relate it.

He began his narration as follows: "Aha!. . . the lion and the mouse. Well now, in Africa there lived a splendid, handsome lion and also—a handsome, the best of them all, a mouse. One day, however, the lion caught this mouse and wanted to cook it like a steak. However, the mouse implored him for so long that there would not be enough for him to eat that he let the mouse go. Then hunters went to Africa by air and took the lion to Europe. . . and together with the lion our old friend the mouse also went to Europe. However, at Orly Airport in Paris the mouse left the plane unnoticed and began to lead its own life. She ran away and walked the streets of the city. Soon she saw crowds of people on the street. She looked—and she saw her friend the lion tied to the columns outside a cinema, where the crowd of Parisians was looking at him. She wanted to set the lion free but all the Parisians were shouting and she could not set him free. . . there was something else, but perhaps I don't need to tell you?" *What else was there?* "Well, now, there was something else, some minor details, for instance the lion went to visit his friend in Paris. . . and some other details that have no bearing on the events. . ."

No, you have not told it correctly. Tell me the story again exactly. ". . . well, now, . . . how can I tell you briefly. . . well it happened in France, in Paris,. . . a foreign train arrived from a seaside town. . . it brought guests to see the French capital. . . no, I shall have to begin again. . ." *Tell me exactly just what was in the story, without any additions!* ". . . well, now, a group of sailors got out of the train and went to see the town. Besides the sailors there came a black mouse. . . and she suddenly saw an enormous lion. . . the lion jumped on her and broke. . . the sailors saw all this and they were very interested. . . no, I have already told you the beginning, I cannot go on without this. . . they went to look at the Père Lachaise Cemetery. . . and some other building. . ."

Although the text of the story was retained to begin with, it later began to be replaced increasingly by irrelevant associations until he was completely distracted by them and was unable to go on with his narration. If we add to this a background of constant retroactive inhibition of the previous elements of the story, the structure of the mnemonic defects will become fully evident.

If the patient is instructed insistently that he keep to the meaning of the story, he can usually do so for a short time, but as soon as he is instructed to tell the story again from memory (i.e., without having it read again), the defects described above appear once more.

"The Lion and the Mouse" story was read again to the patient and he was instructed to relate it without adding anything. He said: "Without adding. . . without taking away. . . this is difficult, I am not used to telling stories without additions of my own. . . well now. . . the lion was asleep and the mouse suddenly ran over his body. . . the lion seized the mouse and wanted to crush it and destroy it. . . later, however, he let it go. . . next day a hunter caught the lion and tied him to a tree. However, the mouse felt gratitude, chewed through the rope, and set the lion free. There, I have tried to tell it without embellishment."

After a second reading with strict instructions not to add anything, the patient was able to relate the story more accurately. After a short pause, however, the situation was different.

A pause of 1 min is allowed, during which the patient smokes, takes a pencil, and begins to draw a face.
Tell me the story again. ". . . a lion was very soundly asleep. . . no, I have started to use my own words. The lion lay down to sleep. . . and a mouse ran over his body. . . he woke up, seized this mouse, and wanted to crush. . . but the mouse implored him to set her free. Later a hunter caught the lion. . . and wanted to take it to France. . . or to the Soviet Union. . . but the mouse became angry and chewed through the rope. . . and set the lion free. The lion himself, of course, could not chew through the rope, but the mouse did so, I consider that the lion himself could not even get the idea. . . there, that is all!. . ."
After a pause of 3 min, the patient was again instructed to recall the story that had been read to him. He said: ". . . you know. . . you told me something. . . but I cannot remember what it was about. . . about a lion and something else. . . but what it was. . . I can't remember!. . . Lion and mouse?. . . Lion and mouse?. . . but the story itself has vanished. . ."
A lion was asleep. . . . "Aha! a mouse ran over its body. The lion woke up, grew angry and wanted to kill it and eat it. However the mouse begged him not to do so and she looked at him with her tiny black eyes. Next day a hunter caught the lion and took him to Europe or to South America. . . and tied him to a trunk. . . however the small mouse ran to him. . . she crept up stealthily and chewed through the rope and set the lion free. . ."

Similar results were obtained in a subsequent test carried out after an operation for the removal of a craniopharyngioma cyst which involved lifting the frontal lobes of the brain, i.e., at the height of the syndrome.

"The Jackdaw and the Pigeons" story was read to the patient and he was asked to retell it. He did so as follows: "A jackdaw wanted to eat well. . . she knew that the pigeons had plenty of food. . . she painted herself with an aniline dye (looks at the assistant carrying out the test), made locks of hair for herself, and flew into the pigeon house at a farm. . . the pigeons accepted her. . . there she lived until the spring, the sun rose higher, our dear little pets began to fly into the yard and they sent the jackdaw away into the forest. They understood that the jackdaw was not a pigeon. . . and the moral I can't understand. . ."

And what happened to the jackdaw? ". . . she had a hard time (looking around). . . she developed appendicitis and had an operation by Dr. K. She lay. . . our bird the jackdaw. . . it was very sad, she was pale, the surgeon looked at her and suggested to her delicately that she should be turned into a woman! Well, now. . . I read all this once. . . she flew somewhere. . . all these different feminine things. . . but they would not accept her, they did not like quarrelsome. . . and she stayed between the sky and the earth. . ."

This record clearly shows that at the height of the syndrome, although the patient completely retained the program of the story read to him, he was easily distracted by random impressions and began to incorporate irrelevant associations into the story. They did not, however, prevent him from returning ultimately to the proper narration of the end of the story.

Similar memory defects can also be seen in patients in whom the tumor itself is far from the frontal lobes but the general cerebral reaction (the toxic effect of the tumor, changes in the cerebral circulation and the flow of CSF) causes the influence of the pathological process to spread far beyond the limits of the focus. The familiar effect can be observed in such cases: The reproduction of the general scheme of the semantic fragment remains intact, despite irrelevant digressions. An example of such a case is:

Patient Chern., a 64-year-old male from whom an intracerebral tumor of the wall of the right lateral ventricle in the region of the trigone was removed. He had a definite Korsakov's syndrome with elements of confusion.

"The Hen and the Golden Eggs" story was read to this patient and he was asked to relate it at once. He did so adequately, but with minor irrelevant additions: "A man—a bad farmer but a good trader—had a hen which laid golden eggs; he wanted her to lay curious golden hens, and so he chopped her up—but the result was a failure. . ." The moral of the story was easily deduced.

"The Jackdaw and the Pigeons" story was read to this patient. He began to narrate it as follows: "A black crow slipped into the jackdaws' house; there was not much difference and she was therefore taken to be a pigeon. . . she wanted to help people and to be one of the useful birds. . . she saw that the pigeons ate fat grain and had no need to dig it up from under the manure. . . she decided to visit them and to eat with them. . . she went off to the man who painted her head with whitewash and after that she flew to the pigeons. . . however, he must have painted her badly—some patches were not properly white and some were striped. . . the pigeons took her in, just as we do, and all credit to them; however, they saw these stripes and realized that she was not a pigeon. They then took council together and decided to send her away! I don't know whether they had made a preliminary flight or whether they simply saw the black color during the feast. The unfortunate crow flew back to her own home, but because of the stripes the crows did not recognize her and would not take her in to their home. . ." The moral of this story also was deduced correctly.

Similar facts were observed when one of these stories was read a second time.

"The Hen and the Golden Eggs" story was read again to the patient and he was asked to relate it exactly, without adding anything irrelevant.

He began to narrate the story: "A villager in a village where most of the inhabitants aimed at getting as much as they could for their work, these little capitalists all trying to increase their personal possessions, or at least persons with improper or bourgeois individual deviations. . . well, one of them bought these hens from another, he tried to obtain hens which, on the one hand, would give eggs for less grain, if the next gave two eggs this one would perhaps give three eggs, the climatic conditions were the same, the area of land was large. . . he bought it and kept it in his own yard. . . he began to feed it regularly, otherwise he could hardly expect to obtain a quarter of an egg as profit. . . she began to lay him a small egg every morning or night, and the hen herself was small. . . the neighbor he saw also had eggs, but these eggs were 1½ or 1¾ times bigger. . . he also wanted. . . then he said to himself: 'From one egg I can have 1½ golden shells, or perhaps even two shells. That is profit. Evidently in this hen's stomach there were large seeds that grew into good-sized eggs,—and he struck her with an axe.' 'There you go,—he said,—soup, and now cut and take out the eggs and cut them and hide them so that nobody can take them. . .' He cut the hen, took off her head, removed the eggs, and they were all ordinary hen's eggs. Moral: when something gives you an income and a decent income, don't behave so like a savage looking for another one for, as you see, it did not turn out. . ." Despite the mass of distractions, the moral of the story was correctly identified.

The situation became much more complicated if, instead of relating the story as soon as it had been read to him, another story was read to him in the meantime. Under these conditions, the disturbance was particularly conspicuous. Instead of slipping into irrelevant details while retaining the general semantic scheme of the story, the patient began to introduce irrelevant associations quite helplessly.

After "The Hen and the Golden Eggs" story had been read to the patient, followed by a second story—"The Jackdaw and the Pigeons"—he was asked to recall the first story. He looked all around and said: "Something about the clock on the wall or about Lunarcharskii's Dem'yan Bednyi?. . . No, I thought so. . . the clock was hanging, it went perfectly, it stopped. . . they set it going. . ." Surely you are making it up? "Perhaps. . ." And what was there really in the story? "Well really it could not go by itself. . ." Well what happened? "They set it going, it went and went. . ." Wasn't it a story about a hen? "I don't remember. . . my memory isn't good enough to say it word for word, but it is alright for seeking the meaning of the story and reaching the essential conclusion. . . of the story-teller, whose meaning I am relating, to introduce the story-teller to this meaning. And if the story-teller says to me that I need not pay special attention to the meaning when I tell the story, I shall give a separate sentence and words, but at the end I shall tell what I understand. . ."

The syndrome just described is seen particularly clearly in patients with circulatory disturbances of the anterior communicating and anterior cerebral arteries, when the pathological process involves the nuclei of the thalamus, as well as the medial zones of the frontal lobes. The distinguishing feature of this syndrome is that recall of a semantic fragment disintegrates completely after the introduction of a second similar story, or during the transition from simple semantic fragments to complex tests incorporating two independent and complete semantic themes. I shall not describe all my material in this book, since it is contained in a separate publication (Luria, Podgornaya, & Konovalova, 1969). I shall content myself with two typical examples illustrating this form of mnemonic disintegration.

Patient Bash., a 38-year-old female with an aneurysm of the anterior communicating artery accompanied by subarachnoid and parenchymatous hemorrhages and spasm of the vessels (severe Korsakov's syndrome with confusion).

"The Hen and the Golden Eggs" story was read to the patient. She related it adequately and deduced the moral easily.

"The Ant and the Pigeon" story was read to the patient. She grasped its moral correctly ("All would give a helping hand to others"), but during its narration contamination appeared and irrepressible associations crept in: "An ant sat on a twig. . . and a pigeon crawled along it. . . the ant very much wanted to make friends with the pigeon. . . oh, I can't. . . let me see. . . they became friends. . . and at the essential moment, when the ant had to be saved. . . the hunter wanted to catch the ant. . . and the pigeon bit the hunter on his hand. . ." and so on.

Contamination of parts of the fragment started to cause the disintegration of the entire scheme. This disintegration became more severe in the attempt to reproduce the theme of stories read previously. The addition of irrepressible irrelevant associations to the phenomena of contamination led to the collapse of mental activity and to inability to recall the stories read previously.

What stories did I read to you before this one? "Before this. . . there was the story. . . 'The poor mother'. . . this was a poem by Bagritskii. . . no, I don't remember!. . . Remind me about it with just one word. . ." Well, was it a story about a jackdaw? "About a jackdaw. . . how it wanted to wear. . . to wear a white coat, but the pigeons did not accept her. . . she flew away and cried 'corr!. . .' " And what were the stories before this one? "There were many stories in envelopes. . ." What was the first? "The jackdaw!" And the second? "The boy. . . the ant and the boy. . ." Tell it to me. "The bear and the boy. . . the ant and the boy. . . the ant and the boy. . . no, I don't know how to begin. . . Once upon a time there was a boy. . . and an ant. . . they got to know each other and became friends. . . no, you began these lessons early, they would be more effective later. . ."

Clearly, reproduction of the story from memory began to be complicated by contamination of its parts, after which it was completely interrupted by irrelevant associations. As a result, all voluntary mnemonic activity ceased, and gave way to apparently aimless repetitions.

Similar observations were made on another patient of this group at the height of his illness.

Patient Iv., a 35-year-old male with a rupture of an aneurysm of the anterior communicating artery followed by subarachnoid and parenchymatous hemorrhage into the mediobasal zones of the frontal lobes and spasm of the siphon of the left internal carotid and anterior cerebral arteries (Korsakov's syndrome with confusion).

"The Hen and the Golden Eggs" story was read to the patient. He related it correctly and easily deduced the moral.

A second story—"The Jackdaw and the Pigeons"—was read to the patient. He also related this story correctly and easily deduced its moral. What story did I read to you before this one? ". . . about an automobile on which a bear was riding. . ." Tell me more exactly. "Well,. . . it was riding along the road. . . and under the automobile. . . further along the road, near to home. . . a bar of gold was buried (fragment from the first story). Well. . . the pigeon with the bear. . . went through the forest. . . they noticed the smell of a jackdaw (fragment from the second story), and the wolves. . . there were all sorts of different changes. . . no I have forgotten a little. . ." Was there a story about a hen? "There was." Tell me about it. "A hen went. . . now I can tell you. . . not with a wolf, not with a bear. . . not with some other animal either. . . and they went in the forest. . ." What happened then? "Then. . . there was a crossing place, but I have forgotten. . . they met a wolf. . . no, not a wolf. . ." And was there something about golden eggs? "In a hen. . . there were precious golden eggs. . ." and so on.

Whereas the theme of each semantic fragment could be narrated without much difficulty, the selective recalling of the theme of the first story after the second had been read was completely impossible. Unlike the patients discussed in the previous sections, however, *Patient Iv.* did not give up his attempts at relating the story. He did not state that he had forgotten what it was about, but instead began to confabulate, interweaving parts of the first and second stories as well as completely irrelevant elements.

This same patient showed more serious deformations of the semantic structure of narration when he attempted to retell a story with two discrete semantic themes.

"The Ant and the Pigeon" story was read to him. Immediately after he exclaimed: "That was a very long story you told me. . . I cannot take it all in. . ." What was the story about? "About an ant and a pigeon." Tell me about it. "I don't know how to begin, there was so much of it. . ." The ant went down to a stream. . . "and not alone. . . there were two things. . . one with a spinning top, the other very quietly. . . who (the patient looks at his fingers). . . crushed his fingers with the top. . . and at home they put him to bed. . . and a hunter. . . ran into the forest. . . to the stream. . . for water. . . then. . . two bears came. . . not one, but two. . . and they also wanted to go to sleep in this den. . . in general. . . they did not share it. . . this den. . . and this sparrow, tapped the white bear. . ." What happened then? "How did they get on together in the same house? . . .I cannot get. . ." Who were they? "The two boys. . . the sparrow. . . and the bear. . ." Have you told me the story correctly? "Tell it to me again so that I can hear from the side. . ."

The story is read to him again. "Aha!. . . an eye for an eye, a tooth for a tooth!" Tell me exactly what you mean. "Well now. . . I can remember. . . in the forest. . . shot. . . what is it called? Now I remember what it's called. . ." Whom are you telling me about? "About the bad and the good. . . now I remember. . . about a horse!. . ." And what else? "About a hare." What happened to them? "The hares ran away. . . now I shall tell you. . . the bear. . . and the hare. . . and the horse."

Even reading the story a third time did not give the required result.

Characteristically, even when the patient could grasp the semantic scheme of a complex story at once ("an eye for an eye, a tooth for a tooth"), attempts to relate details immediately led to digression into irrelevant associations (hunter—forest—bear—horse) or to the intrusion of indirect impressions. Purposive mnemonic activity was replaced by a chain of uncontrolled associations.

The changes in mnemonic processes described above bring us directly to the syndrome of memory disturbances arising in patients with massive lesions of the frontal lobes. The defects are particularly severe if the lesions of the prefrontal region are superimposed on general cerebral reactions as, for example, in patients with massive tumors of this region or with equally extensive injuries of the frontal region. The essential feature of such a syndrome is that all disturbances of mental activity (including mnemonic processes) occur against a background of marked inactivity.

Purposive mnemonic activity is particularly severely affected and attempts to transfer it to a higher level of semantic organization are unsuccessful. These patients can easily retain a volume of material that can be directly imprinted and recalled without special effort. If this volume exceeds a certain limit, selective recall is replaced by irrepressible associations which they make no attempt to correct. This inability to assess performance allows the disturbances of active and selective mnemonic activity to lead quickly to the complete disintegration of recall.

One example of the reproduction of complex semantic structures by a patient with a massive lesion of the frontal lobes, associated with general cerebral disturbances and accompanied by a severe Korsakov's syndrome, is given below.

Patient Kork., a 24-year-old male with a massive injury to the frontal region accompanied by a fracture of the frontal bone and with subsequent atrophy of the substance of the prefrontal zones (severe Korsakov's syndrome).

One month after injury and a long period of unconsciousness, followed by a state of inactivity and confusion, "The Hen and the Golden Eggs" story was read to the patient. He began to reproduce it properly, but then he soon fell under the influence of irrepressible associations.

". . . the man killed it. . . and inside it there was very little gold (echolalic reproduction of the end of the story). He thought, truly, that there would be so much gold inside. . ." Have you finished? "No, soon I shall come to the end. . . inside it. . . it seems he found that there was not as much gold as there should have been (pause). . . . And so they went and began to investigate these places. . . and. . . during the investigation of these places. . . they found. . . that this place. . . is not completely discovered. And so they rejected this place. . . and began to look for a new place (begins to slip into irrelevant associations). . . and so as they searched. . . that is at the inquest. . . of a new place. . . they had to examine the old place. . . but they were not very happy. . . in other words they found that this place is very badly covered. . . having found this place. . . they. . . that is these hunters. . . finding that this place is badly covered. . . and besides. . . not far from this place. . . now I shall tell the number of the dining room. . . 30. . . Now I shall tell you the number of the dining room. . . 31, in my opinion the dining room. . . Well, not finding any number there. . . they. . . abandoned this place. . . they sat on their mules and off they went!. . ." Have you finished now? "Yes, I have finished.`.`. you see that this place is finished (perseveration) and there is nothing good about it. . . these inquests (looks at the tape recorder) go up to these tape recorders. . . they looked, there is nothing new. . . this recorder is switched on, the rest is recorded, the thing that turns round. . . and what are they recording?. . . What this new crowd (shaika). . . I mean Leica. . . have brought out. . . these numbers are twirling round. . . 0.2. . . 0.2. . . 0.3. . . and there 0. . . it turned out that these numbers were recorded and there weren't very many of them. . . that is why they were recorded, all the other numbers. . . and there weren't very many of those either. . . The other numbers were recorded. . . that is all. . . five or six signs were recorded. . ." Have you finished now? "No, I shall finish soon. . . well these numbers. . . five or six were recorded. . . let me tell you more exactly. . . when they sat and went. . . he approaches (further uncontrollable associations). . . along Lefortovskii Val (a street in Moscow). . . . I mean square, Lefortovskii Val, seven point six. . . that will be Lefortovskii Val. . . get on the number five tram, go to the square, change to the tram. . . now I will tell you. . . now I will tell you. . . now. . ." Have you finished yet? "Now I am going to finish, wait just another minute. . . there was nothing there, I go to the square. . . get on the number five. . . or, strictly speaking, I won't take. . . and. . . getting on the number five tram I go the square. . . get on the little tram (continuous perseverations)." Have you finished now? "I shall finish soon. . . change to the little tram. . . now I will tell you. . . now I remember that I must not take. . ." and so on.

In the earlier cases, the general semantic scheme of the fragment remained intact, even though its reproduction was disturbed by irrelevant associations. In the present case, the situation is different. The patient begins to tell the story, he grasps its basic element ("unsuccessful search") and continues to develop this theme passively—repeating it inertly on the one hand ("quest"–"inquest"–"discover"–"cover"–"find a new place," etc.), and on the other hand losing at once the controlled character of mnemonic activity and falling under the influence of irrepressible associations that lead the patient more and more into digressions ("quest"–"inquest"–"dining room"–"tram"). In the last stage of telling the story, the pathological inertia becomes so severe that the whole reproduction of the theme is replaced by the frequent return to the same fragment: "get on the tram. . . change to the tram," etc.

The pathological inertia which is characteristic of this patient appeared not in one, but in two principal forms: First, inertia of the same perseverating associations already mentioned and, second, inertia of the actual process of "narration of the story" when begun, which the patient could not stop (when questioned whether he had finished or not, he invariably answered, "I shall be finishing soon").

The serious disintegration of the scheme to be reproduced (the ease with which he lost the connection between the original motive and the problem) is a basic feature in the defective recall of organized semantic structures in patients with massive lesions of the frontal lobes.

The question will be asked: Can the mnemonic activity of this group of patients be sufficiently organized to make them able to recall a story scheme and block uncontrollable associations?

To answer this question, a test was carried out in which a fragment of a story was read to the patients repeatedly and they were instructed insistently to retell it exactly, without any digressions. Observations showed that in this (acute) period of the disease such attempts cannot succeed.

"The Jackdaw and the Pigeons" story was read to the patient and he was asked to retell it exactly. He began to do so, but very soon lost track and slipped off into a chain of perseverations and irrepressible associations.

"A jackdaw. . . I mean. . . rather. . . a pigeon. . . learned to speak like a pigeon, flew in and told her fellow pigeons that she had learned to speak like a jackdaw, and flew to them. . . and said that she could speak like a jackdaw. She began to speak here and there. . . some time later the jackdaw, you know, asked a jackdaw: 'Where did you learn to speak so that you could finish this job?'" *Tell the story correctly.* ". . . here, I am telling it correctly. . . the jackdaw asked: 'Where did you learn to speak', here and there. . . but they asked the jackdaw: 'For how long can you speak?' The jackdaw said that she could speak for. . . an hour, or two. . . or three (projection of the situation of the patient's own conversation). . . a year, or two, or three. . . later the jackdaw was tired, she did not know what to say next (again projecting the patient's own situation). . . a year, or two, or three later. . . and the jackdaw had exhausted her store of words. . ."

The story was read again. The patient was asked to repeat it absolutely exactly. "A jackdaw painted herself and flew into the pigeon house. . . the pigeons thought at first a jackdaw like a jackdaw. . . I mean, that this jackdaw. . . and they let her fly freely. . . to fly a little there in their own place. . . the jackdaw flew away. . . flew a little around her own home, the jackdaw settled in her own nest." *Was there anything else?* "The pigeons were not clear about this (again the projection of his own state into the story). . . having flown a little around her own home, the jackdaw, I mean (looks at the nurse). . . this girl. . . sat. . . I mean flew. . . and settled next to her own nest. . ." *Which girl?* "No girl!. . ." *Please tell the story correctly!* "I am telling it correctly, just as it was. . . well now. . . the jackdaw was not where she ought to have been. . . some time later. . . well I suppose 15 minutes, the. . . jackdaw, I mean, flew into her own compartment. . . around this porch. . . next to her own railroad car. . . a little later on–the way in was closed to the jackdaw. . . what could she do? There was no way, I mean, for the sparrows–neither this way nor that. . . they could not pass either forward or backward. . . some time later–and they began to let the jackdaw free a little. . ." *Are you telling the story correctly? Have you added anything? I asked you to tell the story exactly as it was read!* "And I am saying what you told me. . . the jackdaw flew into the pigeon house, flew around her own nest. . . and in it there were already some little birds!. . . She flew back to her own nest with a little bird. . . Some time later, I mean, they stopped the jackdaw and made this remark to her: 'Why don't you fly and why don't you behave like yourself?. . . What has happened to you? What has caused you to be in such a state?' The jackdaw was silent, she did not know what to say (again the patient projects his own state into the narrative). . ." *Have you finished?* "No, I shall soon be finishing. . . well soon after that, the jackdaw's state had not worsened at all. . . 10 or 15 minutes passed–the jackdaw's state had improved. . . 10 minutes later her state was no worse. . . another 10 to 15 minutes passed and the jackdaw's state had improved. . ." and so on. Attempts to repeat more of the story were unsuccessful.

All attempts to get this patient to narrate the story exactly were unsuccessful; having once started the process of recalling the theme, it was very quickly replaced either by the inert repetition of previous stereotypes, completely unconnected with the original story, or by the intrusion of the patient's own state into the narrative ("it was not clear to the pigeons," "the jackdaw began to grow tired. . .," "the jackdaw's state became worse and improved. . .," "the jackdaw had nothing to say," etc.).

The traces of the story did not disappear. The difficulty was in translating the theme into an active sequence of recall.

If the patient was asked a series of consecutive questions about the story, relieving him of the necessity of reproducing the theme independently, the subject's memory for the story was completely preserved. An extract from the continuation of this test is given below.

What did the jackdaw hear? "That she heard. . . that the pigeons ate well. . ." *What did she do?* "She changed her color and flew to the pigeons. . ." *What did the pigeons do?* "They in fact did nothing. . ." *How did the jackdaw cry?* "Like a jackdaw. . ." *What did the pigeons realize?* "That the jackdaw was a jackdaw pretending to be somebody else. . ." *What did they do after this?* "They did not allow the jackdaw to cry, and later matters went so far that they turned the jackdaw out. . ." *Where did she go?* "She went back home." *And what did the jackdaws do?* "Now. . . now I will tell you. . . of course, they would not take the jackdaw in. . ."

A further attempt to get the patient to narrate the story by himself still proved unsuccessful. Disintegration of semantic connections during unaided narration was not just the dominant, but also the most persistent phenomenon of the syndrome observed in this patient. It could be observed as long as three or four months after injury, and began to disappear only after four or five months. If a delay was introduced prior to the narration, however, the patient once again failed to stick to the theme of the story. An example illustrating this stage of regression of the disease is given below.

Two months after the test described above, "The Stupid Dog" story was read to this same patient. He now was able to narrate it correctly and also to point out the moral included in the story.

Next day the patient was asked to retell the story he had heard the day before. He began to do so and at first kept completely to the theme of the story; later, however, he slipped into a series of superfluous associations which he could not repress, and near the end he introduced a series of associations inertly reproduced in his earlier attempts. "There was. . . a stupid dog. . . the dog went one night across a stream and saw her own reflection, she thought it was cheese and jumped into the water. . . she found no cheese there, it was only imaginary, and the dog got wet. When she got home she saw her kennel. . . and all that was her home. . . Then she thought that she had foolishly jumped into the water and had foolishly got wet and that there was no sense in it. . . of course she dried herself during the night and when she was dry she returned to her own home (echoes from "The Jackdaw and the Pigeons" story). Then, you know, she thought that people are different and they do harm in different ways, and everything was simpler. . . this dog, it seems, not fully trained and it had been left behind by the rest of its family. After this incident she was forced to live. . . by herself. . . She was, let me see. . . not domesticated, how shall I say it better?. . . Well, generally speaking, she was friendly with a lion cub (fragments from "The Lion and the Mouse" story springing up as uncontrolled reminiscences). . . then, after she had become friendly. . . she decided. . . more exactly it was not she but the cub that decided. . . to feed this dog and took her to her home. . . and said: 'Look, this is my friend, feed him, he has been sent away and there is nowhere for him to go. . .' Of course the cub was asked where he had been taken from, what was his job. . . and other such things. . . he was fed, he thanked his master for the food and was sent off in all directions. . ."

What was the story about? "How a dog became friendly with a lion." Who went across the bridge? "The dog went across the bridge." What happened then? "Well, the dog, you know, saw his reflection in the water and jumped, thinking it was cheese. In fact it was her reflection, she jumped to no purpose." Is this how the story ends or was there something else? "No, after this incident the dog became friendly with a lion, the lion welcomed her. . ." and so on.

At this stage, the traces of the semantic structure were easily followed during direct narration, but if an interval was introduced before the narration, the patient began to reproduce uncontrollable reminiscences of other stories previously read. Although he could reproduce the theme of the story adequately, he easily slipped into random associations and invented confabulatory continuations of the finished story. These irrelevant associations became so strong that, even when the patient was asked "what was the story about?", he mixed these associations with the traces of the required story ("how the dog became friendly with a lion") and could only narrate the story correctly if aided by appropriate questions.

Further regression of the disease led to a new phase in the recovery of mnemonic processes. The patient began to correctly narrate the theme of a simple story he had just heard (without any additions), but he could not recall the theme of a first story after a similar story had been read to him, and incorrectly reproduced the theme of a complex story consisting of two independent and complete semantic themes. In both these cases, the patient could either retain only the theme of the second story (or the second part of the complex story) or he began to contaminate the stories and slip into irrelevant associations.

We are very familiar with these facts. Just as in the tests of recalling sentences, the selective reproduction of two semantic structures was replaced by inert repetition of only one semantic structure (in the earlier tests, the second; in later tests, the first structure). The inhibitory effect of mutually interfering systems was superimposed on pathological inertia and irrelevant associations.

With further regression of the disease, the patient was able not only to repeat simple (or even complex) stories immediately, but could also return to a first story after having had a second similar story read to him. The disturbance of mnemonic processes continued to appear, however, in more complex tests involving the consecutive narration of three isolated stories or attempts to restore the theme of stories read to him one or two days before the test.

Everything I have described so far leads to the conclusion that purposive activity is disturbed, that it is no longer determined by the subject's motive or the problem facing him. He falls too easily under the influence of previous inert stereotypes and irrelevant associations. The structure of his mnemonic processes is also disturbed. The result is a gross disintegration in the recall of imprinted material which spreads to the reproduction of organized semantic systems. The compensatory effect of semantic organization on mnemonic defects, well known in normal subjects, remains intact in patients with mild mnemonic disorders accompanying lesions of the upper zones of the brain stem. It persists, in part, in patients with deep tumors disturbing the "circle of Papez," but begins to recede into the background when the medial and basal zones of the frontal lobes become affected. The compensatory effect finally disappears completely in patients with massive lesions of the frontal lobes.

* * *

Quite different disturbances in the recall of complex semantic fragments can be demonstrated in patients with local lesions of the posterior zones of the hemispheres—in particular, the parietal and temporal cortex of the left, dominant hemisphere. In these patients, purposive mnemonic activity remains completely intact. Their mnemonic defects are modality-specific and they become evident only in certain special circumstances—a disturbance of choice between many possible verbal alternatives in some, and disintegration of the acoustic composition of words leading to literal exchanges or to alienation of word meaning in others. To this must be added a disturbance in the retention of specific logical-grammatical relations, which these patients (especially those with local lesions of the parieto-occipital zones of the left hemisphere) not only cannot grasp immediately, but cannot retain as easily as they should.

Conversely, the change to retaining the meaning of fragments of text arouses no difficulty in these patients. As a rule, they easily grasp the general meaning of a fragment of text, sometimes with the aid of intonation or by selecting individual elements of the narrative that carry the most information, sometimes from the general context, and sometimes by their affective instinct, which as a rule remains intact. If they experience difficulty in grasping the general meaning of a fragment, they seek the meaning actively, they attempt to decode it by examining the component parts in succession and comparing them with one another, and they are never satisfied by "guesses" that come into their head when they have grasped only one single fragment. The process of decoding the meaning of a fragment is converted into a prolonged purposive operation, sometimes taking place in many consecutive stages and frequently taking many minutes or even tens of minutes. The patients of this group differ radically in their behavior from inactive patients with a massive "frontal syndrome," who never begin systematic work on decoding of meaning, but as a rule substitute a simple "guessing" of the general meaning, or simply a flood of irrelevant associations.

Although decoding the meaning of complex verbal fragments may continue over long periods, patients with lesions of the parieto-occipital and temporal zones of the left hemisphere can recall the decoded meaning of the fragment in accordance with the rules which Bühler described for the law of "remembering thoughts." Once memorized, neither a pause nor interfering influences causes these meanings to be forgotten. They can return to the theme of a first fragment of text after a second similar fragment has been read to them.

Their difficulties arise not in the actual recalling of a fragment, but only when they convert this thought into narrative speech process opposite to that they carried out in the primary understanding of the fragment.

The difficulties in speech operations just described differ in patients with parieto-occipital lesions and a syndrome of "semantic aphasia," as well as in patients with temporal lesions of the left hemisphere and a syndrome of acoustic sensory aphasia. In the first, the difficulty arises in choosing the necessary meaning of a word from many possible alternatives, and decoding the meaning of logical-grammatical structures (and in the reverse process, to find necessary logical-grammatical codes for the formation of a narrative). In patients with lesions of the left temporal lobe, the difficulty is in grasping the meaning of a given word and storing this meaning and reproducing it at the required time. The common features are an inability to transfer a spoken expression to the higher, semantic level, to preserve the "memory of thought," and to compensate difficulties in individual operations by the semantic organization of mnemonic activity.

I shall first give an example of semantic fragment recall by a patient with recent and massive disturbances of speech memory resulting from a lesion of the left temporo-parietal region. Then I will analyze this same process in a patient with an old wound in the left parieto-occipital region accompanied by semantic aphasia.

Patient Vig., removal of an arterio-venous aneurysm of the left temporo-parietal region (severe amnesic aphasia).

"The Hen and the Golden Eggs" story was read to the patient. He told the story as follows: "A hen. . . l. . . laid. . . golden eggs, and then the old man thought. . . he must get more eggs. . . and he took. . . he killed the hen. . . and he found. . . only eggs. . ." *Did he do the right thing?* "No, the wrong. . . he should not. . . have killed the hen. . . he would have had more eggs. . . would have obtained more. . ."

Another story—"The Jackdaw and the Pigeons"—was then read to this patient. He immediately recalled that this story had been read to him earlier, and he said: "Yes. . . so it was said. . . she went to. . . (nonsense). . . to a tree. . . and howled, and then they sent her outside. . ." *And what was the first story?* "About a hen. . . and golden eggs." *What happened there?* "The old man killed the hen. . . and there were no golden. . . good. . ." *And what was the second story?* "Ah, I can't tell. . . this. . . begin. . . (nonsense). . . I can't say. . . these. . . came. . . into a garage. . . well. . . they howled. . . they sent them away. . ." *And what is the meaning of the story?* "They made a great din and upset the people. . . they behaved badly. . ."

After an interval, two other stories were read to the patient.

"The Stupid Dog." The patient narrated the theme as follows: "A dog went along a stream. . . she wanted to take the cheese. . . but there. . . she couldn't. . . reach under the water. . . and she fell. . . into the water. . . could not reach. . . there was no cheese. . . and so. . ."

"The Lion and the Fox." The patient narrated this story as follows: ". . . the forest. . . a bear. . . no. . . the biggest of the wild animals. . . forest. . . forest. . . (les = forest; lev = lion) fell ill. . . ill. . . other animals came to him. . . old men. . . these. . . children. . . no. . . came up to him. . . and then eat him. . . children. . . no. . . they ask why nothing will go up to you. . . why. . . there is no need. . . nothing left. . . what he has lost, what is it? Nothing. . . on the scent. . . no. . . in general it was old. . . and ate everything!. . ." *What was the first story?* "Wait a moment. . . I am thinking. . . an old woman. . . an old man. . . he had a golden egg. . . she took his hen. . . he thought he would have more gold. . . but the eggs, he found out, were empty and not gold. . ."

Despite considerable difficulty in finding the correct words, the patient had no difficulty whatever in grasping and retaining the basic theme of the fragment.

When the test was repeated a month later the results were the same.

The "Two Friends" story was read to the patient.[9] He began to tell it as follows: "Two friends went and saw a bear. . . two friends. . . one ran to the village and the other was

---

[9] Two friends were walking in the forest when they met a bear. One of them climbed up a tree while the other lay on the ground and pretended to be dead. The bear came up, sniffed him, thought that he was dead, and went away. The first friend climbed down from the tree and asked the second: "What did the bear whisper in your ear?" He replied: "He said that it is wrong to leave your friend in misfortune."

tired. . . went to sleep. . . or what? He did not sleep, but kept quiet. . . slept. . . (spat')
sowed. . . (seyat') and saw. . . didn't see. . . didn't look. . . pretended to be dead. . . the bear
looked at him, saw that he was dead, and did not eat him and went away. . . the friend came
down from the tree. . . what did the bear tell you. . . he showed me and he said that this. . . I
forgotten. . . this. . . what he whispered into your ear. . . the bear. . . I have forgotten it all
again. . . the bear. . . no, he said, it is wrong to leave your friend in misfortune."

"The Stupid Dog" story was read to the patient. "It is difficult to say the words. . . a
foolish dog. . . an ugly dog or what?. . . a rough dog. . . went. . . no. . . an ugly dog. . . or what
was it. . . stupid!. . . A stupid dog went across a stream. . . on a (vost. . . bost. . . post.–he
means most, bridge). . . and saw in the sky. . . what was it?. . . A dog?. . . forest?. . . the sun?
(solntse). . . no, not the sun. . . (lovko. . . lovkas–meaningless) looked at the water and there
she saw the reflection of the sun. . . not the sun. . . but los. . . los'. . . luna–the moon! lonu!
She saw in the water. . . a heart (serdtse). . . something like (syr) cheese. . . it fell on the
water. . . the cheese fell into the water. . . he thought. . . and there was no cheese. . . just a
reflection. . . m. . . mo. . . on!. . ."

What was the first story? "I have forgotten. . . what. . ." *Walk.* . . "Oh yes. . . two friends
went for a walk. . . I know. . . a bear. . . saw that he seemed to be d. . . d. . . dead, and went
away. . . did not stay to eat. . . and the man asked his friend, 'What did the bear say in your
ear?' He said that the bear told me that you were a bad man. . ." *And waht was the second
story?* "About a dog that fell. . . fell in the stream. . . on the sun. . . I have forgotten again. . .
not the sun, what was it?. . . (Serdtse). . . no, (serdtse). . . he saw cheese on the water. . . from
the sun. . . moon! From the moon! He jumped. . . he wanted to take the cheese. . . and he saw
nothing there. . . he got wet!"

This record clearly shows that all the basic difficulties experienced by the
patient were concerned with seeking the required words. He not only grasped the
general meaning of the story well, but also retained it securely. When recalling an
isolated word series, interfering homogeneous activity had a marked inhibitory
effect on the recall of a previous series, but the inhibitory effect of the second story
was completely abolished if the patient reproduced whole meaningful fragments.

Similar observations were made on patients with a lesion of the
parieto-occipital region of the left hemisphere, but the pattern of the defects was
rather different. As with the cases described above, these patients had no
difficulty in retaining the general meaning of a fragment previously read to them,
and neither a long gap nor interfering activity prevented recall or caused
contamination. Therefore, no loss of selectivity or no irrelevant associations could
be observed in these cases. There were no perseverations. The inhibitory effect of
the homogeneous activity (recalling the second story) was incomparably less
marked than when recalling word series. The main difficulties found in these cases
were connected with the disintegration of logical-grammatical structures, uniting
the separate elements of the semantic structure together, rather than in the lexical
elements, as in the previous group of patients.

What follows is an extract from the records of a test carried out with one such
patient,[10] which exemplifies the difficulties observed in such cases. In doing so, I

[10]This patient was described in my book "A World Lost and Regained," Moscow
University Press (1971).

diverge from my customary plan: To begin with, I describe the process of learning and recalling a fragment with a very complex grammatical structure, and then go on to discuss the usual tests.

Patient Zas., a 48-year-old male with an old left parieto-occipital wound leading to regional atrophy and severe semantic aphasia.

The following difficult fragment was read to him: An old workman came to the school where Vasya was a pupil to tell the children about his own childhood in the Komsomol, which was during the years of the Civil War. The children listened with great interest to the talk given by this man, who had fought for the sake of Soviet power, and they then asked many questions, to which they received the most exhaustive answers.

The patient retold the fragment as follows: "These. . . exhaustive answers. . . something about a boy. . . was because. . . something to do with. . . it was about the Civil War. . . and something lost this. . . what. . ."

The fragment was read again. "Well now, in the ar. . . in the school. . . where Vasya was a pupil. . . an older worker came. . . he had once taken part. . . in this. . . Civil War. . . then. . . he spoke to the children. . . what he said. . . how a long time ago. . . in the Civil War. . . that was when. . . these events happened. . . well the children liked this. . . story. . . about that time. . ."

Another, even more difficult, fragment was read to the patient: To the right and left of the house grew tall trees of a rare species with large fruit, hidden under the leaves and resembling pine cones. Everywhere shone lanterns made of colored paper, resembling happy faces with mouths stretching to the ears; they were reflected in the lake on which four white swans swam.

The patient tried to repeat the fragment: ". . . no, I can't manage it. .,. there was something. . . that spoke, that in this. . . now. . . it is hard to say. . . something about lanterns. . . and about swans. . . on a lake. . . and there. . . on the left and right. . . and there besides. . . the forest. . . what was it? Is that right? No, I can't manage it. . . as well as the swan. . . and the lanterns also. . . and on the left and right. . . trees, is that right? But I cannot manage any more. . ."

The fragment was read again. "Well now. . . they said. . . that. . . on the left and right. . . and. . . on the left and right. . . trees. . . there are trees. . . fruit trees. . . besides pine cones. . . and they. . . look like lanterns, they are bobbing about, that. . . and a swan is swimming. . . swans. . . they are all it seems. . ." *And were there any faces?* "Well now. . . there were lanterns. . . and also some sort of faces. . . no. . . it is all misty. . . resembling happy faces. . . from this lantern. . . or from the water or what? No, I have forgotten. . . lanterns—yes! But whose were the faces? It is all dim. . ."

The patient was asked to recall the content of the first fragment. He reproduced it with the same difficulties of narration: "Well now this. . . this. . . where is it?. . . to the children. . . this old man came. . . this. . . how the events of the Civil War. . . he told them. . . how. . . and they were all very pleased. . ." *And what was the second fragment?* "Now these. . . faces. . . and lanterns. . . and on the right and left. . . how they. . . grew these. . . trees. . . and the swans were swimming. . ." and so on.

The patient's greatest difficulties were concerned with the elucidation of logical-grammatical relations incorporated in the semantic fragments. The whole text was narrated in fragmentary fashion. The details easily "floated away" so that the patient had to make great efforts to unite these fragments into a complete semantic picture. Some components of the story (for example, "lanterns looking like happy faces" or "were reflected in the lake on which swam three swans") could not be grasped. The defects are not defects of memory, however, but defects of logical-grammatical synthesis, and so soon as the patient grasped the meaning of the whole semantic fragment it remained firmly in his consciousness even after long intervals filled with irrelevant activity.

The technical difficulties arising in patients with left temporal lesions were even more marked than those in patients with parieto-temporal lesions and a syndrome of semantic aphasia. Patients with left temporal lesions had difficulty in decoding the meaning of the individual words and in grasping whole continuous series of phrases. During attempts to reproduce semantic fragments, they showed the same phenomenon of alienation of word meaning and numerous literal paraphasias with the replacement of some words by others. These patients could ultimately overcome their difficulties, pick out the general meaning of the fragment, and express its basic thought in words. Although they might substitute individual words (saying "sparrow" instead of "ant" or saying "bird," "crow," or "squirrel" instead of "jackdaw," etc.), they can nevertheless not only tell the story but also keep to the general meaning of the fragment even if the interval between reading and recalling is long or is filled with interfering activity.

The retention and recalling of thoughts (or of organized semantic structure) is much better than the retention of series of isolated words or groups of words. The compensating role of organized semantic sequences remains not only the principal symptom, but also the principal way of retraining these patients.

A few examples are given below which illustrate the distinguishing features of the recalling and reproduction of organized semantic structures by patients with left temporal lesions accompanied by variants of acoustic aphasia.

Patient Freid., a 62-year-old female with hemorrhage into the left temporal region and a syndrome of acoustico-mnestic aphasia [S. A. Soldatova's case].

"The Intelligent Jackdaw" story was read to the patient.

She retold it as follows: "A squirrel (paraphasia) wanted to catch a little squirrel (in the sense of to drink water from a vessel containing only a small amount of water), which could bring water so that she could drink it. . . but there was only a little water and it was difficult to get. . . how could she take some when there was only a little water?. . . she would have to throw something into the water. . . kramyshki (nonsense). . . no. . . krynyshki (nonsense). . . no. . . you understand. . . it lifts it up. . . and she can drink. . ."

Reproduction after 20 min: "A jackdaw wanted to drink. . . but the point was that it was in a small dish. . . that. . . and she had to make the water level rise. . . she threw kamushki (pebbles) in it and the water level rose. . . so that she could drink. . ."

Reproduction after 1 hour: ". . . I remember. . . a dish. . . a cup. . . a jug. . . a ladle. . . no, a cup. . . I can't name it, there was only a little water in it so that it was difficult to reach. . . and so she. . . the little bird. . . threw. . . brought. . . no, she threw pebbles into it. . . until the water level was raised. . . and she could drink. . ."

Reproduction after 2 hours: "A little squirrel. . . no, with ting wings. . . flew and wanted to drink. But there was only a little water. . . she had to. . . throw. . . kishki (paraphasia). . . no. . . no. . . she had to throw them to make the water level rise and then she could drink. . ."

Reproduction after 24 hours: "Of course I remember the story. . . about a little sparrow. . . no. . . something bigger. She started. . . to drink, but couldn't reach. . . because of the narrow neck. . . and she threw something in it and drank!. . ."

Obviously, the chief difficulties experienced by this patient were in finding the necessary words and her performance was frequently complicated by the intrusion of words of similar meaning, leading to paraphasia. Not only had she no difficulty in retaining the actual meaning of the fragment, but she could retain it firmly even after a long interval of time.

Similar observations were made with a second patient.

Patient Bukh., a 62-year-old male with subarachnoid and parenchymatous hemorrhage into the left temporal region (syndrome of acoustico-mnestic aphasia) [S. A. Soldatova's case].

"The Intelligent Jackdaw" story was read to this patient. He reproduced it as follows: "A crow. . . flew and wanted to drink. . . she saw the water far away. . . it was not muddy. . . what shall I say (makes a gesture of throwing stones)?. . . well now, down there. . . there. . . and this, what is it I wonder?. . . I know. . . (gesture of drinking). . . drink!. . ."

Reproduction after 20 min: "The story?. . . of course I remember. . . only now I cannot tell it very well. . . about a bird. . . I have forgotten how it began. . . no, I haven't forgotten. . . it was a magpie. . . the magpie wanted to drink the water but the water was at the bottom. . . she threw everything in it to raise the level, and then she could eat. . . no, of course not eat. . . she began to eat the water greedily. . . is that right?. . . I have told the whole story in a general way but I tell it badly. . ."

Reproduction after 1 hour: "We read a story about a bird, about an intelligent bird. . . about a magpie. . . the magpie wanted to drink, but the water was. . . at the bottom. . . on the lid. . . she threw everything there. . . into the bottle. . . well into this. . . into the vessel. . . the liquid. . . rose. . . and the crow could eat. . ."

Reproduction after 2 days: "A story about a bird. . . about a crow. . . an ingenious crow. . . the crow wanted to drink, she saw a vessel. . . with a narrow bottom. . . she began to throw everything. . . all the rubbish. . . she threw for a long time. . . and then she drank. . . she threw until she could drink, and when she had thrown she was able to drink. . ."

"The Ant and the Pigeon" story was read to the patient. He retold it as follows: "An ant went to a stream to drink. . . he was thirsty. . . he started to drink and he fell in. . . a fish (paraphasia). . . saw him and started to save him. . . and when this. . . he caught the bird that had saved the sparrow (paraphasia) with his net. . . and then bit the fisherman (paraphasia) on his hand. . ."

Reproduction after 20 min: "About a fisherman and a swallow. . . a sparrow flew to a stream to quench his thirst and started to drown. . . the bird. . . the fish. . . impudently caught the bird on a hook and the magpie bit the fisherman and saved his friend who had saved her. . ."

"The Three Loaves and the Biscuit"[11] story was read to this patient. He reproduced it as follows: "A man was hungry and decided to eat a loaf. . . and he ate a second loaf. . . but he

---

[11] A man was hungry and he ate a loaf of bread—but he was not satisfied. He bought a second loaf—but still he wasn't satisfied. He bought a third loaf—and still he was hungry. He then bought a tiny biscuit, he ate it, and said: "What a fool I was—I ate the three loaves, I should have bought the biscuit in the first place."

was still hungry, and then he ate a biscuit... what a fool I was... that I ate the three loaves!"

Reproduction after 20 min: "... about a glutton!... he was very hungry... he bought a loaf of bread, a second, and a third and he still was not satisfied. He then ate a biscuit and was satisfied. Why did I eat the loaves of bread? I should have eaten the little loaf first!"

And what was the first story? "The first story? I remember! About a fisherman and a pigeon... the fisherman caught the pigeon with his net and the magpie bit the hunter... the little bird fluttered out and flew away..."

And what was the second story? "About a glutton... he ate the cakes... he ate the first, the second, the third, and then a fourth—the fourth pie... and was still hungry, and said that it was useless to eat the buns, he should have eaten the cracker in the first place?..."

Reproduction of the story after 24 hours: What were the stories? "I remember... about a magpie, how she ate from a bottle with a narrow neck... at first she threw something into it and then she ate the water... about a fisherman and a fish... the fisherman first saved the fish, and then a hunter caught the fisherman and he was saved by a sparrow... he pecked him on the foot and the bird escaped and flew away... and there was something else about hunger, he ate all the pies, he ate many—one, another, then a third, and finally he ate a cake and was satisfied... finally, he said that he had eaten the cakes in vain, he should have eaten a cracker!"

Reproduction of the stories after 3 days: Try to remember the stories I read to you. "The first was about a cunning magpie, how she ate the water... she wanted to eat, she saw a saucepan but the water was right at the bottom... the neck of the saucepan was narrow and she could not reach... then she started to throw... anything... bricks, and other things and even... kadushki... no... kalushki (confusing kamushki, little stones, and galyushki, little pebbles)... no, well... she threw... and drank... the next was about a bird and a fish, how the bird was drowning and the fish pulled her out... the fish repaid one good deed by another and saved the fish from the fisherman who had used a hook... she bit him and the bird escaped and flew away... I can't remember any more..."

And what about the man, what did he want to eat? "Oh yes, he wanted to eat and he ate a few white loaves but was not satisfied... then he ate a cake and he was satisfied and said that he need not have eaten the three loaves. He should have eaten the French loaf first..."

Despite the continuous paraphasias, the general meaning of the story was firmly retained and could be reproduced even after long intervals of time occupied by interfering activity. The main difficulty observed in the patients of this group was due to the loss of precise meaning of the individual words. Consequently, it was manifested not at the level of the general meaning of the fragment, but at the level of the lexical elements composing it. Purposive mnemonic activity aimed at the selective reproduction of the fragment was intact in all patients with local lesions of the left parieto-occipital and temporal regions. Their main defect was restricted to speech operations. They had difficulty in finding necessary words because they could never repress equally probable alternatives.

CHAPTER III

Syndromes of Memory Disturbances in Local Brain Lesions

General Characteristics of Memory Disturbances in Local Brain Lesions

After examining different levels of mnemonic processes in patients with lesions of various parts of the brain, we can now draw some general conclusions. This closer examination revealed mnemonic activity to be a very complex psychological process, consisting of several components and taking place at different levels of organization. Depending on the localization of the brain lesion; therefore, the disturbance of mnemonic processes may follow a different course and may have a different psychological structure.

In no circumscribed brain lesions were we able to detect a disintegration of memory traces so complete that it led to the rapid and complete disappearance of imprinted traces. Further, active processes aimed at memorizing, retaining, and recalling the material presented remained intact in most types of patients. The exceptions were patients with massive lesions of the frontal lobes, in whom the pathological process involved the diencephalon as well. In such patients, the imprinting of traces of particular events could remain intact to a certain extent, but they were often unable to undertake the active, selective memorizing and, still less, the active recalling of presented material. As a rule, such patients easily lost selectivity. they could not repress irrelevant associations, prevent the intrusion of irrelevant current impressions, or avoid returning inertly to stereotypes imprinted previously.

141

Similar observations can be made during the study of patients with massive deep brain tumors located in the midline and disturbing the hippocampo-mammillo-thalamic · circle. In these patients, however, the disintegration of mnemonic activity is less severe and fluctuates. The patient remains aware of his defect.

* * *

This investigation was undertaken in an attempt to comprehend the physiological mechanisms of the memory disturbances which constitute a principal symptom of virtually every brain lesion. Is the "loss of memory" based on the inherent weakness of traces, their rapid natural extinction (as postulated by the "trace decay" theory), or increased inhibitability by interfering factors? Undoubtedly, these mechanisms are closely connected. One manifestation of weak traces is their instability and greater inhibitability. Nevertheless, the modern approach to the study of memory requires a more precise analysis of the neurodynamic features of retention and recall.

The material collected provides a basis for the solution of this problem. Only in a limited number of cases do traces, once formed, persist for only a relatively short time and easily "decay" or "disintegrate." Rapid decay most likely is a common background feature to all the phenomena observed, but it can be detected in only a limited number of special cases. These included, for example, difficulties in retaining a series of isolated (unconnected) acoustic or verbal traces in patients with lesions of the left temporal region. As we have seen, in such cases even a short pause destroys some of the traces, and later the series disappears completely and does not reappear, even in the form of reminiscence. These defects were restricted to audioverbal memory, and were not by any means found in all brain lesions.

As a rule, the facts were quite the reverse. They showed conclusively that increased inhibitability by interfering factors, on the one hand, and phenomena described many years ago as the pathological equalization of excitability, on the other hand,[12] generally account for these pathological memory syndromes.

By considering the different levels of mnemonic processes, a system of tests was devised in which recall could be compared after "empty" pauses, after filled pauses (heterogeneous interference), and after homogeneous mnemonic activity (the imprinting of a second, similar series of traces).

The results were absolutely consistent. When testing with nonverbal sensomotor traces, unorganized verbal traces, or organized verbal structures, the introduction of an "empty" pause did not cause any appreciable decay of

---

[12] This term was suggested on the basis of the general classical theory of neurodynamics by E. N. Sokolov (Luria, Sokolov, & Klimkovskii, 1967).

traces. Naturally, this fact could be verified only for relatively short pauses (1 to 2 min), for it is impossible to make objective allowance for interfering influences during longer pauses. In recent years, extra-experimental interference has been singled out as one of the chief factors making long-term investigation of "pure" trace decay very difficult. In some forms of organization, for example memorizing a meaningful text, even a delay of one or two days or longer produced no sign of appreciable trace decay. Sometimes the features of reminiscence were manifested, and repetition of the material was actually improved a little (S. A. Soldatova, unpublished investigation). All these facts were evidence against trace decay as the direct cause of forgetting. Conversely, pauses filled with interfering activity led immediately to the "forgetting" of traces imprinted previously, demonstrating the increased inhibitability of traces by interfering factors.

Increased inhibitability of traces could be observed even at the relatively elementary sensomotor level (Konorskii's test of the fusion of traces of two perceived shapes), but only in patients with relatively massive brain lesions. After a pause filled with interfering activity, it could be observed even in patients with relatively mild mnemonic defects (pituitary tumors affecting the system of the hippocampus, deep tumors in the midline), and could be manifested in any modality (the memorizing of series of words, pictures, movements, etc.). This inhibitability of traces by interfering factors was incomparably less serious in tests involving the memorizing of verbal material organized into semantic groups (sentences, fragments of text). The transfer to semantic organization created conditions that, as a rule, increased the stability of the traces and compensated for their increased inhibitability.

This effect was seen most clearly, however, in the inhibitory effect of homogeneous mnemonic activity (homogeneous interference), such as, recalling unaided a first series of picture cards, movements, words, or sentences after the subject had imprinted a second similar series. These tests proved sensitive even to very slight defects of memory. As a rule, patients with local brain lesions who could readily reproduce imprinted traces after a empty pause, or even after a pause filled with interfering activity, were unable to return to the first group of traces after imprinting a second similar group. This phenomenon is well known in psychology as the "inhibition of homogeneous elements" or as "Ranschburg inhibition." As in the other cases, it was particularly clear in tests involving discrete word series. In some forms of disease (deep midline tumors and, in particular, frontal lesions extending into the limbic zone and the walls of the ventricles), it could be manifested just as clearly in recalling organized groups (sentences, fragments of text).

The increased inhibitability of traces by interfering homogeneous activity assumed different forms. In some cases, it led to the simple impossibility of recalling previously imprinted traces. The patient stated directly that he had "forgotten" the first group of traces, that it had "slipped from his memory." In the most severe cases, the patient could not even recall that the corresponding material had ever been given to him for memorizing. In other cases, this increased inhibitability led to the loss of recall selectivity and contamination of elements belonging to different groups of traces (I shall dwell on this form below). The process of contamination, often found in patients in this series of tests, can be explained by a change in the conditions of recall. In all previous tests (including those with heterogeneous interference), the subject had simply to recall a series given previously. With homogeneous interference, his problem was to make the correct choice between the two series of words (or sentences) presented to him. Finally, the increased inhibitability of traces observed in these patients could assume a third form—a pathological inertia of traces. In these cases, when the patient attempted to return to the first group, in fact he simply continued to reproduce the last group inertly.

So far, I have discussed only one neurodynamic factor underlying memory disturbances—the increased inhibitability of traces by interfering factors. There is another neurodynamic factor, however, that prevents selective recall—the equalized excitability of different traces. This phenomenon, well known since Pavlov's time, characterizes the inhibitory or "phasic" states of the cortex which apparently may arise when pathological activity changes take place in the brain. It consists essentially of a distortion of the basic "law of strength" elucidated in the classical Russian literature on the physiology of nervous activity. In a normal state, the cortex gives strong responses to strong (recent, meaningful, or intensive) stimuli and weak responses to weak (previous, less meaningful, or less intensive) stimuli. This law ensures activation of strong or essential traces, and easy inhibition of weak or interfering traces—or, in other words, it lies at the basis of the selective activation of traces. In pathological states of the brain, both strong (recent, meaningful) and weak (old, meaningless) traces may be activated equally easily; this "equalized excitability" of traces begins to constitute a serious obstacle to the selective reproduction of the necessary traces, and thus disturbs organized mnemonic processes.

This mechanism explains why, in many patients, traces of old and irrelevant connections begin to be activated just as easily as the traces of "recent" and important connections. The phenomenon is observed clearly during the repetition of word series, sentences, and semantic fragments, when recently imprinted material begins to be contaminated with interfering associations or direct impressions. It is even more evident in tests with homogeneous interference, when two recently read semantic fragments may be mixed together. In patients with upper brain stem lesions, or with deep midline tumors, these "phasic" states of the cortex may become generalized and the "equalization of trace excitability" is manifested uniformly in all spheres (sensory, motor, audioverbal). Conversely, in patients with lesions confined to the posterior lateral surface of the brain, the loss of selectivity is manifested in only one, isolated modality. This partial "equalization of excitability" was illustrated by the disturbances of the selective word recall demonstrated by the uncontrollable outpouring of a whole series of equally probable alternatives (paraphasia).

The neurodynamic factors described above are primarily reflected in the preservation and recall of recent memory and do not necessarily have any significant effect on the recall of firmly consolidated traces. This dissociation of memory into recent and distant events had long been known in clinical practice and I shall not pay special attention to it.

Under all conditions, equalization of trace excitability must be regarded as one of the most important neurodynamic factors underlying the disturbance of mnemonic activity in pathological states of the brain.

* * *

A second problem undertaken by our investigation was whether the memory disturbances were general or partial, and if partial (specific), what forms this specificity manifested and what lesions evoked them. The results obtained during the investigation also provided a definite answer to this question.

Lesions of the upper brain stem, limbic system and ventricle walls interfering with the "circle of Papez" give rise to general or modality-nonspecific memory disturbances. In very mild cases, they are manifested as increased inhibitability of sensomotor, visual and verbal traces (mainly in series of unconnected elements). In patients with the most massive lesions, when a pathological focus in the medial zones of the hemispheres spreads to the diencephalon, and the symptoms are projected against a background of general cerebral defects (increased intracranial pressure, disturbances of the circulation of blood and CSF), these general disturbances of memory may assume the form of Korsakov's syndrome. They may be superposed on an oneiroid state, and very often assume the form of "fluctuating" states of consciousness accompanied by disorientation in space and time, and confabulation.

These latter symptoms are particularly distinct when the medial walls of the frontal lobes are involved, producing general inactivity and disturbances of critical attitude (defects in the patient's assessment of his own condition). In such cases, all the phenomena mentioned above can be manifested during complex voluntary mnemonic activity—loss of the selectivity, substitution of irrepressible associations, or direct impressions, pathological inertia of established stereotypes, and, above all, serious contamination (mixing traces of different systems). It must be emphasized that these phenomena are totally modality nonspecific.

Totally different phenomena are observed in patients with lesions confined to the lateral surface of the hemispheres. With the exception of massive frontal lobe lesions, none of these cases was associated with disturbances of "personal" memory orientation in space and time, or consciousness.

The mnemonic defects were partial and modality-specific, affecting only one (visual or auditory) sphere, or they were system-specific, manifested in one system (speech) only. If the lesion was situated in the left temporal region, the defects were limited to disturbances of audioverbal memory. If the pathological focus spread posteriorly and involved the occipito-parietal region, the memory disturbances were manifested in the visuo-spatial sphere. The memory disturbances were essentially a continuation of the corresponding disorders of gnosis. They were simply variants of the difficulties in coding information characteristically found in patients with lesions of this type. The mechanisms remained the same as those described above (increased inhibitability), but this time, restricted to one or other modality.

When the frontal cortex was involved, the mnemonic disorders were manifested most clearly in the construction and maintenance of actions, and the ability to retain complex programs of activity. A more significant feature in these instances was the change in the mechanisms of the disturbances. Specifically, with lesions of the lateral convexity of the frontal lobes, the dominant feature was pathological inertia of established stereotypes. With lesions of the orbital frontal cortex, the dominant features were pathological disinhibition and replacement of controlled memory by random fragmentary actions.

The lateralization of the pathological focus in the left (dominant) or right (nondominant) hemisphere is also of great importance. If the focus was situated in the left (dominant) hemisphere, the mnemonic disturbances assumed a particularly severe form during the performance of tasks connected with speech activity. A typical example of this pathology is the disturbance of audioverbal memory in patients with left temporal lesions. Marked disturbances can also arise in such cases in the retention of gnostic or praxic operations, because, in man, speech plays an important role in most memorizing.

Extremely little is known about memory disturbances arising from the right (nondominant) hemisphere. I have seen many cases in which such lesions were unaccompanied by any obvious mnemonic defects, or (as has been shown by Milner and her collaborators) they were manifested predominantly in the retention and recall of nonverbalized experience. An example of such a defect is the inability to recognize faces (prosopagnosia). The reason for the relative lack of information about memory disturbances accompanying lesions of the right hemisphere may be that most of the methods used examine processes based, to a greater or lesser degree, on speech which is unaffected by lesions of the right hemisphere.

The few observations at our disposal suggest that memory disturbances arising from lesions of the right hemisphere are manifested not only in nonverbalized, visual impressions, but also in the formation and preservation of affective, personal relations and/or in the direct investigation of the surroundings. Another possibility (supported by some recent data of E. G. Simernitskaya) is that in the case of memory disturbances in these patients, the defects of rapid consolidation that are not apparent in lesions of the left hemisphere, or are masked by the defect of speech processes, are present in a particularly pure form. The material at our disposal, however, is still insufficient to allow any final decision about the role of the right hemisphere in mnemonic activity.

* * *

We are left to answer the last question raised at the beginning of this investigation: How is the transfer of mnemonic activity to a semantic organization reflected in the memory disturbances arising in local brain lesions?

The observations showed that in relatively mild disturbances of memory arising from lesions of the upper brain stem (pituitary tumors), leaving the cerebral cortex intact, or from lesions of the gnostic zones of the lateral convexity of the cortex, semantic organization of the material substantially improves mnemonic processes. The law of "memorizing of thoughts" formulated originally by Bühler applies in full. We have seen this compensatory effect when patients with local lesions of the left parieto-occipital and temporal regions could not recall individual words, but could easily retain the general meaning of a fragment.

It is quite a different matter when patients have deep brain tumors located in the midline, involving diencephalic structures and associated with general cerebral changes (increased intracranial pressure, displacement of the brain), or in particular when a massive pathological process involves the frontal lobes. In such cases, the pathophysiological factors—increased inhibitability of traces or equalization of trace excitability—are manifested so strongly, that transfer to semantic organization cannot abolish the defects caused by the pathological conditions. That is why these patients are equally handicapped when retaining a discrete element or a precise semantic organization.

The contamination, confabulation, and irrelevant connections apparent during the reproduction of semantic fragments by patients with massive frontal lobe lesions serve as an excellent example of this form of pathology. They also lead us directly to the analysis of the decisive role that these parts of the brain play in the formation and preservation of the highest levels of human psychological activity.

Basic Syndromes of Memory Disturbances in Local
Brain Lesions

I have described the facts obtained by the investigation of different memory disturbances arising from local brain lesions. On the basis of these facts, I shall go on to describe the complete syndromes of memory disturbances in patients with lesions of different parts of the brain.

I shall begin with a general description of mild memory disorder syndromes arising in lesions of the upper brain stem, then go on to analyze the more severe mnemonic disorders associated with massive midline tumors, next cover the syndromes arising when the pathological processes spread to the frontal regions, and end my analysis with a description of the memory disturbance syndromes resulting from lesions of the posterior aspects of the cerebral hemispheres.

Memory disturbances associated with pituitary
tumors

The mnemonic disorders arising in patients with pituitary tumors have attracted relatively little attention, and little information about them has been published. Pathological processes limited to the pituitary itself, as a rule, give rise to metabolic disorders—sometimes a disturbance of sleep, in a few cases a change of interests—but they can occur without any evident disorders of higher cortical functions. For that reason, patients with pituitary tumors admitted to the neurosurgical clinic are rarely subjected to detailed neuropsychological investigation. When pituitary tumors became extrasellar and influenced adjacent structures (the limbic region, the hippocampus, the region of the chiasma, or pressure on the brain stem), the disorders described above are joined by gross changes in consciousness, severe disorders of memory, and, sometimes, by general cerebral changes leading to a marked disturbance of psychological processes.

It must be realized, however, that the effects of a pituitary tumor are by no means confined to changes in metabolism. Tumors located in the sella turcica or spreading outside may directly affect secretory functions and their influence on the reticular formation, thereby giving rise to marked changes in cortical tone. In mild cases, these fluctuating disturbances may be evident only in an increased tendency toward fatigue, but in more severe cases sleep and waking may be disturbed and a primary depression of activity produced. When extrasellar tumors, directly or indirectly (through disturbances of blood and CSF circulation), act on the limbic region and the hippocampus, complications may appear as primary disorders of interest or emotions and, of particular concern to us in the present context, substantial disorders of memory.

As a rule, no disturbances of higher cortical functions, in the narrow meaning of this term, can be observed in patients with pituitary tumors. There are no disturbances of praxis, gnosis, speech, or fine movements. Intellectual processes remain normal. There are no disturbances of purposive activity, formation of plans, or retention of complex action programs.

The main complaints voiced by these patients (disregarding complaints about metabolic processes, or sleep and waking) concern disturbances of memory. Often these complaints are ill-defined. The patients report they have become "forgetful," that "anything said to them disappears immediately from their memory," that sometimes they forget their intentions ("I go to get something and forget what it is"). Although not severe enough to interfere with their principal work, it nevertheless is a matter of concern for them.

In the commonest cases, complaints of a memory disturbance amount to nothing more. In patients with more massive tumors (usually extending outside the sella turcica), affecting the brain stem and medial zones of the cerebral hemispheres, other symptoms may appear—disturbances of tone and waking; dimming of consciousness, sometimes leading to cataleptic states.

Experimental investigations of mnemonic processes in these patients reveal the basic features distinguishing this disorder. Recall of simple sensorimotor and sensory traces remains unimpaired. Neither an empty nor a filled pause produces any appreciable defects. Memorizing a word series does not necessarily produce any noticeable abnormality. Only in patients with massive extrasellar tumors, leading to disturbances of blood and CSF circulation, does learning slow appreciably. When asked to repeat a series of discrete elements in exact order, these patients may have difficulty with as few as four or five words. The defects often persist despite frequent repetitions. Marked defects appear if interfering activity is introduced into the test, particularly homogeneous interference. Sometimes this inhibitory effect is so strong that a patient who had just successfully repeated a series of three or four words was completely unable to return to it after successfully repeating a second similar series. This increased trace inhibition produced by interference is characteristically modality-nonspecific.

Transfer of the mnemonic task to a semantic organization can compensate for the defects just described. These patients are able to recall sentences and stories even after the introduction of homogeneous interfering activity. The only exceptions are patients with massive extrasellar tumors, affecting adjacent structures of the brain stem and the medial zones of the cerebral hemispheres. In such cases, transfer to a higher level of organization does not eliminate the inhibitory effect of interfering factors. These facts demonstrate that tumors of the upper brain stem and, in particular, pituitary tumors can give rise to distinct mnemonic defects which are sometimes the only observable disturbances of higher cortical processes.

Memory disturbances associated with deep midline tumors

Deep midline tumors may be unaccompanied by any definite symptoms or memory disturbances provided they do not involve the thalamus and the medial zones of the hemispheres.

If the tumors are larger and involve certain adjacent structures (the hippocampus, mammillary bodies and thalamus), severe memory disorders may be observed. It was in patients with these lesions that Korsakov's syndrome was first neurologically described.

The severe memory disturbances arising from lesions of the hippocampal system are consonant with numerous investigations which have demonstrated the role of the hippocampus in trace preservation and response to stimulus novelty (Milner, 1958–1970; Ojeman, 1964; Talland, 1965).

The hippocampal system is involved in comparing new stimuli with traces of old excitations and the response to novelty. It thus plays a decisive role in the regulation of elementary investigative mnemonic activity (Vinogradova, 1969, 1970). It is in these parts of the old cortex that neurons respond not to specific (auditory, visual) stimulation, but when a stimulus is either novel, does not correspond to what is expected, or does not coincide with the effect of the action which the subject awaits. Naturally, the functioning of these "novelty neurons" is possible only if the stimulus can be compared with traces of previous stimuli. For that reason, the whole system of the hippocampus plays an important role not only in the mechanisms of attention, but also in the mechanisms of memory.

The same effect can occur after lesions of the mammillary bodies, which act as relays in the hippocampo-thalamic system. Indeed, lesions of virtually any part of the "circle of Papez" can disrupt the normal functioning of this system. That is why brain tumors located deep in the midline, as well as other pathological processes disturbing the normal functioning of these systems, lead to marked disturbances of memory and may sometimes produce a classical Korsakov's syndrome.

The symptoms accompanying massive lesions of these parts of the brain are distinctive.

Even the most meticulous investigations as a rule show no disturbances in gnosis, praxis, speech, or formal-logical intellectual activity. In sharp contrast to the integrity of these processes, there are often severe defects of direct mental activity, orientation to surroundings and self, consciousness, emotions, and (always) memory. The state of these patients may fluctuate considerably, passing from waking to sleep and sometimes manifested as drowsy or oneiroid states of consciousness. The results of mnemonic tests may thus vary on different days, ranging from comparatively mild to very severe memory disturbances.

If the general condition of such patients becomes more severe, as a rule their orientation in space and time becomes vague, and are easily distracted. Very often they cannot say where they are (they may say that they are at the railroad station, in the factory polyclinic, staying with friends), although. they can correctly describe details of their past life. They preserve some general idea of time (chronology), but cannot state the exact time of day, may confuse the date, or even the time of year. Finally, they often have an incorrect idea of their own state. They may say that they are perfectly well, and when asked why they are in bed, answer that they are resting, that they went to bed only a short time ago, etc. Such patients do not remember what happened an hour or two ago, and if asked what they did that morning or the previous afternoon, either fail to answer or fill these massive gaps in their memory with confabulations. Under these circumstances, they frequently give information frankly opposite to the real situation, and become completely helpless if these contradictions are pointed out.

In patients with the severest disorders, the memory defects bear a close resemblance to Korsakov's syndrome, although the syndrome rarely includes the total absence of new memory. Nearly always in the course of a long stay in hospital, the patients start to recognize their doctor, to distinguish familiar nurses from unfamiliar, but they remain unable to say where they are or to clearly identify the people with whom they have to deal.

Neuropsychological tests provide a more precise description of the mnemonic disorders observed in this group of patients. Perhaps the most unexpected fact is that the patients can successfully retain traces of direct impressions even after a delay of one or two minutes, and, in some cases, they can reproduce them as reminiscences even after relatively long intervals (other workers have obtained similar findings: Brion, 1969; Milner, 1969, 1970).

I have observed patients with classic Korsakov's syndrome (very severe disturbances of "current memory") who could retain a series of seven or eight unconnected words and, after some repetition, could reproduce even longer series. A fixed haptic set formed relatively easily in these patients. The illusion persisted for some time provided that the pause between acquisition and test was not filled with any interfering activity. With any type of interfering activity, however, even a short interval (2 min or less) was sufficient to erase the trace of the fixed set so that the patient not only lost the illusion, but, in some cases, he actually completely forgot a test had been carried out. The decisive role of interference in blocking traces of previous experience was perfectly clear.

These phenomena were particularly acute in tests with "homogeneous interference," when patients who had memorized a series of two or three elements were unable to recall them again after they had memorized a second, similar series. It is important to note that frequent repetition of this test did not improve recall of the previous series.

The most important fact distinguishing these patients from the previous group was that transferring the mnemonic process to a higher level did not lead to compensation. Memorizing sentences or semantic fragments continued to demonstrate the same defects as the memorizing of a series of unconnected elements. The patients of this group could easily repeat simple or moderately difficult sentences, or even whole semantic fragments. They could repeat them just as easily after a pause not filled with interfering activity. An exception to this rule was observed with stories including two semantic contexts. In these cases, one semantic context inhibited (pro- or retroactively) the traces of the other semantic context.

The situation changed radically if the patient was asked to repeat a sentence or a simple semantic fragment after a filled pause, particularly after homogeneous interference. As in the previous tests, frequent repetition often did not improve recall or eliminate contamination. It is of some clinical importance to note that the contamination of two semantic systems sometimes appeared before the clinically obvious confusion developed, or it persisted after the syndrome had disappeared. This contamination can thus be regarded as an experimental model for confusion of consciousness and may be of considerable diagnostic importance. A patient who could not reproduce a given semantic fragment immediately after interfering activity could sometimes recall this fragment spontaneously after a very long period. This provides evidence of the dynamic character of these memory disorders.

The disturbances arising in patients with deep midline tumors differ significantly from memory defects observed in patients with bilateral hippocampal lesions (such as those described by Milner).

The memory disturbances described in these patients were relatively isolated (Milner, 1958–1970; Scoville & Milner, 1957), but the syndrome just described was characterized by a general confusion of consciousness and confabulation, on which the memory disorders were superimposed. One explanation for this difference could be that deep tumors giving rise to such disturbances never involve the hippocampus in isolation, but also disturb the thalamus and frequently the medial zones of the frontal lobes. In fact, if the pathological focus is located anteriorly and involves the medial zones of the frontal lobes, the symptoms of confusion and confabulation begin to dominate. This syndrome is described below.

*Memory disturbances associated with lesions of the medial
zones of the frontal region*

Memory disturbances in patients with lesions involving the medial zones of the frontal region have been described in detail elsewhere (Luria, Podgornaya, & Konovalov, 1969).

In common with the previous syndrome, there are profound changes in mnemonic processes bordering on Korsakov's syndrome. What is specific to these cases is that the patients fail to realize the inaccuracy of their mnemonic activity. The process of recalling begins to be mingled with aimless and irrelevant associations, direct impressions, or inert stereotypes. This syndrome is seen most clearly in patients with tumors of the medial zones of the frontal lobes and after rupture of aneurysms of the anterior communicating artery, accompanied by parenchymatous hemorrhage and spasm of both anterior cerebral arteries (which supply the medial zones of the frontal lobes).

Patients with lesions of the medial zones of the frontal lobes likewise do not exhibit symptoms of disturbance of gnosis, praxis, and speech. Only when deep medial tumors of the left hemisphere affect the normal function of the temporal region is it possible to see pre-aphasic phenomena that usually assume the form of difficulty in choosing the necessary word meanings and irrelevant speech associations. As a result, speech becomes particularly over-attentive to detail and readily distracted.

Just as with the previous group, the most consistent feature of this syndrome is a disturbance of memory leading, in the extreme, to a disturbance of orientation in space and time, and sometimes a confused state. In mild cases (when the tumor does not significantly disrupt blood or CSF circulation, or a ruptured aneurysm produces only transient spasm), the disturbances may be paroxysmal, and disappear quickly. If the tumor is accompanied by marked general cerebral reactions resulting from increased intracranial pressure and displacement of the brain, or permanent disturbances of the anterior communicating arteries, the mnestic disorders are intensified, consciousness becomes confused, and confabulations appear. The disturbances are also associated with an impairment of critical attitude and aspontaneity, an important feature of this syndrome. Another common symptom is "double orientation," particularly when the right hemisphere is involved, so that the patient's orientation in space and time becomes impaired. If asked where he is, instead of direct orientation, the patient produces uncontrollable reminiscences and sometimes declares that he is in Moscow and in some other town at the same time, or in the hospital and in his own home. These different decisions are easily interchangeable, and arouse no appreciable sense of contradiction in these patients. Unlike the patients of the previous group, the disorientation in these cases may occur in patients who are relatively or even fully awake. It is conceivable, therefore, that the principal mechanism of this disturbance is loss of selective orientation (possibly as a result of equalization of trace excitability) and, in this particular case, the loss of direct personal experience, rather than a general oneiroid state.

The phenomena just described are also evident during the experimental neuropsychological investigation of mnemonic processes in these patients. If the disturbance is relatively mild, the defects observed will also be comparatively slight. As in the previous group of patients, memory loss is most apparent when interference is introduced, and the loss is not modality specific. One special feature of patients with medial frontal lobe damage is rapid loss of trace selectivity and increased contamination. For instance, after presentation of one word series (dom—les—stol), followed by a second (voda—pen'—shkaf), they cannot repeat the first series selectively, but incorporate elements of the second series in it: "voda—pen'—stol" or "voda—pen'—shkaf," etc. Contamination, superimposed on the rapid forgetting as a result of interfering activity, is also exhibited in tests involving repetition of whole semantic fragments or stories. Finally, these symptoms are exacerbated by the patient's inability to assess his mistakes. In addition, when the pathology primarily disturbs the deep brain functions, but spreads to the anterior cranial fossa, affecting the basal and medial zones of the frontal lobes (as in cases of craniopharyngioma with a cyst spreading anteriorly), the syndrome includes some impulsiveness (difficulty in controlling irrelevant associations), leading to constant wandering from the essential theme to irrelevant details. The loss of selectivity produced experimentally correlates closely with the general clinical features of confusion that are among the early symptoms of a spreading lesion, and are thus of diagnostic importance.

Memory disturbances in patients with massive
frontal lesions

The syndrome just described is intermediate between the memory disturbances found in patients with deep brain lesions affecting the limbic region and ventricle walls and the disorders arising as a result of massive frontal lesions, to which I shall now turn.

In the classical literature, especially that describing experiments on animals, the frontal lobes are invariably connected with memory. This is based on the fact that in amimals delayed responses are clearly disturbed after resection of the frontal lobes (Jacobsen, 1931, 1935). After the work of Malmo (1942), Pribram (1958, 1961), and Weiskrantz (1956), however, it became clear that the memory disturbance resulting after destruction of the frontal lobes derived from increased distraction by irrelevant stimuli. Neuropsychological tests on patients with frontal lesions conducted in our laboratory over a period of many years (Luria, 1962, 1963, 1969; Luria & Khomskaya, 1966; Luria & Svetkova, 1966) also strongly suggest that, although memory disturbances are an essential feature of frontal lesions, the frontal lobes themselves cannot be regarded as the seat of memory.

Observations on animals (Anokhin, 1949; Pribram, 1958, 1969) and on man (our own investigations cited above) suggest that the frontal lobes are an essential apparatus for the stable retention of plans, and for the programing, regulation and control of current activity. In man, they appear to be essential for activity under the control of spoken instructions or the verbal enunciation of tasks. Massive frontal lesions lead to the disintegration of complex goal-directed activity. Organized activity, aimed at performing particular tasks, is easily replaced by uncontrollable random associations, direct impressions, or inert stereotypes arising from past experience. This explains why massive lesions of the frontal lobes also disturb complex mnemonic activity, because the subject must make memorizing and recalling a special task which normally are strictly selective.

In patients with relatively localized frontal lesions situated in the prefrontal zones of one hemisphere, the psychopathological symptoms are difficult to detect. Conversely, massive prefrontal lesions affecting both hemispheres and disturbing CSF and blood circulation may completely disrupt complex activity. As long as the medial walls of the brains are not involved, orientation in space and time remains intact. These patients are dominated by inactivity, sometimes severe aspontaneity, associated with disturbances of the critical faculty. They express no desires, make no complaints, create no firm plans, do not respond to instructions, and carry out necessary actions only after constant stimulation.

Although they retain a simple instruction and can often repeat it even after a period of time, they do not put it into practice. Often, instead of carrying out a spoken instruction, they indulge in echolalic repetition, without making any attempt at movement (Luria, 1962, 1963, 1969, 1970; Luria & Komskaya, 1966). They do not compare the results of their action with the original plan either during execution or after completion of the task. This disturbance of the "action acceptor" mechanism is one of the chief elements in the frontal syndrome.

This characteristic naturally leads to the disintegration of these patients' mnemonic activity. Elementary traces evoked without the introduction of a special mnemonic task can evidently be retained for quite a long time. (Since there have been no systematic tests of such processes in patients with frontal lesions, this cannot be asserted categorically.) For instance, a haptic illusion, evoked by a fixed set, can not only be formed in these patients, but it may be long and lingering (Luria & Bzhalava, 1947). Conversely, the formation of selective traces during a mnemonic task is severely disturbed. The disturbance is not so much the result of defects in trace retention, as the result of deterioration of the mnemonic activity itself.

This defect can be seen clearly in tests which require the learning of a word series. Unable to cope with the task of memorizing (or learning) the series, a patient with a severe frontal syndrome simply repeats three or four of its elements passively (most frequently elements at the beginning of the series). In the severest cases, frequent repetition of the test does not improve performance (Luria, 1962, 1969). The patients make no active attempts to memorize, but simply repeat as much material as they can grasp directly. Rote learning tests with such patients are more in the nature of measures of direct perception than tests of active memory.

The patients of this group, like the rest, have no appreciable difficulty in retaining a series of stimuli (not greater than their capacity for direct perception and retention). They easily repeat them after a pause of 1.5 to 2 min. If this interval is filled with interfering activity, however, recall is replaced by the passive repetition of the interfering material. One such patient, when asked to recall a previous word series, began to repeat passively a number he had just been given. This exemplifies the two major characteristics of this syndrome—the disintegration of voluntary mnemonic activity, and its replacement by inert stereotypes or direct impressions. The ready replacement of selective recalling by stereotypes is particularly evident in tests with homogeneous interference. The patient will first repeat one group of words and then repeat the second group, but in response to the instruction to recall the first group he continues to repeat the last group, with no sign of conflict and quite unaware of his mistake.

Semantic organization cannot compensate for the memory defect. Patients with the severest form of frontal syndrome will repeat a single sentence or a single semantic fragment relatively well, but if required to recall the first of two such sentences or fragments they will inertly repeat the second quite unhesitatingly. Only as the syndrome regresses, do such patients again begin to attempt to recall the first semantic structure. At his stage, contamination becomes a common symptom. Reproduction of semantic fragments by these patients is also disturbed by uncontrollable random associations.

The fact that all these defects are based on the disintegration of goal-directed mnemonic activity is confirmed by a series of tests which I did not include in the general account of my observations because its use was confined to patients with a marked frontal syndrome.

These tests of indirect memorizing, originally suggested by Vygotskii and Leont'ev (1931).* The subject is asked to memorize a word list. To help him, he is allowed to choose a picture card for each word. In the next stage, the patient is shown one card and asked to recall the corresponding word. The process of memorizing becomes indirect, because the subject has first to form an auxiliary connection and then to use this connection as a means of returning to the original word. Naturally, any disturbance of complex mnemonic activity will prevent the subject from establishing an auxiliary connection strictly for the purpose of memorizing a corresponding word (he will replace it by irrelevant associations which distract him from the original word).

---

*Editor's note: This is essentially a paired-associates test.

For example, if in order to memorize the word "evening" the patient was offered a card with a picture of a plate (the association "a plate is necessary for dinner in the evening"), he will either be unable to establish this association or, having done so at the beginning of the test, by the time he is again shown a picture of a plate, the former auxiliary connection is not restored and he drifts into a series of involuntary associations.

Bondareva (1969) has analyzed the results of this test obtained on patients with lesions of various parts of the brain. She found that patients with upper brain stem lesions (pituitary tumors)—i.e., mild memory disturbances but an intact cortex—could compensate for their mnemonic defects with the aid of indirect connections. Mistakes resulted from imprecise repetition but never from uncontrollable irrelevant associations. Even if able to establish a semantic association between the word and a picture card, patients with massive frontal lesions were unable to make use of this association. When the "auxiliary" card was shown to them again, they did not return to the original word but simply described the picture or began a new system of association. In these patients, the auxiliary mnemonic operation breaks up into two separate associative processes and the goal-directed use of the aids is replaced by automatic associations. This provides a convincing demonstration that the memory disturbances are based on the disintegration of goal-directed mnemonic activity, making recall unselective, rather than on a defect of trace imprinting.

Memory disturbances in local lesions of the
left temporal lobe

Mnemonic activity aimed at the selective recall of past experience remains completely intact in patients with left temporal lesions. This ability to imprint traces, however, is greatly impaired. The retention defect and increased inhibitability are modality specific and restricted to the domain directly organized by the affected cortex.

Patients with temporal or parieto-occipital lesions show no disturbances of consciousness. Their orientation in space and time is good, and their behavior always adequate. Only when the accompanying general cerebral disturbances (increased intracranial pressure, displacement) are particularly severe do they become inactive. These patients are always communicative, ready to carry out instructions, work attentively, and are aware of their mistakes and correct them diligently. Their plans are stable. Provided they can understand it, they can keep to an action program and carry it out painstakingly. In all these respects, they differ sharply from patients with massive frontal lesions.

Although their personality, consciousness, and goal-directed activity remain unaffected, these patients have definite disturbances of higher cortical functions, manifested as disorders of gnosis, speech, or praxis.

The posterior lateral convexity of the cortex can be regarded as the central system for the reception, analysis, and storage of information. Temporal cortex functions in acoustic analysis and synthesis, and the parieto-occipital area in the synthesis of spatial experience. For this reason, a temporal lesion of the left (dominant) hemisphere disturbs complex verbal (phonemic) hearing, giving rise to various forms of sensory aphasia, while parieto-occipital lesions disturb the visual-spatial coding of stimuli, destroys the structure of internal spatial schemes, and, finally, upsets operations with logical-grammatical structures, thus producing the most important feature of the condition known as semantic aphasia (Luria, 1947, 1962, 1963, 1970, 1973).

The memory disturbance is secondary and closely linked with the primary gnostic disorders. That is why this memory disturbance is modality-specific and occurs in conjunction with goal-directed mnemonic activity.

The defects affecting audioverbal memory in patients with caudo-dorsal left temporal lesions are characterized by difficulty in phoneme differentiation, alienation of word meaning, and gross acoustic speech defects. Naturally, patients unable to articulate speech sounds clearly and perceive meaning will also be unable to retain verbal traces. Nevertheless, it is difficult to speak of specific disturbances of audioverbal memory, because they are masked by defects of audioverbal gnosis.

When the left mid-temporal region (or the intracerebral zones of the temporal lobe) is damaged, phonemic hearing may remain relatively intact, and the dominant symptom is difficulty with audioverbal retention (acoustico-mnestic aphasia). The main features of this syndrome have been described elsewhere (Klimkovskii, 1965; Luria, 1947, 1962). Essentially, these patients perceive and repeat individual sounds and words relatively easily, but begin to have difficulty when required to memorize series of sounds or words. They cannot retain the order (they usually repeat the last element of the series first) and sometimes cannot reproduce the series completely. This difficulty extends to nonverbal sounds as well. The retention and repetition of visual stimuli or movements present no appreciable difficulty (Klimkovskii, 1965).

The fact that these patients have difficulty only when they try to recall series of sounds, syllables, or words confirms that the mnemonic defects are based on disturbances of the relative order of traces of individual auditory (or audioverbal) stimuli. Although able to repeat a series of two elements, many patients cannot keep them in order but repeat the last element first (retroactive inhibition). Finally, this disturbance is manifested only during oral repetition of an auditory series and does not affect recall of a written series, demonstrating conclusively its restriction to a single modality (Luria, Sokolov, & Klimkovskii, 1967).

The patients of this group also exhibit what has been called "equalization of the excitability of audioverbal traces." When recalling word lists, they substitute; or they exhibit literal and verbal paraphasia.

The audioverbal disturbances observed in patients with left temporal lesions and acoustico-mnestic aphasia give rise to a distinctive pattern of mnemonic disorders. The results can be summarized briefly as follows. The introduction of trivial interfering factors (for example, the simple question: "Well, what did you remember?") caused the previously imprinted traces to disappear. In tests of sentence repetition, the patients understand the meaning, but during its repetition are disturbed by verbal paraphasia and substitution of some words by others of equivalent or similar meaning. For instance, the patients of this group could repeat the sentence "It rained this morning" in a modified version: "The weather was bad this morning." These patients have particular difficulty in tests involving the repetition of semantic fragments (or stories). They are able to grasp the basic meaning of the story and to retain it even after a long interval of time, but are quite unable to recall the proper lexical composition of the fragments and replace the necessary words by others morphologically or semantically similar. The repetition often becomes a continuous paraphasia, in sharp contrast to the adequate preservation of the general meaning.

Memory disturbances following left parieto-occipital lesions

Disturbances of mnemonic process after left parieto-occipital lesions have much in common with those just described. The difference is that the audioverbal organization of speech communication remains intact, but spatial gnosis as well as the semantic and logical-grammatical structure of speech are disrupted. Unlike the temporal lesion patients, they have no difficulty in repeating a short series of sounds, syllables, or words in the correct order. Conversely, many patients with occipital-parietal lesions find it more difficult to memorize written letters or words or geometrical structures than to memorize sounds or verbally presented words. The retention and repetition of structures involving spatial relationships are just as disturbed as is the original discrimination of these structures (Pham Minh Hac, 1971).

As in patients with temporal lesions, those with parieto-occipital lesions can largely overcome their mnemonic difficulties when tested at a higher level of semantic organization (repetition of sentences and semantic fragments). They also exhibit the same dissociation. While able to retain the general meaning of the sentence or fragment, they have difficulty in finding the proper words and substitute others of similar meaning or morphological structure.

Memory disturbances in lesions of the right hemisphere

We still have insufficient facts regarding memory disturbances in patients with lesions of the right (nondominant) hemisphere. Right (nondominant) hemisphere lesions do not lead to any noticeable disturbances of speech activity, so that, as most writers believe (Kimura, 1963; Corkin, 1965; Milner,

1962, 1965, 1970; Prisco, 1963; Warrington & James, 1967), speech memory and memory for logical relations remain intact. Substantial disturbances may be found in the imprinting and recalling of visual, nonverbalized material (remembering faces, tactile discrimination of shapes, the formation of elementary motor skills, etc.). However, these defects are by no means found in every case. Recently, I have observed many patients with right hemisphere lesions who had no difficulty with retention and recall, even afer interference. Only when the lesion is large and accompanied by increased intracranial pressure and symptoms of cerebral displacement may these mnemonic defects become apparent.

Memory for subjective states and orientation to self and surroundings may be disturbed when verbal and logical memory is not (Simernitskaya). I have seen many patients with large lesions (tumors) of the right hemisphere who could easily retain and repeat long series of words, sentences, or semantic fragments, but were unable to retain any clear idea of where they were (within a short space of time they said that they were in Moscow, in Novosibirsk, or some completely different town), and confabulated about the recent past.

Dissociation between the intact verbal-logical memory and the disturbed direct individual memory is unquestionably an important and characteristic feature of the disturbance of mnemonic processes in lesions of the right hemisphere. However, no clear description of this syndrome is yet available.

* * *

Memory cannot be regarded as the simple "recording" and "reading" of traces (so often the starting point in recent attempts to simulate mnemonic processes). The concept of memory includes both the elementary ability to imprint and recall traces of past experience, as well as complex mnemonic activity calling for the selective identification of the necessary material, inhibition of all irrelevant associations, and the comparison of the recalled traces with the original task. Human mnemonic activity can be organized in different ways, and in patients with local brain lesions different components may be affected.

Analysis of the memory disturbances accompanying local brain lesions has demonstrated that neuropsychology is an important method for the study of the memorizing process and the mechanisms of forgetting. The results have shown that memory disturbances arising from local brain lesions may differ in structure. Some result from a general lowering of cortical tone, others from a disturbance of selective activity, and a third group from the corresponding gnostic sphere.

The phenomena of forgetting, associated with nearly all brain lesions, are based less on the weakness and rapid spontaneous decay of the traces (which happens only in special cases) than on the increased inhibitability by interfering factors. The more the interference resembles the material to be memorized in both content and activity, the stronger its inhibitory effect. The use of semantically organized material can compensate for some defects of the mnemonic processes, but in others (primarily in cases of large frontal lobe lesions) it has no effect.

Two principal conclusions can be drawn from these results. First, they have shown that neuropsychological investigation of mnemonic processes can be of practical importance for the early and topical diagnosis of brain lesions. There are some forms of local brain lesion (for example, deep brain tumors located in the midline, disturbing the functions of the limbic cortex) for which neuropsychological investigation of memory is perhaps the only way of detecting symptoms. At the same time, the investigation has shown the extent to which memory disturbances can differ in patients with lesions of identical localization. Finally, the investigation has shown that the basic propositions concerning neurodynamic mechanisms of forgetting can serve as the foundation for methods of testing capable of revealing memory disturbances when the ordinary clinical methods do not.

CHAPTER IV

Memory Disturbances in Patients With Left Temporal Lesions

Lesions of the lateral left temporal region give rise to significant changes in complex auditory analysis. In particular, if the caudo-dorsal left (dominant) temporal lobe is affected, considerable difficulty arises in the analysis and synthesis of acoustic stimuli and in the differentiation of phonemes with similar acoustic properties, the basic feature of acoustic (sensory) aphasia. Investigations in the last few decades (Bein, 1947, 1964; Luria, 1940, 1947, 1961, 1962, 1969) have shown that disturbances in understanding speech, literal paraphasia, or writing are simply secondary symptoms easily derived from this primary disorder.

It remains a question whether similar disturbances arise when the lesion involves those parts of the left temporal region which are not included in the "cortical nucleus" of the auditory system. Many years ago I postulated that temporal lesions outside Wernicke's area may disturb acoustic trace processes without significantly disrupting the analysis and synthesis of direct auditory stimuli (Luria, 1947, 1962; Luria & Rapoport, 1962). I described the syndrome of "acoustico-mnestic aphasia," but left unanswered the question whether it is a distinct form of audioverbal disturbance or simply an attenuated form of the acoustico-sensory aphasia that accompanies lesions of Wernicke's area. In this chapter, I shall describe the results of a more detailed investigation of these disturbances.

Disturbance of Mnemonic Processes in Lesions of the Anterior and Middle (Extra-auditory) Zones of the Left Temporal Region

Lesions of the extra-auditory (anterior) zones of the left temporal region do not necessarily give rise to significant sensory-aphasic disorders.

If such a lesion is confined to the temporal pole, no audioverbal disorders arise whatsoever. If the lesion is so large that it affects the posterior temporal region and creates pathological conditions in auditory speech cortex, it may lead to distinctive audioverbal disturbances which differ sharply from the usual pattern of sensory aphasia.

I shall illustrate this statement by descriptions of two patients with intracerebral tumors of the anterior left temporal region. The first case involved an astrocytoma of the left temporal pole unaccompanied by any lasting audioverbal disturbances.

Patient Dik., a 21-year-old female, right-handed (with a left-handed brother), was admitted in May, 1961 to the Institute of Neurosurgery complaining of fits that started after a "blow on the head," sensations of an electric current running down the right arm and leg, and sometimes by accompanying olfactory hallucinations (a strong "smell of medicine"). These attacks began six months before her admission, and had recently started to be accompanied by micropsia: Visually perceived objects became small and the room appeared incommensurately large. Several times the patient stated that during the fits she could no longer understand unfamiliar speech. She could see that the person sitting in front of her was moving his lips but she could not make out what he was saying. Immediately after a fit she was not always able to speak spontaneously, although she could hear and understand the speech of others. Sometimes during a fit a "cup like a hoof" appeared in front of her eyes and a voice said: "Eat, eat, and then you will die!"

The patient had no speech or memory disturbance. Neurological examination noted a disturbance in odor identification on the left side, slight paresis of the right facial and hypoglossal nerves, and slight exaggeration of the reflexes on the right. The EEG indicated a focus of pathological activity in the left fronto-temporal region. No evidence of increased intracranial pressure was present. Right-sided carotid angiography revealed evidence of a large tumor of the anterior zones of the left temporal region, involving the mediobasal zones; i.e., the vessels were compressed above and medially.

Neuropsychological investigation showed complete integrity of the higher cortical functions. The patient was fully oriented, communicative, and self-critical. She showed no disturbance of kinesthetic or visuo-spatial gnosis and praxis. No disturbance of dynamic praxis was present. The reciprocal coordination of the hand movements was intact. She had no difficulty in perceiving, evaluating, and repeating rhythms, and could easily switch from one rhythm to another. There was no disturbance of her musical ability. She had no speech disorders. She could easily differentiate similar phonemes, understand speech addressed to her, and gave no sign of alienation of word meaning. Her analysis of logical-grammatical relations was excellent. She had no difficulty in naming objects or understanding a story. She had no difficulty in carrying out fairly complex arithmetical operations in her head.

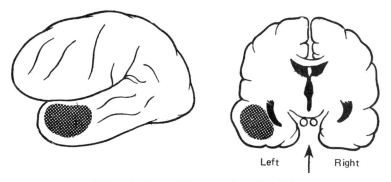

FIG. 7. Position of the tumor in patient Dik.

She could easily repeat series of four or five sounds, words or numbers, keeping them in the proper order, even after a pause of 10 to 15 sec or more, whether or not the interval was filled with distracting conversation. She had no difficulty in retaining complete sentences or groups of sentences.

In May, 1961 an operation was performed and a tumor found in the left temporal pole at a depth of 1 cm, next to the wall of the inferior horn of the lateral ventricle, from which it evidently arose. Histologically the tumor was an astrocytoma (Figure 7). The postoperative course was uncomplicated. No disturbance of the patient's speech could be observed even during the first few days after the operation.

This case demonstrates that, in a right-handed person, a large tumor in the left temporal pole can lead merely to paroxysmal disturbances of speech, inhibition of speech followed by involuntary production of speech fragments, and temporary inability to comprehend speech. The complete absence of speech disorders except during fits and the integrity of rhythm and melody analysis indicate that the acoustic and acoustico-verbal systems may remain completely intact in patients with such disturbances.

In the second case the tumor (an oligodendroglioma) was also located in the left temporal pole, but was connected with a large cyst that compressed the posterior and superior zones of the temporal lobe. This tumor left auditory analysis and synthesis intact, but produced clear acoustico-mnestic defects.

Patient Gorch., a 40-year-old female, right-handed, with some mild features of left-handedness—(Her mother was left-handed. During tests, the left hand was active, but the right eye was dominant.)—was admitted in April, 1961, to the Institute of Neurosurgery complaining of fits with loss of consciousness, difficulty of speaking and writing, and marked loss of memory.

The fits began in 1948. They were accompanied by general convulsions, unconsciousness, and disturbances of speech (she had difficulty in understanding what was going on around her, and her attempts to say or write something were incomprehensible). The fits recurred infrequently, but with the same symptoms. Ten years later, a sensation of

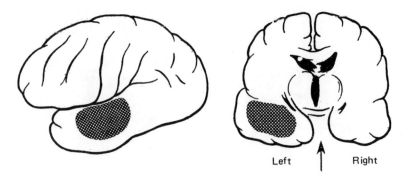

Left   Right

FIG. 8. Location of tumor in patient Gorch.

coldness of the right upper and lower limbs also became a regular symptom. For a long time, her speech remained unimpaired and she continued to work satisfactorily as a translator from and into English. In 1961, the fits increased in frequency and her speech began to be chronically disturbed. She could no longer easily recall the necessary words; her speech became interrupted and filled with word seeking; she had difficulty in naming objects and in writing (these difficulties took the form of inability to find the required combinations of letters). Her English was particularly affected, and she was no longer able to write English words.

Clinical examination revealed the following: Pale discs in the optic fundus; visual acuity with correction 0.7, normal visual fields; weak right optokinetic nystagmus, disrupted experimental nystagmus; some decrease in right superficial and two-dimensional spatial sensation; increased right tendon reflexes; central paresis of the right VII and XII nerves; and considerable speech disturbances (described below).

The EEG showed a marked focus of pathological activity in the left temporal region. Right-sided carotid angiography showed that the left anterior cerebral artery was moderately displaced to the right, but the course of the middle cerebral artery was grossly abnormal: The inferior part at the bifurcation showed little change, but more distally in its course it was raised and displaced upward and medially.

During an operation, the main tumor nodule was located in the antero-dorsal quadrant of the left temporal lobe and a large cyst with traces of blood in the middle zones of the temporal lobe (Figure 8). The brain substance of the caudo-dorsal left temporal lobe remained intact. The tumor was removed within the limits of accessibility. Histologically it was an oligodendroglioma. The postoperative course was smooth; details of symptom regression are described below.

The neuropsychological tests prior to the operation can be summarized as follows. The patient was completely conscious, oriented, and had a critical attitude towards her condition. She was not depressed, but slightly disinhibited and euphoric. She complained of difficulty in speaking, specifically in finding the required words, so that her speech became interrupted, sometimes with verbal paraphasia. Marked difficulty in writing was observed ("I pick all the letters of the alphabet—but I cannot write properly; something makes me take those I don't want.").

Objective testing showed that all forms of praxis were completely intact. There was no disturbance of visual or visuo-spatial gnosis. Acoustic gnosis showed no appreciable evidence of disturbance. She could easily evaluate and repeat rhythmic groups, and had no difficulty in switching from one rhythm to another. She could repeat musical melodies properly and quickly learned to differentiate consistently between two successive groups, consisting of five sounds each of which only the middle ones were different.

The patient's phonemic hearing remained intact. She could distinguish and repeat groups of similar (correlating) sound combinations (such as ba—pa and pa—ba; da—ta and ta—da). There was no sign of "alienation of word meaning." She could analyze the acoustic composition of words and had no difficulty in saying what was the third or fourth letter in the words "Moskva," "gorod," etc. She could easily write such difficult words as "portnoi," "prostranstvo," "skovorodka," and "stroitel'stvo."

Repetition of single words (even such as penicillin) was quite within her grasp. She clearly understood single words and logical-grammatical relations, and had only slight difficulties connected with amnesia—as will be discussed in detail below. She could solve simple arithmetical problems provided that the conditions were in writing and she could get around her amnesic difficulties. Operations with abstract relations did not give her the slightest difficulty.

The main defect in this patient was a severe disturbance in retention of word series or verbal descriptions of figures. As I have said, she had no difficulty in repeating single words, even if they were complex in their acoustic composition. She could repeat them after a pause of 30 sec. A series of two, or sometimes three, words was just as easy. No sooner did she attempt to repeat a series of four words, however, than she found it impossible to retain and recall them. Usually, she repeated three words and sought helplessly for the fourth, saying that it was "lost." If she concentrated her attention on the last word, one of the earlier words disappeared. Similar difficulties arose during the repetition of dictated numbers or when she tried to draw a series of named shapes. A few examples of these difficulties as they appeared during the first test of this patient are given below.

Noch'—igla—luk
Noch'—igla—luk

Zvon—most—krest
Zvon—most and something else. . .
krest

Noch'—zvon—krest—most
(1) Oh, no. . . I forget the first and I can't remember the four words.
(2) Noch'. . . there are too many.
(3) Noch', zvon. . . krest at the end, and something else.

She was able to memorize a longer series of numbers if dictated to her, but the difficulties in this operation were similar in character.

3–0–9–8–2
(1) 3–0–9 and something at the end
(2) 3–0–9... 82...

Try again
(3) 09... oh!... I can't

Naturally, the patient's difficulties were greater if she was instructed to repeat three short sentences, each consisting of two words.

Dom gorit (the house is burning)–luna svetit (the moon is shining)–metla metet (the broom is sweeping)
(1) I have forgotten it.
(2) Dom gorit... I know that... it is difficult for me... luna... svetit... no
(3) Dom gorit... no... I can't go any further... I can't say, but there is... nothing...

Even grouping words into a meaningful sentence did not improve retention.

Apple trees in the garden behind a high fence
(1) In the garden... in the garden... fences... no
(2) In the garden... high... I don't know... I can't put it together.

Similar difficulties arose when the patient had to draw a series of figures after their names had been dictated to her. She could do this easily if two, or sometimes three, figures were named, but she was quite unable to do more. If the same series was shown to her for 3 to 4 sec, and then removed, she had no difficulty whatever in drawing them from memory.

Naturally, the difficulties in trace retention produced corresponding difficulty in carrying out spoken instructions. Although there was no alienation of word meaning and she could easily carry out single instructions (point to your eyes, point to your nose, etc.), the patient soon began to forget if the words were presented in pairs (point to your eye and nose, point to your nose and ear). She was quite unable to obey the instruction if the words were presented three at a time (point to your eye–nose–ear, point to your ear–nose–eye). In such cases, she would either begin to repeat the words in the wrong order, or what is particularly significant, having repeated the instruction correctly, she started to point to the wrong objects. In other words, upon changing to operations with traces she exhibited the phenomenon of "alienation of word meaning" that could not be found in the ordinary test.

The patient had similar difficulty in solving arithmetical problems. Although she could carry out written arithmetical operations correctly, she found it difficult to do them orally. She often named a number incorrectly (for example, after subtracting 7 from 100 she said "97" although at the same time she correctly wrote "93," and so on). For the same reasons, the repetition of a complex story or, more especially, the solution of a complex arithmetical problem, gave rise to considerable mnemonic difficulties. Because she could not retain a system of verbal traces, she could not operate with them. All these defects could be largely overcome by transferring the task into writing.

The mnemonic defects were manifested as another symptom. She was a translator by profession and competent in English. In the advanced state of her illness, however, her English language was severely impaired. Difficulty in finding the necessary words, although mild in her native language, was prominent in English. She was almost totally unable to converse in English because of her failure to find the right words.

The mnemonic nature of the disturbances was particularly obvious when writing in English. Although her phonetic analysis of words remained completely intact, tests showed that the patient had lost the traces of the conventional English orthography. She wrote many English words as they sounded and not as they were written. For example, she wrote the word "light" as "lait," the word "woman" as "wumen," the word "nine" as "nain," etc. When she made these mistakes (at the same time as she wrote other English words correctly), the patient stated that she was not sure about their spelling; the more she tried to recall the proper spelling, the more she had to fall back on phonetic analysis, and since her acoustic analysis remained better preserved, it replaced the traces of conventional spelling.

This temporal lesion did not affect Wernicke's area, but disturbed the function of auditory cortex. It did not directly disturb auditory analysis and synthesis, but produced an instability in verbal auditory traces, which interfered with all operations with verbal memory, creating an "acoustico-mnestic aphasia."

The postoperative course was uncomplicated, and the disturbed mnemonic functions gradually recovered. The syndrome just described persisted, so it was possible to follow the symptoms for about six weeks after the operation, in an attempt to obtain the answer to several important questions.

* * *

Two questions arise as a result of the phenomena described above.

(1) If the disturbances in this patient are confined to defects of audioverbal memory, what is the nature of these disturbances?

(2) Are these defects confined to the auditory sphere or do they extend also to the visual sphere? To what extent can visual aids compensate for a defect of audioverbal memory?

We will attempt to answer these questions with tests carried out when the symptoms were beginning to regress as a result of the operation, although the syndrome as a whole continued in its previous form.

Stability of retention of individual words

Acoustically complex single words are easily repeated by the patient even after a long pause filled with interfering conversation. For instance, the words "sokol," "skvazhina," and "penitsillin" were repeated after an interval of 5 min during which she was engaged in conversation on unrelated topics.

Repetition of numbers

She easily repeated verbally presented numbers consisting of two or three digits, and reproduced them after an interval of 10 sec filled with conversation. She began to have difficulty when repeating numbers consisting of four digits. Although she could repeat them correctly immediately, she was unable to do so after an interval of 10 sec filled with interfering conversation. She began to give fragmentary replies or to contaminate one number with another.

387	2081	2081
387	2081	2081

After a pause of 10 sec:

| 387 | ... 381... (not sure)... | 281... (not sure)... |

Repetition of word series

The patient could repeat a series of three words after an interval of 10 sec, but if conversation was introduced, she occasionally omitted one of the words. Four word series were more difficult, but after the operation she could manage them.

Direct repetition:	Dom–les–zvon Dom–les–zvon	Dom–zvon–rost Dom–zvon–rost
Repetition after a pause of 10 sec occupied with interfering conversation:	Dom... zvon and something else...	Dom–zvon–rost
Direct repetition:	Luch–put'–pero–krest (1) Luch... pero... no (2) Luch, put', pero... krest?... no, something else, I can't remember (3) Luch, put', pero, krest	
Repetition after a pause of 10 sec filled with conversation:	Oh, let me see... put', pero... krest... and wasn't there another?	

The patient exhibited these difficulties for three weeks postoperatively, but they disappeared in the course of her subsequent recovery. During the period when the repetition of four verbally presented words was very difficult, the patient was able to retain visually presented series[13], although she still had difficulty with the proper order after a pause, as before.

[13]The words were shown to the patient in writing consecutively, each for 2 sec, with intervals of 2 sec.

Direct repetition:	*Dom−zvon−les−stol*
	(1) Dom, stol. . . I have forgotten
	(2) Dom−zvon−les−stol

| Repetition after a pause of 10 sec filled with inter- fering conversation: | Les, zvon, sto. . . and something else. . . of course, dom! |

Visually presented words were much more stable and their use led to partial compensation of the defect.

Repetition of Words After Interference

During the auditory presentation of a series of more than two words, the effect of homogeneous interference was so severe that the first series was completely obliterated. The patient could not even recognize the words that formed the first series in a larger list. If the series were presented visually, the retroactive inhibition was much less marked.

The inhibitory effect of interfering factors was highly specific. It was clear in tests with audioverbal series and hardly detectable with visuoverbal series. This pathological retroactive inhibition could still be observed six weeks after the operation, when many of the other symptoms had completely disappeared.

Obeying Series of Instructions. Effect of Pauses and Retroactive Inhibitions

This verbal retention disturbance was clearly manifested when the patient was instructed to draw named figures, but she was able to repeat visually presented shapes from memory. An extract of the records from the postoperative period is given below.

Drawing a series of shapes in response to a spoken instruction	Drawing a series of shapes from visual memory
Circle, minus sign, triangle, two crosses	++○− ++○−
(1) . . . I don't know. . . ○+	
(2) ○ . . . − . . .	
(3) ○− . . .	
(4) ○− . . . and two crosses ++	
(5) ○− ++	
(6) ○− ++	++−○
(7) ○− +++	++−○

When the patient was tired, the quality of her performance deteriorated.

Triangle, two minus signs, dot, circle   ○ + ·

(1) Two or one. . .   (1) + ·

(2) . . . no?. . .   (2) + ·

(3) I can't quite. . . triangle. . . no, I can't (3) ○ + ·
    manage it

(4) . . . no

(5) . . . no. . . nothing   — — · ○

(6) . . . impossible   — — · ○

Traces of a verbal instruction were not only less stable, but they were also more susceptible to fatigue than traces of a visually presented series. Drawing shapes in response to spoken instructions was made completely impossible by retroactive inhibition, but visually presented series were not affected. These tests all demonstrate that the trace instability and inhibitability were confined to the audioverbal sphere.

Follow-up Data

Six weeks after the operation, further tests were carried out on the patient. They showed a very marked improvement in brain function, although the general structure of the disturbances remained.

The patient was able to speak much better and no longer complained of difficulty in finding words. "Whereas before I had to think what to say," she said, "now I can speak like everybody else. . ." Her spoken English was better and her writing had greatly improved.

Musical (pitch, rhythm) and phonemic hearing still remained perfectly intact, as were all types of spatial and kinesthetic gnosis and praxis. As disturbance of her mnemonic functions regressed, the integrity of her intellectual processes became apparent. She could easily carry out mental arithmetic, solve arithmetical problems, understand the meaning of a story, use logical-grammatical relationships, and had no difficulty in naming objects.

In contract to her previous performance, she could repeat a long sentence, or a series of three short (two words) sentences, relapsing only occasionally into verbal paraphasia (for example, instead of "the hunter killed a wolf at the edge of the forest," she repeated: "a hunter killed. . . a hare. . . at the edge. . . in the forest. . . is that how it was?"). She could repeat four word series, but her verbal traces were still unstable. After one minute of interfering conversation, she began to lose the words.

Noch'—zvon—most—krest

"Noch'—zvon, most—krest. . .only I think I have changed the order of the words?"

After a pause of 1 min filled with interfering conversation: Noch'. . . I have forgotten something. . .and then noch', zvon. . .something else. . .and krest.

The patient could repeat a series of five words only after four presentations.

Igla—pirog—lebed'—kreslo—mak
(1) Igla. . . pirog. . . no
(2) Igla. . . pirog. . . lebed'. . . no. . .
(3) Igla—pirog. . . lebed'. . . and krest
(4) Igla—pirog—lebed'—kreslo—mak

Retroactive inhibition remained, but much less severely. The patient could repeat a three word series even under the retroactive influence of another series.

I. *Zuby—pechka—ochki*   II. *Kamen'—ptitsa—ogon'*
   Zuby—pechka—ochki   Kamen'—ptitsa—ogon'

The words were repeated correctly after pauses of 10 and 30 sec:

?/I   *?/II*
Zuby—pechka—ochki   Kamen—ptitsa—ogon'

Only isolated mistakes in writing English occurred.

* * *

Deep lesions of the left (dominant) temporal lobe may lead to disturbances of direct audioverbal memory if the pathological factor (an intracerebral tumor) affects the middle zones without destroying its cells. The considerable residual integrity of auditory analysis and synthesis of incoming speech can be explained both by the location of the focus and by the latent left-handedness that existed in both cases we have examined.

Whether the acoustico-mnestic disorder results directly from the secondary effects of the temporal pole tumor on the audioverbal zones, or whether there is an additional disturbance of tones from the deep temporal structures directly affected by the tumor, is hard to say. The fact that in one case there was no disturbance of audioverbal memory is evidence in support of the first alternative.

Phenomena similar to those just described may also arise in a patient with an intracerebral tumor located in the deep middle zones of the left temporal lobe, but not conpressing the cortex. The mnemonic disorders are limited to a audioverbal memory. Visual and motor memory remain intact.

I have observed a case which, because of its purity, is particularly suitable as an illustration. It shows that even lesions located in the white matter of the mid left temporal region may give rise to these modality-specific disturbances of audioverbal memory without accompanying disturbances of memory, consciousness, or acoustic gnosis.

The patient had a unilocular hydatid cyst situated deep in the middle of the left temporal region, destroying the hippocampus and the amygdala, and compressing the mid-temporal cortex.[14]

[14]This patient was studied in conjunction with T. A. Karaseva.

Patient Kop., a right-handed, 26-year-old male was admitted to the Institute of Neurosurgery in January 1966, complaining of intermittent headaches, bilateral right hemianopia, and severe disturbances of memory.

The first signs of the disease had developed in March, 1965 when he had a sudden attack of headache with nausea and vomiting, which lasted about three days and have recurred frequently ever since. In October, 1965, one such attack was accompanied by a sensation of an unpleasant odor. In December, 1965, he lost the right halves of the visual fields, developed papilledema, and was sent to the Institute of Neurosurgery with the diagnosis of suspected brain tumor. The following observations were made.

The patient was quite alert, with no features of depression or retardation. He complained of headaches, limitation of the visual fields, and marked disturbances of memory: "As soon as I hear something or read something—I have forgotten it!. . ." No disorientation or internal disorders were observed. Objective examination showed papilledema, increased cerebrospinal fluid pressure to 340 mm; the CSF contained 0.87 parts per thousand of protein and the cell count was 34/3. There was incomplete right-sided hemianopia and absence of optokinetic nystagmus downward and to the right. Identification of odors was disturbed and there was a mild right-sided hemi-hypoesthesia.

A large focus of pathological activity in the left temporo-occipital region was seen in the EEG. Left-sided carotid angiography revealed displacement of the middle cerebral artery upward and medially.

Neuropsychological investigation showed no speech disorders. After angiography there was appreciable difficulty in finding words, but this disappeared without a trace after one day. The central symptom was a severe disturbance of audioverbal memory, which will be described below.

On February 27, 1966, the patient had an attack of severe headache, accompanied by vomiting, rigors, and disturbance of respiration and cardiac activity, after which he died.

At autopsy, a large unilocular hydatid cyst was found in the white matter of the left temporal cortex. The cavity of the cyst extended from the anterior left temporal lobe to the posterior end of the genu of the internal capsule. It compressed the internal capsule and pulvinar of the thalamus medially (Figure 9). The cortex of the superior and middle temporal gyri was unchanged. The cortex of the hippocampal gyrus was destroyed. The amygdala and deep white matter of the left temporal lobe were destroyed. The remainder of the temporal lobe was compressed, but not destroyed. The cause of death was the greatly increased intracranial pressure causing pinching of the brain stem in the foramen magnum.

Disturbances of Audioverbal Memory

Neuropsychological investigation of this patient in February, 1966 produced the following description.

The patient was fully communicative, and showed no defects of praxis, gnosis, or speech. His intellectual operations were adequate, he could relate his past history, and he showed no evidence of depression, apathy, or affective disorders. He could recognize a tone and series of two tones 10 sec and 1 min after their presentation. He had difficulty if the series was increased to three tones.

The dominant symptom of the illness was the severe disturbance of audioverbal memory. The patient himself said that he could not retain a conversation or a story read to him: "When I heard or read something it

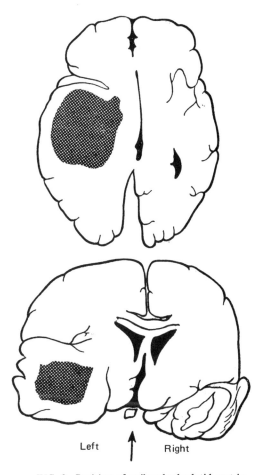

FIG. 9. Position of unilocular hydatid cyst in
patient Kop.

immediately vanished and I could not recall it." These defects were associated
with complete integrity of speech processes (phonemic hearing, writing, reading,
the understanding of speech, the naming of objects). He easily retained and
repeated single words and short sentences. He could just as easily retain series
of three words, but with four or five words the defects of retention became
apparent. Facts showing the defectiveness of the patient's memory are given
below.

Repetition of series of sounds

a–o–i–u	*b–n–r–t–z*	*k–sh–l–p–s*
a–o–i–u	b–n–r–t–z	k–sh–l–p–s

After a pause of 10 sec:

a–o–i–u   b–n–z–g–r   k–shch–z. . . no, I have
                                                              forgotten
After distraction by conversation:
                                                              k–sh–l–p–s
a–o–i–u   No, the order is wrong,
                                 I can't remember. . .

Repetition of word series

Dom–les–stol–kot   *Stol–dom–kot–les*
Dom–les–stol–kot   (1) Stol–dom–les. . . and something else
                                 (2) Stol–dom–les–kot

After a pause of 10 sec:

Dom–les–stol. . . kot   Stol–dom–les–kot

After distraction by conversation:

Dom–les–stol–kot   Stol–dom–les–kot

Kot–stol–dom–les–zvon   *Stuk–prud–noch'–rak–krest*
(1) Kot–dom. . . stol. . . I have   Stuk–prud–noch'–rak. . . svet?
    forgotten
(2) Kot–dom–stol–les–zvon   Stuk–prud–noch'–rak–krest

After a pause of 10 sec:

(1) Kot–stol–les. . . dom–zvon?   Stuk–prud–noch'–rak–krest
(2) Kot–stol–les–dom–zvon

After distraction by conversation:

Kot–stol. . . dom. . . les. . . zvon   Stuk–prud–noch'. . . I have forgotten

Repetition of series of meaningless syllables

Ral–mon–chet   *Zor–min–kul–khon*   *Kom–rach–nis–pel*
Ral–mon–chet   Zor–pin–kul. . . kon   Kom–rach–nis–pel

After a pause of 10 sec:

Ral–mon–chet

After distraction by conversation:

(1) Ral–mon–chet   Zor–pin. . . kul. . . I have   Kom–rav–pil
                        forgotten
(2) Ral–mon–chet

After distraction with conversation:

                                          Kom–ras–pil–chen
                                          . . . no, I can't

Typical defects were either forgetting the last elements of the series or losing the correct order. Distracting the patient's attention with interfering conversation gave rise to particular difficulty. Characteristically, prolonged practice in retaining series did not improve the performance but worsened it—evidence of the early onset of fatigue. Homogeneous interference had particularly severe effects.

I. *Sneg—nul'—rost—versta*   II. *Znamya—ogon'—kust—marka*
   Sneg—nul'—rost—versta   Znamya—ogon'—kust—marka

What was group I?   *What was group II?*
Sneg. . . rost. . . I have forgotten. I don't know, it is all mixed up. . .

Retroactive inhibition also occurred when sentences were given instead of isolated words.

The hunter killed a wolf on the edge of the forest.	*Apple trees grew in the garden behind the high fence.*	*What was sentence I?*	*What was sentence II?*
The hunter killed a wolf on the edge of the forest.	Apple trees grew in the garden behind the high fence.	In the garden. . . I remember this but didn't attach importance to the rest.	A hunter killed a wolf. . . but I can't remember completely. . .

This increased proactive and retroactive inhibition affected memorizing long series of isolated words and narrative speech.

The patient was asked to learn a series of 10 words and repeat a long fragment read to him. Having heard the series of 10 isolated words, he could reproduce not more than 5 or 6 of them. Presenting the same words again did not improve performance. As a rule, the patient could retain either the first or the last elements of the series each time, suggesting increased proactive and retroactive inhibition on the memorizing process. Another characteristic feature was, having repeated a word, the patient could not remember that he had done so, and sometimes he would give the same word several times in succession. Although he could understand the basic meaning of a story, he was unable to retain its concrete details. Having memorized one story, he was quite unable to return to a story read to him previously. An example illustrating this fact is given below.

"The Hen and the Golden Eggs" story was read to him. After it had been read the first time, he could repeat only the beginning: "A man had. . . a hen. . . which laid golden eggs. . . no. . . I can't remember." After it had been read a second time, he said: "A man had a hen which. . . I have forgotten. . ."
"The Ant and the Pigeon" story was read to him. He could not repeat it and said he remembered nothing about it.
Do you recall the story I read to you before this one? "Something about a jackdaw (a week before this test the "The Jackdaw and the Pigeons" story had been read to this

patient)... and about golden eggs... how a hen laid golden eggs... but they would not take her in" (once again, the elements of the story heard long ago could not be repressed).

The defects of memory arising in this patient were based on retroactive inhibition, removed after a long interval by virtue of reminiscence, rather than weakness of the traces.

Memorizing Nonauditory (Visual, Kinesthetic, and Motor) Series

The next question to be considered was: Do similar defects arise in visual and motor memory, or is the pathology confined to the audioverbal sphere? Further tests were carried out.

The patient was asked to memorize and recall material presented visually, and in other tests he was instructed to repeat a series of consecutive movements. He was much more able to repeat nonauditory series and had none of those defects which were observed during the study of audioverbal memory. He remembered the order in which he touched four objects and repeated it correctly either at once or after 10 sec. Distraction with conversation either disturbed the order of the series or led to the omission of one of its components. The patient easily repeated a series of three movements immediately after their demonstration, or after a pause of 10 sec with or without distraction. The presentation of a second group had little effect on his ability to remember the first group of three movements. Usually, the first group was reproduced correctly but the second group was reproduced sometimes in the wrong order. He could easily find five previously presented picture cards in a pack either immediately or after a pause of 10 sec or 1 min.

* * *

Let us evaluate these facts. A patient with a large unilocular hydatid cyst deep in the left temporal region manifested a definite syndrome of audioverbal memory disturbance, evidently based on pathologically increased inhibitability of audioverbal traces. Consolidated traces of previous experience were not disrupted. To the extent that they were independent of operative audioverbal memory, intellectual operations remained intact. Phonemic hearing, writing, reading, and the understanding of speech were normal.

The pattern can be explained on the basis of the fact that the hydatid cyst left intact the gray matter of the superior zones of the left temporal region (Wernicke's area) as well as the adjacent cortex of the left inferior temporal and occipital region, but the mid-temporal cortex was compressed to a much greater degree. The hippocampus and amygdala of the left hemisphere were destroyed, and the connections between these structures and the left temporal cortex were replaced by the cyst. This lesion gave rise to a pathological state of these cortical zones, and to increased inhibitability of the audioverbal traces—or, in other words, to disturbances of audioverbal memory. These memory disturbances differed significantly from the general disturbances of memory arising in patients with bilateral hippocampal lesions and from the acoustico-gnostic disorders resulting from a lesion of the superior zone of the left temporal region.

Disturbance of Mnemonic Processes in Posterior Lesions of the Left Temporal Region

With a lesion of the posterior left temporal region on the parietal-occipital border, audioverbal retention disturbances are also present, but similar disturbances can also be observed in the retention of visual and, sometimes, kinesthetic stimuli.

* * *

Let us first examine the effects of a tumor located in the depth of the left postero-temporal region, after which we can analyze the mnemonic disturbance in a patient with a temporo-parietal wound in the left hemisphere.

Patient Mois., a 46-year-old male, was admitted to the Institute of Neurosurgery in April, 1960, complaining of attacks of intermittent headache, numbness in the right limbs, difficulty in speaking, and a marked loss of memory.

The illness began in 1956 when he noticed weakness, general malaise, headaches, attacks of numbness in the right limbs lasting 1 to 2 min, and fits with generalized convulsions starting with the sensation of an unpleasant smell. The fits were followed by difficulty in speaking. The patient remembered what was said to him but had difficulty in finding the proper reply. The fits were accompanied by anxiety. Because of the increasing frequency of the fits and severity of the speech disturbances, the patient was sent to the Institute of Neurosurgery where examination revealed right-sided hemianopia and diminished visual acuity (R = 0.4, L = 0.8). There was no evidence of increased intracranial pressure. Horner's sign was positive on the left. There was a central paresis of the left facial nerve, and weakness, loss of pain sensation and numbness in the right limbs. Reflexes were increased on the right, the palm-chin reflex was present bilaterally, but the patient had difficulty in speaking, reading, and counting. A pathological EEG focus was present in the left temporal region.

These findings suggested the pathological focus was deep in the left temporal region. This was confirmed by both the speech disorders and the right-sided hemianopia that developed later. The numbness in the right limbs could be explained by the effect of the pathological focus on the sensory pathways. The olfactory hallucinations, anxiety, and alarm accompanying the fits could point to the involvement of the medio-basal zones of the left temporal region. The visual disorders could indicate the focus was situated in the posterior temporal region, on the border with the occipital region. The long course of the disease, absence of increased intracranial pressure, cerebral displacement, or general toxic manifestations, suggested the presence of a slowly growing tumor.

In May, 1960, an operation was performed. Flattening of the convolutions of the brain was observed through a burr-hole in the left temporo-occipital area. A needle was inserted

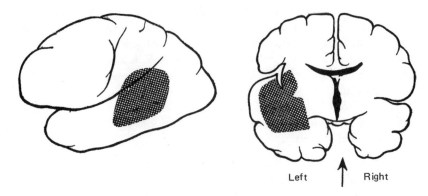

Left   Right

FIG. 10.   Location of tumor in patient Mois.

on the border between the inferior parietal and temporal regions; at a depth of 2 cm, thickening of the brain tissue was detected. The brain tissue there was incised, and at a depth of 3 cm the whitish-yellow tissue of an astrocytoma with no clearly defined boundaries became evident. The tumor spread into the depth of the temporal region toward the occipital border (Figure 10).

During the next two years, the clinical picture increased steadily in severity. In 1961 and 1962, further operations were performed; but in June, 1962, the patient died.

At autopsy, an astrocytoma was found to occupy the white matter of the entire left occipital lobe. The tumor obliterated the inferior horn of the left lateral ventricle and invaded the lumen of the ventricular trigone and the posterior horn. Further growth of the tumor led to the formation of a large nodule in the parieto-temporal-occipital zones in the region of the burr-hole.

A neuropsychological investigation of this patient was carried out during the first weeks of his stay at the Institute of Neurosurgery in 1960, and on several occasions after the operation. The patient was clearly oriented in space and time, communicative, emotionally normal, and acutely aware of his illness. He complained of attacks of paresthesia in the right limbs with olfactory hallucinations, and a state of alarm and anxiety.

He was particularly depressed by the disturbances of speech, verbal memory, reading, and arithmetic. He stated that he found it difficult to speak; he could not find the proper words, although he could understand what was said to him. He had difficulty in naming objects and sometimes gave incorrect names for them. When he started to speak, he often found that he could not say what he wanted to say, and had to stop to seek for the right word. He had considerable difficulty in reading; often he could not recognize the letters. "I can see a word but cannot get the right meaning of the letters. . . I want to form a word but I cannot do so. . ." He also found arithmetic difficult; he could not carry out even the simplest calculations. All these phenomena were greatly intensified when the patient was a little tired, and this gave rise to strong emotional disturbances and depression.

Objective examination showed that his postural praxis was normal. Head's test of mimicing hand positions he carried out slowly, working out successively which hand should be raised and what its position should be relative to the examiner's face. But, as a rule, he performed the test correctly. He had no disturbance of correlated hand movements. He could easily repeat rhythms and switch from one rhythm to another. He had no severe disturbances of visual gnosis. Only occasionally, when looking at pictures of objects, would he identify them incorrectly by picking out one diagnostic sign and not comparing it with the distinguishing features. For example, he would identify a picture of a telephone as a clock (by looking at the dial), or he would take a bench for a stool. He could easily identify outline drawings and silhouettes, but had marked difficulty in identifying crossed out or superposed drawings. Even in these tests, however, he slowly and methodically analyzed the pictures and simply had difficulty in naming them (this will be considered in detail below).

Definite difficulties arose in this patient's spatial gnosis and constructive praxis. He stated that he had difficulty in working with diagrams, which was his occupation: "Even during the examination and discussion of diagrams at work I am less likely to give the right answer. . ." Objective tests confirmed this difficulty. He often found it hard to determine the spatial arrangement of shapes, and would copy ⌐ ⌐ ⌐ as ⌐ ⌐ ⌐. When he tried to draw the position of the clock hands, he made mistakes and represented them as the mirror image. The same phenomenon appeared when he had to transpose a shape mentally. His speech remained phonetically and articulatorily intact, but it was severely disturbed by his word seeking. For this reason, he often substituted artificial constructions for habitual terms of speech: "It seems to me. . . now. . . I have become aware of it. . . that the illness. . . began. . . quite a long time age. . . so. . . I began to consider. . . or to consider. . . I began. . . I was troubled. . . I considered. . . and I began to feel that my memory is poor. . . and for quite a long time. . . I cannot remember. . . and I do not say what I mean to say. . . I forget. . . that is I do not forget. . . but I cannot say. . . this all. . . became. . . a more common event. . .," and so on. In weighted tests, phonemic hearing also was disturbed. For instance, he would repeat a series of syllables da–ta–da as da–da–ta, and when writing words would substitute correlative phonemes, writing sopor instead of sobor.

He had no difficulty in analyzing the acoustic composition of a word, picking out the component sounds, and naming the sounds occupying a certain position in the correct order. When repeating single words, he had no difficulties. He recognized the names of body parts, but began to have considerable difficulty in retaining two such words. He could point correctly to the eye–nose, but could not point immediately to the ear–eye, declaring "Now I am confused," but later pointing to them correctly. With pictures, he could point correctly to groups of two or three named objects, and in that case there was no alienation of word meaning.

Naming of objects gave rise to appreciable difficulty, due partly to difficulty of visual recognition but more especially to difficulty in finding the correct words. Sometimes his word searches were accompanied by verbal paraphasia. "It often happens that. . . I want to name. . . and another object flies into my head. . . and when I am distracted, I recall. . ."–the patient exclaimed. For instance, when shown the picture of a fish, he said: "There now. . . I recognized it, but I could not say what it was. . . and for some reason or other the word duck cropped up, but I know that it is not a duck. . ." Sometimes the patients made typical mistakes of optical aphasia. For instance, he called the picture of a mortar "stand. . . a stand. . . for a pen. . ." In every case, prompting with the first letters of the word helped the patient to recall the required name.

His ability to evaluate logical-grammatical relations was clearly disrupted. For instance, he had great difficulty in understanding the relations between shapes, and would often draw a cross below a triangle as $\frac{+}{\triangle}$ or b below k as $\frac{b}{\kappa}$ and only after much turning it over in his mind and analysis, would he correct his mistakes. Besides logical-grammatical disturbances, however, alienation of word meaning also appeared in these tests. Having heard the instruction to place a triangle under a cross, he drew $\triangle$ then repeated this figure over and over again. He would draw a cross under a triangle as $+$, and would even draw a triangle as $+$. The disturbances of logical-grammatical operations was manifested in a comparatively mild form capable of correction, but appeared worse because it was superimposed on the instability of verbal object naming.

Writing isolated letters, syllables, and words remained relatively intact, but when writing a series of words or sentences the patient started to have difficulty on account of his mnemonic defects, which are examined below.

The patient often confused letters of similar outline, writing н as u, n as н, к as x, and m as φ. A similar difficulty was found in reading words. Because of defective letter perception, he often made mistakes and would declare: "I can see the word... but I take the letters to mean something else... I want to make them into a word, but the word I get is the wrong one..."

The patient's arithmetic was substantially disturbed. He could easily read separate numbers, but when reading numbers formed by several digits he often made mistakes and would perseverate one of the digits. Only by reading out a multidigit number, figure by figure, could be perceive it properly. In order to name isolated numbers correctly, he would often have to recite the whole natural series of numbers until he reached the right one. He could write individual numbers quite normally, and manage simple calculations in single figures. Addition of two-digit figures or, particularly, subtraction requiring carrying over from one column to another or the performance of individual operations "in his head" was very defective. He could not, for example, subtract 31 minus 17; he considered all the possible answers for a long time and said: "30... 17... 16... 4... 6," eventually fixed on the answer "16," then unsuccessfully tested his answer and tried to break up seven into 3 and 4, then to subtract 4 from 11, obtaining 5 as the answer, and then he finally abandoned all his attempts and declared: "I tell you straight—it is very hard for me to count in my head!..." Naturally, the more complex forms of arithmetic were quite outside the patient's grasp, partly because of his inability to retain the component elements, and partly because of the primary disintegration of his numerical schemes.

Tests of the patient's performance of mathematical operations, carried out jointly with Corresponding Member of the Academy of Sciences of the USSR I. M. Gel'fand, showed them to be seriously disturbed. When trying to obtain the powers of 2, the patient (educated in mathematics) wrote: "$2^0 = 0$, $2^1 = 1...$," altered 1 to 2... "$2^2 = 2$; $2^3 = 6...$" and himself commented: "No... 4 must be multiplied by 2 and I can't do it. Recently I have found it hard to calculate... I know how to calculate properly, but I do it wrongly. When given the problem + 2 − 2, he got the correct answer 0, but he hesitated when asked to solve the problem + 3 − 3 and said: "+ 3 − 3... that is 0... no, it must be 1... I cannot reason well..." He was quite unable to solve the following problem. Four people are playing chess. How many times can each of them play with the others? In his attempt to solve it, he carried out the operations 4 x 4, then subtracted 4 from the result and said "12," and not even the suggestion that he draw a diagram helped him to find the correct solution.

More complex intellectual operations could not be tested because of the severe verbal retention defects.

The tests demonstrated that the disturbance of higher cortical functions in this patient was associated with at least two basic factors. First, the patient had marked acoustico-mnestic defects, manifested as inability to retain verbal traces, the perseverative replacement of some traces by others, and the evidently secondary instability of phonemic hearing. Second, there were equally severe disturbances of visual gnosis and spatial synthesis, manifested as defects of constructive gnosis and praxis, logical-grammatical processes, and calculation.

The neuropsychological analysis indicated a primary focus in the left posterior temporal region, affecting the bordering occipital and parietal zones.

The fact that the acoustico-mnestic disturbances were the most severe, while phonetic hearing was relatively intact (defects became evident only during biased tests), and the visual gnosis disturbances were variable, all suggested that the primary focus lay deep in the posteroinferior temporal region and that its influence on the occipital and parietal cortices was secondary.

Disturbances of Mnemonic Processes

The syndrome described above led to concentrated study of the patient's mnemonic processes. The patient himself stated that it was his memory disturbance which upset him the most. The words would not come at once into his head; often he replaced them unexpectedly by others. If many words were spoken to him, he forgot them immediately; and even things he knew before had now disappeared. He could not describe the disturbances more exactly.

Tests showed that these mnemonic disorders were not all equally severe. As already stated, the patient could easily beat time, repeat rhythms, and retain these rhythms for a long time.

He had no difficulty in reproducing tonal relations, easily repeating melodies consisting of five notes (for example ♩♩ ♩♩♩ and ♩♩ ♩♩♩). He could easily make differential responses to tonal stimuli, e.g., he could lift his right hand correctly in response to the first tune and the left hand in response to the second. His rhythmic-melodic (musical) hearing, like his musical memory, thus remained substantially undisturbed.

His long-term semantic memory likewise remained intact, but it was difficult to test it because of his speech defect.

He was perfectly oriented in time, had a clear grasp of chronology (although he could not always find the correct names), recognized his friends and the doctors who treated him, and with the appropriate verbal assistance could clearly describe the events of his past life. He could describe the themes of novels he had read, pick out their essential semantic threads, never went off into irrelevant associations, and had difficulty only in expressing himself properly in words.

He had no difficulty retaining a single word and could repeat it after a pause of 2 to 3 min. He retained and repeated two or even three words. Only as the illness became more severe, and immediately after the operation, did this become so difficult that, having repeated the pair "Dom—les" he could not repeat another pair "Stol—kot," but perseverated the previous word and changed the order: "Les. . . stol."

He had great difficulty in repeating four- and five-word series. He could not keep the words in the correct order but transposed and sometimes substituted them. Usually, even learning a series by heart did not lead to any appreciable improvement. Even a short pause (10 to 15 sec) was sometimes sufficient to make him unable to repeat a series he had learned. A few examples are:

A series of five words was recited to him (the words were given at intervals of 1 to 1.5 sec) and he was instructed to repeat it at once. This test was repeated several times in succession.

Dom—les—stol—kot—zvon

(1) Dom—les—skot—zvon—stol
(2) Dom—les—stol—skot—zvon

(3) Dom—les—stol—skot. . . I have forgotten the last one.
(4) Dom—les—stol—skot—stol. . . and the last is zvon.
(5) Dom—les. . . but. . . dom—les—stol.
(6) Dom—les—zvon. . . but. . . not zvon . . . I am confused.
(7) Dom—les—stol—skot. . . zvon
(8) Dom—les. . . stol. . . skot. . . kot. . . I remembered them very badly.

After a pause of 10 sec:

Stol. . . zvon. . . no, I can't.

Put'—most—stul—krot—svet

(1) Put'—most—stul—stol—svet
(2) Krot—svet. . . put'. . . stol. . . this is bad.
(3) Put'. . . most—stul. . . svet

(4) Put'—most—stul. . . the third one I have forgotten.
(5) Put'. . . no, will you repeat them.

(6) Put'—most—stul—krot—svet

After a pause of 10 sec

Put'—most. . . stul. . . no

After a pause of 10 sec:

Pust. . . stol. . . there, it won't come.

Similar results were obtained with long number series. The introduction of a short pause (especially if filled with irrelevant stimuli, such as conversation) was sufficient to make repetition impossible

(The intervals between the numbers read out were 1 to 1.5 sec.)

5—6—1—2—7

(1) I can do this: 5—6—1—2—7
(2) 5—6—1—2—7

After a pause of 10 sec filled with interfering conversation:

2—6—1—5—6—. . . no. . .

3—8—1—6—2—4

(1) 3—8—1. . . 4—6—1
(2) 3—8—1. . . I don't know anymore.
(3) 6—2—4. . . 3—4—1
(4) 3—8—1—6—2—4

5—2—7—6—1

(1) 2—5—7—6—1
(2) No, I can't
(3) 5—7—6—7—1. . .
(4) 5—2—7—6—1

After a pause of 10 sec:

5—6. . . 5—6. . . 7. . . 1

After a pause of 10 sec filled with interfering conversation:

6—8—1. . . I don't know.

Attempts to repeat a long sentence or a fragment of text gave very poor results. Having listened to the story of "The Jackdaw and the Pigeons (Golubi)," he could only repeat: "Jackdaw. . . and (golovnoe). . . (golovno). . . no, this is the wrong relationship. . ."

These facts differ only slightly from those described in the previous section. Other observations, however, point to substantial differences between the two syndromes.

Lesions located in the depth of the anterior left temporal zones cause considerable audioverbal memory disturbances but do not affect the retention of kinesthetic and visual series.

This dissociation does not take place in patients with lesions of the posterior zones of the left temporal lobe. A focus deep in this region, affecting the occipital and parietal lobes as well, leads to mnemonic disturbances which involve acoustic, visual, and kinesthetic stimuli equally.

This patient had no difficulty in reproducing single positions of the hands, but was unable to repeat a series of three different positions. This alone showed that the repetition of kinesthetic series caused considerable difficulty. Difficulties were even more pronounced during the repetition of visual series. I did not test the patient's ability to memorize visually presented word series, because his residual aphasia made such tests unproductive. The memorizing of visually presented number series gave results not greatly different from tests with verbal stimuli.

Much clearer results were obtained during the repetition of a visual series of geometric shapes. In the first test, a series of shapes was shown to the patient for 15 to 20 sec; the paper was then covered and the patient had to draw the shapes from memory. If the test was unsuccessful, it was repeated several times. The results are shown below.

$\triangle \ \square \,-\,-\,+$
(1) $\triangle \ \square$ ... I don't know
(2) $\triangle \ \square -\,-$ ... and what next?... I have forgotten.
(3) $\triangle \ \square -\,-$ And the last... I have forgotten... perhaps $+$

Draw this again

$\triangle \ \square -\,-\,+$

In this case the patient could examine all the shapes at once. In the next test, the shapes were presented consecutively. Performance was much worse in this case.

$+ \ \bigcirc \ \bigcirc \ \cdot$
1) $\triangle -\,-$.
2) $\triangle \bigcirc \bigcirc :$
3) $+ \bigcirc \bigcirc :$

* * *

Gunshot wounds of this region can give rise to similar findings.

Patient Krap., a 45-year-old male, right handed, disabled since the Second World War.

In 1944, he received a penetrating splinter wound of the left hemisphere with a point of entry in the inferior parietal region and the splinters lodged in the left posterior temporal region (Figure 11). The wound was treated immediately after injury, but the postoperative course was complicated by local inflammation and delayed healing. After it had healed, for two years the patient's condition frequently worsened, he developed meningeal symptoms, and the cell count in his cerebrospinal fluid was increased. Epileptic fits began 4 or 5 months after wounding, and later recurred with variable frequency.

In January, 1947, an operation was carried out to excise a scar affecting the meninges and brain, together with a granuloma and metallic fragment. A few months after the operation, however, the patient again began to have epileptic fits, recurring every two months.

After the wound, the patient had severe aphasia, which gradually regressed (studied by Professor S. M. Blinkov). After the operation the patient was registered as disabled. He worked at home, carving wooden chess pieces. During this period, he was communicative, self-disciplined, fully adapted to his situation, and lived with his family.

In May, 1961, he was admitted to the Institute of Neurosurgery because of prolonged epileptic fits. He had residual manifestations of a left parieto-temporal lesion: Signs of right pyramidal insufficiency with intact sensation, asymmetry of the right naso-labial fold, and tendon reflexes stronger but abdominal reflexes weaker on the right side. As before, he had epileptic fits with an aura consisting of paresthesia with auditory, visual, and vestibular hallucinations ("something like birds appear in front of my eyes... everything falls over sideways and moves to the right... all sorts of strange thoughts arise"). The EEG revealed marked diffuse cortical irritation with a focus of epileptic activity in the left parieto-temporal region.

Neuropsychological tests indicated the patient was rational, organized, and purposive. Despite his disability, he remained at work, kept in touch with events, and enjoyed the respect of his neighbors. Everything in his room was tidy. He was aware of his increasing difficulties and strove diligently to overcome them. He had no difficulty in visual gnosis or in carrying out tests of kinesthetic praxis. He managed reciprocal coordination tests well.

He had real difficulty with spatial organization of movements: Sometimes he confused the basic coordinates of space and substituted the sagittal plane for the frontal. The difficulties were particularly evident when he was instructed to copy the relative position

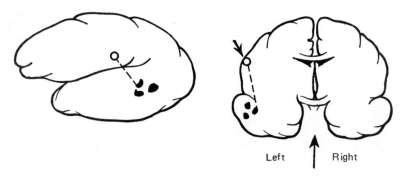

Left   Right

FIG. 11. Location of lesions in patient Krap.

of the two hands. For a long time, he tried to find the correct position of the hand and finally exclaimed: "No, it is too difficult for me: if there is only one hand it is easy, but when both hands—it is difficult, I have to think about this and that. . ." Difficulties with simultaneous operations were obvious in Head's test or tests of constructive praxis (for example, making shapes out of matches). In these tests, the patient could never solve the problem immediately. He always tried to do so in stages, breaking it up into consecutive steps and subjecting each step to verbal analysis. If this was forbidden, he soon fell under the influence of direct impression and he produced a mirror image of the required shape. Similar difficulties were observed during his assessment of the position of the hands on a clock. He could tell the time easily if the clock was in its ordinary position, but could not do so if the clock was placed upside down and the number 6 had to be taken conventionally as 12. No difficulties of constructive praxis, in the narrow meaning of this term, were present in this patient. His main difficulty was simply that he could not immediately grasp spatial relations and operate with them as ideas.

The patient had no disturbance of elementary auditory gnosis. He could distinguish and repeat tones and the relations between two tones of different pitch easily; as a rule, he could easily evaluate simple rhythmic groups and repeat them.

The situation changed considerably when he was required to analyze and compare pitch or rhythmic relations under more complex conditions. For instance, after successfully repeating two tones separately, he had great difficulty when he was given the same two tones as conditioned stimuli (in response to one tone raise your right hand, in response to the other raise your left hand). In this case, he gave correct responses only once or twice, after which he began to be confused and exclaimed: "They are both so alike, I don't know what each one means. . ." The patient could not discriminate more complex combinations unless verbal analysis was allowed.

Similar phenomena were observed during evaluation and repetition of rhythms. Although repeating simple rhythms immediately after their presentation was possible (‖ ‖ or ‖‖ ‖‖)[15], he was quite unable to cope with more complex rhythm (for example, ‖. . . or . . .‖‖) or to compare different groups of rhythms (for example, ‖ ‖ ‖–‖‖ ‖‖ ‖‖ or ‖ ‖ ‖‖–‖ ‖ ‖‖). In these cases, he began to have great difficulty as soon as he tried to compare the rhythmic structure he had just produced with the current model. He could not retain the precise model sufficiently and, consequently, the operation of comparison became impossible.

The patient stated that it was "difficult for him to remember what he had to tap" or that he "could not remember so many taps": He therefore resorted to verbal analysis, and if he could immediately estimate the number of taps in a rhythmic group with the aid of speech rhythms, he found he could perform the task satisfactorily, although even then he tapped out the rhythm slowly. His ability to reproduce rhythms in response to a spoken instruction, despite considerable difficulty in doing so from auditory traces, was a distinctive feature of his disability.

If the patient was not allowed to make a verbal analysis of the rhythms, if they were presented quickly, or if he was instructed to tap them out as quickly as possible, his difficulties became particularly apparent. The patient abandoned the task and said: "Well now, I can't do it at all, I can't work it out. . ."

Difficulties in comparing a visual stimulus with a model were also observed.

In the absence of any purely sensory disturbance (for example, in color discrimination), he exhibited serious defects of complex discrimination. After establishing a stable differentiation between two pairs of colors, if all four colors were presented in random order, an unexpected phenomenon occurred: He began to say that the colors were new and had not been shown to him before, that the green or the red color was not the same as he

---

[15] Strokes denote loud taps—dots, weak taps.

had seen earlier, that they were of a different shade, that he did not remember whether he had seen them before, or that they were "darker" or "deeper" and he did not know how to react to them. This difficulty consists essentially of inability to compare a present stimulus with the past model.

These tests reveal a dynamic instability of sensory processes that may be the physiological basis of the higher cortical disturbances arising in this patient.

Disturbances of Mnemonic Processes

This patient had no severe disturbances of speech. He readily understood when spoken to if he listened very attentively. He often had to request the speaker to talk more slowly, so that he could "grasp the meaning," and not to say so much at once ("if there is too much I cannot understand it all at once"). His own speech contained no articulatory defects, but he had to seek the necessary words constantly and this interrupted the fluency of his conversation. Often he would say: "Well, it is like this. . . I seem to know it all. . . but I cannot remember. . . how shall I say it. . ."

The patient's phonemic hearing was not noticeably disturbed. He could easily repeat single sounds of speech and did not confuse similar (correlative) phonemes. If he was instructed to repeat three correlative phonemes (for example, t–t–d or t–d–t), he was unable to do so. Often he would repeat the phonemes in the wrong order, stating that he did not remember the order in which they were given to him. He had no difficulty in repeating pairs or trios of sharply different sounds (for example, k–m, r–n or r–m–n, k–s–n), but repetition of four sounds (for example, l–s–k–n or r–p–s–d) caused considerable difficulty. Even if he was able to repeat the series properly after several presentations, he forgot it after a pause of 10 to 15 sec.

The patient had no difficulty in retaining single words after a long pause, even those with a fairly complex acoustic composition. He could just as easily write single words. He had appreciable difficulty in repeating a series of words. He usually repeated a first pair of words without difficulty, but when asked to repeat a second pair he would repeat only one and forget the other:

Sneg–noga	*Grom–most*
Sneg–noga	I have forgotten. . . grom. . . and something else

The repetition of 3-word series invariably gave rise to considerable difficulty. Although he could sometimes repeat the first series, he was quite unable to repeat a second and third series. The traces were inhibited so easily that he could not even identify the words in a group:

Stol–les–kot	*Noch'–krug–ten'*
Stol. . . les. . . and something	(1) Noch'. . . then. . . ten'. . . and another
else. . . dom? No, kot	one besides
	(2) Noch'–krug–ten'. . .

Stul—zvon—rak

(1) It is. . . stul. . . no. . . rak, I mean stul, isn't it?

(2) Stul. . . stul. . . I have forgotten one, I seem to remember rak. *Could it be krug?* No. *Snop?* No. *Zvon?* I was confused, no, I think not. . . *Kust?* No. . . *Noch'?* There was another one, or was there?. . . I can't remember.

Krik—snop—rost

(1) Kirk. . . snop. . . krik. . . no, krik was the first one

(2) Ah, rost!. . . snop. . . krik. . . Oh, I have forgotten the third now. *Could it be kust?* I don't know. *Zvon?* No, another one, no. . . *Krest?* No. . . *Rost?* No certainly not.

The patient was quite unable to repeat a series of four words.

To try to discover if these difficulties were connected with ecphoria or with trace retention, control tests were carried out in which the patient did not have to repeat words but simply to pick out named objects by choosing them from a pack of picture cards. The results of these tests were similar to those already described and demonstrate that auditory traces of words were not retained by this patient.

Similar results were obtained in tests in which the patient was instructed to draw three named shapes. At best, he could retain the first such series with three shapes or pictures; however, he could not retain a second series. He could hardly ever retain a series of four named shapes.

Cross, dot, circle[16]

(1) +

(2) + · ○

After a pause of 10 sec filled with conversation:

+ · I have forgotten

Circle, minus sign, triangle

(1) ○

(2) ○+. . . no, triangle, what can it be?

(3) Triangle

(4) No, I have quite forgotten.

(5) ○···+ I can't go on.

Circle, dot, cross

(1) Circle. . . I have forgotten.

(2) Circle, dot, and something else. . ." ○

(3) Circle, dot and minus sign? ○

(4) Circle, dot. . . that is what I remembered but I have forgotten the rest. . .

An essential difference betwee this patient and the patient with a lesion of the temporal pole is that a change to visually presented stimuli does not improve performance. Extracts from the record are given below.

---

[16]The patient's spoken replies are given as text; the shapes he drew are shown graphically.

Successive presentation of shapes □ + −	*Simultaneous presentation of shapes* △ + ○	*Simultaneous presentation of shapes* + ☽ □
(1) □ + and something else	(1) There was a cross. . . I can't remember. . . besides a square but. . . there was a triangle first, and then. . . I don't remember	(1) ☽ cresent in the middle
(2) □ + and something else? dot?, no, not dot	(2) · +	(2) ☽ and something else . . . I very soon forget.
(3) □ + . . . what can this be?	(3) △ and then this. . . but I have. . . +	(3) ☽ it is a crescent. . . I remembered it well, but there was another shape: a quadrilateral, but I am not sure whether it came in front or behind.
	(4) +	(4) + ☽, □ but I am not sure.
	(5) I can't. . . + No, I am not sure △, . .○. . . No. . . ○ +. . .	

When the patient repeated the shape, he accompanied his drawing with speech and sometimes showed alienation of word meaning (when he drew a triangle, he called it a "cross," and so on).

Alienation of word meaning can also be seen in tests requiring the carrying out of spoken instructions. The patient easily carried out the instruction to point to particular named objects. If instructed to name pairs of objects, he began to have difficulty. He began to exhibit alienation of word meaning, as observed frequently in patients with lesions of the speech areas of the temporal lobe, if the object corresponding to the words was not visually present, e.g., if parts of the face are named and if a combination of the same words is repeated. An extract from the records is given below.

Glaz−nos ukho−nos *(Eyes−nose ear−nose)* (Points to them correctly)	*Ukho−glaz* *(Ear−eye)* Ear. . . the first one is ear. What can the other be. I don't know. . . ear and eye, there it is!	*Nos−ukho* *(Nose−ear)* Nose. . . nose. . . well it is nose and something else. . . I have forgotten.

Nose−ear
(1) It is much the same. . . but
I cannot
(2) The first is nose. . . nose. . .
nose. . . nose. What about the
nose?. . . Nose. . . foot, nose. . .
nose. . . something else I can't
remember, where my nose is. . .

The inability to retain a series of named words suggested mutual inhibition of stimuli and indicated the need for an investigation of retroactive inhibition.

Just as in the case discussed above (*patient Gorch.*), retroactive inhibition was greatly intensified. After repeating a second group of words, traces of the previous group disappeared and he was unable to recall them. The difference from the case discussed above is simply that the severe retroactive inhibition in this patient appeared not only in tests involving verbally presentation of word pairs, but also in tests with visual stimuli.

Repetition of pairs of words

I. *Nozh–pero*	II. *Sosna–ochki*	?/I
Nozh–pero	Sosna. . . and something else	I have forgotten.

I. *Stol–noga*	II. *Grom–most*	?/I
Stol–noga	Grom–most	I have forgotten. . . although I just remembered. . . it seems, about noga. . . after it there was noga, and something else. . . and there was grom

After a pause of 5 min, the patient was able to recall both words of the first series by way of reminiscence.

As already stated, at the time the patient was tested he had hardly any difficulty in naming single objects. If required to name pairs of objects, however, the phenomenon of amnesic aphasia was fully apparent. A few examples confirming this statement are given below.

Naming single objects

Key	*Matches*	*Window*	
Key	Matches	Window	
Beard	*Razor*	*Chin*	*Eyelashes*
Beard	Razor	Chin	Eyelashes

Naming pairs of objects

Spectacles–Matches
This is. . . well, that is interesting . . . why is it difficult? I have just told you the separate words. . . but I cannot. . . this was. . . spectacles. . . and. . .

Beard–Ear
Beard. . . the first one. . . well, yes beard. . . and then. . . it seems. . . ear

Razor–Key
Key. . . and the first. . . well, how can I. . . no. . . not knife. . . something like it. . . razor

Eyelashes–Matches
The first was. . . what is it. . . well. . . I can't remember. . . beard. . . that's what it was. . . key. . . no. . . what then? This is something new! When you name two things I can't answer. What can it be? I have always been able to say.

The increased proactive and retroactive inhibition, which disturbed verbal memory, proved to be one of the important mechanisms accounting for the syndrome exhibited by this patient. These defects became apparent only when the patient had to recall visual or verbal forms from memory. If required to pick out a previously presented set of visual stimuli from a larger sample, all his difficulties disappeared and he showed no abnormality whatever. For instance, he could easily recall a series of four or five picture cards from among many others shown to him even 24 hours after the original exposure.

* * *

The disturbance of higher cortical functions in *patient Krap.* has a number of features that resemble the syndrome of audioverbal memory disturbance mentioned above, yet at the same time they differ substantially. The common features are the absence of direct sensory (particularly audioverbal sensory) disorders, severe disturbances of audioverbal memory, and pathologically increased retroactive and proactive inhibition. Both patients could distinguish sounds perfectly and retained the ability to carry out phonemic analysis of speech, to write words, etc. The distinguishing feature in *patient Krap.* was that the trace instability and inhibitability extended to visual as well as auditory stimuli. This fact can be fully explained on the grounds that the lesion present in this patient involved both the posterior temporal and the inferior parietal structures of the dominant hemisphere at their border with the occipital region.

Disturbance of Mnemonic Processes in Lesions of the Fronto-Temporal Systems

So far, I have discussed cases in which mnemonic processes were disturbed as a result of lesions restricted entirely to the temporal region.

Lesions in many patients, however, extend beyond the temporal region to affect the anterior temporal lobe, as well as the posteroinferior and basomedial zones of the frontal lobe. As we have seen, the anterior temporal region maintains intimate connections with the cortical auditory system and can affect the integrity of audioverbal traces. The basomedial cortex of the temporal and frontal region influences diencephalic and reticular systems regulating the general state of cortical excitability. A lesion of this region can result in diverse symptoms including aspontaneity, disinhibition, affective changes, altered consciousness, and inability to plan or carry out actions (Gamper, 1928; Milner, 1958, 1970; Penfield & Milner, 1958; Scoville, 1954; Scoville & Milner, 1957).

I shall analyze two cases with lesions of the fronto-temporal zones of the left hemisphere, who manifested a distinctive syndrome including mnemonic disturbances of speech activity superimposed on a general disturbance in the regulation higher forms of behavior.

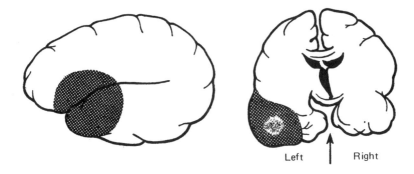

Left ↑ Right

FIG. 12. Location of tumor in patient Shchuk.

Patient Shchuk., a 57-year-old male, was admitted to the Institute of Neurosurgery in April, 1959, with protrusion of the left eyeball, headaches, severe papilledema, and optic atrophy. Neurological investigation showed amaurosis of the left eye with a severe concentric narrowing of the visual field of the right eye, left-sided hypo-osmia, defective function of cranial nerves III, IV and VI on the left, and left amaurosis. Craniography revealed destruction of the greater and lesser wings of the sphenoid bone on the left side, but the shape of the sella turcica was unchanged. The CSF pressure was 360 mm, the protein content 1.32 parts per thousand, and the cell count 2/3. Arteriography showed displacement of the left anterior cerebral artery upward and the middle cerebral artery, posteriorly.

Neuropsychological tests revealed no appreciable disturbances. The patient's praxis, gnosis, and speech were within normal limits. He was slightly inhibited, sluggish in his replies to questions, and very occasionally showed isolated disturbances of the word seeking type, with paraphasia.

The final diagnosis was an arachnoidendothelioma of the lesser wing of the left sphenoid bone. An operation was performed on May 13, 1959, and a large tumor (an arachnoidendothelioma) of this bone was in fact removed. The tumor measured 5 x 6 x 7 cm, and compressed the left frontal and temporal regions. During removal of the tumor, the vessels were not damaged (Figure 12).

After the operation, the patient was apathetic and inactive, but he answered questions. After a week, the disturbances became more severe, the patient became untidy and dirty, he no longer understood what was said to him, and responded by laughing. He ceased to speak and a state resembling total aphasia developed. He became sharply negativistic. This state continued throughout the following weeks.

Three weeks after the operation, two injections of 0.5 ml of 0.5% galanthamine were given 24 hours apart. After the injections, the patient became more lively, he started to articulate individual words clearly, but his speech was limited to echolalic repetition and perseveration. In the days following, stereotyped sentences began to appear: "I don't understand anything at all...," "I beg your pardon...," "God knows...," etc. He remained negativistic and difficult to test. At this time, his praxis remained intact but performance was very unstable and was soon replaced by mirror-image performance or perseveration. He incorporated stereotyped phrases in his actions: "No, I shan't, I shan't any more... there is something I can't understand..." Conversation with the patient was very restricted. He would usually reply to questions with echolalic repetition of the question or a stereotyped reply which was repeated after all subsequent questions.

A detailed investigation showed that he could clearly differentiate between similar phonemes and repeat pairs of correlative phonemes correctly. He could easily repeat single words and sentences, with a remark such as: "I shall always tell you, rest assured. . ." He could repeat series of three, or sometimes four words, but when he attempted to repeat three short phrases, each consisting of two words, he lost some of the components and exhibited contamination (for example, instead of "the house burns, the moon shines, the brush sweeps," he would say "the house burns. . . the brush shines. . ." or "the house burns, the moon shines. . . and something else. . ."

He could understand single words and point to the objects they represented, but if required to do the same with pairs of words (teapot–ball, table–teapot), he could point to only one of the objects and began to show evidence of alienation of word meaning (for example, when saying "ball" he would point to a table, etc.). He could easily name separate objects, but if he had to point to two objects he showed severe features of amnesia. For example, when pointing to separate pictures of a cap and a cupboard he exclaimed: "this is a cap, but this. . . what do they call it. . . it is. . . how shall I say. . .," and when shown the pair table–elephant, he said: "This is a table. . . a child's table. . . and well. . . of course a child could name it. . . and the other one is just as well. . ."

The patient's speech became much more fluent five weeks after the operation although he remained passive and negativistic. He was communicative, but his conversation with people around him was very restricted. Usually his speech would begin only when accompanying an action. He would then say an appropriate phrase quite distinctly, although often habitual expressions crept in: "I don't know. . . I can't understand. . ." or "Well now, as you say, but this is worse," etc. In his attempts to answer questions, the patient usually produced only stereotyped phrases.

Investigation of Mnemonic Processes

The systematic investigation of the patient's mnemonic processes began one month after the operation. At this stage, he could easily copy movements presented visually. On the basis of his visual memory, he could draw copies of two or even three figures. He tired quickly, however, and after a few tests could retain only one figure.

Irrelevant stimuli often intruded into his performance.

For example, on one occasion *patient Shchuk.* was drawing a series of figures from memory and the experimenter said to his assistant: "He does it like Negin (another patient)." The patient immediately introduced the letter "N" into his drawing:

$$\frac{+\bigcirc\triangle}{+\triangle\bigcirc}$$

The experimenter says: like Negin, the patient draws: N$\triangle\bigcirc$. All attempts were accompanied by multiple stereotyped spoken expressions: "No. . . I can't recall. . . why this happens. . .," etc.

Although the patient was capable of copying drawings shown to him, he was almost totally unable to draw in response to spoken instructions. He could draw a circle correctly in response to a spoken instruction, but could not draw a $+$ (cross). Instead, he would draw a letter "y" or an equals sign. He could perform only a few simple tests correctly, and spoiled his performance frequently by perseveration.

Circle ○ It is the letter *o*...	Cross y	Cross =	Cross −	Triangle y	
Window ▭	*Star* +	*Dot* ○	*Plus* +	*Four* 4	*Seven* 7
Zero 0	*Cross* I don't know.	*Eight* 8	*Eleven* 11	*Six* 6	*z* z
B B	*S* S	*N* N	*R* R	*Circle* 6	*Triangle* T
Circle kr	*Circle* k				

(circle = kruzhok)

Carrying out two serial instructions was totally impossible.

By this time, writing was potentially possible but severely disturbed by perseveration and anticipation. For instance, when instructed to write his surname (familiya), he wrote the letter "F," and when asked to write "Shchukin," wrote "Faum..." (contamination with the word "familiya"). Nevertheless, he could write single words or even simple sentences from dictation, only occasionally introducing perseveration.

Write your surname F		Shchukin Faum	Stol Stol	Kot Kot	Okno Okno

Similar perseverations occurred when he wrote numbers from dictation:

24	117	329	1362
24	107	119	1364

By this time, the patient was able to repeat short word series and sentences, to name objects, and to understand the meanings of words (although the difficulties mentioned above still remained). He could repeat a number series echolalically, but had great difficulty in transposing the series into the opposite order. He had difficulty in reciting the months, and he echolalically repeated the rhythm of the original sample. Tell me the months—January, February, etc. "January, February..." and what next... "March, April... I can't rem... I can't remember..." He was quite unable to recite the months backward and soon abandoned all attempts to do so.

Two months after the operation, the patient's speech became much more fluent. He could easily take part in conversation and answer questions. He could repeat single words, sentences, three or four word series, and name individual objects. He found it easy to name pairs of objects and understood the meanings of two words presented as a pair. In spoken conversation, however, he still exhibited some instability, and any interfering stimulus could insinuate itself into the theme of the conversation. For instance, in reply to the question whether he found it difficult to tell a story, he said: "I don't know, it is such a long time since I looked in a mirror" (the patient's glance had fallen on a mirror hanging on the wall).

The same phenomena appeared when he repeated a story. For instance, having repeated the sentence "A hunter killed a wolf on the edge of the forest," the patient told "The Hen and the Golden Eggs" story as follows: "Somehow I can't retain it. . . it is all mixed up. . . on the edge of the forest a hunter lived with a hen and a parson. . ." Only after the second reading could he tell the story: "A man had a hen. . . it had many eggs. . . the eggs were used up. . . and the hen was empty. . . it was almost the same. . ."

He could not develop a theme or tell a story by himself if shown a picture. In such cases, his speech became impoverished and limited to a recitation of direct impressions.

For instance, he described the picture "The hunter" as follows: "A lake in the morning. . . and a dog. . . and everything there. . ." and when asked to develop the theme, he added: "What I told you there. . . the lake in summer. . . a hunter set out to battle (association with the gun). . . well whatever there is. . . the lake, the light. . . shining in the sun. . . some ducks and geese flying, dogs barking. . ." The insistent request that he develop the theme of the picture did not give the desired result, and even after he had been prompted with the opening remark "Early one morning," he said "Early one morning the hunters decided to go for a walk. . ." Go on! "Then they went to a lake. . . they stayed there and went away."

The aspontaneity of his speech processes, the ease with which they were inhibited by interfering influence, and the rapid loss of selectivity remained a characteristic feature of the "dynamic frontal aphasia" which accompanied the symptoms of temporal (acoustico-mnestic) speech disorders.

In the year after the operation, considerable recovery had taken place although the core of the syndrome remained.

At the time of his second examination, the patient was quite well and readily submitted to the investigation. His main complaints were impairment of his memory: "I cannot retain anything. . . I cannot tell a story coherently. . . my wife begs me to tell her something, and I cannot. . ." These complaints were confirmed when the patient was tested. He showed no disturbance of gnosis or praxis.

His hearing was completely intact. He could repeat single words and sentences, name objects, and understand words. No alienation of word meaning was observed. Reading and writing presented no difficulty. He could calculate, although he recited the operations aloud. His understanding of long fragments of speech remained somewhat impaired. Deviations from the text occurred during repetition, although the story as a whole was narrated coherently, without any articulatory, lexical or grammatical difficulties.

The patient showed substantial disturbances in tests requiring the repetition of long word series or a change to spontaneous narrative speech. In such cases, he revealed the central core of the syndrome: Weakness of audioverbal traces superimposed on appreciable defects of spontaneous speech.

As stated above, the patient could repeat a series of four words but was unable to repeat five at a time. Even if he managed to repeat the series after several attempts, the process soon disintegrated. If a short pause was introduced, he lost the order of the series or forgot it altogether. Fatigue had the same effect. The patient was given a series of five words which, after many successive presentations, he repeated as follows:

Dom—les—kot—stol—zvon
(1) Dom—les—kot—zvon—stol
(2) Dom—les—kot—stol—zvon
(3) Dom—les—kot—zvon—stol—zvon

   After a pause of 5 sec, without any additional presentation of the series:

(1) Dom—les. . . no. . . I have forgotten
(2) Dom—les—kot—zvon—stol
(3) Dom—les—zvon. . . no not like that
(4) Dom—les—kot—zvon
(5) Dom—les—kot—zvon—stol, no. . . something is wrong
(6) Dom—les—kot. . . no, I am confused. . .
(7) Dom—les—zvon. . . skot? zvon? dom?

   After a pause of 10 sec:

(1) Dom—les. . . no, impossible. . .
(2) Dom—les—znak. . . no, impossible. . .
(3) Dom—les—zvon. . . but I can't. . .

   After a pause of 10 sec:

(1) Dom—les—zvon. . . no. . .
(2) Dom—les—kot—zvon—stol

A similar pattern was seen if the patient was instructed to write down a series of words dictated to him. Transpositions and the rapid disintegration of the series were observed after a pause.

In contrast, visual presentation of word series was followed not only by their full reproduction, but by much greater stability. An example is given below.

Put'—most—stul—krest—svet (visual presentation)
(1) Put'—most—stul—krest—svet
(2) Put'—most—stul—krest—svet

   After a pause of 10 sec:

Put'—most—stul—krest—svet

   After a pause of 10 sec filled with interfering conversation:

Put'—most—stul—krest—svet

Verbally presented number series were remembered better than words, but a filled pause still obliterated the memory.

3–0–9–8–2	*8–6–1–2–7–4*
After a pause of 10 sec:	After a pause of 10 sec:
3–0–8–9–2	8–6–1–2–7–4

After a pause of 10 sec filled with interfering conversation:

I have forgotten. . .	I don't know. . . I have forgotten. . .

Similar results were observed with repetition of geometrical shapes in response to a dictated instruction or to pictorial presentation. Although a series of dictated words was poorly retained and repeated, spoken instructions about geometrical shapes were retained much better, and if shapes were shown to him, he could repeat them perfectly well.

These observations suggest that not only visual traces, but also traces of verbal instructions remained very stable in this patient, provided they contained a substantial visual representation (like numbers). Instability of audioverbal traces remained the essential component of the syndrome developing after injury to the fronto-temporal zones of the left hemisphere.

These disturbances were associated with severe defects of spontaneous narrative speech, a characteristic feature of the residual-fronto-temporal system. Although the patient could repeat single words and sentences, name objects, and carry out operations requiring manipulation of simple logical-grammatical relations quite well, he was no longer capable of spontaneous narrative speech. When asked to say how he had spent the year since his operation, he could only produce fragmentary stereotypes. The same adynamia of verbal thinking was clearly manifested when he was instructed to give a connected account of a familiar theme. This was quite impossible for him, and he could only undertake the task in the form of answers to questions. An example of the records demonstrating this fact clearly is given below.

Tell the story of "Evgenii Onegin. "I don't know. . . it is very difficult for me to say. . . I can't find. . . it is all wrong. . ." *Tell me the main features. . .* "I don't know what to call the main. . . I don't know how to start. From the beginning to the end. . . now I am confused. . . I know it all but I can't tell you. . . my wife is always trying to make me tell, but I can't." However, the theme of the "Evgenii Onegin" story was easily told as answers to questions.

When does the action start? "One summer morning." *What happens?* "A new friendship." *Who becomes friendly with whom?* "The guests, among them Evgenii Onegin, become friendly with the Larins.", and so on.

Now tell me the whole story from the beginning to end. "Once upon a time. . . now it is all wrong. . . oh dear, I can't understand. . . everything has vanished. . ." One summer day. . . "Do you think I can tell you?. . . I have no idea. . ."

We still do not know the physiological basis of this curious phenomenon—why answers to separate questions are possible although the coherent, complete narration of the story is completely disrupted. The explanation of this phenomenon as a disturbance of the patient's activity (Kleist, 1936), widely accepted in clinical practice, is not adequate because it is contradicted by the preservation of other, nonverbal forms of active behavior. More probably the disturbance of internal speech disrupts the conversion of the original draft plan into expanded external speech.

* * *

If fronto-temporal lesions involve the hippocampus and amygdala, the preceding syndrome may be complicated by severe disturbances of consciousness, although the symptoms of diminished activity and audioverbal traces instability remain prominent. As an example, I shall describe a patient with an intracerebral tumor of the left fronto-temporal region.

Patient Neg., a 46-year-old male, right-handed, was admitted in February, 1959, to the Institute of Neurosurgery in a serious condition with signs of depression, adynamia, constant headaches, and obvious disturbances of mental activity.

In November, 1958, he began to have headaches accompanied by nausea and vomiting, loss of vision, and severe worsening of memory. In December, the patient's condition deteriorated; his memory changed so much that he forgot the names of his friends, was unable to find the way out of the garage, and had to give up his job as a driver.

In January, 1959, at the Neurological Hospital, he was inhibited and apathetic. Examination revealed slight paresis of the right facial nerve as well as hyperreflexia and pathological reflexes on the right side. Sensation remained normal. The optic discs were hyperemic with commencing papilledema, and later the discs became choked. The CSF pressure was 160 mm; the CSF itself was xanthochromic and contained 1.98 parts per thousand of protein and a cell count of 81/3.

Additional examination at the Institute of Neurosurgery indicated he was slightly disoriented and confused. He had a bilateral Kernig's sign and neck rigidity, his field of vision was limited slightly in the upward direction, with paresis of ocular movements to the left and coarse nystagmus to the left. There was paresis of the right facial nerve with a slight diminution of strength in the right hand, and tremor of the hands with increased tone in the right hand. Electroencephalography revealed a distinct focus of pathological activity (slow waves) in the left fronto-temporal region combined with severe general cerebral changes reflected in slowing of the rhythms. The patient evidenced speech disorders with word perseverations, and difficulty understanding speech. Besides his disorientation, he was insufficiently aware of his own state.

Diagnosis: Intracerebral tumor of the left fronto-temporal region.

Upon operation, a large tumor and cyst were found subcortically at a depth of 4 cm in the middle zones of the left frontal region, extending anteriorly to the premotor area. The cyst communicated with the anterior horn of the left lateral ventricle. The tumor involved the dorsal, lateral, and part of the ventral wall of the left lateral ventricle and spread toward the base of both the anterior temporal lobe and basal ganglia (Figure 13). The tumor was removed subtotally; the part in the temporal lobe was left behind. Histologically, the tumor was an angioreticuloma.

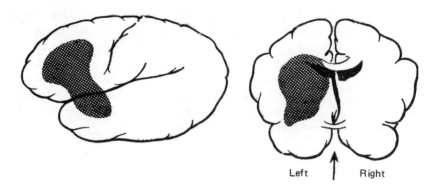

Left   Right

FIG. 13. Location of tumor in patient Neg.

Neuropsychological investigation of this patient disclosed a distinct fronto-temporal syndrome which was followed after the operation. Before the operation, the patient was apathetic, adynamic, and inadequately oriented in time. He knew he was in the hospital but could not state clearly why he was there and of what he was complaining. He could not tell his age, nor state he had recently come to Moscow from Kishinev. He said he had been in Moscow since the age of 18, and was born in 1912, but at the same time stated he was 35 years old. He could not give the date of his examination, gave the wrong month and year and, finally, he declared: "No... I am confused about everything..." His replies to questions were often mixed with perseverations. When asked from where he had come, immediately after he had been instructed to write down the word "okoshko," he answered, "from Okoshko," quite unaware of the absurdity of his answer.

In Head's test, he often substituted mirror-images or perseverations for the correct position of the hands, but sometimes corrected his mistakes. He could copy rhythmic groups satisfactorily, but when required to change from one group to another he often began to perseverate. His phonemic hearing was undisturbed, but immediately slipped into different combinations of sounds (for example, replacing the meaningless combination "na-ba" by the meaningful "pal-ka (a stick)?...."). He could repeat single words without any articulatory difficulty. The repetition of word series was very difficult. He found it hard to retain the proper order, and having once made a mistake, repeated it stereotypically. He perseverated, replaced a word with one of similar sound, and mixed systems of words.

Dom–stol–kot–les
(1) Dom–les–kot–stol
(2) Dom–kot–stol–les
(3) Dom–kot–stol–les
(4) Dom–kot–stol–les

3–0–9–8–2
(1) 3–9–0–9–9–9, les
(2) 3–9, lebed, stol
(3) 3–9–lebed–dom... 9

Similar difficulties appeared when he attempted to repeat a sentence.

Apple trees grew in the garden behind the high fence.
Apple trees grew in the garden behind the high fence.
A hunter killed a wolf on the edge of the forest.
(1) Wolves at the edge of the forest... no, once again
(2) Okushchik (he means okhotnik a hunter) killed a wolf at the edge of the forest...
What is an "okushchik"? I don't know.

These defects could be overcome after several repetitions.

The naming of pictured objects was not particularly difficult, but if asked to name a pair of objects (or pictures), he could name one but not the other. If he then moved to another pair, he began to exhibit perseveration.

Naming pictures of single objects

Baby	*Table*	*Thermometer*	*Tumbler*	*Spade*	*Plane*
Baby	Table	Thermometer	Tumbler	Spade	Plane

Naming series of two pictures

Beetle–Goose	*Fort–Cock*	*Puppy–Clock*
Rock... rocket	Goose... and fork	Clock and... rocket... I mean clock... I am confused.

Naming pictures of single objects

Melon	*Bicycle*	*Fork*	*Cock*	*Clock*
Melon	Bicycle	Fork	Cock	Clock

The patient could understand single words, and perseverated only if tired. Retention of two words was much more difficult. When instructed to point to his eye—nose, ear—eye, etc., he usually could carry out only one of these instructions, declaring he had forgotten the second, or pointing incorrectly to the second object (most frequently with perseveration).

Having performed the first simple instruction, he was often unable to carry out any subsequent instructions, but inertly repeated the same action, quite unaware of his mistakes. This pathological inertia was also evident in tests involving writing words. Often just picking up a pencil was sufficient to cause him to repeat habitual expressions ("uvazhaemyi" is the usual opening word of a letter, i.e., "Dear...""). A record of one such test is given in Figure 14.

The perseveration and weakness of audioverbal traces so acutely obvious when carrying out spoken instructions were much less distinct and sometimes absent altogether if he had to copy from a visual specimen.

The graphic record of tests in which the patient either copied shapes directly or drew them from visual memory after the specimen had been shown for 3 to

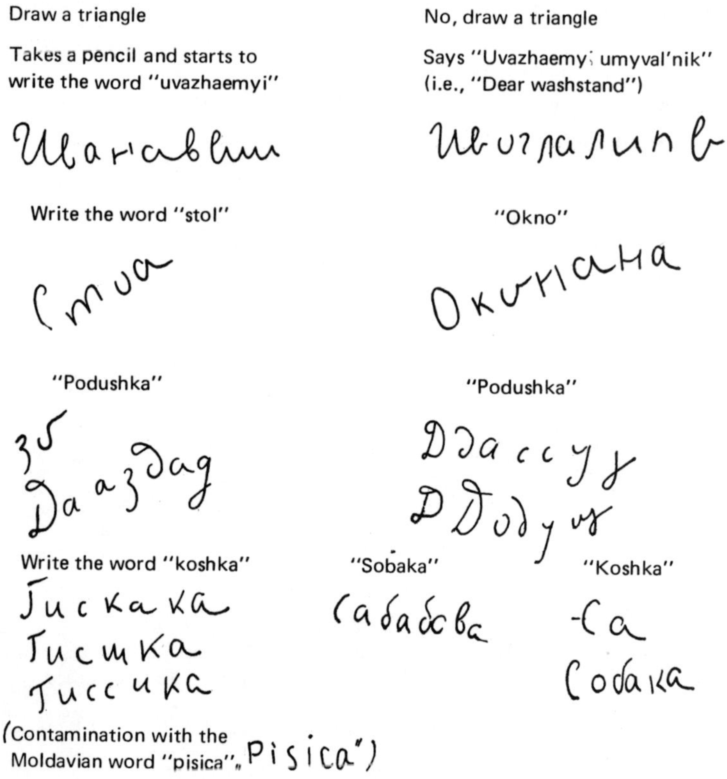

Draw a triangle

Takes a pencil and starts to
write the word "uvazhaemyi"

No, draw a triangle

Says "Uvazhaemy; umyval'nik"
(i.e., "Dear washstand")

Write the word "stol"

"Okno"

"Podushka"

"Podushka"

Write the word "koshka"   "Sobaka"   "Koshka"

(Contamination with the
Moldavian word "pisica", Pisica")

FIG. 14. Inert stereotype writing by patient Neg. (having written a word
once, he perseverates it and cannot change to drawing).

4 sec is illustrated in Figure 15. Clearly, the elements of perseveration are
manifested only during copying of a series of several shapes, and even then they
were less marked than when carrying out spoken instructions. The pathological
inertia was manifested particularly strongly when he was tired, especially if he
had to switch from one system of actions (writing) to another (drawing).

The pathological inertia affected not only movements, but also perception
and, in particular, reading. He could easily read single digits and even numbers
consisting of two or three digits. He found it difficult, however, to switch from
one number to another. Inertia could be observed between systems, with the
result that words presented after numbers were often read as numbers if there
was some slight graphic similarity between the individual elements of the
problem.

24	47	64	25	108	219
24	41	62	25	401	419
214	Kot	Noch'	Most	Okno	Kot
214	Kat	401	400	Four noughts	Three noughts

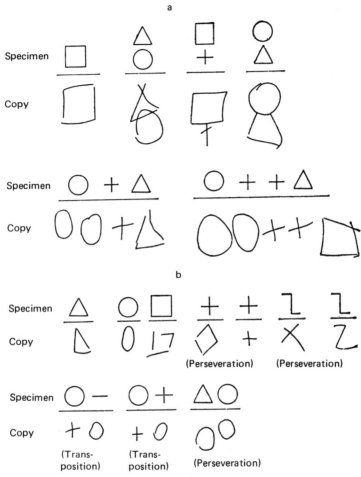

FIG. 15. Copying shapes by patient Neg.: a) drawing geometrical shapes from a specimen picture; b) repeating geometrical shapes from memory after visual presentation.

Pathological inertia of previous stereotypes led to considerable disturbance of more complex intellectual processes. In principle, the patient could perform elementary arithmetical operations in his head (12 + 6 = "18"; 14 + 7 = "21"; 12 + 6 − 2 = "12 + 6..."; 18 − 2 = "16"). The pathological inertia soon began to interfere with performance, and these operations were replaced by the inert repetition of a previous reply.

   12 − 15 = "17"; 8 + 1 = "12... and 8... and 11..." 8 + 1 = "8..." 23 − 6 = "23 − 6... 23... I mean, 23... 23 − 6... that will be 23"; 31 − 14 = "31 − 14... 31 − 14... 31... how many? 6?... is that 14?... take away 14... that will be 31... 14 − 31... 31 − 14... that will be 14... I was so confused."

The disturbances of higher cortical functions observed before the operation constituted a definite fronto-temporal syndrome. Besides distinct adynamia of his psychological processes and pathological inertia, his audioverbal memory was unstable but visually guided behavior better preserved. The patient's lack of critical awareness and inability to correct his mistakes added to these defects.

* * *

The syndrome just described could result from both local influences and much more general factors (increased intracranial pressure, displacement of the brain, toxic effects) that created an unfavorable environment for the higher cortical functions. It was extremely interesting, therefore, to study the changes in these symptoms after the operation, which greatly reduced the intensity of these supplementary factors.

After the operation the syndrome continued even when the patient's condition improved and his confused state of consciousness had regressed considerably. When the patient was tested one month and six weeks after the operation, his consciousness was fully restored. He knew that he had been in the hospital for a long time, although he could not state how long. He remembered nothing about the operation and considered that he had very probably met with an accident. He could not name the month or the year and he very quickly drifted into perseverations (what year is it now?) "1960. . . no, 1951. . . now it is from the first year. . . ," etc.). He knew he was in Moscow, but could not state exactly either the name of the hospital or its address, but simply remarked that "he could not remember anything in his life."

As before, the principal types of praxis were intact, although the movements that he copied were quickly replaced by perseveration or mirror-images. He could repeat rhythms, but they also were quickly replaced by perseveration. He repeated separate words faultlessly, but soon became tired when repeating word series. He had no difficulty in naming single objects or pictures of them, but if required to name two pictures shown simultaneously he would either transpose them or perseverate.

Elephant—cup		*Cap—bucket*		*Automobile—scissors*	
It is a cup.	It is an	It is an	It is a cup.	It is a body.	It is a pair
	elephant.	elephant.			of scissors.

Flag—elephant
It is an elephant. . .
I am confused.

As before, the patient could understand the meaning of separate words, and point to objects named. After frequent repetition of the same words, however, he soon ceased to point correctly and began stereotyped repetitions. He soon gave up pointing to pairs of named objects, and instead he said inactively: "There isn't one here."

When requested to do so by the experimenter, he correctly drew a circle. The stereotype became so inert and the instability of verbal meanings so pronounced that he began to carry out all subsequent instructions incorrectly. He repeated the same shape without being aware of any mistake. These defects were in sharp contrast to his ability to perform actions in response to visual stimuli. Even the repetition of a complex series of visual instructions (for example, pointing to the second, third, and fifth or to the fourth, first, and sixth objects of a row) was quite within his capacity despite the fact that pointing to named objects led to rapid alienation of word meaning and perseveration. The patient could easily draw a series of two shapes, but had some difficulty with three, particularly, when required to draw them from memory. These symptoms match the previous syndrome quite closely.

One year later, the patient was readmitted to the Institute of Neurosurgery in a much worse condition, with severe depression, inhibition, untidiness, right-sided hemiparesis especially of the upper limb, reflexes of oral automatism, and gross speech disorders which made communication impossible. The electroencephalogram revealed gross pathological slow waves, especially marked in the left fronto-temporal region.

On January 15, 1960, the patient died from congestive cardiac failure. Autopsy revealed a tumor (angioreticuloma with a cyst) occupying nearly the entire left temporal lobe and spreading into the frontal lobe. It obliterated the anterior horns of the lateral ventricles and replaced the caudate nuclei and the centrum semiovale.

* * *

In both patients with left frontal-temporal lesions the syndrome consisted of unstable audioverbal memory, superimposed on general adynamia and defects of spontaneous, narrative speech. In both cases, defects appeared only when the patient had to repeat series of words, or perform operations requiring a switch from one element (word or action) to another. Under these conditions, clearly defined perseverations appeared. The mnemonic defects were manifested predominantly in the audioverbal system and the repetition of series of shapes (letters or numbers) in response to visual stimuli was much more reliable. The syndrome has clearly distinguishable components of both temporal and frontal dysfunction.

Each patient also showed distinctive features which, in all probability, were attributable primarily to the character and situation of the lesion. In the first patient, the disturbance resulted from trauma inflicted during the removal of an arachnoidendothelioma of the sphenoid bone. In the second patient, there was a rapidly growing intracerebral tumor, located by the ventricle. In the first patient, this complex series of disturbances was superimposed on a lucid state of consciousness, but in the second patient, consciousness was grossly upset, orientation in place and time was clearly disturbed, and he was unaware of his state and surroundings.

Conclusions

We have examined data based on a consecutive series of cases in which the focus (usually a tumor) was located in the depth of the anterior, middle, or posterior temporal region, as well as the left fronto-temporal system. Unlike most patients with deep brain lesions involving medial cortex and the upper brain stem, none of the patients with deep temporal lesions had disturbances of consciousness associated with their mnemonic defects.

Except those with massive frontal-temporal lesions, these patients were afflicted to some degree or other with acoustico-mnestic aphasia.

Their primary symptom was a disturbance of modality-specific audioverbal memory. Although their motor, visuo-spatial, and emotional-personal memory remained relatively intact and their motives and plans were well preserved, they were unable to retain audioverbal stimuli. These defects were usually only slightly evident with single sounds or words, but became clear in tests involving series of several (usually three or four) audioverbal elements. Characteristically, the basic group of patients could not repeat a fairly long series of audioverbal elements, but they had no significant difficulty in repeating a similar series of visual stimuli (for example, drawings of shapes). This basic fact indicates that the mnemonic disturbances were specific disturbances of audioverbal memory.

The basic mechanisms of these modality-specific forms of memory disturbance appear to be similar to those responsible for the more general memory defects described earlier in this book. Recall, rather than acquisition or retention, appears to be the primary difficulty, and increased inhibition by interfering or competing stimuli the primary cause of that difficulty.

In the patients described in this chapter, the basic factor disrupting recall of audioverbal traces (the inhibitory effect of interference) may perhaps be combined with direct weakness of the audioverbal traces themselves and/or their increased decay. At present, this suggestion lacks proof and will require further investigation (Klimkovskii, 1965).

This investigation demonstrates the way in which the character of the mnemonic disorder depends on the location of the pathological focus. If the focus is in the left temporal pole and does not involve the middle zones (as in the first patient I described), audioverbal memory may not be disrupted at all.

If the focus involves both the anterior and middle zones of the left temporal region, no acoustico-gnostic disturbances arise, but modality-specific disturbances of audioverbal memory are manifested in full. Similar cases have been described both by myself and my colleagues in my laboratory (Klimkovskii, 1965; Luria, 1947; Luria & Karaseva, 1968). When a focus in the middle zones of the left temporal region spreads posteriorly, involving structures in the occipital and parieto-occipital region, the modality-specific memory disturbances become more complex and involve both audioverbal and visual stimuli (optical aphasia) (Luria, 1969).

Finally, if the pathological focus includes areas deep in the left frontal lobe as well as the anterior temporal region, the mnemonic disturbance is superimposed on general adynamia and an inability to maintain plans and intentions—typical of patients with massive lesions of the frontal lobes (Luria, 1962, 1963, 1969; Luria & Khomskaya, 1966). The patients replace active recall with inert stereotypes. The disturbance of memory in this case is not so strictly modality-specific, for disturbances of motor traces are also present, but the disruption does not necessarily lead to general disturbances of consciousness.

* * *

The material described above is only the first stage in the neuropsychological study of the basic forms of mechanism of memory disturbance arising in patients with local brain lesions.

In the second part of this book, I shall examine the clinical syndromes of memory disturbances in patients with deep brain lesions, attempt to describe the variants of disorders of memory and consciousness arising in such patients, and relate them to the parts of the brain involved in the pathological process.

Introduction to the Second Part

In the first part of the book I described and analyzed the forms of memory disturbance arising from local brain lesions. I showed that active memorizing starts from definite motives, that the memorizing process may differ in complexity, and that it often includes organization of the material into known systems. I also showed that the reproduction (or recall) of the material is distinguished by a complex psychological structure. As a rule, the recalling process involves choosing from a series of possible alternatives and inhibiting interfering associations. Finally, we saw that the structure of recall and repetition does not remain constant, but may vary in complexity at different levels of memory. Each brain system makes its own special contribution to mnemonic activity, so that lesions in different parts of the brain give rise to different disturbances of memory.

The description of the various forms and mechanisms of memory disturbances arising in patients with local brain lesions represents only half of the neuropsychological investigation of mnemonic disorders. The other half consists of describing the syndromes of disturbances in memory, consciousness, and psychological activity that arise from local brain lesions. A general syndrome analysis was presented in chapter 3. Detailed analyses of specific cases which typify particular syndromes will be presented in the chapters that follow. These descriptions go far beyond the narrow study of mnemonic processes into the wider sphere concerning relationships between memory and consciousness as a whole. The syndrome analysis of memory disturbances in local brain lesions also provides better perspective on the clinical reality that is the essence of neurological science.

As is well known, classical neurology used the detailed monographic analysis of syndromes arising in particular local brain lesions as the principal method of its work. This detailed analysis of individual cases, describing the logic of syndrome construction, provided the classical neurologists with an approach to the understanding of the role of particular brain structures in human psychological activity, and identified characteristics necessary for the diagnosis of brain lesions.

This was the method followed in the classical investigations of aphasia, notably in the work of Broca and Wernicke, Jackson and Head, and Goldstein and his school. One example of the same approach to the study of memory disturbances in local brain lesions is given by the work of Scoville and Milner (1957), who described the syndrome of memory disorder in hippocampal lesions that serves as the basis for many modern views on the neuropsychology of memory.

Clinical investigation always rests on a limited number of cases with clearly marked variations in the observed symptoms. That is why the ordinary methods of statistical analysis are not generally useful in this branch of science. The detailed description of syndromes, with comparison and correlation of the disturbances composing those syndromes, provides another way of ensuring reliability despite the relatively limited samples. I have argued in support of this approach elsewhere (Luria & Artem'eva, 1970).

In the present analysis, I have deliberately disregarded the pathogenesis of the syndromes studied and have included patients with brain tumors and injuries as well as those with memory disturbances resulting from ruptured aneurysms accompanied by hemorrhage and spasm of the blood vessels.

The general principle of investigation remains, as before, the neuropsychological analysis of syndromes of memory disturbance in local brain lesions. Therefore, when describing these syndromes we need consider only those clinical symptoms that owe their origin to the location of the focus, to its size, and to the disturbances of the circulation of the blood and cerebrospinal fluid that appear on account of the focus.

There is strong reason to suppose that tumors or hemorrhages leading to a disturbance around the "circle of Papez," to lesions of the hippocampus, or involving various parts of the frontal lobes, may give rise to different syndromes of memory disturbance. The comparative analysis of the syndromes arising in such patients must assist with the analysis of the role of each of these formations in human memory processes. The same analysis will assist in differentiating the syndromes of memory disturbance and indicate the essentially different forms of mnemonic disorder that are included in what was previously described as the single "Korsakov's syndrome."

* * *

All that remains is briefly to discuss the concrete problems to be considered in the ensuing pages and to underline those details on which I shall dwell in my subsequent analysis. We are well aware that all disturbances in the function of deep brain structures inevitably lead to lowered cortical tone and fluctuations between sleep and wakefulness, and that these changes affect the course of mnemonic activity and lead to modality-nonspecific disorders of memory. In some cases, these memory disturbances are apparently of a primary, isolated character, unaccompanied by any general disturbance of consciousness. Pathologically increased inhibitability of traces is not accompanied by disorientation in place and time, or by confusion or confabulations. In other cases, the memory disturbances form part of a different syndrome associated with disorientation and confabulations.

The description of these two syndromes could greatly increase our knowledge of modality-nonspecific disturbances of memory and could help to shed light on one of the most difficult problems in neuropsychology and clinical neurology—the relationship between memory and consciousness. This problem cannot be solved by a single investigation, but it is one of the main purposes of this volume to make an initial approach.

Pathologically increased inhibitability of traces by interfering factors is an important physiological mechanism of the memory disturbances in pathological states of the brain. Facts confirming this statement were described in sufficient detail in the first part of this book. The form of these memory disturbances observed in different syndromes, and the mechanism through which selective recall is disturbed, remains a problem. In some cases, the inhibitory effect of interfering factors produces only temporary blocking of previous traces. If the subject is distracted by interfering activity, he will be unable to recall traces just formed, yet at the same time they are not replaced by interfering irrelevant associatons. It is in such cases that we can speak of "pure" or "primary" disturbances of memory.

These cases differ sharply from others in which attempts to recall soon begin to be replaced by the uncontrollable outpouring of irrelevant associations. In these cases, the memorizing process is easily contaminated with traces of past experience, or with traces of direct impressions, so that memorizing loses its selective character. I have already postulated that the physiological mechanism of this disturbance of selectivity is a pathological "phasic" state of the cortex in which the excitability of traces of different strengths becomes equalized and their recall loses its organized character.

Finally, in the first part of this book, I included cases in which the main obstacle to the active, organized recall of traces was a disturbance of the normal mobility of nervous processes; when excitation, once it had arisen, became so inert that the traces easily replaced all the other newly formed associations. In these cases, the actual process of trace formation remained unaffected, but the main obstacle to recalling was the pathological inertia of established stereotypes.

The three forms of disturbance of general, modality-nonspecific memory just described are different. They are based on different mechanisms, and can be components of different syndromes of memory disturbance associated with lesions of different parts of the brain. My plan in writing this book was to first examine syndromes in which a predominant place is occupied by primary disturbances of memory, which may be temporary and fluctuating, or permanent and constant; next, to describe cases in which memory disturbances are accompanied by the loss of selectivity as a result of the equalization of excitability of the various systems of associations; finally, to consider cases in which the disturbance of memory is based on the pathological inertia of established traces.

Although these three mechanisms of memory disorder may be intimately connected, in some cases one of them will be dominant. If we can relate these cases to the location of the focus, its size, or general dynamic background we will have made a significant contribution to the syndrome analysis of the disturbances under consideration.

I shall turn to these problems when I examine my data, but for the time being I shall concentrate on the syndromes of memory disorders arising in a patient with fluctuating cortical tone, after which I shall turn to the description of static memory disturbances in patients with massive deep brain tumors, giving rise to general disorders of consciousness. I shall finish my analysis with an examination of cases in which the deep zones of the frontal lobes are involved in the pathological process.

In my description of syndromes, I shall adhere to the methods used in the first part of my investigation. My plan is to test the retention and recall of traces of different modalities, to study the retention and recall of material differing in degree of semantic organization, and then test reproduction after various intervals, in some cases occupied by interfering factors.

CHAPTER V

Primary Disturbances of Memory in Tumors of The Third Ventricle

Of all forms of memory disturbance, those of the purest character are the primary modality-nonspecific disturbances observed in patients with deep brain tumors located chiefly in the upper levels of the brain stem, the third ventricle, and the limbic region. These disturbances are closely linked with changes in cortical tone. They are characterized by fluctuations between states of sleep and wakefulness, and therefore, may be somewhat unstable, ranging from the almost total absence of mnemonic defects to gross disturbances of memorizing and recall. As a rule, they are associated with adequate preservation of consciousness and are unaccompanied either by disorientation or by confabulations. The patients remain critically aware of their disability. Their memory defects are associated with only minimal disturbances of selective, goal-directed, intellectual activity and with the full preservation of gnosis, praxis, and speech.

I propose to give a detailed analysis of one patient with such a memory disturbance whom I had under observation for a long time. I shall describe the fluctuations in the mnemonic disorders observed in this patient, and then go on to discuss similar patients in whom the syndrome of primary memory disturbances occurred in a stable form.

Patient Snyatk.[17], a 35-year-old female (a senior researcher at an academic chemical research laboratory), was admitted to the Institute of Neurosurgery in

[17]This patient was studied by Drs. T. O. Faller and L. I. Moskovichute.

March, 1971, with the diagnosis of a suspected cystic tumor of the third ventricle.

On her first admission, her symptoms were very vague and she was discharged without an operation. She was readmitted two months later with signs of increasing intracranial pressure and definite worsening of her general clinical condition, but again no operation was performed. After a further two months, the patient was admitted for the third time to the Institute of Neurosurgery with symptoms indicating compression of the brain stem. This time, an operation was performed and it revealed a cyst in the cavity of the third ventricle. Tests carried out during the three weeks after the operation reflected regression of the symptoms. Finally, six months after the operation, the patient was admitted for the fourth time to the Institute of Neurosurgery because of impairment of vision, indicating that the pathological process had spread to the basal zones of the frontal lobe.

First Admission. Mild Memory Disturbances

For 10 years, she had complained of migraine headaches. In January, 1970, she developed amenorrhea, insomnia, general weakness, and impaired eyesight, and she noticed some disturbance of memory. In the 2½ months before admission to the Institute of Neurosurgery, metabolic disturbances appeared and she became very stout. At the same time she observed changes in the character of her sleep, the vivid dreams that had usually been a feature of her sleep disappeared and she became emotionally placid.

On admission to the Institute of Neurosurgery, examination revealed a marked right-sided temporal anopia (R 0.7, L 0.03), but the results varied from one test to another. There was no evidence of papilledema or of increased intracranial pressure (CSF pressure 170 mm water). Sensation was diminished in the nose and there were distinct disturbances of identification of odors on the left. Marked paresis of the left facial nerve of the central type was present and there was slight weakness of the left upper limb. Sensation was normal.

Pneumo-cisternography revealed narrowing of the space between the cerebral peduncles and chiasma. The lateral ventricles were slightly hydrocephalic and no air entered the third ventricle (Figure 16). These findings indicated the presence of a tumor in the third ventricle acting on the hypothalamus and diencephalon.

Neurophysiological tests (N. A. Filippycheva), during the first admission when her mental state was quite normal, showed a marked decrease in bioelectrical activity of the ascending reticular activating formation (very high amplification was required to record the EEG). Synchronous groups of δ-waves were obtained in the frontal regions. Desynchronization of cortical electrical activity was considerably depressed by both meaningless and meaningful stimulation. No psychogalvanic, electroencephalographic, or plethysmographic response occurred to a spoken instruction to shake hands. Sometimes when responses to instructions did arise they disappeared abnormally rapidly, but motor responses became pathologically protracted.

It was concluded that this patient had marked signs of diencephalic dysfunction.

Neuropsychological tests carried out at this period showed clearly defined memory disturbances associated with some flattening of the emotions, but complete preservation of praxis, gnosis, and intellectual activity.

The patient was fully oriented in place and time and critically aware of her defects. All she complained of was loss of memory ("I have started to forget

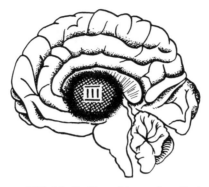

FIG. 16. Position of tumor in patient Snyatk.

everything; I can keep nothing in my mind; I have to write everything down; often I forget people I have met."). These defects were clearly apparent in hospital—the patient did not recognize members of the staff who had tested her the day before, she denied that her relatives had visited her a few hours previously, etc. All these defects fluctuated, being worse on some days and milder on others.

Mnemonic Disorders

The usual experimental psychological investigation of the patient's memory during this period showed no appreciable evidence of mnemonic disorders. Learning a 10-word series was within high normal limits (7-7-9-9-9-9-9-9-10).

She easily memorized a group of three geometrical figures, three phonemes or three words, and after memorizing a second similar group she could easily recall the first. None of these tests revealed any signs of disturbed memory or pathologically increased inhibition. Similar results were obtained in a test of story recall except that when required to relate three stories consecutively she showed signs of forgetting the third story. This was aggravated by the introduction of interfering factors. A record of this tests is given below.

Test 1

Three stories were read to the patient: "The Jackdaw and the Pigeons"[18], "The Lion and the Mouse"[19], and "The Lion and the Fox"[20]. The patient easily repeated each story,

[18] A jackdaw heard that the pigeons had plenty of food, and so painted herself white and flew to the pigeon house. The pigeons thought that she was a pigeon and took her in. She could not restrain herself, however, and cried like a jackdaw. The pigeons then saw that she was a jackdaw and sent her away. She flew back to her own family but they did not recognize her and they also sent her away.

[19] A lion was asleep. A mouse ran over his body and awoke him. The lion seized the mouse who begged him to let her go. The lion laughed and did so. Next day a hunter

(Footnotes continued on page 216)

and had no difficulty in drawing the appropriate moral. When next she was asked to repeat each story separately, she could easily do so for the first and second, but said that she had forgotten what the third story was about. With a little prompting, however, she was able to recall the third story also.

The patient was then given interfering tasks (repeating sounds or letters, remembering geometric figures). When, immediately after, she was asked what stories had been read, she exclaimed: "No, I have forgotten. . . something about a crow, painted herself a different color. . . nothing else. . . but. . . it seems there was a mouse, a lion and a hunter. . . but I can't tell you anything else. . ." *What was the third story?* "I can't remember." *Was it about a lion?, about a hen?, about a bear?, about a fox?* "One story was about a lion. . ." *And what about another story?* "No." *Something about a lion and a fox?* "Yes, of course, it was. . ." (She then recalled the story and told it correctly.)

Tests on this patient, at this period, thus revealed only very mild defects of memorizing, especially under the influence of interfering activity, when she easily forgot the theme of the story, although in fact her performance was within normal limits.

Much clearer disturbances of memory were revealed two days later, when the patient complained that she felt unwell (a "bad day"). When asked what stories had been read two days previously, after a pause of reflection, she answered that only one story, "The Lion and the Mouse," had been read, and no others. Tests on that day showed that the efficiency of memorizing material was much lower than in the previous test, and the ease with which recall of verbal material was inhibited by interfering factors was much greater. For instance, the patient was no longer able to recall a group of three words after repeating a second similar group; she mixed up the order of words in a series, and only after the third repetition of the test was she able to perform it correctly.

A test of repetition of three sentences gave similar results.

Test 2

Three sentences were read in succession to the patient: (1) In Tashkent there was a severe earthquake and many houses were destroyed. (2) In Tushino there was an air display with parachute jumps from airplanes. (3) A hunter killed a wolf on the edge of the forest. After the patient had repeated each sentence separately, she was asked to repeat them again in order. She had no difficulty in recalling the first two, but when asked for the third sentence she explained: "Something about a wolf, but what I have forgotten."

(Footnotes continued)
caught the lion and tied him with a rope to a tree. The mouse came up stealthily, gnawed through the rope, and set the lion free.

[20] A lion grew old and could no longer catch animals for food. He decided he must live by cunning: He lay in his lair and pretended to be ill. Animals came up to him and he ate them. A fox approached but did not enter the lair. The lion asked, "Why don't you come in?" The fox replied, "I can see footprints going into your lair but I cannot see any coming out."

The defects of her memory were more obvious in story recall. The stories "The Hen and the Golden Eggs"[21] and "The Ant and the Pigeon"[22] were read. She easily repeated each story, but when asked to recall the first story again, she hesitated and said she had forgotton it. Only after prompting (*something about a hen?*) was she able to repeat it.

Second Admission. Marked Disturbances of Memory

Three months later, when the patient was readmitted, the general pattern of neurological symptoms was much more marked and the memory defects had become much clearer.

She complained of headaches, increased general weakness, and proneness to fatigue. The optic discs were choked. The patient's range of interest was narrowed; she no longer read, her emotional reactions were weaker, she often fell into a state of drowsiness, was inactive and less critical of her condition. These phenomena were still not constant, but fluctuated from day to day. A tremor of the hands was present, more severe on the left, and accompanied by hypomimia. As before, the reflexes were normal, and sensation and movements were undisturbed.

Ventriculography with Myodil revealed a nodular filling defect of the third ventricle, narrowing its lumen. The exit from the third ventricle was partly blocked. Electroencephalography showed definite deterioration. The predominance of slow activity was more marked, indicating the effect of a deep tumor. On July 14, 1971 Torkildsen's operation was performed without significant success.

Mnemonic Disorders

Neuropsychological tests still showed no disturbance of higher cortical functions, but revealed considerable disturbance of memory and an increased general tendency toward fatigue. The memory disturbances continued to fluctuate, and in response to additional stimulation partial compensation was possible.

The patient was still able to learn a series of 10 words and the learning curve did not differ from the previous one. Tests involving memorizing two groups of words and then recalling them separately showed appreciable worsening of her memory. She could not retain a 3-word series securely, and additional interfering activity led to marked inhibition of the traces. Records illustrating this fact are given below.

---

[21] A man had a hen which laid golden eggs. But he wanted to get more gold at once. He cut open the hen but found nothing inside. It was just like any other hen.

[22] An ant went down to a stream to drink. The water covered him and he began to drown. A pigeon flew by and threw him a twig into the river. He climbed on to the twig and was saved. Next day a hunter spread nets to catch the pigeon. When the hunter took the pigeon from the net, the ant crawled up and bit him on the arm. The hunter cried out, the pigeon freed itself and flew away.

Test 3

The patient was asked to repeat two groups of three words and to recall them later.

		?/I	?/II
I. *Pen'—metla—myach*	II. *Krug—luch—zvon*		
(1) Correctly	Correctly	Correctly	Correctly

(Interfering activity introduced—counting backward from 102 in 13s)

		?/I	?/II
(2) Correctly	Correctly	Correctly	Stol—kot. . . no, zvon

(Interfering activity introduced—mentioned five pointed objects)

		?/I	?/II
(3) Correctly	Correctly	Stol—metla— myach	Luch. . . I can't remember

		?/I	?/II
		Correctly	Correctly

(Interfering activity introduced—counting backward from 100 in 13s)

		?/I	?/II
		Krym. . . more. . . myach. . .	. . .

This phenomenon was seen more clearly still when the test was repeated a week later.

		?/I	?/II
I. *Son—okno—myach*	II. *Zvon—luch—les*		
(1) Correctly	Correctly	Correctly	Correctly

(Interfering activity introduced—counting backward from 100 in 7s)		?/I Son—okno—luch	?/II I have forgotten. . .
(2) Correctly	Correctly	Correctly	Correctly

(Interfering activity introduced—choose 5 words starting with the letter K)		?/I I have forgotten.	?/II I have forgotten.
(3) Correctly	Correctly	?/I Correctly	?/II Correctly

(Interfering activity introduced—solving arithmetical examples)		?/I Zvon—okno—luch	?/II I have forgotten.
(4) Correctly	Correctly	?/I Correctly	?/II Correctly

(Interfering activity introduced—solving arithmetical examples)		?/I There were numbers? *No, words*. There were no words.	?/II I don't know. (The patient had forgotten she had been given words to memorize.)

This record shows that the introduction of interfering activity was sufficient to make the patient unable to recall words retained previously. On her first admission the patient could easily recall series of words she had repeated previously, but on the second admission this was no longer possible. Repeating the same series five times did not improve her performance, but worsened it. It was a particularly characteristic feature that in the last two tests the patient not only was unable to recall words presented, but she actually began to believe that no words had been given to her.

Similar disturbances were found in tests of the recalling of two sentences.

Test 4

Two sentences were read to the patient and she was asked to repeat each one separately, then to recall the first sentence first, followed by the second.

I. *In Tashkent there was a severe earthquake and many houses were destroyed.*	II. *In Tushino there was an air display with parachute jumps.*	?/I	?/II
(1) Correctly	Correctly	Correctly	Correctly
(Interfering activity introduced – solving problems)		?/I I can't remember what the sentence was.	?/II I can't remember ... I have forgotten.

Prompting with the beginning of the sentence did not help the patient who could not even recall that any sentences had been read to her.

(2) Correctly	Correctly	In Tashkent there was an air display and many houses were destroyed.	Correctly
(3) Correctly	Correctly	In Taskhent there was an air display and many houses were destroyed.	In Tashkent there was an air display with parachute jumps.

The record shows that direct repetition of sentences was still possible, but if interfering activity was introduced the patient completely forgot the sentences or even began to doubt whether any sentences had been read to her at all.

Similar disturbances of memory were seen in tests involving the retelling of complete stories. Whereas the patient had no difficulty in repeating one story directly, followed by another, she was quite unable to recall a story read to her previously; it was either completely obliterated or replaced by contamination of fragments from both stories.

Test 5

"The Hen and the Golden Eggs" story was read to the patient. She repeated it easily. Another story, "The Intelligent Crow"[23], was then read to her and she also repeated this story correctly. *What was the first story?* "Let me see. . . I have forgotten it all." *What was it about?* "Something about a jug. . ." (a fragment from the second story). *And what was the second story?* "A crow and a golden jug. . . golden eggs. . . (fragment from the first story). . . The sun shone and its rays fell on the jug in which there were golden eggs. . . she put the jug in the sunlight and the eggs rose to the top. . ." (contamination of the meaning of the two stories).

What was the first story? "Something about golden eggs and a jug. . ." *Do you mean that both stories were the same?* "Yes. . . evidently the same. . ."

This contamination between the themes of the two stories, followed by the conclusion that they were identical, indicates a profound disturbance of the recalling process, with loss of selectivity when repeating previously imprinted associations under more complex conditions or during fatigue. Characteristically, these defects appeared despite the patient's lucid consciousness.

Third Admission. Severe Disturbances of General Activity and Memory. Evidence of Regression of the Syndrome

Two months later, the patient was readmitted for the third time to the Institute of Neurosurgery with signs of continued growth of the tumor and considerable worsening of her condition.

The patient was now apathetic and adynamic, the hypertensive headaches were almost continuous, on standing up she fell, and she had brief losses of consciousness. There was definite loss of vision on the right side (indicating spread of the pathological process to the chiasma) and deep paresis of upward movement of the eye (indicating its effects on the corpora quadrigemina). Well defined papilledema of both discs was present. The visual acuity of the right eye was about 0.6, and the left 0.7. Paresis of the abducens nerve was present. Pressure on the brain stem was indicated by the loss of optokinetic nystagmus. Caloric reflex nystagmus was increased and there were signs of disturbance of bulbar functions. There was weakness in the left limbs; central paresis of cranial nerves VII and XII on the left, a positive Babinski's sign on the left, and a bilateral Oppenheim's sign. Tremor of the fingers and sometimes a grasping reflex appeared.

The patient remained oriented in place but frequently her orientation in time was disturbed. As before, there were no confabulations. She answered questions with monosyllables. She slept frequently, although easily aroused. Sometimes she showed signs of anxiety about her state.

These observations all clearly indicated growth of the tumor (or cyst) of the third ventricle to affect the region of the chiasma, the rhombencephalon and the mesencephalon.

---

[23] A crow wanted to drink from a jug but the jug had a narrow neck and the crow could not reach the water. She therefore dropped pebbles into the jug to make the water level rise, when she was able to drink.

A neuropsychological investigation undertaken during this period revealed a marked worsening of the patient's general condition. Usually she slept all the time, awakening only if stimulated. She was inadequately oriented in her surroundings. Although she knew she was in hospital, she did not recognize people around her. She was poorly oriented in time.

Her gnosis and praxis, as before, remained intact, but speech was sluggish and monosyllabic—with no aphasic disturbances. She had no difficulty in performing simple imitative movements. In response to an instruction, she would shake hands twice, three times, or six times easily, and was able to draw isolated figures (a circle, cross, or triangle) as well as series of figures (for example, two circles, a cross and a triangle) as before, with no evidence of hyperkinesia or pathological inertia of an established stereotype. She could draw objects named to her (for example, a house).

She exhibited appreciable defects only if the conditions of the problem were made more complicated. For instance, when instructed, "When I raise my fist you show your finger, and when I raise my finger you show your fist," she started to carry it out correctly, but she very quickly drifted into the echopraxic repetition of the examiner's posture although she retained the spoken instruction.

Mnemonic Disorders

The memory disturbances were severe at this stage. She was now unable to recall two groups of two words or two sentences.

Test 6

(1) Recalling pairs of words

I. *Dom—les*	II. *Klei—stol*	*?/I*	*?/II*
Correctly	Correctly	Correctly	Correctly
(Interfering activity introduced—calcula-tion)		Correctly	I have forgotten.

(2) Recalling sentences

I. *In Tashkent there was a severe earthquake and many houses were destroyed.*	II. *In Tushino there was an air display with parachute jumps.*	*?/I*	*?/II*
Correctly	Correctly	Correctly	...I don't know, I have forgotten.

In this period, the patient became fatigued even after minimal effort. She fell asleep during the test, which made it very difficult to carry out a systematic neuropsychological investigation.

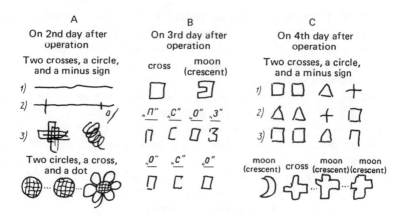

FIG. 17. Drawings by patient Snyatk. in response to a spoken instruction on consecutive days after operation.

The main phenomenon characteristic of this period was the sharp decrease in the patient's tone, the ease with which she passed into a state of drowsiness and sleep, and her proneness to fatigue. Against this background, her program performance remained unimpaired; i.e., there was no sign of any marked perseveration or repetition of inert stereotypes. An increasingly severe amnesic syndrome with pathologically increased inhibitability of trace recall by interfering factors dominated the clinical picture. There was no evidence of any marked contamination and confabulation.

On September 28, 1971, a right-sided ventriculotomy was performed on the patient and a large cyst in the third ventricle was drained.

On the first day after the operation, spoken communication with the patient was impossible; a detailed neuropsychological investigation capable of determining any regression of the disturbances of memory could not be initiated until the second day after the operation. These tests then continued for a month.

On the second day after the operation, the patient was grossly inactive and all her behavior pointed to inability to carry out any instruction. This was clearly apparent in tests requiring drawing in response to instruction (Figure 17). When instructed to draw two crosses, a circle, and a minus sign, she took the pencil lethargically and drew just one continuous line, following the border of the piece of paper (Figure 17, A, 1). In response to the second instruction, she again drew a similar horizontal line, crossed by two short vertical lines, after which she added a small circle and an oblique line which was supposed to represent a minus sign (Figure 17, A, 2).

At her third attempt to perform this test, she began to draw two crosses, a circle and a minus sign, but each action was accompanied by the repeated inert repetition of the same strokes (Figure 17, A, 3).

When instructed to draw two circles, a cross and a dot, she started to draw a circle, then shaded it in, and while she did so she said "cross," followed by "cross," and then she again repeated the same drawing. Finally, having repeated the same figure again, she surrounded it by petals to form a flower. When the instruction was repeated, the patient again drew a similar sort of picture, but this time she drew a trapezium and shaded it.

Naturally it was impossible to test the patient's mnemonic processes in the presence of such severe aspontaneity.

On the third postoperative day, the patient's condition improved considerably, although her general apathy and inactivity remained.

When asked to state the date (October 1, 1971), she began to say, "Today it is the 30th... 31st... 32nd... 33rd," and then remarked critically, "But surely there is no such thing." After reciting the days of the week, when asked to repeat the natural series of numbers (1, 2, 3...), she began to confuse the two series ("1, 2, 3, Thursday, Friday," etc.). The patient had definite diplopia, the severity of which she realized; when one of a group of doctors started to move toward her, with alarm she said, "Why do they move separately?", evidently taking the two figures of the doctor as a single divided figure. The patient retained her pathological inertia when carrying out graphic tests, but its character changed. When, having drawn a cross, she attempted to draw a moon (crescent), she inertly repeated the straight lines. The same features of inertia also appeared when she wrote the letters of the alphabet, and only when she wrote the familiar word "Ol'ga" was this inert graphic stereotype abandoned.

On the fourth day after the operation, the general manifestations of inactivity and pathological inertia were less severe. The patient was fully oriented in place and she remembered she had had an operation, but she was still incompletely oriented in time. Very gradually, she started to correctly perform the graphic tests. To begin with, she had difficulty in drawing a series of two circles, a cross, and a dot; instead, she drew two squares, a circle and another square. On repeating the test, she drew two dots, a cross and a dot. With further stimulation, however, she carried out the test correctly, although she did continue to exhibit some features of pathological inertia.

At this stage, therefore, it was possible to begin observing the gradual recovery of the previously disturbed mnemonic activity.

The results of the appropriate tests are described below.

Test 7

Repetition of a series of figures. The patient could easily reproduce single figures (square, cross, circle) from memory. However, repetition of series of figures from memory remained beyond her grasp. When shown a series consisting of two crosses, a circle and a dot, she did so correctly only immediately after its presentation. After a pause of 1 min, she repeated it as "two circles, a square and a dot," and after another pause of 1 min, as "two squares, a circle and a square." Later she was quite unable to repeat the series of figures and instead she drew a series of identical figures (squares).

Recalling words. Prior to the operation, repetition of this test led to fatigue and worsening performance. After the operation, on the contrary, repetition led to improvement.

Recalling sentences. The familiar test of memorizing and recalling sentences was carried out with the patient.

I. *Apple trees grew in the garden behind the tall fence.*	II. *A hunter killed a wolf on the edge of the forest.*	*?/I*	*?/II*
Correctly	Correctly	Behind the high streetcars in the garden... I have forgotten.	... No, I have forgotten.

Recalling stories. "The Ant and the Pigeon" story was read to the patient and she was asked to repeat it. She said: "Behind the tall fence (perseveration from the previous sentence). . . behind the tall fence. . . there lived a pigeon. . . a boy wanted to catch her and he shouted her name. . . the pigeon spread her wings and flew away."

The same story was read a second time to the patient and she was asked to repeat it exactly. She said: "An ant saw a pigeon drowning and wanted to save her. . . he went up close and shouted. . . at once they let the pigeon go. . ." *Who let it go?* "Whoever had caught her." *But who had caught her?* "Whoever let her go." The patient made no further attempt to repeat the story more correctly and said: "Why is it that your thoughts will stick together whereas mine won't. . . it is surprising." After a pause of 1 min filled with conversation, the patient was asked what story had been read to her. "I can't recall. . . something about a little ant. . ." *About a jackdaw?* "No." *About an owl?* "No." *About a fly?* "No." *About a pigeon?* "Apparently not. . ."

The test carried out on the fourth day after the operation thus still showed very considerable inactivity and very definite instability of all the patient's traces (visual and verbal, discrete and organized), with a marked tendency for their contamination, despite the general preservation of the patient's consciousness.

By the sixth to tenth day after the operation, when the manifestations of edema had subsided, it was possible to undertake a systematic neuropsychological investigation of the patient. During this period, there was a residual syndrome of primary memory disorders which subsequently underwent definite regression. The patient's condition became much better, her inactivity disappeared, her voice became clear, and she no longer spoke in a whisper. She became fully oriented in place and time, and the features of pathological inertia disappeared. On the sixth day after the operation, she still showed some inertia in drawing the details of figures and letters, but by the tenth day these phenomena had completely disappeared.

As before, the patient's gnosis, praxis, and speech were intact. Her critical attitude towards her defects was complete. A primary disturbance of memory, in the form of increased inhibition of recall under the influence of interfering factors, now dominated the clinical picture.

As before, the memory disturbances were modality-nonspecific. They were manifested as slight contamination of traces, especially old ones, although the patient's consciousness was lucid, and they could be abolished to some extent by additional stimulation.

The results of tests involving repetition of figures, words, sentences, and stories are given below.

Test 8

Recalling figures. The direct repetition of a series of visually presented figures ("two circles, a dot and a cross" or "two squares, a triangle and a minus sign") at this stage was within the patient's capability although after a pause of 1 min the traces of the figures presented to her were unstable. After the series of figures had been presented a second time, however, the patient could retain them relatively well, and even interference with irrelevant activity did not disturb their repetition.

Recalling words. The patient was given two groups, each consisting of three words, and asked to recall them. She had no difficulty in repeating each series of words, and after a second repetition of the series she could easily recall both series; however, the introduction of even slight interference (counting forward and backward) was sufficient to make the patient unable to recall words just presented, so that either she simply said, "I can't remember. . . ," "I have quite forgotten," or she repeated only one series, contaminating it with elements from the other series. Repeating the test six times did not overcome this defect.

Characteristically, the increased inhibition by interfering activity continued to be observed in tests with verbal material organized into semantic structures (sentences and stories).

Recalling sentences

I. *In Tashkent there was a severe earthquake and many houses were destroyed.* Correctly	II. *In Tushino there was an air display with parachute jumps.* Correctly	*?/I* In Tashkent there was an air display and many houses were destroyed.	*?/II* I can't remember.
I. *Apple trees grew in the garden behind the high fence.* Correctly	II. *A hunter killed a wolf on the edge of the forest.* Correctly	*?/I* I can't remember.	*?/II* I have forgotten.

"For some reason or other I wanted to say a hunter killed a wolf in the garden behind the high fence but it is impossible for both sentences to start in the same way." *How does the second sentence start?* "The second—a hunter killed a wolf in the garden behind the high fence." *And the first sentence?* "That was the second, the first I can't remember. . ."

Recalling stories. The two stories—"The Hen and the Golden Eggs" and "The Intelligent Crow"—were read to the patient and she repeated each of them perfectly well immediately. She was next asked to repeat the first story and then the second.

What was the first story? "I can't remember." *What was the second story?* "About a crow. The crow wanted to drink on a hot day. . . she flew to a stream (reminiscence of a fragment from "The Ant and the Pigeon" story read some days earlier) and started to throw pebbles into it, she throws—drinks, throws—drinks. . ." *And what was the first story?* "I can't remember. . ." *A man had a hen. . .* "No, I don't know. . ." *Which laid golden eggs.* "No, I can't remember anything. . ."

The patient could thus repeat the stories perfectly well immediately, but when she tried to recall them later, she either contaminated fragments of it with fragments of a story read previously or she had forgotten the story to such an extent that not even prompting led to its recall.

The same test, when carried out three days later, yielded similar results.

A definite syndrome of primary memory disorder was found in a patient with intact orientation in place and time, awareness of her condition, no disturbance of gnosis, praxis, speech, or goal-directed activity. It was exhibited as pathologically increased trace inhibitability by interfering factors, and affected equally the reproduction of discrete material (figures, words) and organized material (sentences, stories). Repeating the second semantic structure (a sentence or story) was sufficient to cause the traces of the first semantic structure either to disappear completely or to be contaminated with traces of the second structure, leading to a curious amalgam of the two structures ("A hunter killed a wolf in a garden. . ." or "The hen wanted to drink. . ." or "A crow laid golden eggs"). Fragments of a story read on a previous day could also be introduced by way of reminiscence. The inhibition was so strong that not even insistent prompting helped the patient to recall the "forgotten" story.

By the end of the second week after the operation, her ability to repeat stories read to her immediately was perfectly good, but when she tried to recall stories read one or two days previously she still showed evidence of instability, changes in the order of events and contamination, of a sort never found under normal conditions.

In the fourth week after the operation, these memory defects had disappeared completely. Only during attempts to repeat stories read previously were certain mnemonic difficulties and signs of contamination still noticeable. During subsequent tests, these mild defects persisted, and when the patient was admitted to the Institute of Neurosurgery the fourth time—six months after the third admission—it was still possible to notice very slight defects of involuntary memorizing which the patient herself described in her own words: "If you give me something to memorize, I will memorize it; if I am not told to memorize something, I easily forget it, even though it is something I should remember."

* * *

I have described mnemic disorders in a patient with a tumor of the third ventricle and have traced their course over a period of time. Let us now summarize these observations:

A patient with a tumor and cyst in the third ventricle, whose illness began with marked metabolic disturbances, disorders of sleep and waking, and general primary asthenia revealed a clear picture of primary dynamic disturbances of memory. Her gnosis, praxis, and speech remained intact throughout the period of investigation. Her goal-directed activity and critical attitude to her own defect likewise remained intact. This patient had no features of general disorientation and no confabulations were observed.

When tested for the first time, the patient's memory appeared reasonably well preserved, in sharp contrast to her complaints ("I forget everything. . . I cannot keep anything in my memory. . ."). Subsequent tests, however, showed the presence of marked primary disturbances of memory, manifested as pathologically increased inhibitability of traces by interfering factors. These defects were nonspecific and affected different levels of organization of material equally (series of isolated words, sentences, stories). In every case, complete inhibition of recall and/or contamination of one system with another could be observed.

The memory disturbances were fluctuating in character to an extent that depended largely on the patient's fatigue, which aggravated the memory disturbances, or on stimulation, whereby the patient was mobilized to some extent and the results of the test were improved. Gradual growth of the tumor and an increase in the severity of the hypertensive syndrome led to a successive increase in severity of the disorders. Drainage of the cyst was followed by regression of the syndrome and the gradual disappearance of the memory disturbances.

The fact that the tumor was in the third ventricle and affected the reticular formation, combined with the marked depression of the level of wakefulness, suggests that the primary memory disturbances are due to involvement of these nonspecific structures and, perhaps to some degree, the limbic region. As we shall see later, the complete integrity of the patient's consciousness (even in the period when she was most seriously ill) sharply distinguishes this syndrome from others in which the memory disturbances were accompanied by confused consciousness and marked confabulations.

In order to assess the reliability of this syndrome, let us describe the corresponding disturbances of memory in two similar patients.

* * *

Patient Volk., a 42-year-old male (a designer by profession), was admitted to the Burdenko Institute of Neurosurgery on May 10, 1971, with the diagnosis of a tumor of the floor of the third ventricle.

His illness began in fall of 1969 when the sight of his left eye started to deteriorate and he developed metabolic disorders and polydipsia. He put on 15 kg in a short time. A year later, he began to have headaches and nausea.

Examination at the Institute of Neurosurgery revealed visual acuity of the right eye 0.7, left 0.07, pallor of the temporal halves of the optic discs, and a paracentral scotoma in the temporal zones of the visual field. Pneumocisternography showed a space-occupying lesion in the region of the chiasma. The cerebrospinal fluid contained 0.5% protein and a cell count of 23/3.

Neurophysiological investigation of the patient by N. A. Filippycheva gave the following results. Cortical electrical activity was sharply depressed, indicating a disturbance of the ascending reticular activating formation. The gradient of decreasing amplitude of the α-rhythm from the occipital to the frontal regions was gentle, and pathological delta-waves were present in the frontal region. Little, if any, response of the cortical electrical activity, psychogalvanic reflex, and plethysmograph was obtained to indifferent stimuli. They did respond, however, to informative stimuli, although the electrophysiological and plethysmographic responses began to diminish very quickly (after the fourth stimulus) and the motor response became protracted and inert in character. These findings point to a pathological state of the diencephalic systems. No evidence of involvement of the frontal lobes could be detected.

On August 16, 1971, an operation was performed to drain the cyst in the cavity of the third ventricle. After coagulation of the blood vessels, a skin incision was made in the

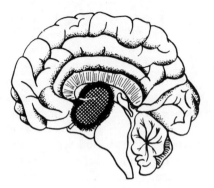

FIG. 18. Position of tumor in patient Volk.

region of the middle frontal gyrus, the anterior horn of the right lateral ventricle was opened and a grossly dilated foramen of Monro was discovered, through which a large cyst could be seen. The wall of the cyst was grasped with forceps and excised to provide free drainage of the third ventricle. The patient died on the eleventh day after the operation with signs of edema of the brain stem and cardiac arrest.

Postmortem examination of the brain showed a large tumor nodule (craniopharyngioma) occupying the anterior portion of the third ventricle, displacing its floor dorsally and penetrating into the hypothalamic region (Figure 18).

Neuropsychological tests gave the following results. Throughout the period of observation, the patient was inactive; he could be induced only with difficulty to carry out instructions, and he did not display the necessary interest in carrying them out. He knew that he was in a hospital but thought it was the Institute for Eye Diseases, or he stated that he did not remember where he was. His orientation in time was inadequate and on May 9 he said that it was November. He knew the names of his wife and son, but when asked his daughter's name he said he had forgotten it. When asked if he had a headache, he replied that he evidently had, because he had just taken tablets. He couldn't remember the name of his doctor and said that his memory was "evidently changed for the worse."

The patient's condition fluctuated. Sometimes, for example, if the conversation turned on radio receivers, in which he was interested, he became more lively and said that he had invented a radio receiver himself.

He could walk but usually lay in bed, having little to do with people around him, making no complaint, quickly exhausted by the smallest effort, and quickly abandoning the performance of a task.

The patient's gnosis, praxis, and speech were completely preserved. He showed no signs of confusion or confabulations, except occasionally—such as, when asked in what city he was, he answered, "In Odessa," but immediately corrected himself: "No, in Moscow, the fact was I was going to go to Odessa."

The patient's intellectual processes and his assessment of his own situation were completely intact; he could solve problems given to him, and abandoned only the most complicated problems requiring some degree of effort.

Mnemonic Disorders

The central symptom of this patient was the severe disturbance of his memory, manifested as pathologically increased inhibitability of traces by interfering factors. Different modalities and different levels of organization were all equally affected. Learning a 10-word series showed no improvement over trials (4-3-4-5-5-3-4-5) and remained unchanged after an injection of 0.05 ml caffeine.

The patient could easily reproduce two groups, each consisting of three geometrical figures, but in his attempts to repeat these figures from memory he forgot the composition of the groups and omitted the components or mixed them up. The same thing happened in tests to repeat two groups of movements, each consisting of a pair of movements. He had difficulty in memorizing two groups of three words, and then repeating each group separately. Even after seven or eight repetitions, there was no improvement and he continued to contaminate or forget the groups.

I. *More–zvon–luch*	II. *Son–okno–myach*	?/I	?/II
(1) Correctly	Correctly	I have forgotten.	Correctly
(2) Correctly	Correctly	More–zvon–myach	I have forgotten.
(3) Correctly	Correctly	More–zvon–okno	Son–myach
(4) Correctly	Correctly	More–grom–luch	Grom and something else
(5) Correctly	Correctly	More–grom–luch	Son and something else
(6) Correctly	Correctly	More–grom–luch	Okno–son–myach
(7) Correctly	Correctly	More–grom–luch	Correctly

Other tests gave the same results.

Repeating sentences also causes this patient considerable difficulty.

I. *Apple trees grew in the garden behind the high fence.*	II. *A hunter killed a wolf on the edge of the forest.*	?/I	?/II
(1) Correctly	Correctly	Apple trees grew in the garden. . .	A hunter killed a hare on the edge of the forest.

(2) Correctly	Correctly	Correctly	Correctly
(3) Correctly	Correctly	I have forgotten.	I have forgotten . . . no, I have remembered.
(4) Correctly	Correctly	I have forgotten.	Correctly
(5) Correctly	Correctly	So, I have forgotten.	I can remember the second but I have forgotten the first.
(6) Correctly	Correctly	I have forgotten.	Correctly.

The test involving repetition of the two stories revealed a very significant defect. As a rule, the patient could not repeat the entire story, and he was quite unable to repeat any of the first story after the second story had been read to him.

"The Jackdaw and the Pigeons" story was read to the patient. He repeated it as follows: "A jackdaw flew with some pigeons and heard that they had plenty to eat, but they would not receive her. . . she was black and she cried not like. . . she should have been white. . . she flew back but they did not take her in. . ." *Why?* "Because she had forgotten to cry. . ." *What is the moral?* "In strange company, with its own laws, white will not go with black or black with white."
A second story ("The Ant and the Pigeon") was read to the patient. He tried to repeat it: "The pigeon and ant. . . ant and pigeon. . . no, I can't remember, I have forgotten it already." *What was the first story?* "No, I can't remember. . . I have forgotten." *And what was the second story?* "I have forgotten the second story as well. . . maybe about a pigeon, but I can't remember what." Repeating the test produced no improvement and the patient was still unable to recall the stories read to him.

Similar results were obtained in tests with other stories.
A similar picture of primary memory disturbances accompanied by sharp fluctuations from sleep to wakefulness, but with the lucidity of consciousness and goal-directed critical behavior unimpaired, was given by the third patient.

* * *

Patient Zueva., a 35-year-old female (a nurse by profession) was admitted to the Burdenko Institute of Neurosurgery on June 15, 1971, complaining of double vision, attacks of muscular weakness, headaches, and metabolic disorders.

The neuropsychological investigation of this patient revealed apathy and aspontaneity. She yawned or dozed very frequently during the investigation. She was fully oriented in place and partly in time. She knew where she was and reacted adequately to her condition. She was bewildered and had lost her emotional motivations. Her state fluctuated sharply—sometimes she lay in bed with her eyes closed and responded in a slow half-whisper; sometimes she got up and walked along the corridor. Her main complaints referred to her severe memory defects: "I forget everything, I sometimes say the same thing several times over. . ." She could not remember whether she had eaten her lunch or whether she had answered questions. There were no confabulations or other features of confusion.

All forms of gnosis, praxis, and speech were intact in this patient; her movements were free from perseveration, and only occasionally in the most difficult tests did she reveal elements of echopraxis, which she at once corrected.

Mnemonic Disorders

Gross defects appeared in tests involving the repetition of material. As in the patients described above, these defects were modality-nonspecific and observed equally in discrete series (figures, movements, words) and semantically organized material. These defects were manifested as the familiar phenomena of increased inhibitability of trace recall by interfering factors, by contamination, by changes in the order of the elements, etc. In this case also, the defects fluctuated depending, to a marked degree, on how fatigued the patient was. They could be overcome, to some extent, by increased stimulation.

Learning 10-word series was very depressed (3-3-4-4-5-5-6-4). Memorizing two pairs of words presented no particular difficulty, but the introduction of interfering activity made it impossible for the patient to recall previous words. In the test involving memorizing two groups of three words, even without interference she could not recall the words she had repeated previously.

The corresponding test, when carried out on the patient on a "bad day," when she lay passively in bed with her eyes closed and when her inactivity and exhaustion were particularly severe, gave worse results still.

Similar defects in the repetition of traces imprinted previously were observed—also in tests involving the recalling of series of isolated picture cards, figures drawn by her, or movements. Some typical results are described below.

Recalling picture cards. The patient was first shown a group of three picture cards, then a second group. The cards were turned face downward and the patient instructed to name the cards in each group twice. The test was repeated seven times in succession and it gave the following results:

I. *Grusha–divan–silva*[24]	II. *Vishnya–yagoda–mal'chik*	*?/I*	*?/II*
(1) Correctly	Correctly	I have forgotten.	Mal'chik– yagoda
(2) Correctly	Correctly	Devochka and yagoda	Mal'chik and yagoda

---

[24]Grusha = pair, divan = sofa, sliva = plum, vishnya = cherry, yagoda = berry, mal'chik = boy, devochka = girl. The names of the objects shown on the picture cards are indicated in the record of the tests.

(3) Correctly	Correctly	Devochka grusha— vasilek	Mal'chik. . . no, I have forgotten.
(4) Correctly	Correctly	Devochka— grusha	Mal'chik. . . no.
(5) Correctly	Correctly	Grusha— devochka	Mal'chik
(6) Correctly	Correctly	Devochka— grusha	Mal'chik
(7) Correctly	Correctly	Devochka— grusha— sliva— yagoda	Mal'chik— yagoda—no, I have for- gotten.

Characteristically, repeating the experiment many times did not improve the results.

Recalling figures. The patient was asked to draw first one group of three figures and then a second group; she was then asked to recall which figures she had drawn in the first group and in the second group.

I. *Circle–cross–triangle*	II. *Square–minus–dot*	*?/I*	*?/II*
(1) Correctly	Correctly	Square–minus –dot	Circle–minus –dot
(2) Correctly	Correctly	Triangle– minus–dot	I have for- gotten.
(3) Correctly	Correctly	Circle–cross– circle	. . . I have forgotten.

Recalling movements. The patient was first instructed to carry out a series of three movements, then another series of three movements, and then asked to show the movements in the first group followed by those in the second group.

I. *Threaten with the finger–show a fist– clap hands.*	II. *Make a ring from your fingers–make a cup– stretch your palm.*	*?/I*	*?/II*
(1) Correctly	Correctly	Shows a fist, stretches palm.	Ditto
(2) Correctly	Correctly	Threatens with fist, threatens with palm.	Ditto, in op- posite order.
(3) Correctly	Correctly	Threatens with fist, threatens with palm,claps hands.	Threatens with finger, makes cup, claps hands.
(4) Refuses to repeat	Refuses to repeat	Threatens with finger, stretches palm, claps hands.	Threatens with finger, shows horns, claps hands.

The defects of this patient's memory were seen more clearly when she attempted to repeat sentences or, in particular, whole stories.

"The Hen and the Golden Eggs" story was read and she was asked to repeat it. She answered: "... and he killed the hen..." (stating that she could not remember anything more).
"The Jackdaw and the Pigeons" story was read. She at once exclaimed: "No, this too much, I cannot tell it... I remember only that the pigeons would not take the jackdaw in and killed her..."
What was the first story? "About gold..." *A man had...* "He had a lot of gold... because of his gold someone wanted to kill him..."
In both cases, the patient was unable to retain the whole theme of the story, and only those fragments that were freshest in her mind could be repeated.
The test was repeated three days later. She was asked to recall whether a story had been read to her three days before. By way of reminiscence, she recalled: "The little hen laid golden eggs."
"The Hen and the Golden Eggs" story was read to her again. This time she repeated it completely, even after interference with mental arithmetic.
The second story, "The Jackdaw and the Pigeons," was read to the patient and she was asked to repeat it. She said: "... a jackdaw... no I can't... everything has gone out of my mind." *Nevertheless, try again to repeat it.* "A man had a hen, she laid golden eggs..." (repeats the first story). *No, that is the first story, what about the second?* "... I can't, I am all confused..." *What was the story about?* "About a jackdaw." *Repeat it.* "Now I am all confused: about a jackdaw and about a hen... no, I can't."

Even direct repetition was thus beyond the patient's grasp, and she could remember only the end or the beginning of the story, or else she interwove fragments of the previous story into it by way of reminiscence. As a rule, she was quite unable to recall the first story voluntarily after the effort of repeating the second. Her difficulty was even greater if she was asked to recall unaided stories read to her several days previously. In such cases, she usually could recall nothing; only if prompted (with the names of the stories or their beginnings) could she recall the theme. She then either repeated the story reasonably accurately or her performance was affected by the now familiar contamination.

Conclusions

We have examined primary memory disturbances in a group of patients with tumors of the third ventricle and can now draw some general conclusions characterizing this syndrome as a whole.

In all the patients described, the pathological process in the third ventricle gave rise to metabolic disorders, marked disturbances of cortical tone, and distinct fluctuations between states of sleep and wakefulness. On certain days, they showed virtually no symptoms of higher cortical disturbance, but on others, these disturbances were much more conspicuous. The patients were easily fatigued and as a result the prolonged repetition of the same test, as a rule, led to worsening rather than improvement of the disability.

Gnosis, praxis, and speech remained completely intact and, what is particularly important, ·their consciousness remained unimpaired, their orientation in place and their awareness of their condition were complete, and their emotional experiences and their emotional attitude toward their defect remained intact. No permanent signs of confusion or confabulation were observed.

Primary disturbances of memory were the central syndrome in all these patients. These disturbances did not lead to Korsakov's syndrome and usually fluctuated in severity from day to day. The structure of the disturbances was identical in all patients.

All patients complained of loss of memory ("I forget everything, I cannot retain anything"), but the ordinary psychological investigation of memory (learning a series of 10 words) revealed no gross abnormality in some patients, and in others pointed merely to a slight reduction in the volume of material remembered.

Clear defects appeared during recall after interfering activity (for example, the imprinting of a second similar group, i.e., "homogeneous interference," or distraction by irrelevant activity, or "heterogeneous interference"). Although the patient could repeat material perfectly well, immediately after presentation, he was quite unable to recall it after interference. He either stated that he had "forgotten" the material or he retained only the first part of the material and forgot the second (the "primacy" factor), or he reproduced the second part and forgot the first ("recency" factor). Contamination often occurred.

As a rule, the patients of this group were well aware of the defects in their memory. Sometimes they expressed their defect precisely in words ("when it is necessary you cannot recall it... it sits somewhere in your head but you cannot recall it...."). Repetition of the required material was never replaced by irrepressible outpouring of irrelevant associations or inert stereotypes.

These defects were modality-nonspecific and manifested in various forms of activity (remembering cards, drawings, or words) and at different levels of the semantic organization (during memorizing series of discrete words, sentences, or complete stories). Finally, another characteristic was that in all cases the phenomena described fluctuated in intensity, and increased stimulation within certain limits increased the patient's performance.

This completes the account of the syndrome of primary memory disturbances observed in patients with tumors of the third ventricle. I have given a detailed analysis of only 3 of these patients, some of whom were examined periodically; however, I have at my disposal the records of another 12 cases which substantially repeat the picture described above.

Very probably, the physiological basis of this defect is a reduction in cortical tone arising, like the fluctuations in the state of sleep and wakefulness, as a result of a disturbance of the normal activity of the thalamic reticular formation, and the accompanying profound metabolic disturbances produced by the pathological process in the diencephalic and hypothalamic region.

CHAPTER VI

Disturbances of Memory at Consciousness in Patients With Massive Deep Brain Tumors

Another group of patients with tumors of the third ventricle present a clinical picture that differs from the one just described. In these cases, a larger tumor invades the floor of the ventricle, destroys the hypothalamus, compresses the mammillary bodies, sometimes influences the limbic structures and, in certain cases, is accompanied by increased intracranial pressure.

The distinguishing feature of this group of patients is that their mnemonic disturbances are much more severe and persistent, and they sometimes closely resemble Korsakov's syndrome. As in the previous group, the basic mechanism of the memory disturbance is pathologically increased inhibitability of traces by interfering factors. The main difference between this and the previous group of patients is that traces of incoming information lose their selectivity and become intermixed with traces belonging to other systems, so that recall is characterized by contamination and confusion more characteristic of an oneiroid state than a state of normal wakefulness.

In the patients I shall now describe, the memory disturbances are associated with marked disorders of consciousness. As a rule, the patients of this group lose their clear orientation in place and time; they do not know exactly where they are—they often suppose they are at home, at work, or in some temporary situation (at the polyclinic or railroad station). They cannot give the date or even the time of year. Even the time of day gives rise to confusion. These patients confuse people around them with others they have met before. For example, they consider that they met the doctor looking after them in some other period of their previous life. Often these patients not only do not remember events in the immediate past and become unsure of themselves when asked where they were an hour or two hours ago, but contamination appears and they state that they had gone into town or they were at the place where they used to work. They begin to confuse reality with imaginary pictures. The defects of their memory thus begin to resemble disturbances of consciousness, so that the typical picture of a state of incomplete cortical wakefulness is produced. The disturbances observed in such cases reflect a marked lowering of the general tone of cortical processes. A detailed account of two cases belonging to this group follows.

Patient Rakch., a 40-year-old female (an economist by profession), was admitted to the N. N. Burdenko Institute of Neurosurgery on March 7, 1967, in a serious condition with gross disturbances of memory, disorientation in place and time, and severe confabulations.

In January, 1967, she began to complain of headaches, mainly in the fronto-temporal region. The optic discs were indistinct; no abnormality of the cranial nerves was found; she had no pareses or disturbances of sensation; her reflexes were equal; no pathological reflexes or disturbance of tone was found; and her speech was completely intact. Soon after discharge, she continued at her previous job.

On March 1, 1967, while watching a motion picture, she felt unwell. She became excited and disoriented, and in that state she was readmitted to a neurological hospital. Significant clinical findings were discovered: The patient was depressed, did not respond to questioning, did not carry out instructions, and was incontinent in bed. Examination revealed bilateral pathological reflexes, clonus of both ankles, and pathological automatisms on both sides. No meningeal signs were present, but muscle tone was raised and reflexes were increased on the left side. After a few days, the patient's condition improved. She now responded to questioning, but she remained apathetic. A bilateral Oppenheim's reflex was observed, as before. She was transferred to the Burdenko Institute of Neurosurgery with the diagnosis of a suspected brain tumor.

On admission to the Institute of Neurosurgery, the patient was severely disoriented. She had no anxiety about her state and exhibited a very severe amnesic syndrome. She did not recognize the doctors or patients, and thought she was at work or in the polyclinic that she had just visited on the way from home. During the day, she was apathetic but not depressed; at night, she sometimes got up and showed features of psychomotor excitation. She would get into the wrong bed, and urinate in the middle of the ward.

Objective examination revealed: Indistinctness of the borders of the optic discs and dilated veins of the optic fundus, narrowing of the visual field, especially on the right side; hemiptosis on the left side, central paresis of the right facial nerve, reduced strength in the left arm, a positive Babinskii's sign on the left, a bilateral increase of muscle tone of the plastic type (more marked on the left), absent abdominal reflexes, a positive Marinesco's reflex on the right, a bilateral grasping reflex, and elements of a sucking reflex. No sensory disturbances were found and her speech was completely intact.

The cerebrospinal fluid contained 0.45% protein, the cell count was 4/3, and the pressure normal (180 mm water). The roentgenogram of the skull showed no evidence of increased intracranial pressure. The EEG showed reduction of the α-rhythm on the left and epileptiform discharges also on the left, more marked in the posterior zones. Left-sided carotid angiography revealed some spasm of the middle cerebral artery, but no visible displacement of the blood vessels.

On ventriculography air entered the hydrocephalic ventricles; the right ventricle was wider than the left; air would not pass from the right ventricle into the left. The anterior horns of the ventricle were incompletely filled and flattened. The foramen of Monro was displaced posteriorly and the posterior horns of the lateral ventricle were hydrocephalic. Due to occlusion of the foramen of Monro, air had not passed into the other ventricle after 24 hours. The cerebrospinal fluid in the ventricles was hydrocephalic (0.13%).

The results of a combined neurophysiological investigation (N. A. Filippycheva) pointed to a marked lowering of cortical tone, a weakened response of the EEG to stimulation, and definite evidence of disinhibition of cortical activity and psychogalvanic reflexes to any random stimuli, leading to disturbance of the regulation of the cortical rhythm by the speech system.

At the beginning of the investigation of cortical activity, constant rhythmic fluctuations of cortical potentials were observed, independently of stimulation; these were intensified during the application of any random stimulus. The orienting reaction to indifferent stimuli was considerably weakened with respect to all tests, and after one or two repetitions of the stimulus it disappeared. The motor response to an informative stimulus was sharply reduced in amplitude and increased in duration. It was very unstable and disappeared after the second presentation of the stimulus. The verbal response shows that the patient quickly forgot the informative value of the stimulus. Characteristically, although selective motor responses to informative stimuli were absent, the patient developed diffuse motor responses and the responses to informative stimuli were almost indistinguishable from those to uninformative stimuli. These findings suggest considerable inhibition of the ascending activating system, and a gross disturbance in regulation of the basic physiological activity level by the speech system, suggesting a large tumor in the deep structures of the brain in the midline.

Neurological investigation by Professor Yu. V. Konovalov revealed the following: Steady paresis of upward movements of the eye coupled with a marked dynamic character of all the other signs, notably the reflexes. This fact may indicate that the pathological process was at the tentorial level and exerted its effects most constantly on the corpora quadrigemina. The very severe disturbances of memory, taking into account the visual field defects (at least on the right), suggest a lesion of the posterior part of the corpus callosum spreading to the hippocampus, particularly on the left. Considering the interference with the circulation of cerebrospinal fluid in the region of the foramen of Monro, the initial site of the pathological process was probably in the posterior part of the septum pellucidum.

The patient stayed in the Institute of Neurosurgery for two months, when she was transferred to the Neurological Hospital where she died. No postmortem findings are available.

Mnemonic Disorders and Their Investigation

The neuropsychological investigation of this patient, which continued intensively for two months, showed that the patient was not depressed, was perfectly accessible for testing, and engaged willingly in conversation. Her state fluctuated sharply—some days she was apathetic, inactive, and sleepy; on other days, she was lively. Her attitude toward her condition also varied—sometimes she was unconcerned and did not respond emotionally to her illness; sometimes her emotional reactions were quite clear and she stated that she was "all confused... look what I have become. I am no good for anything, just stupid... can't someone help me quickly?"

The central features throughout the whole period of testing continued to be her severe disorientation in place and, in particular, in time, and her well-marked amnesic syndrome. Extracts from a record of conversations with the patient illustrating this fact are given below.

Where are you? "I am at present in a hospital... in an institute." *What institute?* "It must be gynecological." *How did you come here?* "I used to give blood there... and probably the blood was not correct... or else it was too correct..." *Where do you work?* "In an institute..." *Which institute?* "At present I don't work every day... I don't work for some reason or other, but I will enjoy working..." *At what institute do you work?* "At an institute... where I am now... I don't know... they give blood... to others..." *Where does your husband work?* "At an institute... he helps you and me..." *At what institute are you now and why?* "Because of my mind... I can't grasp anything... I used to be normal all the time—but now suddenly—please..."

When did you come here? "A month ago" (in fact it was three days). *What is the date today?* "The 29th." *And the month?* "The seventh." *And the year?* "The 40th... the 40th... no, the 60th... I have forgotten everything." *When were you born?* "In 1925... no, in 1920..."

The patient was almost completely unable to retain impressions of current events and her answers to questions about these events were confabulations. For instance, 30 min after a painful ventriculography, she could tell nothing about herself and when asked what she did a short time before, she said, "I went out for a walk," "I was listening to music," "I was writing notes..." And when further asked whether she had had an injection, she replied, "No, I don't think so. I said that I don't feel well and don't want to listen to music any more."

When asked what she had done that morning, she often replied that "she had gone out for a walk along the street," "she was at home where repairs are in progress," and so on. When asked what she had eaten in the morning, she would answer, "Soup and fish cutlets." If the same question was repeated 5 min later, she answered, "Soup, porridge, and cocoa"; 5 min after that she said, "Chicken soup, meat cutlets, and stewed fruit," and after another 5 min, "Soup with forcemeat balls, pieces of meat, and stewed fruit." She was quite unaware of the contradictory nature of her answers, and every time the question was asked she regarded it as an entirely new one.

It must not be supposed, however, that impressions of current events left no trace whatever. After two or three weeks of almost daily exercises, she began to recognize the doctor who tested her, she smiled when he came into the room, distinguished him clearly among the others, but could not remember his name. She could find her way to the ward, although with difficulty, and sometimes said that a puncture had been carried out (she remembered the word from the previous test). Characteristically, on being asked what the doctor had said to her, she replied, "There is something wrong with *his* memory," so that she repeated the theme of the conversation but transferred her own complaint to the doctor.

* * *

The neuropsychological tests at this time indicate that some aspects of the patient's psychological activity were more severely disturbed than others.

Despite the severe disturbance of orientation in place and time, she had no disturbance of gnosis and praxis. She recognized drawings (even when crossed out) and repeated the position of the doctor's hands correctly. She made mistakes only occasionally when, for instance, she had to recode the instruction before she could carry it out. She corrected her mistakes relatively easily by means of verbal analysis of the instruction. In the reciprocal coordination test, she showed evidence of unawareness of the left hand and had a tendency to slip into symmetrical movements. She perceived rhythms correctly and reproduced them well in response to both visual and verbal instructions.

She could solve relatively complex problems involving a choice reaction even if the conditions of the test were conflicting (for example, showing a finger in response to a fist or vice versa, or tapping once in response to two taps and twice in response to one tap). She retained the instruction in her memory throughout the test and only occasionally found it necessary to assist herself by repeating it aloud. She forgot the instruction only if the test was interrupted by a pause or by interfering conversation, and on those occasions asked again what she should do.

She could easily draw named figures, and if the instruction could be carried out without delay, could even draw a series of named figures, with mistakes only at the end of the series. For example, when asked to draw two circles, a cross, and a dot, she drew the first three figures correctly, repeating, "two circles, a cross... and what else?" She had no difficulty in tests requiring preliminary recoding on the instruction; she drew "a cross under a circle" or "the letter *b* under the letter *i*," and she quickly suppressed the tendency toward incorrect echopraxic performance of the instruction.

She had no disturbance of phonemic hearing. She could easily repeat single words or series of three or four words, even after a pause of 10 to 15 sec. She had no difficulty in understanding words and easily pointed to named objects (even if the names were given in pairs). As a rule, she had no difficulty in naming drawings shown to her, although sometimes she would have slight difficulty in finding the necessary names. These difficulties usually appeared, however, only when she had to use comparatively unfamiliar words and as a rule the defects were easily compensated. Only rarely did she exhibit paraphasia when naming objects.

She willingly examined thematic pictures shown to her and gave her interpretation of them, although, admittedly, this was not always correct. For instance, looking at "the broken window" picture often used in clinical practice, she said, "Well, in my opinion, this boy came home and another boy was there already and he could not understand why there was no room for him... and his father persuaded him that the position was already filled by the other boy and he would have to go and work somewhere else..." However, she was able to correct this mistake; after she had examined the broken window, the key thematic element of the picture, she corrected her original guess and said, "Obviously they have caught the other boy here, not this one... he had gone to school, to be sure, because he has his satchel..."

This patient had no difficulty in understanding logical relationships (e.g., relationships of opposition). She could solve relatively simple problems involving the selection of analogous relationships, and carry out simple arithmetical calculations (e.g., simple addition of two numbers each with two digits—24 + 17 or 34 + 12; subtraction—41 − 27; or multiplication—12 x 7). She could solve arithmetical problems, and if her impaired memory prevented doing this mentally, the difficulties were overcome by solving the problem in writing, in which case she could solve even comparatively difficult problems. This distinctive process of the patient's struggle with forgetting the elements of the task and drifting into irrelevant associations will be analyzed further below.

The neuropsychological tests thus revealed the relative integrity of this patient's higher cortical functions, although this was accompanied by a severe amnesic syndrome with marked disorientation in place and time and with definite confabulations.

We can now move on to the central problem of the nature of these memory disturbances without the risk that they could be masked by additional defects.

Structure of Mnemonic Disorder

The first question investigated was, is the amnesic syndrome described in this patient based on weak traces or, in other words, their rapid spontaneous decay? This would be a natural suggestion; however, the contradictory data mentioned above make it doubtful, and call for a more precise definition of the conditions under which existing traces are "forgotten." To answer this question, a series of tests was carried out and we shall now examine their results.

Konorski's test. One of the most suitable tests for our purpose was that suggested originally by Konorski (1969). (See Chapter 2.)

To investigate the stability of existing traces, Konorski presented the subject with a visual stimulus (e.g., a blue square), and then after an interval (30 sec to 2 min) he presented another stimulus, sometimes identical with the first, sometimes differing from it in shape or color (e.g., a blue rhombus or a green square). The subject had to say whether the two stimuli were the same or not. If the traces of the first stimulus had decayed, naturally this comparison would be impossible.

The test was carried out on this patient, and in order to analyze the stability of different traces, it was carried out in several series. In one series, the stimuli differed in only one dimension (color), and in other tests, in several dimensions (color and shape). In another series, the figures were replaced by sounds of speech (*a, o, u*), but the conditions of the test were the same.

The test gave perfectly clear results: The patient was able to retain the trace of the first stimulus for 30 sec, 1 min, 1.5 min, or even 2 min; however, if an interfering factor was introduced or the patient herself was instructed to perform an interfering task during this interval, she could no longer compare the two stimuli and, in some cases, she even forgot that the first stimulus had been presented. Let me give a few examples.

a–(pause of 5 sec)–a	*a–(pause of 5 sec)–o*
The same	Different
a–(pause of 15 sec)–a	*a–(pause of 15 sec)–o*
The same	Different
o–(pause of 1 min)–o	*u–(pause of 1 min)–a*
The same	One was *u* and the other *a*
u–(pause of 2 min)–u	*u–(pause of 2 min)–o*
The same	Different

a–(pause of 15 sec filled with conversation)–a
Now I didn't recognize anything. . . you gave me *a*.

u–(pause of 30 sec filled with conversation)–u
I was distracted, I can't remember.

Similar results were obtained in tests involving comparison of figures differing either in color or in shape.

Tests with a fixed set. In the second series of tests to study the stability of traces, the method of the fixed set suggested by Uznadze was used. (See Chapter 2.)

This method is as follows: The subject was asked to close her eyes and then to feel two spheres of different sizes (4 cm and 6 cm in diameter) with both hands several (12 to 15) times, after which she was given two equal spheres. The set produced by feeling the larger sphere with the left hand leads to an illusion of contrast, in which the equal spheres were assessed as unequal, the sphere in the right hand being considered to be the larger. In normal subjects, this illusion is stable, persisting after an interval of 2 to 5 min (or sometimes much longer), and disappears only gradually.

In these tests, the patient gave results that differ substantially from those found ordinarily. She retained a fixed set for quite a long time, for it disappeared only gradually even after an interval of 2 min, but if that interval were filled with interfering activity, the fixed set quickly disappeared. These observations tend to confirm the hypothesis that this patient's forgetting was based not so much on weakness of the traces as on their inhibitability by interfering factors.

Investigation of Speech Memory

Memorizing series of words. After these preliminary tests, we come now to the series of tests that forms the central part of this investigation. The patient could easily memorize series of three or four isolated words and retain them after an interval (2 to 3 min). The introduction of interfering activity, however, was sufficient to prevent repetition of the recently memorized series.

A series of four words was given for the patient to repeat—at first after an unfilled pause, and later after a pause filled with irrelevant activity.

Repetition of series of words after "empty" pause

House–table–bell–forest
    Correctly
(Pause of 30 sec)
    Correctly
(Pause of 2 min)
    Correctly
(Pause of 3 min)
    Correctly

Repetition of series of words after pause filled with solving
arithmetical problems

House–table–bell–forest
    Correctly
(Pause of 1 min)
    I can't remember. . . it seems like house–table. . . no, I have forgotten.

    (The words are repeated; pause of 1 min filled with arithmetical calculation.)
    I have forgotten it all.

Similar results were obtained in tests to study the effect of "homogeneous interference."

The patient was instructed to memorize and repeat a group of two or three words and she was warned that she must memorize this group. She was then given a second similar group of words, which she also had to memorize. Next she was asked to state the words that formed the first group, and then those that formed the second group.
If she was unable to do this, the test was repeated several times.

The results of this series of tests were quite clear: The patient easily retained a series of two, three, or even four words, but was quite unable to recall the first series after being given a second similar series. This phenomenon did not occur when memorizing single words. It began to be manifested in tests of memorizing pairs of words, and it assumed a severe form with 3-word series. In this last case, not even a long period of learning series by heart could overcome the effect of retroactive inhibition of the second group of words of the first. Let us consider some examples.

Recalling single words

I. *Box*	II. *Spectacles*	*?/I*	*?/II*
Correctly	Correctly	Correctly	Correctly

        (Pause of 30 sec)

?/I	*?/II*	*?/I*	*?/II*
Correctly	Correctly	Correctly	Correctly

Recalling pairs of words

I. *Sun–cat*	II. *Knife–forest*	*?/I*	*?/II*
(1) Correctly	Correctly	Correctly	Sun. . . cat
(2) Correctly	Correctly	Scissors and forest	Sun. . . and cat

(Pause of 30 sec)

What words did I speak to you? "Just now you didn't say anything. . . you said cat when you came. . . before this you said. . . no, even then you said nothing, you only said that there would be some words." *Maybe, but what words did I speak to you?* "What?. . . it is very difficult to remember."

Recalling series of three words

I. *House–forest–cat*	II. *Night–needle–pie*	*?/I*	*?/II*
(1) Correctly	Correctly	Correctly	I have forgotten.
(2) "	"	House–needle. . . pie	Just now. . . I can't remember.
(3) "	"	House–table. . . no. . .	Something else . . . table

I. *House–forest–cat*	II. *Night–needle–pie*	*?/I*	*?/II*
(4) Correctly	Correctly	I don't remember.	I still don't remember.
(5) "	"	House, table. . . and this (looks at the doctor) one writes with his hands.	House, table. . . and something else
(6) "	"	Correctly	Now I have forgotten the second word. . . needle. . . pie and a third
(7) "	"	"	. . . I don't know. . .
(8) "	"	"	. . . house– night. . . needle, pie
(9) "	"	"	. . . needle. . . pie, and some-thing else

The inhibitory effect of interfering activity provides an explanation of the fact that memorizing a long series of words (e.g., a series of 10 unconnected words) was outside the patient's grasp. This was because of the inhibitory effect of the elements of the series on each other. This hypothesis is also confirmed by the fact that although this patient could not actively repeat a series of words given to her, she could recognize many more elements of a series than she was able to repeat in each attempt.

Recalling sentences. As a rule, it is easier to remember sentences, each consisting of a single semantic entity, than to remember a series of discrete words. The situation was quite different, however, with our patient (with a marked amnesic syndrome). Although she could easily memorize and retain one sentence, she was unable to recall it after another sentence had been given to her. The second sentence exerted such strong retroactive inhibition on the first that the patient either could not recall the recently imprinted traces at all or she perseverated the second sentence or mixed elements of both sentences; or, as a final alternative, she started to drift into irrepressible irrelevant associations or impressions.

A sentence was read to the patient for her to repeat; she was then given another sentence, after which she was instructed to recall the first sentence followed by the second. This test was repeated 10 times.

I. *Apple trees grew in the garden behind a high fence.*	II. *A hunter killed a wolf on the edge of the forest.*	?/I	?/II
(1) Correctly	Correctly	We saw. . . a wolf at the edge of the forest. . .	Just now. . . the second. . . we saw with our. . . we saw wolf at the edge of the forest. . .
(2) "	"	At the edge of the forest. . . what did we see?	And the second. . . we saw. . . what?
(3) "	"	In the garden. . . wait. . . we saw a wolf at the edge of the forest. . .	And the second. . . we killed it.
(4) "	"	Well, we saw. . . wait. . . my brains aren't working	I don't recall the second at all. . . sometimes I can't remember the first, sometimes the second.
(5) "	"	The first was that at the edge of the forest. . .	And the second. . . that we killed a wolf at the edge of the forest, we saw a wolf . . . we saw and I mean we began to kill.

(6)	"	"	The first, I mean, we saw something at the edge of the forest. . . what did we see there?	And the second, what the person who killed the wolf himself says.
(7)	"	"	I don't even know what the first was.	Gives up
(8)	"	"	I have forgotten already.	Gives up
(9)	"	"	I have forgotten. . . I mean, a hunter killed a wolf at the edge of the forest.	And the second? Whom did they kill?
(10)	"	"	I have forgotten.	Could it be that somebody or something was killed?

Memorizing stories. This marked disturbance of recall by interfering factors and drifting into irrelevant associations suggest that this patient retained more complex systems less well than simple ones. This conclusion was confirmed by tests of memorizing stories.

The patient could memorize simple stories consisting of a single theme relatively easily but was unable to memorize more difficult stories containing two themes. Naturally, she was unable to recall a first story after having had a second story read to her.

L. N. Tolstoy's story, "The Hen and the Golden Eggs," was read to her. She repeated it relatively easily although not absolutely accurately: "There was. . . a hen, and she laid eggs. . . but the master wanted all the eggs to be gold. He took the hen and killed her. . . and everything stopped."
What is the moral? "That you mustn't hurt hens. . ."
L. N. Tolstoy's story, "The Jackdaw and the Pigeons," was read to her. She immediately said: "No, it did not work. . ." And she went on to repeat the story as follows: "Just now. . . now. . . a pigeon. . . they added a jackdaw to their number. . . she listened and then she flew to them. . . but she could not change her color. . . and nothing turned out right for her. . . they flew away. . . then he took a pigeon—and it was made a pigeon already. . . and flew somewhere. . . no, it is difficult."
(The story was read again). *Tell the story?.* . . "A jackdaw. . . wait a minute now, it is all confused. . . the jackdaw decided. . . that she. . . would make. . . how do they cry? How do jackdaws cry? I am telling this story badly. . . my brains are not working properly. . ."
Can you recall the first story? "About these. . . about a hen. . ." *And what happened to the hen?* "What indeed? The hen brought. . . something. . . now what did she bring? This one. . . was it a chicken?. . . but everything is wrong. . . for some reason I cannot recall it. . ."

The ease with which recently imprinted traces were inhibited and replaced by irrelevant associations became more evident still if the repetition of the story was delayed for 1 to 2 min. As we have seen, this delay had no effect on the retention of short series of words or sentences. It severely impaired the repetition of complex sentantic structures, each of which evokes many irrepressible associations. After a long time interval (3 to 4 days), the patient could recall details by way of reminiscence of what was apparently a forgotten theme. This confirms the view that the defects described above were the result, not of trace decay, but of inhibition of their immediate repetition.

* * *

We have studied the defects exhibited by this patient when repeating verbal material (series of isolated words, sentences, and stories). Similar observations were made in tests with visual material. In these cases also the patient could easily retain isolated pictures or pairs of pictures. If the patient was given two pairs of pictures to memorize in succession, however, she could no longer recall the first pair. She either recalled fragments of material presented earlier, or abandoned the task, declaring that she had "forgotten it all," that she was confused and could not recall what had been shown to her.

Characteristically, in both this and the previous series of tests, a few minutes after examining the pictures or completing the drawings the patient would be unable to recall what she had done. When asked, "Did you look at pictures?" she said, "No, I have not see any pictures today..."

Recalling verbal associations. The tests described above bring us to the next problem: To what extent could this patient with an amnesic syndrome retain associative connections in the verbal system and under the influence of what factors were these connections broken?

To investigate this problem, a series of tests similar to those described above was used. The patient was given words to which she had to respond with a verbal association (e.g., "light—darkness" or "pen—book"); she was then given the first word of each pair and instructed to respond with the second. The test was carried out under various conditions, with pauses of different lengths between presentations and response, and with the presentation of a second pair of words before the first pair of associated words was recalled.

These tests gave a similar result to that already described. Although a single verbal association could be retained for a long period of time, the recalling of this system of associations was grossly impaired after the recalling of a second system. Even if the association was subsequently reinforced (this was very difficult), it again disintegrated after a pause.

The patient was instructed to respond to the word "light" with the word "darkness," and to the word "pen" with the word "book." The first verbal association was easily consolidated and was retained reasonably firmly, for it was still present after long time intervals; however, the second association was unstable and disintegrated more easily after a pause.

Light—darkness   *Pen—book*
Light—"darkness"   Pen—"I can't. . . what is it?"

    (The instruction is repeated; pause of 1 min.)

Light—"darkness"   Pen—"science"

    (Pause of 2 min)

Light—"darkness"   Pen—"science"

    (Pause of 5 min)

Light—"darkness"   Pen—"It is harder now to respond
                                             to pen."

The same test was carried out with another pair of associated words, this time without any direct semantic connection ("table"—"tooth" and "willow"—"heron"), and again the results were the same.

Test of indirect memorizing. The investigation of the retention and recall of verbal associations leads us to the question of whether the defects of memory could be compensated by indirect memorizing. Under normal conditions the use of logical associations is an important method of widening the natural limits of memory. Could this tactic be used to compensate the defects observed in this patient? The fact that she could easily form associations but could not recall them selectively suggests that her ability to utilize semantic associations as aids to memorizing would be very limited in this case, or perhaps even nonexistent.

To study indirect memorizing, the methods described by Leont'ev (1930) were used. For instance, the patient had to memorize a given word (e.g., "coffee") and she was instructed to use a picture (e.g., a "cup") to help her, by forming an association between them. The cards were then presented again and she was asked to recall the words of which they reminded her.

These tests confirmed the hypothesis. They showed that the patient could in fact easily form an auxiliary association and that her intellectual processes remained intact. After a short time, however, when these auxiliary cues (picture cards) were presented again, they either evoked no associations whatever, or irrelevant associations sprang up and distracted the patient from the original meaning.

Appropriate results are described below (Table 29).

The patient was given 8 words in succession and instructed to make use of an appropriate picture card in order to memorize each of them. She was asked what association she would use to help her. Then she was shown the separate picture cards and asked to recall the words she had learned with their aid.

The patient could easily form semantic associations between the word and the picture card, but when the cards were presented again later she either

TABLE 29

INDIRECT MEMORIZING OF WORDS WITH THE AID OF PICTURE CARDS

Word to be memorized	Auxiliary picture card	Indirect association	Process of recalling words*
1. *Coffee*	(Cup)	"It will be coffee, I remember."	(5) "Here is a cup of coffee." *What was the word?* "We must give some coffee to the boy athlete."
2. *Village*	(Hen)	"Cock and village"	(2) "Hen?" *And what was the word?* "I had to say hen for team. . . or game. . . but this is a team. . . I never played football. . ."
3. *Morning*	(Bed)	"I can easily recall that. . . a sofa. . ."	(4) "Sofa." *What was the word?* "The word was sofa. . . I should add with a pillow. . ." *Is it really?* "Yes of course, a sofa. . ."
4. *Shop*	(Dog)	"About a dog. . . a shop. . . and here is the dog. . ."	(1) "Dog." *And what was the word?* "Only it isn't a dog. . . no, in my opinion, it is a dog. . . I can't remember. . ."
5. *Field*	(Melon)	"Melon—and there it is in the field. . . yes, the melon is growing in a field. . ."	(6) "Melon—this one was left. . . our athlete. . ." *And what was the word?* "He must not have been chosen, our boy athlete."
6. *River*	(Flag)	"I have to remember. . . a flag flying—that means a river. . ."	(7) "We need a place for the flag, somewhere to put it. . ."
7. *Caucasus*	(Grape)	"There is a grape here—this must be the Caucasus. . ."	(3) "Grape. . ." *And what was the word?* "Besides grape, what else could there be?"
8. *Boy*	(Football match)	Football, we need a football boy. . . The word has to be memorized because they play football and not girls. . ."	(8) "It is a football match."

*Figures in this column denote the order in which the pictures are presented.

simply named the picture or perseverated the "frozen" association ("football team"). The picture card was never used as an aid for recalling the required word.

Further tests showed that the patient could not recognize the significance of the picture card used as an aid, even having picked it out from the possible alternatives.

Tell me: What word did you memorize with the help of the picture of a melon? Was it the word "boy"? "No... perhaps, a boy as well, it was a game of football..." *Was there perhaps a shop?* "No... a boy but not... I missed out the shop..." *Was it field?* "No, not field... perhaps a small field, where a few people were lying on the ground..."
What word did you memorize with the aid of the picture of a grape? "I don't know." *Was it an apple?* "No." *A shop?* "No." *The Caucasus?* "No... he was born in the Caucasus..." *Are you sure it wasn't the Caucasus?* "Quite sure."

The facts described above suggest that this patient could not form the necessary associations and she could not therefore recall the word designated by the picture card.

To verify this hypothesis, a control test was carried out during which auxiliary associations were formed by the examiner and expressed in expanded form (e.g., "field—melon," the melon grows in the field; "shop—dog," the dog guards the shop, etc.), after which the patient was shown the picture cards again and she had to recall the necessary word. The expanded semantic associations given to the patient did not change the situation. When shown the corresponding picture cards, the patient was still unable to recall the required word and instead she either abandoned the task or produced other random associations.

Similar results were obtained also when the patient was given ready-made associations (e.g., when given the instruction: You must remember the word "school" when I show you the picture of "a button"—in school you learn how to sew on a button; or: You must recall the word "theatre" when I show you the picture of a "comb"—the actresses comb their hair with a comb; etc.). Even in this case, the subsequent presentation of the picture card aids evoked only further random associations and she hardly ever recalled the required word.

Sharply reducing the number of words which the patient had to memorize with the aid of the pictures did not change the results. In some tests, even the attempt to memorize a single word with the aid of a picture card was unsuccessful, for presenting the card after a short interval (1 min) was followed, not by recalling the necessary word, but by the arousing of associations unconnected with it.

This gross disorder of indirect memorizing occurred, not because the patient did not form the necessary auxiliary association, but because the associations which appeared inhibited the preceding word and continued to evoke fresh irrelevant association.

The case described above (*patient Rak.*) is typical of the picture of the disturbances of memory and consciousness appearing in patients with large deep brain tumors disturbing the normal function of the diencephalon and hypothalamus and of adjacent zones of the limbic region.

Unfortunately, the location of the lesion of *patient Rak.* could not be verified postmortem. This gives particular interest to the detailed neuropsychological investigation of the second patient (*patient Bel.*)[25], in whom the pattern of the mnemonic disorders was similar, and the location of the lesion was verified at autopsy, so that the gap in our information can be filled. In this case, very severe mnemonic disorders were caused by a tumor (craniophyaryngioma) replacing the hypothalamus and mammillary bodies and compressing Broca's periolfactory area and the region of both hippocampal gyri (which themselves showed no visible changes). The detailed postmortem findings make this case particularly demonstrative.

Patient Bel., a 36-year-old female who worked at a kindergarten, was admitted to the Burdenko Institute of Neurosurgery in May, 1967, in a serious condition with gross disturbances of memory, incomplete orientation in time, and anterograde amnesia.

Her illness began in the spring of 1966, when she developed headaches accompanied by vomiting. Since December, 1966, she had been forgetful, sleepy, and untidy; sometimes she had fits and lost consciousness. Definite metabolic disturbances were noted: She had put on considerable weight and had ceased to menstruate. At the Institute of Neurosurgery, to which she was sent, she was apathetic and drowsy, she was unperturbed about her condition, and exhibited a very severe amnesic syndrome. She did not remember the doctor or her neighbors, she could not say confidently where she was, and she was disoriented in time.

The following neurological picture was observed. Examination of the optic fundus revealed primary optic atrophy with obliteration of the outlines of the disc and dilatation of the fundal veins; she had bitemporal hemianopia, visual acuity was reduced to 0.1, there was paresis of the upward movements of the eye, and the corneal reflexes were diminished. Tone was reduced in the left limbs and the tendon reflexes in the upper limbs were diminished. A sucking reflex was present, together with a bilateral Marinesco's reflex, and there was gross asymmetry of Babinski's sign. Sensation was normal and speech remained intact. The cerebrospinal fluid contained 1.31% protein, the cell count was 12/3, and the pressure normal. Roentgenograms of the skull showed no evidence of increased intracranial pressure and there was only slight displacement of the pineal gland to the left.

Comprehensive neurophysiological investigation (N. A. Filippycheva) showed the following: The amplitude of the patient's respiratory movements alternatively rose and fell; during fatigue, which developed rapidly, the inspiratory waves were arranged in groups of four or five, separated by pauses. A pathological state of the cortex was revealed, with widespread, generalized brain-stem effects on the respiratory harmonics reflected both on the plethysmogram and the electroencephalogram. Generalized delta- and theta-waves were characteristic of the latter.

[25]This patient was studied by N. K. Kiyashchenko and T. O. Faller. For the physiological analysis, I am indebted to N. A. Filippycheva and for the postmortem findings, to S. M. Blinkov.

All this clearly indicates a marked decrease of cortical tone and a severe disturbance of corticofugal regulation of afferent excitation arriving from brain stem structures. This state of the cortex disappeared during stimulation and reappeared in a resting state. No evidence of increased intracranial pressure could be found. The whole picture pointed to the existence of an inoperable glial tumor arising from the inferolateral portions of the left lateral ventricle.

The patient died on November 26, 1967, from cardiac and respiratory failure.

At autopsy, a huge cystic tumor (craniopharyngioma) was found to occupy the cavity of the third ventricle, displacing the chiasma anteriorly and compressing it. The tumor, with a cyst measuring 40 x 35 mm, replaced the hypothalamus and pressed the thalamus upward, stretched Broca's periolfactory zone, and severely compressed the mammillary bodies. The medial aspect of the right hippocampal gyrus was compressed. The limbic region macroscopically remained intact (Figure 19).

Neuropsychological tests carried out by N. K. Kiyashchenko over a period of one month gave the following results. The patient's state was one of apathy and primary aspontaneity and she was incompletely oriented. Her condition fluctuated noticeably. Sometimes she was more lively and concerned about her state; however, this concern was fleeting and quickly disappeared. No clearly marked disturbances of gnosis or praxis were ·found but there were distinct disturbances of reciprocal coordination with backwardness of the right hand. Her speech was intact and she carried out intellectual operations without any appreciable difficulty. She could correctly interpret a thematic picture, calculate, and solve relatively difficult arithmetical problems. These findings point to primary integrity of the temporo-parieto-occipital and frontal zones of the cortex.

The central feature of the syndrome was a severe disturbance of cortical tone, with marked fluctuations in her general condition, primary disturbances of activity, and flatness of the emotions, dominated by severe disturbances of memory.

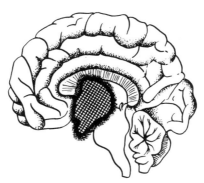

FIG. 19. Position of tumor in patient
Bel. (from postmortem findings).

She retained good memory for personal details. She knew where her husband worked and the names and ages of her children. Nevertheless, her orientation in place was unstable and in time, severely disturbed. She thought that the year was still 1957, that she was at the factory where she had worked 10 years previously, she called the patients by the names of her workmates at that time, denied that she had recently worked in a nursery, but the character of her replies varied sharply depending on her general condition. A few extracts from the records are:

Where are you now? "At the No. 12 factory." *What year is it?* "1958 or 1957." *How old are you?* "27... Oh!... you moved me to Khot'kovo, why couldn't I stay at the factory?... I came to work only this morning, but my head ached..." *Who are these people here?* "They are all people who work at our factory." *And who am I?* "You are somebody from our factory, Valya is my friend... shall we go with you to a movie today?" *How long have you been here?* "One day" (in fact, a week). *Where are you?* "At the factory." *Why are you in bed here?* "I am just resting for a minute... but lying down isn't allowed... (looks at the stopwatch held by the examiner)... I have just finished a time-study—now I have come to lie down..."

Mnemonic Disorders and Their Investigation

Investigation of memorizing revealed considerable defects but, at the same time, also yielded convincing evidence that these disturbances were due to pathologically increased inhibitability of traces by interfering factors rather than to primary weakness of the traces. The results of the test also showed that the defects were not confined to a single modality, but were apparent at all levels of organization.

As in many other similar cases, the retention of a series of isolated elements (words or numbers) reflected only slightly this patient's gross disorders. Recall of 10 isolated words remained at a relatively low level (5-5-3-4-7-4-4-6) despite the patient's altering the order of the components in an attempt to organize the words into particular groups.

Konorski's test. The patient was shown a figure (e.g., a red rhombus), and after an interval of 1 to 2 min she was shown a second figure, either the same or one differing from it in color (a blue rhombus) or in shape (a red triangle), and she was asked to state whether the second figure was the same as the first or different.

The patient had no difficulty retaining the features of the first figure and comparing them with those of the second and she gave the right answer if the interval between the presentation of the two figures was not filled with interfering activity. If interfering activity (e.g., naming objects) was introduced, however, the first shape shown to her disappeared from her memory and not only did she forget what it was, but she actually forgot that any shape had been shown to her.

Memorizing series of discrete elements. In this test, the patient was given a series of two or three words or picture cards which she had to recall, in some cases after an "empty" pause of 1 to 1.5 min, or in other cases after a similar pause filled with interfering activity (solving simple arithmetical problems, naming pictures, etc.). Next followed the familiar test in which the patient was shown one group of two or three words (or pictures) which she had to recall in turn, after which she was asked to recall the two series again in the proper order.

The patient had no difficulty in retaining and recalling series of two or three words (or pictures) or even two groups, each consisting of two words (or pictures), and she was able to go back and recall them again. If the interval between the presentation and repetition of the groups was filled with interfering activity, the traces of the words or pictures disappeared and she declared helplessly that she could not recall them. An increase in the size of the groups to be memorized to three elements made it impossible for her to recall the first group after repeating the second, even in the absence of any interfering activity.

Recalling sentences and stories. Similar results were obtained in tests of the memorizing and recalling of material organized into semantic systems.

Unlike patients with relatively mild mnemonic disorders, in whom the disturbances observed in the recalling of discrete material disappeared with the change to semantically organized material, in this patient such a change revealed the same defects as before. For instance, she had the same difficulty in recalling whole sentences as she had in recalling series of isolated words, pictures and movements.

As a rule, she had no difficulty in grasping the meaning of even a complex story. For example, after hearing "The Ant and the Pigeon" story, she said: "First the pigeon saved the ant, and later the ant saved her." When instructed to repeat the story in detail, however, she often introduced elements of her immediate situation or elements of a previous story into her narrative. For example, when repeating "The Ant and the Pigeon" story, she suddenly said: "The ant came across a lump of sugar" (mixing impressions of a lump of sugar in a sugar basin). When repeating "The Ant and the Pigeon" story after "The Jackdaw and the Pigeon" story, she said: "The jackdaw flew to the hunter (from the previous story), who caught him; he began to beg him, 'Let me go' (fragments from the story read previously–"The Lion and the Mouse"); he did not let him go and he hid himself. The hunter then caught the pigeon, and he began to ask to be set free; he let them go and was left with nothing. . ." (from the earlier story, "The Hen and the Golden Eggs").

Conclusions

We have examined the results of memory tests in two patients with deep brain tumors associated with a massive amnesic syndrome. In both cases, the pathological process involved the system of the corpus callosum, septum pellucidum, hypothalamus and limbic region and caused dysfunction of the deep structures of both cerebral hemispheres. This pathological process led to a marked amnesic (Korsakov's) syndrome, accompanied by general disorientation in place and time and by definite confabulations, in both patients.

The memory disturbances in both patients took the form of severe impairment of memory for current events, difficulty in recalling selective associations of past experience, and a marked disturbance of consciousness with confabulations. It was this last feature that distinguished the patients of this group from those with a tumor of the third ventricle, whose memory disturbances were not accompanied by any gross disturbances of consciousness or confabulations.

The structure of mnemonic disorders, mainly pathologically increased inhibitability of traces by interfering factors and equalized excitability of traces in different systems were similar in both types of lesions. The loss of association selectivity and the ease with which the patient drifted into irrelevant associations, which led to total disintegration of recall, was a new phenomenon distinguishing the syndrome of massive memory disturbances just described, and bringing it closer to a disturbance of consciousness.[26] As we shall see below, a closely similar syndrome can be found in patients after rupture of aneurysms located in the deep zones of the brain, disturbing the blood supply to the brain structures mentioned above.

---

[26] I have presented an analysis of facts obtained by the study of two patients with this syndrome. I have made many more observations on patients of this group, and these observations will form the subject of a special publication that is under preparation by T. O. Faller, N. K. Kiyashchenko, L. I. Moskovichute, and N. A. Filippycheva.

CHAPTER VII

Disturbances of Memory and Consciousness After Rupture of an Aneurysm of the Anterior Communicating Artery

We have analyzed disturbance of memory and consciousness associated with a general asthenic state produced by a massive deep brain tumor located in the third ventricle, the hypothalamic region, and the limbic region. These disturbances are usually superimposed on a syndrome of general lowering of cortical tone, increased proneness to fatigue, and frequent fluctuations between states of sleep and wakefulness.

Cases in which disturbances of memory and consciousness are associated, not with depression of cortical. tone, but with normal cortical tone or even with general irritation are no less interesting. This picture is seen particularly clearly in patients with no evidence of increased intracranial pressure or dislocation, when the state of depression typical of patients with brain tumors is absent. Such a state may result after local spasm of blood vessels or a local hemorrhage.

In these cases (Luria, Konovalov, & Podgornaya, 1970), even very early after the hemorrhage patients may revert to their ordinary state—signs of asthenia and reduced wakefulness may no longer be found—but the disorders of memory and consciousness may persist unchanged.

When the operation on the hemorrhage led to spasm of the anterior cerebral arteries, the disturbance of memory can be superimposed upon lasting disorders of consciousness and general disorientation to place, time, and current events.

When the anterior cerebral arteries remained patent, the general state of confusion can disappear, leaving only severe disturbances of memory with unimpaired consciousness. Nevertheless, sometimes the memory disturbances can be severe enough to resemble Korsakov's syndrome.

As in the cases described above, gnosis, praxis, and speech remained intact. The only differences between the pattern observed here and that described earlier were that the memory disturbances now began to appear even in the absence of general asthenia and exhaustion.

I intend to take advantage of the opportunities provided by this group of patients and analyze the two alternative forms of memory disorder. I shall begin by examining the acute period after rupture of an anterior communicating artery aneurysm, accompanied by gross disturbances of memory, confusion, and confabulations. I shall then turn to an examination of a case of a relatively transient circulatory disturbance in the region of the anterior communicating arteries in which the lasting disturbances of memory, unaccompanied by any disorder of consciousness, were connected with a massive deep brain hemorrhage.

Disturbance of Memory and Consciousness in the Acute Period
After Rupture of an Aneurysm of the Anterior
Communicating Artery

We shall commence by analyzing those mnemonic disturbances which occur in the acute period immediately after the rupture of an aneurysm of the anterior communicating artery.

Patient Koch., a 45-year-old male (engineer), suddenly became ill in the middle of January, 1968. He had an abrupt attack of headache and lost consciousness. He received emergency treatment at home. The loss of consciousness was of short duration, but his headache was severe and accompanied by vomiting and by hyperesthesia to sound and light. On the second day, his temperature rose to 38°C and he was excitable, euphoric, and uncritical of his state. After 10 days, on attempting to get up, he had a second, similar attack with severe headache and the same manifestations. Twelve days later, the patient's condition again worsened suddenly and he lost consciousness, developed spasms in his right limbs, a meningeal syndrome, and severe mental disturbances. He became disoriented in place and time, confabulated, and was euphoric.

On admission to a hospital, examination revealed hypo-osmia on the right side, lowered visual acuity to 0.3 in both eyes, and congestion of the veins and narrowing of the arteries in the optic fundus. A central paresis of the right facial nerve was present, tone was increased in the right upper limb, pathological Oppenheim's reflexes were present on the right side, but the muscle power and sensation remained intact. The cerebrospinal fluid contained blood. Arteriography revealed an aneurysm of the anterior communicating artery.

With this diagnosis, the patient was transferred to the Burdenko Institute of Neurosurgery on May 27, 1968. The clinical picture at that time was as follows: No physical abnormality was present, the patient was communicative and could walk about the clinic unaided, but he was confused and disoriented. He confabulated and immediately forgot his confabulation. A well-marked Korsakov's syndrome was present, and it is on this aspect that I shall concentrate.

Neurological examination revealed contraction of the occipital muscles, features of oral automatism, a positive sucking reflex, a bilateral Marinesco's sign, a plastic increase in muscle tone (more marked on the left side), a bilateral grasping reflex (more marked on the right), and a Mayer's reflex on the right. Power was reduced on the right, but the tendon reflexes were increased on the left; the knee jerks were inhibited, a marked tremor was present in the fingers of both hands, and a bilateral positive Babinskii's sign was present. The EEG showed a focus of pathological activity, mainly in the left temporo-central region. Arteriography was repeated and the diagnosis of a saccular aneurysm of the anterior communicating artery was confirmed.

The following conclusion was drawn from these findings: Three hemorrhages had occurred, accompanied by loss of consciousness and development of a meningeal syndrome. The third attack, the most severe, was accompanied by epileptic fits and gross mental disorders, which persisted unchanged, and by a marked Korsakov's syndrome with disorientation in place and time, and confabulations. These observations suggest dysfunction of the medial zones of the frontal lobes (the limbic zone). The extrapyramidal symptoms (increased plastic tone, especially in the right upper limb, pathological signs, and deep reflexes) suggest that the lesion affected the deep structures of the brain, predominantly of the left hemisphere. The presence of complex pyramidal reflexes in the left upper limb, however, indicates that the possibility of involvement of the corresponding zones of the right hemisphere cannot be ruled out.

These findings are evidence of a complex clinical syndrome caused by general hemodynamic disturbances, affecting blood vessels supplying the anterior zones of the subcortical formations and localized in parts of the middle cerebral artery system.

On June 5, 1968, an operation was performed. The cortex of the right frontal lobe was displaced with a spatula to reveal the olfactory nerve, surrounded by deep arachnoid adhesions, after which a saccular aneurysm of the anterior communicating artery was identified. The base of the aneurysm projected into the cortex of the left frontal lobe where, after aspiration, a focus of hemorrhagic softening was found. The operation was uneventful and was attended by no additional complications.

The postoperative course was smooth, and quite soon the patient was able to walk about the clinic unaided. No significant changes in his behavior occurred throughout the period of investigation. Angiography four months after the operation showed no evidence of spasm of the anterior cerebral arteries. This suggests that those pathological changes, which were caused by spasm of the blood vessels accompanying the hemorrhage, had now subsided, leaving behind only residual phenomena of hemorrhagic softening of the brain substance.

The neuropsychological investigation of the patient began after the operation and continued for two months, during which tests were carried out almost daily.

Now for a detailed analysis of the syndrome observed in this patient. He was a man with no physical abnormality, who greeted us warmly, obligingly offered a chair, and was perfectly prepared to talk. He easily gave his surname, his place of work, described what he usually had to do in the course of his work, and indicated the criteria by which the quality of his work could be estimated. He had no difficulty in describing his family, the occupations of his two children, and the usual conditions of their family life at home. He had a good memory of the period during the war in which he served.

The patient's previous knowledge, including logical operations, was equally intact. Quickly, and without any apparent stress, he could perform ordinary operations of multiplication, division, addition, and subtraction (even with numbers consisting of two or three digits), and frequently found the solution before the doctor examining him did. Tests relating whole to part and part to whole, or finding analogies, were not particularly difficult. He easily interpreted the meaning of proverbs and filled in missing words from sentences. He had no appreciable difficulty in understanding the meaning of a picture, and indeed it became clear that he could easily distinguish not only the external concept, but also the emotional quality of the picture. The instruction to name five red or five pointed objects, or to recite the names of the month in the correct or reverse order, gave the patient no difficulty whatsoever. He had no difficulty either in solving harder problems requiring the integrity of expanded solutions and active thinking. For example, he easily discoursed on the subject of "the north." No defects could be detected in the patient's speech; his motor skills remained completely intact and he showed no defects of gnosis.

These findings left an impression of complete integrity of the patient's higher levels of gnosis and praxis, speech and intellectual activity. It appeared that the lateral zones of the cerebral hemispheres (including those of the frontal lobes) reamined untouched by the pathological process.

Mnemonic Disorders

This impression of the considerable psychological integrity vanished completely as soon as tests were carried out to study the patient's memory and his orientation in his surroundings, in place and time, and in his own state. Even superficial observation revealed the memory disturbances of a very severe Korsakov's syndrome with well-marked confabulations. The patient's severe defects came to light as soon as he was asked questions requiring memory of current experience, instead of questions based on firmly established previous knowledge.

A profound disturbance of consciousness was discovered. A normal subject (like a patient with a lesion of the lateral zones of the hemispheres) automatically recalls traces of his direct experience and at once assesses his place, the time, and his own state. This patient was forced to pick out from situations in which he found himself some particular cue and to interpret its importance, and thus eventually to reach logical conclusions regarding the whole circumstances of the situation. Naturally, this led to marked defects in the evaluation of the surrounding situation and of his own state or, in other words, to a profound disturbance of consciousness. These defects were even more conspicuous in the evaluation of time, or recall of the immediate past. This severe disturbance in fixation of traces from the direct situation created a state of confusion in the patient. Absence of traces from incoming information led him to look for probable associations, which assumed the form of confabulations. Let us examine facts illustrating this state of affairs.

The patient knew quite well that his permanent address was in Irkutsk, and he had no difficulty in stating his address as well as that of the place where he worked. Asking where he was now, however, brought him into a state of utter confusion. His surroundings told him that he was not at home, but in some sort of institution. The beds and the patients suggested that the institution was a hospital. The group of doctors and students suggested that it was some sort of institute where teaching was perhaps carried out. Finally, the patient's own experience made it likely that the students were learning some sort of technical subject, perhaps working toward higher qualifications, perhaps on refresher courses. The patient's answers to the question where he was, confirmed this idea. The answers were not consistent. Sometimes he replied that he was taking a course himself, that he had arrived recently, that we (the examiners) were the teachers. Sometimes he said that he was evidently in a hospital, most probably in a railroad hospital at one of the stations. Later, after the name of the institute had been told repeatedly to the patient, he replied that he was in the Burdenko Institute but that he could not say exactly whether this institute was in Irkutsk, in Moscow, or in Leningrad. He was unable to say what sort of an institute it was—teaching or medical. Sometimes he answered that it was a "technical institute," sometimes an "educational institute." If asked what he was doing there, he suggested that he was studying. Characteristically, the patient was unsure of himself when stating these conclusions, and it soon became clear to the observer that he was simply making suggestions of possible places.

In his assessment of place, the patient sometimes came close to reality, but his assessment of time and the immediate past was particularly lacking in confidence, and often represented pure guesses, sometimes becoming confabulations. The patient still retained some diffuse traces of his direct experience. Soon be began to recognize the doctors who visited him, at first purely emotionally but later more definitely. He recognized his own doctor (although not always recollecting his name), and he could say which of the people working in that part of the hospital he met more often than the rest. He recognized the present writer and sometimes asked, "When are you going to bring the professor to see me?" Nevertheless, he never obtained any clear impressions of the order of events. When asked how long he had been in the hospital, he gave answers completely at random. He could not state the time of day, and would either note the absence of clocks or try to guess on the basis of how light it was. He could not give the date, but gave purely random guesses for the day, the month, and the year, and he immediately added that he was quite unsure about this and would ask with curiousity, "Why, how far out was I?"

Similar difficulties arose during attempts to obtain information from the patient about events of the preceding days. When asked how he came to be in the hospital, he said humorously, "Through disrespect to my parents," and at once added, "No, I am joking" and produced a version evidently linked by association with the group "parents": "I brought my daughter here, she was ill. . . and I was ill myself. . . and by chance I came with them myself. . . then they suddenly had to go to Khabarovsk and returned to Irkutsk. . . now it is all over and they have gone to study. . . and here am I. . . sent by the district committee to see about the grain storage. . . and that is how I came to be here. . ." All these hypotheses were expressed without any sense of confidence, more as logical suggestions than as answers to questions about actual events, and within a minute he could produce a totally different version and deny that he had ever suggested anything else.

The patient's confusion and his substitution of confabulations for the recalling of real events were particularly conspicuous when he was asked what he did the same morning or the night before. In such cases, he was distinctly unsure of himself and quickly slipped into confabulations, sometimes arising under the influence of direct impressions and sometimes the repetition of some well consolidated previous experience.

A few examples to illustrate this state of affairs are:

The patient was asked, *What did you do yesterday morning?* "This morning. . . at 8 or 9 o'clock,. . . I got ready and went out. . . out of town. . . I went to the grain store. . . and then walked on further. . . they said that some wheels have been thrown away and the children could use them. . ." *And before that where did you go this morning?* "To the farm to get some milk. . ." *But you said you went to the grain store?* "To the grain store? No. . . I never said that," and so on.

No better description of the patient's condition can be given than this fragment from his conversation. The patient had no clear idea of events that had just taken place and filled the gaps in his memory indiscriminately with associations which, in turn, became forgotten. If these associations came into direct conflict with the other elements, the patient began to sense the contradiction and his intact logical operations led him to try to find a way out of the conflict. The hypotheses disappeared almost as soon as they appeared, however, so the patient reverted to fresh confabulations having forgotten the old ones.

Naturally, under these conditions the patient's assessment of his own state was very poor. He was unable to answer exactly whether he was fit or not, and instead simply guessed. If he interpreted the surrounding situation as a hospital, he would conclude that he was ill—he then had to form an hypothesis about the part of him that was affected. If certain features of the situation suggested to him that he was in an educational establishment, he would postulate that he had come there to study, that he was taking part in a refresher course, and no idea of illness entered his head.

The phenomena of confusion just described were evident not only during conversation, but also in behavior. As a rule, the patient's behavior in the clinic was that of a confused, disoriented person. Sometimes he asked when his wife would be coming (although she was then in the hospital, in the corridor). Sometimes he began to seek the way out to the street, in order to go somewhere. One Sunday he actually found the way out to the street, hailed a passing taxi, and asked the driver to take him "to the sanatorium," and only when, instead of money, the patient offered him a temperature chart did the driver realize that he was dealing with a person with a disturbance of his faculties, and took him back to the institute.

This picture reveals the intimate connection between the states of consciousness and the disturbance of memory. It is not sufficient to allow conclusions about the nature of this connection or the mechanism underlying the disturbances. Were true disturbances of trace fixatiort from direct experience present in this case, or were there other conditions that prevented trace recall and led to disorders of selectivity? These questions are crucial to the rest of the investigation. I shall try to answer them by examining, in turn, the degree of preservation and retrieval of, first, the most elementary sensory and sensorimotor traces, then more complex verbal traces, and finally the conditions under which the precise recall of traces becomes impossible.

Tests with a Fixed Set

Analysis of the patient's mnemonic processes began with tests that showed to what extent he preserved his elementary sensorimotor traces and under what conditions their preservation began to be impaired. The most adequate test to answer this question is the well-known test with a fixed set, introduced by Academician D. M. Uznadze. The patient was able to retain traces of the fixed set for a long time, even if a pause of 1 min was introduced between the set and the control test. The important fact was that traces of an induced fixed set remained virtually intact in this patient even though, on questioning, the patient could actually have "forgotten" that the test had been carried out with him, and he insisted that he was seeing the balls for the first time. This association between the firm retention of traces of a sensorimotor set and loss of the ability to give a verbal account of the tests was the most important result of this test. Similar observations have been made previously by other workers (Claparède; later, A. N. Leont'ev).

The results of the tests make it necessary to look for conditions under which the retention of an existing sensorimotor trace becomes unstable and its recall becomes difficult, if not completely impossible. Evidence obtained by many investigators studying patients with Korsakov's syndrome has led to the hypothesis that the disturbance of the mnemonic processes in these cases is based not so much on the weakness of traces, as on their inhibition by interfering agents, preventing their recall. To test this hypothesis, a special series of tests was carried out in which the pause between the conditioning and control tests was filled with interfering activity, in some cases of a completely different character (mental arithmetic), and in others of a sensorimotor character (tapping out a rhythm).

The tests showed that whereas a pause not filled with interfering activity (empty) did not disturb the retention of the fixed set, filling the pause with interfering activity, as a rule, caused the traces of the fixed set to disappear, and the illusion exhibited immediately after production of the set was no longer retained. This was observed equally when the interference was heterogeneous (mental arithmetic) or homogeneous (tapping out a rhythm).

An important conclusion can be drawn from these facts. It now seems probable that the amnesic syndrome observed in this patient was based, not so much on weakness of direct sensorimotor traces, as on their inhibition by interfering factors, and that this occurred even with very elementary forms of sensorimotor experience.

In the tests, the issue was the retention of very simple sensorimotor traces induced by objects (balls) presenting only one feature (volume). In this case, as the tests showed, the fixed trace (difference in volume) persisted even after a pause separating the conditioning tests from the control, and it disappeared only if the pause was filled with interfering factors. The question must next be asked: Does this picture apply also under more complex conditions when the objects compared have several features and when the subject has to pick out one particular feature as the basis for comparison?

One fact in the previous tests suggested that the selective distinguishing of one feature caused this patient considerable difficulty even in the simplest test. In some cases, when the patient had to compare objects (balls) by their size, in the course of the test he forgot this condition and began to compare them by weight. This suggested that much more serious complications could be produced if the patient were given the task of fixing pairs of objects differing in several features.

For this purpose, the test described above was repeated, with one difference—instead of the equal balls, he was given two cups or a cup and a glass stopper to assess on the basis of size. The results of this series of tests justified our expectations. During tests with complex objects (having several features), the retention of the evoked trace (the fixed set) was less stable. Even a simple pause, not filled by interfering activity, was sufficient to lead to the disintegration of this more complex trace.

These results suggest that retention of the trace of the fixed set for a relatively long time was possible in this patient only under the simplest conditions, when fixation of the trace did not require any preliminary choice. Under more complicated conditions, extinction (or inhibition) of the fixed trace began much sooner.

Tests with Fixation of Sensory Traces

In the fixed set tests, we studied the fate of sensorimotor traces arising without premeditation in the form of involuntary illusions. What, if anything, distinguishes the higher forms of mnemonic processes arising from verbal instruction? The most convenient way of testing sensory forms of mnemonic activity is by the method suggested originally by Konorski (previously described). The tests carried out on our patient, like those described earlier, differed in only one feature; in addition to the classical Konorski's test, in which the interval between the two shapes was not filled with any form of activity (an empty pause), a series of tests was carried out in which the interval between presentation of the two figures was filled with interfering activity, such as mental arithmetic (multiplying a number consisting of two digits by one consisting of a single digit).

The two series of experiments on this patient gave precise results. The patient was able to retain the visual form of the shape presented, and to carry out the operation of comparing the second shape with the first, provided that the interval between them did not exceed 1 min. He could do so partly if the interval was 2 min, but in this case errors appeared, suggesting that trace of the first figure was starting to disappear.

The series in which the interval separating the presentation of the two figures was filled with interfering activity gave quite different results. Even when this interfering activity was completely different in character, when it differed from the activity of comparing the visual forms (mental arithmetic), it had a strongly inhibitory action on the recall of the trace of the first shape and on the performance of the task. If the interval did not exceed 30 sec, the patient made mistakes in half of all the cases, for he failed to retain either the color or shape of the first figure and substituted guesses for true comparison. If the interval amounted to 1 min, the number of correct answers was reduced and in some cases presentation of the second shape did not even arouse an attempt to compare it with the first figure. Finally, if the interval was increased to 2 min, the task of comparing the two shapes was completely forgotten and the patient helplessly asked what he ought to be doing, or he began to carry out one of the instructions given in previous tests, which sprang up by way of reminiscence. The results of the corresponding tests[27] are given below.

Tests with empty pause

(Pause of 30 sec)
(1) GR–RR: "Different, the first was green"

(2) BT–BT: "The same"
(3) RR–BR: "The first was red, that means this must be different"

(4) GR–GT: "Different in shape"
(5) GT–GT: "The same"

(6) RR–BR: "Different in color but the same in shape"

Tests with intervals filled with interfering activity (multiplication)

(Pause of 30 sec)
(1) GR–RT: "This is different, the first was blue"

(2) BT–BT: "This is the same"
(3) RR–BR: "The same" *Are you sure?* "Quite sure"

(4) GR–GT: "Different in shape"
(5) GT–GT: "Different in shape, the first was a square"

(6) RR–BR: "The same"

---

[27]GR–green rhombus; RR–red rhombus; BT–blue triangle; GT–green triangle, etc.

(Pause of 1 min)
(1) GR–RT: "Different, the first was green"

(2) BT–BT: "The same"
(3) RR–GR: "Different, the first was red"

(4) GT–GR: "Different in shape, the same in color"
(5) GT–GT: "Both the same"
(6) RT–BR: "They are quite different"

(Pause of 2 min)
(1) GR–RT: "Different. . . the first was apparently blue"

(2) BT–BT: "Exactly the same"

(3) RR–GR: "Exactly the same. . . both squares. . . but color–I have forgotten"

(4) GR–GR: "They are the same color, but different in shape"
(5) RT–GR: "The same. . . one was blue. . ."
(6) GR–RT: "This is different, the first was green. . . and they are different in shape"

(Pause of 1 min)
(1) GR–RT: "What am I supposed to do?. . ."

(2) BT–BT: "The same"
(3) RR–GR: "This is the same, it is blue also"

(4) GT–GR: "The same" *What about shape?* "The same"
(5) GT–GT: "The same"
(6) RT–RR: "I have forgotten. . . compared with green?. . ."

(Pause of 2 min)
(1) GR–RT: "I am listening. . . what must I do?" *You must compare the two figures.* "When was that? We have never spoken about it. . ."
(2) BT–BT (raises hand): *What must you do?* "I must lift my left hand" (from previous tests with a reaction of choice)
(3) RR–GT (patient confused): "The same?. . ." *How are they the same?* "It is like the blue one. . ."
(4) GR–GR (patient confused): "I don't know what to do. . ."
(5) RR–GR: "What must I do?"

(6) GT–BT (raises left hand): "Ought I to do it twice?. . ." (reminiscence of a previous test)

The results of this series of tests are summarized in Table 30.

The inhibitory effect of interfering activity, leading to inability to retain the traces is revealed perfectly clearly by these tests.

Tests of Conditioned Motor Responses

In the series of tests just described, traces from sensory stimuli could be retained by this patient for 1 to 2 min, but they were inhibited by interfering factors. The question arises: Is a similar situation observed in the retention of complex conditioned motor responses formed to a spoken instruction? Claparède observed that the conditioned motor response to nociceptive stimulation, if evoked in a patient with Korsakov's syndrome, remained intact even though the patient had forgotten the fact that such a connection had been formed (A. N. Leont'ev made equivalent observations).

Similar tests were carried out with this patient; the only difference from tests referred to above was that the conditioned motor response was formed

TABLE 30

NUMBER OF CORRECT PERFORMANCES OF KONORSKI'S TESTS
OF COMPARING SHAPES (PERCENTAGE OF TOTAL
PRESENTATIONS)

Type of pause	Length of pause		
	30 sec	1 min	2 min
Empty	100	100	100
Filled (mental arithmetic)	50	34	0

with the aid of a spoken instruction, after which the patient was tested without verbal reinforcement.

The patient was instructed to raise his hand (or make a fist) in response to a tap, or to raise his right hand in response to one tap and his left hand in response to two taps. In some cases, the test was made more difficult; the patient was instructed to point with his finger in response to being shown a fist, and to show his fist in response to being shown a finger. By such a test, it was possible to determine to what extent the patient's conditioned motor response was preserved if the traces of the verbal instruction were in conflict with the direct visual signal. After direct testing, showing that this conditioned motor response had been formed, two series of tests were carried out. In the first series, before application of the corresponding stimulus, a pause of 30 sec to 2 min, unfilled with interfering activity (an empty pause), was introduced. In the second series, the pause was filled with some form of interfering activity (usually multiplying numbers of two digits by numbers of one or two digits), after which the conditioned stimulus was presented, without any reinforcement by the instruction.

As the results of these tests showed, a simple conditioned response (raise the hand in response to a tap) was easily formed to a spoken instruction and was preserved after an empty pause of 1 or 2 min. The same result was found in tests of a complex reaction of choice (raise the right hand in response to one tap and the left hand to two taps). The patient performed the reflex movement easily and with adequate stability, and could still perform after an empty pause of 1 to 2 min. One interesting fact was found; after a pause of 1 to 2 min, the patient sometimes could no longer retain the system of the responses but replaced it by the opposite (raising his left hand to one tap and his right hand to two taps). This easy loss of selectivity was manifested both in his practical repetition of the reflex movement and also in his verbal account. It is significant, however, that a pause of 1 to 2 min did not cause the traces of the motor response to disappear. In one test traces of the motor response were still present (although slightly deformed) after 24 hours. The results were completely different if the pause was filled with interfering activity. A stimulus applied after such a pause not only no longer evoked the necessary conditioned reflex, but the patient asked in confusion: "What is it all about? What ought I to do?", without even attempting to give any conditioned reflex movement. As in the previous tests, interfering activity led to complete inhibition of the patient's motor response, and it was only after a long period (sometimes 24 hours) that this inhibitory effect could be abolished, so that the stimulus once more evoked a conditioned response (which could be incomplete). Records of a test confirming this statement are given below.

The patient was instructed: When I give one tap, raise your right hand; when I give two taps, raise your left hand. Tests immediately after presentation of the stimuli showed that the motor response of choice was preserved.

(1)	*(2)*	*(1)*	*(2)*	*(1)*	*(1)*	*(2)*	*(2)*[28]	
R	L	R	L	R	R	L	L	etc.

When asked what he should do in response to the stimuli, even though he had just successfully completed the test, he frequently gave incorrect answers: "Of course, when you tap I have to raise my hand!..." Later, however, this dissociation disappeared and the verbal account assumed the correct form.

Filling the pause with interfering activity immediately caused the disappearance of the newly formed connections.

(1) "Ah... what must I do?"   *(2)* "Two. Maybe I should point with my finger?"

(2) Shows four fingers.   *(1)* "One finger"   *(2)* "Two fingers"

What should you have done when I tapped once? "I don't know, I can't say at once..."

Presenting the conditioned stimuli after 24 hours (without warning) led to the appearance of the previously stabilized motor response (raise your right hand in response to one tap, your left hand to two taps), but no traces of the instruction given previously could be detected in the verbal account.

Similar, although somewhat more complex, results were obtained in tests with "conflicting" motor responses (showing a fist when the examiner shows his finger, and vice versa). If the patient was given an instruction in which the conditioned meaning of the stimulus conflicted with the examiner's direct action, and if the stimuli were presented immediately after the instruction, the patient gave the correct conditioned responses, and these continued even after an empty pause of 30 sec or 1 min. As soon as the pause was filled with

[28]The numerator shows the number of taps given by the examiner; the denominator shows the subject's response (L–left hand, R–right hand).

irrelevant interfering activity, the response completely disappeared and was either replaced by the echopraxic repetition of the examiner's movements or the patient remained in a state of confusion and was unable to recall the gist of the instruction.

These facts show that the patient easily formed a system of motor reflexes in response to a verbal instruction. These responses remained firmly intact even after a short pause, but interfering activity was sufficient to cause the system of newly formed reflexes to disappear completely. The patient forgot the verbal instruction, and even the fact that an instruction had been presented. Partial recovery took place only by way of reminiscence.

Investigation of Verbal Memory

Let us now turn to the central portion of our analysis, i.e., to the investigation of the voluntary memorizing of verbal material.

Memorizing series of words. Tests of memorizing series of isolated (unconnected) words, carried out under ordinary conditions, did not yield clear results. A test of memorizing 3 or 5 words showed that the patient could retain them quite well and had no difficulty in recalling them after an empty pause of 10-30 sec to 1 min, or even 1.5 min. Traces of a recently presented verbal series could evidently be retained in the absence of interfering activity. Learning a long series (10 words) gave results that were not particularly demonstrative. The patient could at once recall 5 or 6 of the 10 words, but further repetition led to only a very small increase in the number of words repeated (5-5-6-5-6-6-6).

To discover conditions that prevented the normal recall of verbal traces, the process of recall was studied after the introduction of interfering activity. To study trace recall after interfering activity, the patient was instructed to repeat, first, a group of 3 words, and then another similar group, after which he was instructed to recall the first and the second group of words, in turn. The results of this test showed that interfering activity caused severe disturbances of the patient's recalling even of such a short series of words. Although he could repeat the first and the second groups of words immediately, at first he was quite unable to recall any of them again. Repeating the test many times over was not followed by appreciable improvement. Under these conditions, the selective recall of the two word groups was so difficult that the patient either abandoned the attempt and simply said that he had "forgotten" the words, or he began to repeat them and contaminated traces of the first and second groups.

I. *House–forest– stable*	II. *Water–stump– cupboard*	*?/I*	*?/II*	*?/I*	*?/II*
(1) Correctly	Correctly	"I don't know please excuse me. . . house –stump. . . table. . ."	"Water. . . and something else"	–	–

(2)	"	"	"Water—stump—table..."	"Forest—table ...and something else"	–	–
(3)	"	"	"Water—stump—table"	House...and something else"	–	–
(4)	"	"	"House...table ...forest...table"	Correctly	"Water—stump—school"	"I don't know"
(5)	"	"	"Water—stump—table..."	"...I have forgotten..."	–	–
(6)	"	"	"House—stump—table"	"Forest—table—stump..."	"Water—forest—school..."	"Stump—forest—school"
(7)	"	"	"Water—stump—school"	"Forest—stump—school"	"I have forgotten"	"I have forgotten"

As a result of prolonged exercises, this test could eventually be carried out successfully (evidently this happened on the patient's "good days" when the general level of brain activity, which fluctuated from day to day, was at its highest). Even in these cases, however, the mere introduction of further interference was sufficient to prevent recall of previous groups of traces once again.

Memorizing sentences. Tests carried out with the patient showed that he could easily memorize a sentence read to him and could repeat it either at once or after a pause of 1 to 2 min.

If immediately after the first sentence the second sentence was read to him (he was then asked to recall the first and second sentences in turn), he began to experience the familiar difficulties. In this case (which never happens normally), contamination of the elements of the two sentences appeared. The frequent repetition of these tests as a rule did not lead to the selective recall of each sentence.

I. *Apple trees grew in the garden behind the high fence.*	II. *A hunter killed a wolf on the edge of the forest.*	?/I	?/II
(1) Correctly	Correctly	What was it... a hunter killed a wolf... at the edge of the forest.	What was the second... on the edge of the forest... something else...
(2) "	"	The first was... I have forgotten... a hunter killed a wolf at the edge of the forest...	What could it be?... I have forgotten.

(3)	`"`	`"`	A hunter killed a wolf in the forest behind a fence.	I have forgotten it again. . .
(4)	`"`	`"`	Wolves were feeding in the forest. . . behind the fence. . .	. . . something I can't recall. . .
(5)	`"`	`"`	A hunter killed a wolf in the forest behind a fence. . . does that seem right?	. . . what was it? I can't remember. . .

Characteristically, when, after a pause of 3 min, the patient was asked what he had just done, he was unable to answer, and helplessly exclaimed: "It seems I was counting letters, what the letters were. . . they were different: E and Z. . . it seems like that. . ." *What have we just been doing?* "We talked about counting letters. . . then we began to arrange. . ." *Did you memorize anything?* "Something I don't remember. . ."

Another significant fact is that even the presentation of one of the sentences memorized did not lead to its recall. *Try to recall: Apple trees grew in the garden behind the high fence. Is that sentence familiar?* "It is." *When did you hear it?* "A long time ago." *Not today?* "No, not today. . ." *Does any other sentence come into your head?* "Apple trees grew in the garden behind the high fence. . . it seems to me that not long ago you said. . ." *What about the sentence: A hunter killed a wolf on the edge of the forest?* "No there was no such sentence."

The second group of words was often imprinted so strongly that it began to cause retroactive inhibition of the first. After frequent repetition of the test, both groups of traces were stabilized, but the selective repetition was still quite impossible. The patient contaminated the two groups. It is interesting to note that he could not even repeat a sentence immediately after its presentation. Another characteristic feature was that even a short pause after the test was sufficient to make him unable to recall activity in which he had just taken part; he recalled earlier tests by way of reminiscence, but could not recall traces of a test he had just done.

Memorizing stories. Tests of memorizing whole semantic fragments (stories) take us a step further in our description of the mnemonic difficulties experienced by this patient.

Memorizing semantic fragments (stories) is a psychologically complex process with a dual character. On the one hand, the semantic fragment is a single semantic entity and after its decoding it is converted into a single thought (the sense of the fragment), which is retained much better than meaningless material or a chain of disconnected semantic units. On the other hand, a semantic fragment consisting of many sentences and embodying a whole chain of semantic units contains an extraordinary quantity of information.

In order to study the degree to which whole semantic fragments were retained and recalled by our patient, I used the methods described earlier. The patient was instructed first to repeat the stories immediately after hearing them; then, to repeat them under complicated conditions, such as recalling the first story after another story had been read.

As a rule, the patient grasped and retained the general sense of the story very well, retained it for a long period of time, and could repeat it after a considerable pause. He repeated the end of the story worse than its beginning. Sometimes detailed repetition was impossible. Finally, sometimes irrelevant elements were interwoven and the recall lost its selective character.

The sense of a story could sometimes be retained even after interfering (usually irrelevant) activity, such as mental arithmetic. Frequently, I have observed that the traces of a semantic fragment were retained for a very long time. The theme of a story was sometimes recalled involuntarily by the patient several days later, often as strongly as the newer and more recent traces.

In sharp contrast to this, if a second story was read to the patient immediately after the first, he was unable to recall the first story. He either said, with perplexity, that he had forgotten what it was about, or he mixed up the themes of the stories. Let us examine the appropriate material.

"The Hen and the Golden Eggs" story was read to this patient. He repeated it without any difficulty and easily deduced the moral: "Do not take everything at once. . ."

"The Jackdaw and the Pigeons" story was read to him. He repeated the substance of the first part of the story, but did not retain the second part. He deduced the moral easily. "So. . . the jackdaw went where the pigeons were spending the night and cried. . . and so she stayed. . ." *Did she go back to her own home?* "No, she stayed. . . perhaps they would kill her (perseveration of elements of the first story). . . especially Siberian pigeons. . . they can kill. . ." *What is the moral?* "Don't intrude where you haven't been invited." After attempts to recall the first story, the second was forgotten. *What was the first story?* "This is the first story." *But wasn't there another story before it?* "No, there wasn't." *Was this the first?* "Yes." *Have I ever told you any other stories?* "No. . . I didn't know that you knew any others to tell. . ."

Characteristically, after the second story had been read, traces of the first story disappeared completely. Even leading questions, which should have evoked recall by recognition, did not lead to ecphoria for the appropriate traces. Moreover, after questioning in this manner the traces of the second story also disappeared, and even after prompting the patient could no longer recall them.

Did the traces of the stories disappear completely or were they just temporarily inhibited? To answer this question a tests was carried out the next day.

Did I read you any stories? "No, none of the doctors has read me a story... still, there were some." *What were they?* "I can't remember them." *Try to recall them!* "I will try... (taps his forehead)... what can I tell you?" *Well, I will prompt you: "A man had a hen..."* "Have I to go on?" *Yes.* "She was a good hen, not simple, but a golden hen, she laid eggs, the man did not take good care of it, somehow the hen was killed, the man cried bitterly, but he could not get the hen back..." *Who killed the hen?* "The man's enemy, he simply destroyed it, they were enemies all the time, he decided to get his revenge..." *Was there another story?* "No." *About a jackdaw and pigeons?* "I can't remember..." *The jackdaw heard that pigeons had plenty of food.* "... she decided to join them, but she wasn't like a pigeon, the master chased her away, she was left by herself, the pigeons were a group but she was alone..." *And before that was there a story about someone?* "Counting things at the market and in the room." *What exactly?* "Something of the sort... I did not think that I should have to recall it..."

This record shows conclusively that a day after gentle prompting of the patient, elements of stories read previously could be recalled. The interfering factors did not completely destroy the traces but simply inhibited them temporarily, and their general scheme could be repeated by way of reminiscence. Although the patient could repeat the theme of a particular story reasonably accurately, if he were even slightly fatigued one story began to be interwoven with another. Selective repetition was soon converted into repetition of the confused (contaminated) themes of the two stories and irrelevant associations.

For instance, if, after hearing "The Hen and the Golden Eggs" story "The Ant and the Pigeon" story was read to him, he began to repeat it as follows: "A pigeon breeder decided to catch a pigeon and laid a net. However, a little pigeon was caught in the net. He then decided to set a trap. He put wheat in it and the pigeons came into the trap... and when the hunter ate the pigeon later, he was fat and he ate the wheat. Having once started on wheat he grew very fat..."

The active recall of the theme of the previous story activated uncontrollable irrelevant associations, arising from direct impressions. For instance, if the patient was asked which story had been read to him previously, he unexpectedly said: "The first?... the first there were so many... the first... you showed me picture cards... something climbed into the house... someone climbed into the apartment... they would not let him go..." (the patient looks at the nurse sitting in front of him). This... pigeons... and girls... counting the girls... she lived as an orphan in a good peasant's family and she looked after the house well... just like..." (the patient was confused).

This loss of selective recall, made worse after the introduction of interfering factors, led to contamination and confabulation during repetition of the stories, and was the central feature of the whole syndrome in this patient. Loss of selectivity increased when the patient became tired, so that at the end of the experiment the selective recall was completely replaced by the involuntary production of irrepressible associations.

Investigation of Indirect Memorizing

As is well known, the development of memory during ontogeny can be summarized briefly by saying that elementary direct memorizing is superseded by complex, indirect, logical memorizing, in which the subject begins to use various auxiliary methods in order to perform a mnemonic task. The observations indicating that individual groups of traces were subjected to marked mutual (proactive and retroactive) inhibition suggest that this patient was unable to use indirect aids that constitute the basis of indirect memorizing, and that these higher forms were no longer within his grasp. This conclusion was confirmed by a series of special tests.

The patient was instructed to memorize five words and, to make it easier for him to retain them, each word was accompanied by a picture. Although the patient had no difficulty in establishing the required association, when the pictures were presented subsequently he could not recall the original word. The association used to recall them was completely forgotten.

The appropriate observations are given below:

Word given for memorizing	Auxiliary picture	Connecting association	Repetition of original word
(1) Hen	Goose	"Let this represent a sort of hen."	"It is a goose." *What was the word?* "There was no word." (Even after presentation of the series of words he could not recognize it.)
(2) School	Drum	"A drum and two sticks. . . this should mean school."	"Drum with sticks. . . two sticks. . . something else is required."
(3) Medicine	Apple	"Apple—it is medicine, they use it as medicine."	"Apple. . . I can't remember any word. . ."
(4) Steamship	Knife	"Let this stand for some sort of steamship."	"Knife. . . what is the word?. . . I don't know"
(5) Dog	Athlete	"Striped like a zebra, dogs also are like that."	"It is an athlete. . . what else. . . I can see that it is an athlete." *What was the word?* "There wasn't one. . ."

The same result was found in another variant of this experiment in which words were read to the patient and he had to draw a picture representing each of them. The words were chosen so that their meanings could be represented only in conventional (and not literal) form. The drawings were then shown to the patient and he had to recall the word that each picture represented.

The results of this tests are given below.

Word given for memorizing	Auxiliary picture	Connecting association	Repetition of original word
(1) Rain	Draws a series of verti-cal lines		"It is snow. . . around the house."
(2) Illness	Draws an elbow	"The elbow will be bandaged, there is an abcess."	"Most probably this man should have gone to work yesterday but he didn't go out, and we have two people's work to do. . ."
(3) Meanness	Draws a large house	"Meanness—that means he is rich."	"A house. . . but this house is on three stories." *Then why did you draw it?* "I didn't draw it, some-one else must have drawn it. . ."
(4) Winter	Draws a road	"The sun shone. . . in the forest. . ."	"Here is a road. . . a horse with a sleigh. . . no, I don't remember. . ."

Clearly, the drawings not only did not help him to recall the original word, but sometimes the patient could not remember even the fact that he had drawn them himself, still less the motive for which they were drawn.

* * *

We have examined a case in which rupture of an aneurysm of the anterior communicating artery caused acute circulatory disturbances in the system supplying the medial zones of the frontal lobes and the diencephalon. Although his long-term, well-consolidated reminiscences were unchanged, the patient showed very severe disturbances of current memory, making him completely unable to recall recent events, and replacing them by irrepressible confabulations. The confabulations were seen not only in the clinical findings but could be produced experimentally by giving the patient the task of repeating an excessive volume of information (outside the limit of his capacity for direct repetition) or by presenting the patient with two semantic systems. This conversion of a closed semantic system, capable of being recalled, into a system open to all interfering factors, was the feature that united this group of patients with those described below.

The case of *patient Gavr.* is a clear example of what happens when the disturbances of memory produced by a burst of an aneurysm of the frontal connecting artery become closely related with very pronounced disturbances in retention of given behavioral programs, and when the above-described mnemonic disturbances occur on a background of a pronounced "frontal syndrome."

Patient Gavr., a 38-year-old male (a railroad car checker, with a secondary education in engineering), was admitted on May 11, 1971, to the Burdenko Institute of Neurosurgery after three acute brain hemorrhages.

On February 1, 1971, while asleep, the patient suddenly awoke with a severe occipital headache, loss of use of the lower limbs and the right upper limb, and transient loss of vision. After 10 to 15 min, the limb movements recovered and his eyesight returned. Only a residual disturbance of sensation in the feet, nausea sometimes turning to vomiting, and disturbances of memory remained. On February 4 and March 17, 1971, similar attacks occurred, but after the last attack he was unconscious for 7 hours, and retrograde amnesia continued for a week.

The patient was admitted to the Burdenko Institute of Neurosurgery on May 11, 1971, with the diagnosis of a suspected aneurysm of the vessels at the base of the brain, which had ruptured three times to give rise to hemorrhage. At this time, the patient was well oriented and communicative, although his critical attitude toward his own condition was impaired. The neurological diagnosis revealed symptoms that clearly pointed to a lesion of the upper region of the brain stem coupled with pathological changes in the frontal lobes.

The patient's corneal reflexes could not be elicited. Evidence of bilateral paresis of the abducens nerve was present, but sensation remained normal. The tendon reflexes were increased, more so on the right side. Inconstant pathological reflexes were present on the right, while on the left there was a hint of positive Babinski's sign, the middle and lower abdominal reflexes could not be elicited, and a distinct sucking reflex was present. The alpha-rhythm in the occipito-parietal region of the right hemisphere was slowed, and in the left, it was reduced. Diffuse polymorphic slow waves, usually a theta-rhythm, were particularly obvious in the anterior region. Bilateral synchronized theta-waves were seen periodically. Fast waves of the theta-type were present in all regions, especially on the fronto-central leads. Considerable general cerebral changes were thus present, giving rise to a slowed rhythm, interhemispheric asymmetry with reduction of the alpha-rhythm in the left hemisphere, and features of irritation resulting from the action of the pathological process of the subcortical brain structures.

Neuropsychological investigation of this patient revealed the following. The patient was communicative, oriented, and recalled the history of his illness. He complained only of physical weakness. He was by no means always aware of his mistakes and did not give the appropriate negative affective response to them. Postural praxis was marked by active searching and by a mirror-image phenomenon, but he did not realize his mistakes and did not correct them. In tests of spatial praxis, only the most elementary tasks could be accomplished. Reciprocal coordination tests were performed properly. No disturbance of optic gnosis was found. He had no speech defects. His writing, reading, and calculation were intact. He had great difficulty in solving problems despite the integrity of his elementary arithmetical operations. The patient could not grasp the conditions of the problem immediately, could not produce a plan for its solution, and his replies were impulsive. These findings point to a deep brain lesion, possibly involving both hemispheres, and evidently affecting the frontal lobes.

Left-sided carotid arteriography showed a saccular aneurysm of the anterior communicating artery. An operation on May 26, 1971, revealed a large saccular aneurysm arising from segment "A" of the internal carotid artery. The main bulk of the aneurysm stretched toward the third ventricle. The aneurysm gave off a cyst which penetrated into the white matter of the left frontal lobe and reached as far as the anterior horn of the left lateral ventricle.

The operation was difficult to perform and was accompanied by trauma to both frontal lobes. The aneurysm was clipped and the cyst removed. In the acute period after the operation, the patient showed considerable aspontaneity, he was incontinent, his emotions were grossly disturbed, and at times he lay in a state of complete indifference. Slight paresis of upward eye movements, paresis of both abducens nerves, increased tendon reflexes of the left side, oral automatism, and very severe disorders of memory with contamination, confabulations, and marked echolalia, were observed. The echolalia soon regressed, but the memory disturbances and confabulations continued for a long time. Investigation of this patient began two weeks after the operation and continued for six weeks.

Mnemonic Disorders

The patient's physical condition was good, with no evidence of increased intracranial pressure and no headaches. He was sufficiently active, took part willingly in the investigation, and performed the tests with no sign of negativism. Fairly soon, after the second or third session, he began to recognize the examiner, although he could not by any means always say by whom he was being tested.

He knew he was in a hospital and that an operation had been performed on his head, but he had no clear idea where this hospital was, or when the operation was done, even at the end of the investigation. Sometimes he was not even quite certain that he was in a hospital, and although clearly aware that he was not at home, he said, "I can't tell exactly where I am or why I am in this place."

Where are you now? "I am at a clinic in Novaya Tula district. . ." *Why are you here?* "Because I had an operation on my head. . . last year. . ." *You had an operation?* "Yes. . . the day before yesterday. . ." *But you have just told me it was a year ago!* "That can't be right, a year ago. . ." (Later the same day), *Where are you?* "Evidently not at home. . . I must be in a teaching hospital. . ." *How did you get here?* "It is very difficult to answer that question. . . they must have kept me. . ." *But why?* "I suppose I must have done something wrong. . ." *What? What could you have done?* "Well, I may have gone where it was not allowed. . ." *Are you well or unwell?* "It is hard to say. . . perhaps I might seem well—or unwell." *Have you had an operation?* "No, no operation. . ." *But you just told me you had!* "No, no operation."

His disability was particularly severe if he was asked questions about his immediate past. In such cases, he could say nothing definite and soon his true recollections of the past were replaced by confabulations, to which his attitude was completely uncritical.

What did you do this morning? "I was at home. . . I was working there. . . but what I can't say. . . then I went to Novaya Tula on the bus. . . (sees the assistant looking at a drawing). No, I was reading some sort of plans or maps there. . ." (Pause), *What did you do this morning?* "This morning the nurse introduced me to the director of a club of metallurgists. . . we joined and s̈aid a few words. . ." *Why then are you in the hospital?* "This is the hospital of a metallurgical factory. . . since it doesn't have a permanent situation it is forced. . . how shall I say it. . ." *What might happen to you if, while a patient in the hospital, you go out to a club? Surely these things are not permitted?* "Well, how can I say. . . I am just an independent person, and as an independent unit I took the decision, it was not the decision of a group. . ."

This gross disturbance of orientation in space and the marked confabulation as regards the patient's immediate past remained unchanged during six weeks of testing. Even at the end of the period, the patient was still uncertain whether he was in a hospital or in some sort of educational establishment.

The patient was not fully aware of the defects just described. He did not realize that his memory was much different from previously. When he produced confabulations instead of recalling events correctly, sometimes he said, "I am certainly making this up," although then added at once, "I am quite sure about what I am saying."

How is your memory? "My memory is not bad. . . I don't complain of any loss of memory. . . I consider that my memory is normal. . ." *Why then do you tell me now sometimes that it is August, sometimes that it is May?* "I don't know."

Despite the severe amnesia for events in the immediate past, the patient's ability to recall the distant past still remained intact. This dissociation is clearly visible in the records given below.

Tell me where you lived, studied, and worked previously. "Well, when I was a child I went to primary school; I went up into the next class every year. . . in 1944 I began to study at an industrial school. I studied there for two years. At the end of that time I was sent to work on the railroad, at a wagon depot. Wagons were repaired there. . . then I went into the army, I was in a light infantry regiment. . . ," and so on.

Tell me where you are now and what you did yesterday. "I am at present in hospital for treatment. . . having tests. . . I had an operation on my brain. . . the operation was done last year." *And where were you yesterday?* "I spent the whole day partly at the stadium and partly in the department. . ." *Did you really go to the stadium?* "Yes, I was taking part in athletics. . ." *Are you sure or not very sure about that?* "Not very sure. . . I don't know exactly, or else I am making it up. . . it was found. . ." *What was found?* "A burial." *Where?* "There, near the stadium. . . and we did an excavation. . ." *And what did you do this morning?* "This morning I. . . I went into town. . . shopping. . ."

This pattern of severe disturbances of memory for recent events with confabulations and an uncritical attitude continued throughout the period of investigation and constituted the center of this patient's syndrome.

Let us first examine the results obtained by testing his verbal memory at his various levels, and then make a close analysis of the disturbances of his nonverbal mnemonic processes.

Memorizing Series of Words

Learning a series of ten isolated words gave the typical flat, plateau-like learning curve (5-6-5-5-6-6-5-7).

The patient repeated the same words on each trial without making any effort to enlarge the series of words memorized.

The patient had no difficulty in memorizing a group of two words, retaining them after a pause of 1 min, and recalling the first group after being given a second group.

Memorizing groups of three words was different. He could easily repeat one group of three isolated words immediately, followed by a second similar group. If he was then asked to recall the words of the first group, followed by those of the second, he either mixed up (contaminated) the two groups or added new words of his own to them, and gave totally inadequate guesses. Even repeating the test several times did not lead to any improvement in the result. He had no misgivings about his performance.

If a further complication was introduced into the conditions of tests, in the form of interfering activity (such as mental arithmetic), he was completely unable to recall the words he had just learned. Sometimes, he actually no longer remembered that he had in fact learned any words at all.

I. *House−table− night*	II. *Oak−needle− pie*	*?/I*	*?/II*	*?/I*
(1) Correctly	Correctly	Oak−table. . . I have for- gotten	Correctly	Oak−table
(2) Correctly	Correctly	House−table− chair	House−needle −pie	House−chair− table

(Interfering activity introduced: *2 x 7 = ? 3 x 8 = ?*)
   What was the first group? "Something about 14. . ." *No, what were the words?* What were the words?" (the patient was confused).

Memorizing Sentences

To determine whether these difficulties were experienced at all levels of verbal material, tests were carried out to study memorizing and recalling sentences.

The patient mixed up the elements of two sentences, and after a short period of interfering activity (mental arithmetic) he was unable to recall the sentences selectively and started to make them both the same.

The patient was given two sentences:

		?/I	?/II
I. *In Tashkent there was a severe earthquake and many houses were destroyed.*	II. *In Tushino there was an air display with parachute jumps.*		
(1) Correctly	Correctly	Airplanes fell	An air disaster
(2) Correctly	Correctly	In Tushino. . . no, in Tashkent there was an air display with parachute jumps. *This was the second sentence. What was the first?* Correctly	I have forgotten already.

(Interfering activity introduced—solving arithmetical problems for 15 sec. The patient was then asked to recall the sentences presented previously).
What was the first sentence? "16 + 2." *No, that is arithmetic, and before that I told you some sentences. What were they?* "16 : 2." *No, sentences. What was the first?* "In Tashkent there was a severe earthquake and many houses were destroyed." *And the second?* "In Tashkent there was a severe earthquake. . . and the houses there. . . were not destroyed." *No, that is wrong. What was the first sentence?* "In Tashkent there was a severe earthquake and many houses were destroyed." *And the second sentence?* "In Tashkent there was a severe earthquake and nothing was destroyed there." *No, that is wrong. The first sentence was correct. What was the second sentence?* "There wasn't a second sentence." *Are you quite sure?* "In my opinion there wasn't."

The facts just described were verified over and over again under different conditions. Contamination accompanied by irrelevant associations and direct impressions continued unchanged in this patient.

Memorizing Stories

The patient had even greater difficulty with memorizing and reproducing stories than he had with words or sentences. His recall of stories was interspersed with irrelevant associations and impressions which the patient could not control or inhibit. These defects were particularly severe in the acute postoperative period. Later, this disturbance of selectivity could still be detected in the more difficult tests, such as when he had to recall stories "from traces" or when he was instructed to repeat two stories given to him previously.

"The Lion and the Mouse" story was read to the patient and he was asked to repeat it. He began: "A hunter was going for a walk. . . he saw a lion and arrested it. . ." (He started with the end of the story and the beginning underwent retroactive inhibition. He was then unable to control the association "caught"—"arrested".)
Tell it more accurately! "A hunter was hunting lions and he caught a lion. . ." *Go on!* "Because the lion did not hunt wild animals, did not creep up to them stealthily. . ."

(attempts to correct his mistakes by substituting negative for positive). *What happened next?* "He arrested him and put him in a cage. . ." (irrepressible associations: "lion–cage"). *What else was there in the story?* "There was also a mouse. . . who became ʾattached to the lion. . . she stayed with the lion." *What is the moral of the story?* "That a mouse doesn't go with a lion. The mouse is something very small, but the lion is huge?" (replacement by habitual associations).

(The story was read a second time and the patient asked to repeat it) ". . . a hunter hunted a lion. . . he took a rope, tied him to a tree. . . and that is all!" (the last fragment of the story bursts out). "He hunted, but the lion got away from him. . . there was also a mouse. . . or perhaps a cat with the lion. . . and they hunted. . ." (irrelevant association "mouse–cat"). "He hunted the cat. . . with this mouse. . ." *Tell the story more accurately.* "They hunted, hunted. . . went up to the cat with the request. . ." (the patient was confused).

(The story was read a third time). "A hunter was hunting these. . . snakes. . . mice. . . the mouse met with misfortune. . . she went and asked. . . the hunter did not believe the mouse. . . and then. . . ate this. . ." *This what?* "His mistrust. . ." (The coherent narration was replaced by individual fragments and the patient was confused.)

Naturally, the recalling of this story under more complex conditions was completely impossible. If a second story was read to the patient immediately after the first, the request that he recall the first story simply evoked continuous confabulations.

"The Jackdaw and the Pigeons" story was read. He repeated it with the defects already described. Another story, "The Ant and the Pigeon," was read to him. He also repeated this story in the same way. He was then asked: *Did I tell you a story before this one? Try to recall.* He said: "Yes. . . perhaps there. . . was a story. . . about a gypsy!" *And what happened in it?* "I have forgotten. . . but something seems to tell me that it was about a gypsy. . ." *Perhaps it was about a hen?* "Perhaps it was about a hen. . . the hen laid an egg, not a simple egg but a golden egg. . . the old man hit, but did not smash, the old woman hit, but did not smash. . ." ("The Hen and the Golden Eggs" story, read a week before, was replaced by the habitual variant.) *Perhaps it was about a bear?* "Perhaps it was about a bear. . . I can't remember what followed. . ." *Perhaps it was about a jackdaw?* "Perhaps it was about a jackdaw, only I don't remember. . ." *What were we talking about?* "A lion fell into misfortune and a jackdaw was set free to release him. . ." (contamination with "The Lion and the Mouse" story read a few days previously).

The first story was evidently forgotten. Incorrect prompting of the patient had exactly the same effect on him as correct. In every case, his answers were mingled with irrepressible reminiscences, sometimes of stories read a long time ago.

Traces of previous systems (both recently imprinted and long-standing) were recalled with equal probability, so that selective recall of the required material was sharply disturbed. Selective recall was also disturbed by the pathological inertia of the most recent memory, with resulting retroactive blocking of the previous traces, but without upsetting the uncontrollable outpouring of reminiscences.

Finally, the third factor is a disturbance of active goal-directed mnemonic activity, with no attempt to compare irrelevant associations and impressions with the material to be recalled.

All these factors were manifested in the early period of the tests in the direct repetition of stories. Later, as the pathological process regressed, they appeared only under more complex conditions—in tests requiring the active recall of previously presented material.

Memorizing Pictures

The memory defects found in the memorizing and recalling of isolated words and verbal structures were also evident in the memorizing of isolated drawings and thematic pictures. Let us examine appropriate records.

The patient was shown two pictures in turn: "horse" and "cornflower." He named each picture; they were then turned over and he was asked to say what was drawn on each card.

I. *Horse*	II. *Cornflower*	?/I	?/II
Correctly	Correctly	Correctly	Correctly

(Empty pause of 30 sec)

?/I	?/II
Correctly	Correctly

(Pause of 30 sec with interfering activity—mental arithmetic)

?/I	?/II
Woman	Youth

The patient was given a pack of cards and asked to choose the ones that had been shown previously. He correctly picked the cards showing the horse and the cornflower. *But what did you tell me?* ". . . I said 'woman' and 'youth'."

The pictures were again turned over; an empty pause of 1 min then followed.

?/I	?/II
Horse	This is—an urchin

Are you sure? "No. . . not a hundred percent certain." *What about the horse?* "I am a hundred percent certain of that." The second picture was turned up again. "Yes. . . of course. . . a cornflower."

The cards were again turned over. An empty pause of 1 min was given.

?/I	?/II
Correctly	Correctly

Interfering activity for 30 sec was introduced: *Recite the days of the week and the months of the year in the proper and reverse order.* The patient was then asked what he had been doing previously.

What were you doing before this? "Working with signals" (reminiscence of previous test with conditioned reflexes.) *What sort of signals?* "To do with production" (slipping into irrelevant associations). *And what were we doing before that?* "Reciting something. . ." *And before that?* "Well, how can I put it in words. . ." *What were we doing?* "Turning cards over" (confused recalling of choosing cards from a pack).

You remembered the cards! There they are, two cards turned over! What is this one first? "A boy—fishing. . ." *And the second?* "A woman." *Are you sure?* "The first is a woman. . . and the second a boy. . . or a dog. . ." The pictures were shown again and a pause filled with interfering activity for 30 sec introduced: reciting the names of five round objects. *What were we doing just before this?* "Working with signals" (attempts to get the patient to recall the cards were unsuccessful).

The results of this test show that the patient could easily recall two isolated cards and retain them after an empty pause of 30 sec to 1 min. The introduction of interfering activity altered the situation considerably and the patient started to confabulate in his answers ("woman," "youth"), although he could still recognize the pictures, and to choose them from the pack.

The tests just described were concerned with recall of single pictures. The defects were seen more clearly in tests with a series of pictures.

Although he could easily recognize pictures shown to him previously and pick them out from the pack of cards, the patient was quite unable to recall actively which pictures had been given. Instead, he simply confabulated. Gross disturbances of active mnemonic searching, manifested as a loss of selective recall, continued to be the central features of his memory disturbances.

Similar defects were revealed in tests of memorizing and recalling of thematic pictures. He had no difficulty in grasping the meaning of a thematic picture, retaining it for a short time, and reproducing it, provided that the pause between presentation and recall was not filled with interfering activity.

The patient was shown a picture, "The hole in the ice," showing a man who has fallen through the ice. He easily grasped the meaning of the picture and memorized it. He was then shown another picture. "The broken window." He also understood this picture quite well.

He was then asked: *What was shown on the first picture?* He answered at once: "A river, a boy drowning, people on the bank, they want to save him. . ." *And what was the second picture?* He said confusedly: "I have forgotten. . ." *Try to remember!* "Now, now. . . a woman. . ." *And what else?* "A boy. . . he grabbed the woman by her arm. . . well, he was certainly responsible for breaking the window. . . and the true culprit was hiding behind a tree. . ."

He thus had an adequate understanding of the meaning of the two pictures. The results were very unstable, however, and when the patient was asked the same questions a second time, recall of the themes was replaced by confabulations.

Are you sure there were two pictures? "Yes." *What was the first picture?* "There was a fire and they saved the buildings. . ." *And the second picture?* "A group of pupils. . . they were marching along the street. . ." *Are you sure?* "Not quite." *And what was the first picture?* "They saved the buildings after a fire. . ." Other tests gave similar results.

Recalling Movements and Actions

The tests of memorizing and recalling the patient's own movements were carried out with a view to answering two questions. Were the mnemonic defects described above observed in this sphere of activity also, and was a dissociation between ability to retain a movement in practice and an inability to express the corresponding recollections in speech also apparent? We have already seen elements of this dissociation when studying the patient's visual memory and can expect it will be seen more clearly still in movements.

To answer the question we used the familiar methods for formation of reactions to a spoken instruction, on the one hand, and the performance of a series of manipulations with objects, on the other. The patient was able to develop and retain a sufficiently stable system of movements, but was quite unable to express in words the movement he had just performed. Characteristically the instruction to tell in his own words what he had just done caused him to be completely confused and he produced only irrepressible associations or confabulations. The results of the tests are given below.

Oral instruction was given: *When I give one tap, raise your right hand; when I give two taps, raise your left hand.* He understood the instruction perfectly well and easily performed the necessary movement. He was able to perform the action even after an empty pause of 2 to 3 min. He was then given a second instruction: *When I say "M," put out your tongue; when I say "Zh," touch your knee.* He carried out this instruction and retained it perfectly well. All these four instructions were then given to him at random. He gave the correct responses to each instruction. Only after a short "empty" pause did he begin to mix up the responses to the last two instructions, tapping on his knee in response to "M" and putting out his tongue in response to "Zh."

The extent to which the reactions were reflected in the patient's speech was next tested. He was asked: *Tell me what you were just doing?* (Patient confused) "... I was solving these... what do you call them... examples or this..." *I just asked you to do something, what did you do?* "I repeated the movements..." *What movements?* "Physical" (the questions were put in a more concrete form, showing the cues). *When I tapped once, what did you do?* "Raised my right hand!" *And when I tapped twice?* "Then I raised my left hand." *And when I said "Zh"?* "I put out my tongue..." *And when I said "M"?* (The patient was confused, he could not remember.)

Now let us repeat it all in order. What were we just doing? "We studied a system..." *What sort?* "Signals..." *What sort of signals? Repeat everything.* "We had another person with us—Pogozhev gave us the job of... testing the system... what is it called... signals..." *Tell me exactly what we were just doing?* "Well now... we invited our friend... (looks at the tape recorder) Nadelya... that is not Nadelya, and they fixed this... tape recorder... to it... in the region... they began to communicate with him..." *How?* "With the aid of sounds..." (goes on to give continuous confabulation).

All the instructions were again given to the patient. He evidently retained them to some extent, although he responded to the letter "M" by tapping on his knee; the response to the letter "Zh" was forgotten.

He was again asked to say what he had just done. He answered: "There were signals... there were signs... they should have operated a right hand side system..." He was given more precisely worded questions: *What should you have done when I tapped once?* "Raised my right hand, and if you tapped twice, raised my left hand?" *And if I said "M"?* "Put out my tongue. . ." *And if I said "Zh"?* The patient did not know and could not recall the answer.

After a pause of 2 min, he was again given the cues. He responded to them with the correct movement, except that he had forgotten what he should do in response to the letter "Zh" (tap on the knee).

He was next instructed to say what action he had just carried out. He again became confused and began to confabulate. "Well. . . when my friend requested the signals that should have been given to him. . . I had to answer. . ." *How?* "Positively!" *No, tell me exactly what you did?* "When he signalled requesting permission to land. . . I permitted him to land. . ."

Continuation of the test did not abolish this dissociation between the integrity of the practical actions and the inability to express them in the form of words.

The movements themselves continued to be performed even without reinforcement one week later, whereas attempts to obtain an accurate verbal account of the actions he had just performed were unsuccessful, and continuing the test simply caused the patient to be confused.

Similar results were obtained in tests in which the conditioned character of the movements was removed, and they were replaced by direct manipulations with objects.

The same features were revealed even more clearly when the patient was asked to draw named figures, and then after a short period of distraction, to express in words what he had just done.

He was asked to draw a star, an axe, and a stream. He did so; the drawings were removed and he was asked what he had just done. He replied correctly that he had drawn a "five pointed star, an axe, and a stream."

After a short pause (30 sec), during which he was asked to list five red objects, the question was repeated: *What were we doing together immediately before this?* "Before giving the names of the objects?. . . we. . . we were busy studying objects. . ." *What sort of objects?* "We were at your country cottage. . . and (he looked at the tape recorder). . . we built a radio. . ." *What else were you just doing?* (He looked at the paper on which he had drawn pictures) ". . . we were doing examples. . . arithmetical." *And what else? Did you draw something?* "I didn't draw anything. . ." *Well, who did draw?* "You drew. . ." *And what was it?* "I think a squirrel. . . and a tree. . ." *And you yourself drew nothing?* "I drew something this morning!" *But what was it?* The patient was confused (his drawings were shown to him). *Who drew this?* "Oh yes. . . a star and an axe. . . that is certainly my work. . ." *And when did you draw it?* "Certainly yesterday evening. . ." *And what were you just doing this morning?* "I was busy with many things. . . we went on a trip. . . looking for fruit. . . at the Bogucharovo State Farm. . . or a division of that farm. . . then we were preparing. . . the lists of objects. . . like the liquor-vodka system. . ." This was followed by a continuous stream of confabulations.

In the tests just described, the same defects were found as previously except that inability to express his actions in words was joined by complete forgetting—even that he had performed the acts ("You drew this, not I".)

284 NEUROPSYCHOLOGY OF MEMORY

The clinical picture is very similar to that described many years ago by Claparède and by Leont'ev (1930) in patients with Korsakov's syndrome. These patients may respond relatively normally to a pinprick or give a conditioned response to nociceptive stimuli, but they cannot voluntarily recall the tests. They declare time and time again that nobody else was in the room, they did not see the person inflicting pain upon them, or the apparatus used in the conditioning tests. The only difference was that our patient replaced the adequate recalling of the recent action by well-marked confabulations.

This suggests that the basic mechanism of the defects in this case was inability of the patient himself to choose the required alternative from a large number of possible associations and direct impressions, which is evidently the fundamental condition for spontaneous, active recall.

Investigation of Indirect Memory

We have discussed above the unique dissociation observed in this patient. Although he could recognize pictures shown to him and could select them from a large number of others, this patient could not himself recall what pictures had been shown to him. He could firmly consolidate and retain appropriate movements and actions; he could not express in words what action he had just performed. Does this dissociation amount to integrity of visual or motor skills combined with a disturbed verbal memory, or were the disturbances of a totally different form, and could both intact and disturbed components be found within his speech activity?

To answer this question it was necessary to use tests that would be strictly confined to verbal memory, but would enable two forms of this memory to be compared—one determined by organized connections; the other, requiring active choice of the necessary connections from a large number of alternatives. This could be done by tests using auxiliary connections for indirect memorizing, on the one hand, and by the active recall of recently imprinted verbal connections, on the other.

Despite a well-marked Korsakov's syndrome, the patient could establish and retain verbal connections relatively securely, but, as before, he was totally unable to recall actions he had just performed, or even that he had established the verbal connections. The results of these tests are given below.

He was asked to memorize ten words, and while memorizing each word he was given an aid consisting of a card with a picture totally unconnected with the word itself. Using this card as a mnemonic aid, an appropriate semantic connection was established between it and the word to be memorized. He was then shown the card and asked to state what word he had memorized with its assistance.

The patient was quite capable of performing this task, and after two repetitions the use of the auxiliary connections became sufficiently stable to enable him to recall the word when shown the picture. The most striking fact was that the patient could still recall the appropriate words when shown pictures two days or a week later.

Attempts to obtain the patient's active recall of the actions he had recently performed were in sharp contrast to the results just described. After a test of indirect memorizing, when the patient was asked to relate what he had just done, he became totally confused and was quite unable to answer the question. To begin with, he could only say "I have forgotten what I did" or, instead of answering, produced confabulations.

What were we just doing together? "We were learning a story about the fox and a crow... the fox ran across the field, and above the field a crow was flying..." etc. (reminiscence of a test carried out a few days previously).

The test was repeated many times, and each time the question "What have we just been doing?" caused the patient either to become confused or to perseverate his recollections of interfering activity (... "we did calculations..., we told a story," etc.).

A patient with a severe Korsakov's syndrome, associated with substantial lesions of the frontal lobes, was able to imprint and recall a system of verbal connections only when the first member of the pair was presented so that recall of the connection was strictly determined, like signal and response. Conversely, if the patient was requested to recall by himself what he had just done, or, in other words, if he was placed in a situation of indeterminacy, so that he was forced to choose the necessary association from many possible alternatives, he was quite helpless and his active recall was replaced by irrelevant associations or reminiscences.

Conclusions

We have examined disturbances of memory arising in patients with lesions of the medial zone of the frontal lobes, on the one hand, and structures of the diencephalon, on the other hand. In neither case was the pathological process accompanied by manifestations of increased intracranial pressure or brain displacement, nor was there any sign of the asthenic syndrome characteristically found in patients with massive tumors of the upper portion of the brain stem and diencephalic structures. Neither patient showed pathologically increased proneness to fatigue or an undue tendency to fluctuate between sleep and waking. They were fully awake, and indeed showed distinct signs of increased irritation, affecting nearly all forms of mental activity.

Despite these basic features distinguishing this group of patients from those described earlier, many aspects of the syndrome recalled the picture found in patients in whom analogous disturbances resulted from deep brain tumors. As in the cases described earlier, the patients of this group had no disturbance of gnosis, praxis, or speech—as characteristically found in patients with lesions of the lateral zones of the hemispheres. Their formal intellectual operations were intact.

The disturbances of memory were general (not modality-specific) and manifested equally in the memorizing and recall of visual material, movements and actions, and verbal traces. Just as in the patients described earlier, these disturbances were manifested as pathologically increased inhibition by irrelevant, interfering factors rather than by decay of established traces. The severe disturbance of recall was equal for series of isolated, unconnected elements (pictures, movements, words) and organized semantic systems (sentences, stories, thematic pictures).

A special feature of these patients was that when required to recall previously imprinted material, they very soon began to slip into irrelevant associations. These disturbances were found in tests involving recently presented material (stories, thematic pictures) as well as in recalling events in the immediate past. Both situations revealed contamination, irrelevant impressions, and confabulations, in sharp contrast to the otherwise apparent slight disability of these patients.

Perhaps the most interesting fact discovered during tests on these patients was the sharp dissociation between the relative integrity of involuntarily imprinted connections and the gross disturbance of their active recall. The patients were quite unable to express in words what they had just done, despite the fact that they actually retained the traces of this action.

This dissociation between the preservation of skills and the inability to recall previously imprinted traces voluntarily has frequently been described in the literature (in the classical observations of Bergson, and subsequently by Claparède, and by Leont'ev). This dissociation shows that active selective recall is a completely different psychological process from the preservation of an established skill. The success of recall is largely dependent on the type of activity involved.

Disturbances of Memory in the Residual Period After Operation for an Aneurysm of the Anterior Communicating Artery

The study of a large number of patients with rupture of an aneurysm of the anterior communicating artery (Luria, Konovalov, & Podgornaya, 1970) shows that the fate of these patients may differ considerably.

In some of them, the disturbances of memory and consciousness, after a sharp exacerbation in the postoperative period, regressed to such an extent, as the spasm of the anterior cerebral artery disappeared and the collateral circulation was restored, that two or three months after the operation no evidence of a disturbance of higher cortical processes could be found.

In other patients in whom the spasm of the anterior cerebral arteries was so persistent that they were completely excluded from the circulation, and in whom the collateral circulation could not compensate for the defect, the disturbances of higher cortical processes remained stable. The defects of their memory and consciousness described in the acute period of the disease remained substantially unchanged.

Finally, there is a third group of patients which, although much smaller numerically, is of particular interest. I am speaking of cases in which rupture of an aneurysm of the anterior communicating artery is accompanied by massive hemorrhage spreading to the region of the floor of the third ventricle, and gives rise to acute disturbances of memory and consciousness accompanied by signs of disorientation and confusion. When the spasm of the anterior cerebral arteries disappears, however, the circulation in the area is restored and the general picture changes appreciably. The disorientation and confusion undergo regression, but the severe disturbances of memory, evidently the result of structural damage in the hypothalamo-thalamic region caused by the hemorrhage, continue unchanged.

The disorders of consciousness and the memory disturbances are dissociated and after a certain period, sometimes a fairly lengthy one, a fully developed Korsakov's syndrome of vascular origin may be observed. The principal pathological changes are localized to deep zones of the hemispheres in the midline and extend to the medial zones of the cortex and diencephalic structures.

Let us now turn to the analysis of one of these rare cases.

Patient Kur., a 30-year-old male (an electrician by trade), was admitted to the N. N. Burdenko Institute of Neurosurgery in July, 1970 on account of hemorrhage caused by rupture of an aneurysm of the anterior communicating artery.

On June 13, 1970, the patient suddenly lost consciousness, vomited, developed meningeal symptoms, and was admitted to the Burdenko Institute in a confused and disoriented state. Communication with the patient was impossible. Examination revealed a positive Kernig's sign, neck rigidity, primary disturbances of olfaction, central paresis of the facial nerve, and depression of the tendon reflexes. Right-sided carotid angiography revealed a saccular aneurysm of the anterior communicating artery.

After recovery from unconsciousness, the patient was grossly disoriented and showed severe disturbances of memory. Neuropsychological investigation showed the following picture: The patient was accessible and communicative, his gnosis, praxis, and speech were fully intact; however, he was imperfectly aware of his state and was completely disoriented in place and time: He thought he was at his factory, that he had just gone to rest for a short time, etc. He had a fully developed Korsakov's syndrome with very severe mnemonic defects and confabulations, which persisted right up to the time of his operation.

On July 29, 1970, an operation was performed during which the anterior part of the right hemisphere was incised and the sinus was opened in its anterior part, to which the anterior cerebral arteries were adherent; the vessels were clipped and the saccular aneurysm of the anterior communicating artery with its thin floor and the daughter aneurysms removed. During the mobilization of the aneurysm, its floor was torn and hemorrhage followed. Clips were applied for a short time to both anterior cerebral arteries and then removed.

Control arteriography carried out a few days after the operation showed that both anterior cerebral arteries were patent, but both clinical and neurophysiological investigations indicated that the deep brain structures in the midline had suffered severely as a result of the hemorrhage.

The features of confusion described above gradually passed off although the severe memory disturbance remained unchanged. The patient was readmitted to the Institute of Neurosurgery for follow-up examination one year later. By this time, the neurological signs were very slight, there was no disturbance of sensation or movement, the functions of the cranial nerves were intact, the tendon reflexes were brisk and equal on both sides, and bilateral Babinski's, Rossolino's, and Marinesco's signs were present. Electroencephalography showed some decrease in electrical activity and an increase in amplitude of the alpha-rhythm with absence of a falling gradient of amplitude from the posterior to the anterior zones of the cortex and with incomplete desynchronization of the alpha-rhythm in response to photic stimulation. In the anterior zones of the cortex, a combination of low, pointed delta-waves, epileptic complexes, and beta-waves was observed. These findings pointed to a pathological state of the diencephalon, as a result of the disease.

The mild neurological changes contrasted sharply with his very severe memory disturbance. This assumed the form of a massive Korsakov's syndrome in a patient remarkable for the integrity of his gnosis, praxis, and speech, and also of his consciousness, his orientation in place and time, and his awareness of his own state.

All forms of praxis were intact in this patient. He performed all the tests at once without any difficulty, mentally reversing the position of the examiner's hands during the test. He easily performed tests of dynamic praxis and reciprocal coordination. There was likewise no disturbance of copying rhythms, whether directly or in response to a spoken instruction, and no difficulty in acoustic analysis of rhythms or in switching from one rhythm to another. He could easily carry out conditioned responses (following the instruction to raise your right hand in response to one tap and your left hand in response to two taps) and had no difficulty if the instructions introduced some response conflict (e.g., raise your fist when I raise my finger and raise your finger when I raise my fist). His performance was always faultless.

The patient's visual gnosis was fully intact: He could easily recognize simple and crossed-out figures, had no difficulty in distinguishing the figures in Poppelreuter's test, and he readily identified the meanings of thematic pictures. The patient had no disturbances of speech. His phonemic hearing was unimpaired. He could easily repeat sounds, words, series of words, and short sentences. He could name objects and had no features of "alienation of word meaning." His writing and reading were undisturbed.

He could draw figures in a specified spatial arrangement, showing no trace of constructive apraxia, and he could continue an asymmetrical series of figures started by the examiner. His elementary arithmetic was intact. He could perform operations, such as counting backward from 100 in 17s; he could solve problems in finding opposites and analogies. He had no appreciable difficulty in logical operations.

Superimposed on this picture of apparent normality, the patient had very severe disturbances of memory, and we can now go on to describe their structure.

Mnemonic Disorders

It was easy to communicate and converse with the patient. He knew quite confidently that he was in the Burdenko Institute. He had a very good memory of his distant past. He knew the nature of his work and the surname of his manager, his senior assistants, his team mates, and his shift foreman. He remembered his previous pass number. In all these areas, he displayed a very clear and precise memory.

Nevertheless, he could not tell the address of the apartment to which he had recently moved shortly before his illness began. "I moved house but I can't remember the new address. I used to live at Novodachnaya Station, but then—I find it difficult to recall the name of the place where I now live, I do not know the address. . . I do not know what happened to me or from where I was admitted to hospital."

The patient's memory for current events was more seriously affected. "I have no memory of the present," he said, "I cannot retain anything and cannot deny anything. . . I do not know what I have just done or from where I have just come, . . . I can recall my past very well, but I have no memory of my present. . . ." When asked whether he had ever seen the person testing him, he said: "I cannot say yes or no, I can neither affirm or deny that I have seen you. . ." The patient gave the same answer when asked how long he had been in the hospital and what he had done that morning; he had difficulty in saying even what time of year it was. Since he had no direct sense of time, into which mnemonic coordinates are always interwoven, in reply to any such question the patient would always begin to make a detailed analysis of the situation, attempting to discover its minutest features and to draw the necessary conclusions from them. For instance, when asked "What time of year is it?"—he looked carefully through the window and began to argue; "Well, there is snow on the rooftops. . . not much of it. . . certainly winter or fall. . . still a few yellow leaves on the trees. . . if it were winter they would all have blown away. . . it must be late fall."

It would be wrong, however, to conclude that the immediate past left no traces in this patient's memory. Some relatively indistinct traces remained, but he could not recall them voluntarily. His recall was vague and diffuse, and he was completely unable to relate the traces to any definite time.

During a demonstration of the patient in the large lecture theatre, he could not say from where he had come or where he had been the day before. On the day after the demonstration, however, he was directly asked whether he remembered that he had been taken from the Institute and had appeared in front of a large audience. He answered, "I do remember something. . . I certainly was taken somewhere. . . and the students were sitting there. . . you were there also. . . but when this was or where it was I really don't know."

When he was asked the date of his operation, he could not answer and said, "Perhaps a day or a month ago. . . I can neither affirm nor deny this. . . it was certainly sometime, but when I have no idea. . ." He had equal difficulty in estimating the time of day; instead of estimating it directly, he guessed and made serious mistakes. This happened also when he estimated the time that had elapsed after the beginning of the test. "Certainly about ten minutes. . . perhaps even half an hour. . . I really cannot say. . . ," he exclaimed.

During his long stay in the clinic, he began to form a "sense of familiarity": The patient recognized the doctors he met frequently, but he could easily make a mistake and confuse strangers with people he had met previously. He remained unable to form a clear opinion of the time that corresponded to any of his reminiscences.

Investigation of verbal memory. The test of learning a series of ten isolated words produced unstable results. Sometimes he remembered three or four words and occasionally he was able to repeat seven or eight words (6-8-3-5-3-3-3). The patient could retain only the first two or three words reliably, and the rest he repeated in an unstable, random order. He did not show the confident recall of the first and last words of the series usually found in such patients. Equally undemonstrative results were obtained with this patient when his direct repetition of a successively increasing series of words and sentences was tested.

Recalling series of words and sentences. The patient could easily repeat one, two, three, or four words and retain them in the same order after a pause of 30 sec, 1 min, and 1.5 min. Significant disturbances appeared only if the pause between memorizing and repetition was filled with interfering activity, such as mental arithmetic. In that case, he was not only unable to repeat the words he had just learned, but often forgot that he had learned anything before the mental arithmetic. This indicated that the gross disturbances of this patient's memory were based on pathologically increased inhibitability of traces by interfering activity.

Going back to the first pair of words after recalling a second pair was not particularly difficult, which distinguishes him from many other patients of this group. An empty pause of 30 sec or 1 min likewise was not reflected in his retention. Introduction of interfering activity, however, led to marked inhibition of trace recall. If the test was made more difficult by requiring him to memorize 3-word series, his performance was impaired further. He could easily repeat each group of three words, but was unable to recall the first group after memorizing a second group. He could not even say confidently how many groups of words he had been given. When the test was repeated later, he was able to return to a group memorized earlier, but even then the introduction of interfering activity again caused severe disturbance of his recall. An extract from the records is given below.

I. *House—forest—cat*	II. *Night—needle—pie*
Correctly	Correctly

How many groups were there? "Two groups, each with three words." *What was the first group?* "I can't remember." *Roughly?* "Roughly it was house—forest—cat." *And the second group?* "There was the word stump, but I can't remember the first word."

What did we do with you just now? "I had to memorize some words." *How many groups were there?* "I can't say exactly." *But how many words in each group?* "Three. I can't remember them."

Interfering activity was introduced: The patient was asked to subtract from 100 in 9s for 30 sec.

What were we doing with you before? "Before you gave me some words, then for some time you tapped your stopwatch (pseudoreminiscence), some part of the time had passed. . ." *What were the words?* "House, forest, cat, I can't remember. . . the rest I cannot remember. . ." *And the second group?* "The second group ˋI have completely forgotten. . ."

What changes were introduced into the memory disturbances by a change from memorizing a series of discrete words to memorizing organized verbal material? To answer this question, tests involving memorizing sentences were used.

Memorizing sentences. The results were similar to those of the previous tests.

I. *In Tashkent there was a severe earthquake and many houses were destroyed.*	II. *In Tushino there was an air display with parachute jumps.*	*?/I*	*?/II*
Correctly	Correctly	Correctly	In Tushino there was an air display.

And the end of the sentence? "I can't remember anything else." *You have to memorize these two sentences. What were we doing?* "We memorized two sentences." *What was the first?* (Gives the correct answer.) *And the second?* "In Tushino. . . and many houses were destroyed. . ." *No, jumps!. . .* "Parachute jumps. . ." *Memorize these two sentences; I shall ask you about them.* "I will try."

Interfering activity was introduced: The patient was instructed to subtract from 100 in 4s for 30 sec.

You have just been counting. What did you do before that? "Before that I repeated some words. . ." *What words?* "I can't remember the words. . . house, forest. . . and something else. . ." (reminiscence of an earlier test). *And did you repeat any sentences?* "I can't deny it. . . I cannot say yes. . ." *Perhaps there were some sentences?* "I can only remember the words: house, forest, cat. . ." *And what about sentences?* "Do you mean words?. . . House. . . forest, mare?" *But whole sentences?* "No sentences will come into my head. . ."

Next day a similar test was carried out with other sentences.

The records show that there is no difficulty in the direct retention of sentences. If the patient has to recall a second sentence after recalling a first sentence, however, difficulties begin to arise and they increase in severity after the introduction of interfering activity.

Memorizing stories. Like the preceding patient with severe disturbances of consciousness, this patient as a rule could not repeat a story that had just been read to him. He could retain the general sense of the story quite well, but he repeated the story itself fragmentarily: usually he recalled only the beginning or sometimes only the end. The rest of the story completely vanished from his memory. Unlike the other patient, however, no confabulations appeared and he did not drift into irrelevant associations. The introduction of interfering activity into the test made it impossible to recall the story. The same was observed if, after two stories had been read, and each had been repeated separately, the patient was asked to recall the first story. Characteristically this "forgetting" was so severe that often he could not even recall the fact that a story had been read to him. Let us examine the results of the test.

The story "The Lion and the Mouse" was read to him and he was asked to repeat it. He attempted to do so as follows: "One day a lion was asleep and a mouse ran over him. . . the lion awoke and caught her. . . she was running of course. Why she was running I cannot say. . . She ran away and then there was something else. . . something about a tree. . . I can't remember any more. . . something about a tree and there were some consequences. . ." *What is the meaning of the story?* "The meaning is that there was some sort of relationship between them . . ." *What sort?* "I can't remember who the characters were. . . I can remember there were two. . . One did something first, and then the other answered him. . ."

After the story had been repeated in this way, an empty pause of 1 min was introduced in order to test the stability of the retained traces. This pause was sufficient to prevent spontaneous recall. Only if prompted, could he begin to recall the story, and then only the first part.

What have we just been doing? "You told me a story." *What was it?* "I can't remember. . ." *Was there a theme of the story?* "There was a theme, but I have lost it. . ." *Can you tell me roughly what the story was about?* "No, I can't. . ." *Was it about a dog?* "I can only remember that there were some animals. . ." *What sort of animals?* "A lion and. . . an elephant." *What happened?* "I can't remember the theme. . . I don't even know what they quarreled about, so that I could recall. . ." *The story was "The Lion and the Mouse."* "Aha, a mouse ran over a lion. The lion woke up. . . I think he caught her. . . I can't say for sure. . . I don't know what happened next. . ." *What was the meaning of the story?* "The meaning?. . . Well I don't remember exactly, I couldn't catch the meaning. . . I don't remember the meaning. . ."

The story was repeated a second and a third time. After each reading, a pause of 1 min was introduced. The patient said he could not remember the story. The story was read a fourth time. This time the patient's attention was distracted toward the end of the story, but its beginning disappeared from his memory: "I can't remember the end, the mouse crawled up stealthily, and showed mutual aid and set the lion free. . ." *What about the beginning?* "At the beginning the lion let the mouse go. . . but in what situation or condition I cannot remember. . ." *The lion was asleep. . .* "And a hunter tied him to a tree and then went on with his hunting, and during this time the mouse ran up to the tree and chewed through the rope with which the mouse was tied. . ." *That is the end of the story. What was its beginning?* "The beginning I cannot recollect. . ."

Since the introduction of an empty pause made it difficult for this patient to repeat a story, the next step was to examine the effect of a pause filled with interfering activity.

The familiar "The Hen and the Golden Eggs" story was read to him and he was asked to repeat it immediately. He did so quite well, except for a little uncertainty about the end. After a short pause, the story was read once more, and he again repeated it well. Interfering activity was then introduced (simple mental arithmetic).

The patient was then asked: *What did we do together before the mental arithmetic?* "I remember that you said count upward in 3s and in 8s, and I did so only in 8s." *What did you do before the arithmetic?* "Before the arithmetic, I can't tell you. . ." *But surely you were doing something?* "I can't deny it. . ." *Before the arithmetic did you memorize a story?* "Maybe I did. . ." *What was it?* "I can remember there was a hen. . ." *Tell me about it!* "I can't tell you what it was about, I have forgotten." *Nevertheless, try!* "No, a hen. . . let us suppose she was. . . but no, it is pure invention. . . There was evidently a hen. . . but what she was doing. . . I suppose she was laying some sort of eggs." *What sort of eggs?* "Oh, possibly golden eggs, or perhaps something even more expensive. . ." *What next?* "What next I can't remember. . . Well here is the story, let us say I remember that a man had a hen which laid golden eggs. . . but after that I can't say. . ." *When we read this story, had you heard it before or was this for the first time?* "No, I'm not sure. . . you reminded me about it. . . but I have completely forgotten."

The test showed that the theme of the story, although sufficiently firmly retained, disappeared after the introduction of interfering activity, so that not even the production of the fragment "There was a hen" could enable him to recall the theme as a whole (as happens usually). The patient, being unable to recall the recently imprinted theme, tried to reconstruct the story logically; however, the story he tried to reproduce was not the one that had just been read to him, but something he had heard before.

These results make it unnecessary to make a detailed analysis of the next, more complex series of tests, in which the patient was given two stories in succession, asked to repeat separately, then to recall unaided the theme of the first story. As might be supposed, this task was completely beyond his ability. Having repeated the second story, he completely forgot the theme of the first and usually said that he could not even remember that another story had been read to him. At best, he said that all he had was some sort of vague recollection, but he could not clarify it.

The main feature of the disorder is that a comparatively short series of words could be easily memorized and repeated. Even a short empty pause, but particularly a "filled" pause, however, completely prevented recall. These difficulties of recollection were uncomplicated by confabulations, consciousness was perfectly lucid, and the patient retained a normal critical attitude toward his mnemonic defects. Inability to recall sometimes assumed the form of forgetting the very fact that he had just performed the activity. The memory defects were connected with a disturbed temporal perspective. He always experienced a "sense of familiarity" with recent material, but placed it in the distant past.

Memorizing visual material. In order to determine whether the mnemonic disorders were restricted to the verbal sphere, or were modality-nonspecific, a series of tests was carried out with isolated pictures, organized thematic pictures, and finally movements and actions. These experiments yielded results similar to those just described.

The retention of single pictures was within the patient's grasp, although traces of the cards shown to him were somewhat unstable. Different results were obtained when the tests involved recall of two pairs of pictures.

I. *Dress–poppy*	II. *Horse–jug*	?/I	?/II
Correctly	Correctly	Correctly	Correctly

(An empty pause of 30 sec introduced)

?/I	?/II
Horse and jug	Dress and poppy

Test repeated.

I. *Dress and poppy*	II. *Horse and jug*	?/I	?/II
Correctly	Correctly	Lily of the valley and jug	Dress and poppy

(Pause of 30 sec introduced, filled with interfering activity, counting from 100 in 6s)

What were we doing together just now? "We repeated some words, then there was a pause and we looked to see what I could keep during the pause. . ." (reminiscence of previous test). *But now, immediately before this what were we doing?* "I counted from 100 every three or four I can't remember. . ." *That is correct; but before you counted, what were we doing?* "I can't remember. . . (looks around vaguely; sees the picture cards turned over on the table). . . . Ah yes, we were remembering picture cards. . ." *And what was on them?* "I can't remember." *Try to recall!* "There were flowers. . . or children's toys. . . or articles of children's clothing. . ." *And what was in the first pair?* "In the first. . , I think children's clothes. . . an overcoat and teddy bear. . ." *And in the second pair?* "Some sort of flowers—I can't collect my thoughts. . ."

The phenomena just described were repeated in the memorizing and repetition of thematic picture cards. Although he could identify them perfectly well, if a second card was shown to him immediately after the first, he was able to retain only one of them.

Similar data were obtained in experiments with memorizing and recall of movements and actions.

Clinical observations showed that once an action had been performed, it soon disappeared from the patient's memory. He was therefore quite unable to answer if asked what he had done the same morning or two days ago. He invariably replied that nothing remained in his memory. He had to make logical deductions when we tried to make him recall events or actions that had taken place.

What were you doing this morning? "I can't say. . . certainly I was doing something, but what it was I really cannot say. I am in a hospital, so that it must have been some sort of treatment. . ." *Did you see a motion picture?* "Perhaps. . . I can't confirm it or deny it. . ."

This was seen in an even simpler form in tests involving tapping out rhythms and then repeating them later.

He was asked to tap out rhythms of varied complexity, either in response to a pictorial representation or a spoken instruction. As noted above, he had no difficulty in carrying out this test. He could easily repeat a rhythm both immediately and after an empty pause of 30 to 45 sec. When asked what he was doing, he had likewise no difficulty in saying that he was "tapping like the Morse code," and repeated the last rhythm.

A completely different picture was seen if tapping out rhythms was followed by interfering activity–for example, if for 30 sec after receiving the instruction he had to carry out a reaction of choice, such as raising the right hand in response to one tap and the left hand in response to two taps. After tapping out the rhythms correctly, followed by the reaction of choice, the patient was asked what he had been doing before the interfering activity. "I can no longer remember. . ." *But I told you to remember!* "Ah yes, I tapped out some sort of tunes. . . but I don't know what they were–I don't even know if there were any!. . ." *And what did you do after tapping out the tunes?* "I have told you I don't know. . . I probably made a sentence out of two sentences (traces of previous tests recalled as reminiscences). . . but I can't say definitely. . ." *But don't you know what you did after tapping today?* "I can't even remember what or where it was, and what happened after. . ."

As in the tests examined above, interfering activity grossly impaired his recall of a previous action, and if he could recall the previous action, that disturbed his recalling of the later action. As in the previous test, there was gross disturbance in retention of the temporal sequence.

Two questions remained unanswered: Was the recalling of movements and actions inhibited only by another motor task or was it inhibited by any other type of activity? Was this inhibitory effect of interfering activity confined to the verbal account of the previous activity or did it extend to the repetition of the action itself? Some examples follow:

The patient was instructed: *When I show my finger, you must touch your cheek; when I show my fist, you must hold your left ear.* After the instruction had been repeated twice, he carried out the test perfectly. An empty pause of 1 min was introduced. The patient could easily continue to carry out this instruction and to describe it in words. The pause was then filled with interfering activity (mental arithmetic).

After this "filled" pause the patient was asked: *What were we doing before this?* "We were adding two numbers, and then subtracting." *And what did we do before that?* "I can't say. . ." *Perhaps we were doing something with our hands?* "I can remember using my hands, but I have no idea what for. . ."

The process of recalling was transferred to a practical plane: The examiner raised his finger and asked what must be done. The patient tapped with his finger on the table. He gave the same response when the examiner raised his fist. *Did you recall what you had to do?* "I can only remember that there were these movements, but what I was supposed to say about them I don't know. . ." *Try to recollect!* "When you tapped once I had to make some sort of movement, but what it was I can't say exactly. . . When you tapped twice I had to make another movement. . ." (By way of reminiscence, fragments of the test involving the reaction of choice carried out a few days previously began to reappear in his memory.)

The instruction was repeated a second time. The patient easily repeated the instruction and just as easily carried it out. An empty pause of 1 min had no effect on his performance of this task.

Interfering activity (the solution of arithmetical problems for 1 min) was again introduced into the pause. The patient was then asked: *What were we doing before counting?* "Before that I was repeating some words." (Reminiscence of the previous test.) *And what were we doing with our hands?* "We were doing something but what I can't remember. . ."

The test was transfered to a practical plane. The patient was shown a finger and he clenched his fist. He was shown a clenched fist. He looked at it helplessly and said: "I have to do something but I don't know what."

These findings show that both the practical recalling of traces of previous motor responses and expressing the instruction in words were inhibited by interfering activity—not only motor, but also of any other type (especially intellectual). The intensity of this inhibition was so strong that it extended both to the verbal recall and the practical repetition of the previously consolidated action.

Conclusions

I have described a syndrome of massive primary memory disturbances observed in the residual period, one year after the acute stage of a lesion involving the deep connecting structures of the brain. It differed from many of the disturbances described above in that the disturbances of memory were associated with complete preservation of consciousness, they were unaccompanied by contamination or confabulations, the mobility of the primary processes remained completely normal, and there was no evidence of pathological inertia. The tests showed that these disturbances were modality-nonspecific in character, affecting auditory, visual, and motor processes, and verbal and nonverbal processes equally. These disturbances also were manifested at all levels of mnemonic activity.

As in the previous tests, the severest memory disturbances occurred as a result of the inhibitory effect of interfering activity and, consequently, they were associated not so much with defects of imprinting (recording) as with defects of retrieval. They were particularly conspicuous when the patient was given the special task of returning to his past and recalling a certain fact. The patient was quite unable to extract what he thought from his memory, but at the same time he could activate, by way of reminiscence, impressions received two or three days previously in the course of an earlier test. This reminiscence, associated with a severe disturbance of voluntary recall, was one of the characteristic features distinguishing the disturbances of this patient's mnemonic activity.

As in others described in the classical literature, the mnemonic disorders of this patient occurred in association with a severe disturbance of the temporal arrangement of traces. Often he did not know to what period a trace referred ("I don't know whether it was just now or a long time ago").

These primary memory disturbances were reflected neither in the patient's logical thinking nor in his intellectual behavior. As the clinical data showed, this syndrome of mnemonic disorders associated with the preservation of consciousness and unaccompanied either by irrelevant associations or by confabulations can arise in patients with local lesions of the deep zones of the brain and it differs sharply from the cases described earlier in which the frontal lobes also were involved in the pathological process.

CHAPTER VIII

Disturbances of Memory in Lesions of the Diencephalic Systems of the Brain (Intermediate Forms)

So far I have analyzed primary, modality-nonspecific disturbances of memory and consciousness arising in patients with pathological processes affecting the diencephalon and limbic region. Such lesions lead to pathologically increased inhibition of traces by interfering factors and equalized excitability of traces, with the consequent introduction of fragmentation and contamination. In all cases described so far, the patients were motivated to perform the mnemonic tasks, however poor their actual performance might be.

A completely different picture arises when the pathological process spreads to the frontal lobes. In such cases, pathologically increased inhibition and equalized excitability of traces is joined by a disturbance in the regulating function of speech sets and goal-directed activity, characterized by the abandonment of organized programs and their replacement by irrelevant associations, echopraxis, or inert stereotypes (Luria, 1962, 1969, 1970; Luria & Khomskaya, 1966). If these components are simply added to the pathology described earlier, the changes observed may be in the nature of a compromise. If the frontal lobe lesions become the dominant factor, the disturbances of memory and consciousness become part of a general disturbance of goal-directed activity.

In this chapter I deal with intermediate forms of memory disturbance arising in a patient with a deep brain tumor (craniopharyngioma) after a traumatic operation during which the frontal lobes were elevated. In the subsequent chapters I shall examine disturbances of mnemonic activity arising in patients with massive lesions of the frontal lobes.

The case of the patient that we will now discuss is of special interest. Massive impairment of memory resulting from lesions in the deep parts of the brain is combined here with the ready tendency to slip into uncontrollably occurring secondary associations whose occurrence the patient can suppress so as to return to the execution of a given program.

Patient Avot., a 34-year-old male (a research worker in economics by profession), was admitted to the N. N. Burdenko Institute of Neurosurgery on June 7, 1968, with the diagnosis of a suspected tumor in the anterior zones of the 3rd ventricle.

The illness began in 1967 when the patient noticed the appearance of headaches, increased thirst, and a gradual loss of eyesight, which quickly became the dominant feature of this complaint. He was admitted to the ophthalmological department of one of the Riga hospitals, from which he was quickly transferred to the neurological department, where, besides loss of eyesight and pain in his eyes, attention was directed to his increased thirst, bulimia, and a marked decrease in tone of the limbs without any appreciable difference on each side. Pneumoencephalography revealed changes in the anterior zones of the 3rd ventricle. Due to the suspected brain tumor, the patient was transferred to the Burdenko Institute of Neurosurgery.

Neurological investigations did not provide a clear-cut picture. The patient was fully oriented and communicative, he had no definite complaint of a disturbance in his intellectual activity, but noticed some diminution of his memory. As before, the central factor was the impaired eyesight (which by this time had become particularly severe) and the headaches. Ophthalmological examination revealed a primary pallor of the optic discs. Visual acuity was sharply reduced, especially in the left eye (in which vision was limited to the perception of movements of the hands in front of his face). On the right side, visual acuity was reduced to 0.09 and the temporal part of the visual field was lost. These facts pointed to a lesion of the chiasma and optic nerves, especially on the left side. An otoneurological examination showed a disturbance of the functions of the central vestibular system at the level of the diencephalon.

The cerebrospinal fluid pressure was normal, the protein concentration 0.8 parts per thousand, and the cell count 73/3, with an increased number of neutrophils. Electroencephalography showed only general cerebral changes. The roentgenogram gave no indication of a prolonged increased intracranial pressure, but it did show flattening of the anterior wall of the 3rd ventricle and marked evidence of calcification. Angiography showed no clear changes in the lumen of the vessels. On the basis of this syndrome a tumor (craniopharyngioma with a cyst) was diagnosed. The progressive worsening of the patient's vision was an indication for operative treatment.

Two weeks after admission, an operation was performed. A cyst was found in the region of the chiasma and was drained. Continued worsening of vision, however, made a further operation necessary. On August 30, 1968, a second operation was performed, when the left frontal lobe was elevated. Gross scarring was found in the region of the chiasma and the left optic nerve. A cyst found in this region and the anterior part of a tumor (craniopharyngioma), evidently spreading posteriorly, were removed (Figure 20).

This operation did not arrest the development of the disease, and at the beginning of September the patient's eyesight showed further deterioration, with loss of olfaction of both sides, increased thirst, and loss of caloric nystagmus.

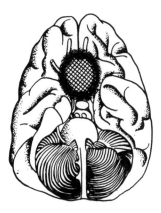

FIG. 20. Position of tumor in patient Avot.

At this period the changes in the patient's behavior began to increase in severity. He became apathetic and drowsy, less communicative, and disoriented, so that he mistook people around him for his relatives. Gradually the apathy and drowsiness disappeared and gave way to restless movements and to disinhibition. The patient became good-natured, somewhat disinhibited, and grossly disoriented. Sometimes he thought he was in Hungary, sometimes in Leningrad, sometimes in hospital "because of a disturbance of his nervous activity." He was untidy and sometimes went into the corridor undressed, but did not get into people's way. Disturbances of sleep and the emotions appeared. During this period the patient developed severe disturbances of memory and consciousness with confabulations, and these constitute the main subject of my investigation. Later all these phenomena began to regress and by the end of October, after a series of punctures, the features of disorientation and the general uncritical attitude disappeared. The patient began to behave much more adequately, but the memory disorders continued.

It was concluded from a comparison of all the symptoms of the disease that the tumor affected the chiasma with the adjacent parts of the optic nerves, and was undoubtedly spreading into the floor of the 3rd ventricle, i.e., mainly into the hypothalamic region. The base of the frontal lobes was not damaged directly by the tumor. The approach to the tumor during the second operation inevitably led to considerable trauma to the basal frontal cortex and to bleeding, which were followed by scar formation in the meninges, already adherent to the brain surface as a result of the first operation.

On clinical grounds, the cytopathological disorders were most likely to be due to the progressive lesion in the floor of the 3rd ventricle, i.e., in the hypothalamic region, where connections with the frontal lobes could also be damaged. It is worth noting that this patient had no significant symptoms of increased intracranial pressure. Furthermore, throughout the period of observation no secondary quadrigeminal symptoms were noted, nor any manifestations of brain-stem displacement.

Neuropsychological investigation of the patient before the operation revealed a relatively mild disturbance of higher psychological processes, similar to those described earlier in this book. The patient was completely oriented and communicative. He readily took part in the investigation. He complained only of the visual disorders and his loss of vision, and mentioned that he had recently begun to notice something wrong with his memory. There was no disturbance of gnosis, praxis, or speech; he knew exactly where he was; he had no difficulty giving the date; and he was rather depressed by his condition. The ordinary memory tests gave no indication of any marked changes. More sensitive tests of memory revealed relatively mild increased inhibitability of traces by interfering factors.

A few days after the second operation, the patient was disoriented and had severe memory disturbances. In this period he was not depressed, his movements were brisk and adequate, and he was even a little euphoric. His orientation in place was badly affected, for sometimes he thought he was "in Hungary," in hospital "because of a disturbance of his higher nervous activity," or sometimes that he was in Riga or Moscow. He knew he had had an operation, but was uncertain whether it had happened twice or three times. He had no special complaints and thought he would easily be able to get on with the work of writing his dissertation. He did not even mention that he had almost lost his eyesight, but simply repeated in stereotyped fashion: "Well of course. . . I soon get tired. . . I still can't make out with my eyes. . ." He could not recognize people around him, took the people in the ward as his relatives, did not remember the doctors treating him. He immediately forgot that he had met people, introduced himself afresh to the doctor who had just left the ward 3 to 5 min ago and returned. Sometimes he confabulated and started to discuss with his wife the question of buying a car (which he did not have) and said that the day before he had driven somewhere. He eagerly started a conversation; he was very talkative, but his answers were filled with irrelevant details or limited to stereotyped phrases and flat jokes.

The patient's memory was severely disturbed. Although, after the first 2 or 3 weeks, he began to recognize the doctor testing him, he had no idea of the time elapsing between two conversations. For a long time he remained unsure of his estimation of time.

His memory for long past events and his previous store of knowledge remained much more intact than his recent memory. Nevertheless, when discussing subjects previously very familiar to him, he easily slipped into irrelevant stereotypes. For example, when relating the story of "Evgenii Onegin," with which he was very familiar, he began properly but ended by saying that "Tat'yana, as usually happens in such cases, married Evgenii, and their love ended in marriage," etc.

The patient's behavior was uninhibited and subject to uncontrolled orienting reactions to every irrelevant stimulus, each of which induced him to emit uncontrollable actions or remarks. For instance, when he was invited into the laboratory and sat on a chair, he looked around, reached for a piece of paper lying on the table, picked up the files, looked through them, observed the notebook in the doctor's hands and asked: "Perhaps you would give me some sheets of paper, I may perhaps need them." His reactions to every chance impression were so brisk and uncontrolled that before the tests began everything had to be taken from the table otherwise they would have distracted him so much that it would have been impossible to start the test. When the doctor accompanied the patient back to the ward, these uninhibitable reactions to any impression were exhibited particularly strongly. For instance, as he went out of the laboratory door, he made for the half-open doors into the opposite room. Going past the door with the notice "Investigation of Cerebrospinal Fluid," he read the notice out aloud and asked, "Doctor, can you also read Latin names?" When he found the open door of the elevator, he immediately entered and said, "Now, doctor, shall we go!", although he did not need to take it because the way was in the opposite direction. This overresponsive, uninhibited and impulsive behavior was at that time the most characteristic feature of this patient, and together with his amnesia, confabulations, and lack of concern, formed the basic syndrome.

During this period he could perform most of the neuropsychological tests perfectly well. He had no difficulty in carrying out tests of praxis and could easily transpose the spatial relations involved in copying the position of the doctor's hands. Reciprocal coordination was intact. He could easily estimate rhythms and repeat them either directly or in response to a spoken instruction. Choice reactions were performed well, and no mistakes were made in such "contradictory" tests as: When I tap once you must tap twice, but when I tap twice you must tap only once; or, when I show my fist you must point with your finger, but when I point with my finger you must show your fist.

He could easily repeat separate words and short series of words or phrases. He had no difficulty in understanding words or simple logical-grammatical relations or in naming objects pointed out to him. He could calculate well, made very few mistakes in arithmetical examples, and could solve simple problems. In this last case, the only disturbing feature was that he was invariably distracted by irrelevant associations. He asked many unnecessary questions unconnected with the conditions of the problem, and easily fell under the influence of irrepressible stereotyped arguments. The perception of logical relations (genus-species, part-whole, simple analogies) presented no particular difficulty. He could interpret relatively successfully the meaning of a simple picture, actively examining the picture for this purpose and picking out its details. He could draw well, and still preserved the skill of a caricaturist (which he had learned before his illness). His drawing technique was excellent and no perseverations or forced movements were observed.

Structure of Mnemonic Disorders

Tests with a Fixed Set

A fixed haptic set, in Uznadze's terminology, was produced in the patient (he was instructed to feel a large sphere 5 cm in diameter with his left hand and a small sphere 3 cm in diameter with his right hand); a control test was then carried out in which he had to feel two spheres of equal size, each 3 cm in diameter, and to estimate their size.

After preliminary experiments, a stable illusion of contrast was created in this patient, so that if two spheres of equal size were subsequently shown to him, the sphere in the right hand appeared larger to him than the sphere in the left hand.

The test was then carried out under different conditions. The patient was instructed to feel two unequal spheres 10 times (the large sphere, again with the left hand), but this time the two parts of the experiment were separated by an interval of 1 min, which was kept "empty" in some cases but filled with interfering activity, such as arithmetic, in others. In both cases, the traces of the fixed set (the illusion that the right sphere was larger) were retained by the patient for one or, at most, two presentations. A short "empty" pause led to a sharp decrease in the stability of the traces, and a pause filled with interfering activity abolished them almost completely.

Konorski's Tests

Similar results were obtained in previously described series of tests by Yu. M. Konorski.

The patient was shown a figure (e.g., a blue triangle), followed by another similar or different figure (e.g., a red triangle). He was asked to say whether the figures were the same. The second figure was presented either immediately (3 to 5 sec) after the first, or after a longer pause unoccupied by interfering activity (30 sec, 1 min, or 1.5 min) or, finally, after a pause of 1 min filled by interfering activity (mental arithmetic).

When the second figure was presented immediately after the first, the patient had no difficulty in assessing differences in its color or shape. If the second figure was shown after an "empty" interval of 30 sec, the patient could also correctly compare the second figure with the traces of the first. Increasing the interval to 1 min led to occasional mistakes and, in some cases, the patient declared that "he seemed to forget what the first figure was," but even so his mistakes did not exceed 10–12%. Finally, in tests in which the second figure was presented 1.5 min after the first, the number of doubtful answers ("Was there a first figure?") or mistakes increased to 30–35%. When a pause of 1.5 min was occupied by irrelevant activity, the patient either could not remember that the first figure had been shown, declared that he had forgotten its color, or made a mistake.

Memorizing Pictures

In tests described above, the subject was not faced with any special mnemonic task. The question therefore arises how pauses and interfering factors would affect the simplest forms of voluntary memorizing of visual material. To study these problems, a series of tests involving memorizing drawings was carried out. Without interfering factors, a drawing was retained sufficiently firmly and could be distinguished from irrelevant associations, but with homogeneous interference the traces easily disappeared. Instead of repeating the required figure, the patient could not repress irrelevant associations. This phenomenon was particularly conspicuous as the patient grew more tired.

He was shown a card with the picture of a frying pan. He identified the picture correctly. The card was covered and 1 min later he was asked what was the picture on the card. "This is where I can use my imagination. . . or a pile of books or. . . no, a frying pan. . ." The patient was shown another card depicting a drum with drum sticks. He said: "This is an interesting tank with two guns!" *Isn't it a drum?* "Yes, of course, a drum. . ." *What was the first picture?* "A frying pan." *And the second?* "Not a frying pan, no, something else. . . no, I can't remember. . ." *And the first picture?* "A frying pan." *The second picture?* "A pile of something, but what I have forgotten." The same test was repeated. This time the patient named the two pictures correctly. *Did you remember them well?* "Yes!" *What was the first picture?* "A frying pan." *And the second?* "A drum, male or female."

The test was continued and the patient shown another pair of pictures—an apple and a knife. After the pictures had been presented, there was a pause of 1 min during which the patient looked around him and tried to start a conversation with the doctors sitting there. After the pause, he was asked: *What was the first picture?* "Some sort of. . . interesting. . . I can't remember any more. . . some sort of pile. . ." *And the second?* "I can't recollect. . . I am having a chat with them. . . I can't remember anything. . ."

The test was repeated. After the two pictures had been shown there was another pause of 1 min during which the patient said: "In fact my memory became worse during this time," and he again tried to start a conversation with his neighbor. *What was the first picture?* "A frying pan" (the trace of a picture shown previously, by way of reminiscence). *And the second picture?* "Some sort of household utensil."

The memorizing of pictures, like the patient's own actions, obeys the rules described above. A pause, especially if filled with interfering activity, leads to rapid decay of the traces. Sometimes he could not even remember that he had been asked to carry out a particular task.

Investigation of Verbal Memory

Learning a series of 10 unconnected words was unexpectedly good for a patient with a fully developed Korsakov's syndrome. In consecutive repetitions, he recalled 4-4-5-6-7 of the 10 words. His chief disability was repeating the same word several times over (evidently he forgot just having said it). The integrity of direct repetition was in harmony with tests of his operative memory, in which he correctly carried out complicated calculations requiring the retention of intermediate operations.

What then were the defects of our patient's memory that were so clearly manifested in the clinical picture? To answer this question, I carried out a number of recall tests beginning with unconnected words and ending with meaningful sentences and complete stories. Each of these tests was carried out under three different conditions: Direct repetition, repetition after a delay, and repetition after a delay occupied by interfering activity.

Direct repetition of 3 (or even 5) word series was easy for this patient. He could repeat the series even after a delay of 1 min. If this period was occupied by interfering activity, however, the words just given were forgotten. Similar results were obtained when repeating sentences. Normally a sentence, as an organized semantic entity, can be remembered and recalled much more successfully than a group of isolated words. But in this case, traces of sentences were also readily inhibited by interfering activity.

As we saw above, the operation involved considerable trauma to both frontal lobes, and led to marked changes in the patient's behavior. Any irrelevant stimulus began to evoke a strong orienting reaction and a whole chain of uncontrollable actions. Any object or problem given to him set in motion a chain of irrepressible associations, which led to a flood of irrelevant questions, a demand for unnecessary details, and phenomena described in psychiatry as sterile "rationalization."

The patient had no difficulty in grasping the general sense of a story, but perceived it in fragments. Sometimes he forgot the second part of the story, if it constituted a separate semantic theme. When repeating the story, he began to introduce irrelevant associations, adding numerous superfluous details, and finally drifting into a new subject altogether. Usually he did not completely lose the theme but managed to adhere to the general theme of the story, or eventually, to return to it. Only in the acute period of the illness, or while fatigued, did this cycle repetition of the story give way to total distraction and loss of the assigned program. This fact is so interesting that I shall discuss it in detail.

L. N. Tolstoy's "The Jackdaw and the Pigeons" story was read to the patient. He retold it as follows.

"A jackdaw very much wanted to grab some food from the pigeons, who had plenty of good food to eat... She went and painted herself white and flew to the pigeon house. They let her in and she ate her fill of tasty and nutritious food. However, she suddenly cried out 'Caw' and the pigeons saw that their visitor was one of the wrong kind, and they chased the jackdaw away. She shed many bitter tears, changed her clothes (!) and went back to her own home." (Moral of the story was correctly deduced.)

When Tolstoy's "The Ant and the Pigeon" story, which has a more complex structure, was repeated, the disturbances became more evident.

"Once upon a time a pigeon lived in the forest... and an ant. They were mutually sympathetic: The ant liked the pigeon and vice versa. One day a wicked hunter with fascist views (!) went into the forest and caught the pigeon. When the hunter seized the pigeon the ant became angry, bit him on his arm, and set her beloved pigeon free..." *Tell the story more fully!* "Yes, I didn't tell it completely... but I can't remember the beginning..."

These features were seen more clearly still in later tests, carried out at the height of the syndrome. L. N. Tolstoy's "The Lion and the Mouse" story was read to the patient. He retold it as described on page 123.

The same drift into irrepressible and irrelevant associations occurred during further attempts to get this patient to retell the story properly.

This record is extremely interesting. The patient started to retell the story correctly and grasped its basic theme. When switching to the second part, however, he could not distinguish the correct details ("the hunter") from the irrepressible associations ("lion hunters—Africa") and he introduced these irrelevant associations into the text of the story, being unable to inhibit them, although he was aware of their presence all the time.

If the story were simply read a second time without a delay, the patient was able to retell the story correctly. A pause of 1 min was sufficient for irrelevant associations to be introduced into the repetition. After a pause of 3 min, it was completely impossible for the patient to recall the traces of the story.

Another test, also carried out at the height of this syndrome, yielded similar results. This test was carried out by a female member of the writer's staff, to whom the patient paid close attention all the time.

The "The Jackdaw and the Pigeons" story was read to the patient and he was asked to repeat it. He started as follows.

"A jackdaw wanted to eat well. . . she knew that the pigeons had plenty of good food; she painted herself. . . with aniline dye,. . . (looked at the examiner). . . turned her hair into locks. Then she flew to the farm. . . to the pigeon house. . . the pigeons welcome her. . . she stayed there until the spring, the sun rose higher in the sky, our dear little bird began to fly out into the farmyard and they chased the jackdaw into the forest. . . they realized that the jackdaw was not a pigeon. . . but I can't remember the moral. . ."

What happened to the jackdaw? ". . . she found it hard to live. . . she. . . (looks around). . . developed appendicitis. Dr. X did the operation. There she lay, our little bird Galka (jackdaw) very miserable and pale, and the surgeon looked and looked at her and felt very tenderly toward her. . . and proposed she should marry him! Let me see. . . I must have read all this somewhere. . . she flew away. . . you know, all these different female things. . . but they would not accept her there, they did not like noisy birds. . . and she had to stay somewhere between the sky and the ground. . ."

This record adds a great deal to those discussed above. All through the tests the patient looked attentively at the female examiner, and although he retold the story correctly at first, he soon started to introduce irrelevant impressions into the narrative, and these significantly distorted the theme ("combed her hair into locks," "lay in hospital," "the surgeon began to feel tenderly toward her," etc.). The ease with which irrelevant impressions were introduced into the repetition of the story, impressions which this time had a distinct emotional flavor, is further evidence of the instability of the memory traces and the ease with which they were distorted by irrelevant factors.

As we shall see below, this basic defect persisted for a long time after the manifestations of general disinhibition and the introduction of irrepressible associations had disappeared.

Subsequent Course of the Illness

All symptoms described were observed, to a very slight degree, before the second operation, but intensified in the postoperative period, when additional effects of trauma to the basal zones of the frontal region were present. It was this factor that led to the production of a unique symptom-complex. Not only did any random stimulus inhibit recall of previously imprinted traces, but also irrelevant associations could not be inhibited. The patient's narrative was distorted by these irrepressible associations, so that the theme as related by the patient often lost all connection with the original material. At the height of development of the syndrome, this phenomenon also affected the patient's behavior, causing confusion, disorientation in his surroundings, and marked confabulation.

This uncontrollable flow of thoughts corresponded clearly to the basal-diencephalic syndrome I have described fully elsewhere.

The distinguishing feature of the present case was that he was unable to recognize the inadequacy of these intruding associations, or to a certain extent, control their course. As illustrated in the transcripts, having drifted into additional irrelevant associations when retelling a story, the patient exclaimed: "I am making this up!"—and as the test continued he began to ask whether he was following the theme of the story correctly, without any "adornments," or whether he was giving free reign to his random impressions.

The postoperative period was accompanied by a marked exacerbation of the syndrome. Three weeks after the operation there was a sudden change in the patient's condition. After puncture with the withdrawal of a considerable volume of cerebrospinal fluid, all the signs of disorientation, evident earlier on the same day, disappeared. His wife remarked that "he had become sensible again." The confabulations ceased, and his behavior became much more rational. At this stage, the patient was tested again. There had been a definite regression of the syndrome, considerable strengthening of the memory traces, and some reduction in the intrusion of irrelevant associations and excessive details. These phenomena continued to undergo slow regression and careful observation revealed several stages in this process.

In the first stage, the contamination and intrusion of irrelevant associations began to assume the form of talkativeness and frequent intrusion of habitual stereotypes. Easy inhibition by interfering factors continued, and was particularly marked during the performance of the more difficult tests, such as the repetition of a cycle of stories. (An example is given below.)

The patient was asked to repeat the "The Lion and the Mouse" story read to him four days previously. He did so without difficulty, adding only a number of habitual stereotypes that did not occur in the original.

"The Clever Rat" story was read to him. He retold it with superfluous details, not occurring in the original (e.g., "Once upon a time there were two mice—one was cleverer and the other a bit more stupid, in short—a man and his wife. Once they both went into the kitchen and saw an egg lying somewhere where I won't tell you. Each thought of carrying off the egg for itself, so as to have an egg flip and other good things to eat...," etc.). Despite this intrusion of irrelevant verbal stereotypes, the theme remained intact. It was only at the end of the story that the patient began to introduce completely irrelevant details: "A crow was flying around there (from "The Crow and the Crab" story read to him four days previously) and they began to think that it might eat this egg...," etc.

The patient was asked if he remembered "The Jackdaw and the Pigeons" story read to him a few days earlier. He easily repeated this story also, but with the introduction of irrelevant associations ("the jackdaw wanted to go back to her own home, but her people refused to take her, as a betrayer of her own people").

Having repeated this story, the patient was asked to recall stories he had repeated earlier. He said, helplessly, that he was unable to do so: "Did you really read me any stories today?! I can't remember... Perhaps there was something about a boy and something else... Perhaps some animals..." Even prompting (about a dog?, about a cat?, about rats?, about mice?) did not help. Only more insistent prompting (How did the mice propose to carry away the egg?) enabled the patient to recall the theme. As before, he was unable to recall the traces of the other stories and said: "Perhaps there were other stories but I can't remember anything about them..."

The next tests on the patient were carried out during November and December, 1968, i.e., two and three months after the operation. The intrusion of irrelevant associations and stereotypes, and the inhibitability of traces by interfering factors, were both reduced a little in intensity, but the general picture still remained. Further regression of the syndrome was manifested by interfering activity no longer preventing recall of previous traces but still led to their mixing with traces of other systems. In other words, a disturbance of selectivity remained although in much milder form.

Conclusions

The investigation showed that the operative trauma to the frontal lobes added new and very important components to the already familiar syndrome of memory disturbances. The symptoms incorporated definite components of the frontal syndrome characterized by increased orienting reactions and by the irrepressible intrusion of irrelevant associations. This intrusion of irrelevant associations was purely a temporary phenomenon. Despite it, the patient did not lose the basic theme of the story and eventually returned to it. The disturbances in this syndrome are intermediate between the primary disturbances of memory and consciousness already described and the disturbances of goal-directed mnemonic activity found in patients with massive lesions of the frontal lobes (examined in the next chapter).

CHAPTER IX

Disturbances of Mnemonic Activity in Massive Lesions of the Frontal Lobes

After the classical observations of Jacobsen (1935), who first observed that delayed responses are disturbed after resection of the frontal lobes in monkeys, investigators were inclined to connect the frontal lobes with memory. Subsequently, the idea developed that the lesions of the frontal lobes lead primarily to a disturbance in the normal inhibition of orienting reactions, to the appearance of pathological hyperreactivity, or pathological inertia of existing stereotypes (Anokhin, 1949, 1958(a), 1958(b), 1959, 1962(a), 1962(b); Konorski et al., 1967, etc.; Malmo, 1942; Pribram, 1958–1961), and that the relationship of the frontal lobes to memory is much more complex and indirect. The views just mentioned were expressed on the basis of animal experiments. Observations on memory disturbances in patients with frontal lobe lesions provided less impressive material from which no definite conclusions could be drawn.

A careful structural analysis of the mnemonic disorders following massive lesions (tumors, traumatic lesions, hemorrhage) that have inactivated various zones of the frontal lobes may provide some answers to the role of the frontal lobes in mnemonic activity. It is particularly valuable to analyze cases in which the pathological process disturbing the normal functions of the frontal lobes is accompanied initially by considerable general cerebral disturbances due to increased intracranial pressure or displacement of the brain.

I shall analyze the disturbances of mnemonic activity in two patients with massive lesions of the frontal lobes, the first a patient with an extracerebral tumor (arachnoidendothelioma) of the basal zones of the frontal lobes, and the second a patient with a large traumatic lesion of the frontal lobes. I shall attempt to trace the changes observed in both these patients at successive stages of regression of the disease.

Disturbances of Mnemonic Activity in Patients with Massive Tumors of the Frontal Lobes

We will first show data obtained upon analysis of disturbance of mnemonic activity in a patient with a massive tumor in the frontal parts of the brain.

Patient Sar., a 60-year-old male (a history teacher and lecturer), was admitted to the Burdenko Institute of Neurosurgery on March 6, 1972 with the diagnosis of resumed growth of an arachnoidendothelioma in the basal zones of the frontal lobe.

The illness began in the fall of 1966 and led to an operation for the removal of a sarcomatous arachnoidendothelioma located in the parasagittal zones of the frontal region, more especially on the left side. During the next four years, he felt fit and continued to work and to give lectures, and later after retiring he had undertaken special duties.

In November, 1970, his behavior changed. He became apathetic, indifferent, and drowsy. Examination of the optic fundus revealed papilledema more marked on the right. A course of dehydration therapy was given which resulted in temporary improvement only. The symptoms then increased in severity, and he was sent to the Burdenko Institute of Neurosurgery with the presumption that the tumor had continued to grow. On admission, he was apathetic, adynamic, untidy, and confused. He was unable to relate the history of his case, and was disoriented in place and time. Examination showed neck rigidity, a positive Kernig's sign, and low visual acuity (right eye 0.5, left eye 0.02). The pupils were equal, but the pupillary reflex was absent on the right. Papilledema was severe, paresis of the abducens nerves and central paresis of the right facial nerve were present, the right palpebral fissure was narrower than the left, and the tongue deviated to the right.

The patient had symptoms of a disturbance of the primary olfactory structures on both sides and secondary symptoms of brain-stem defect, indicating a lesion of the posterior cranial fossa of dislocation origin. Sensitivity was intact except for hypoesthesia of the left lower limb. Movements were intact, apart from a slight Barre's sign on the left. The reflexes were uniformly brisk, but the abdominal reflexes were absent on the left and a positive Gordon's sign was present on the right.

The roentgenogram showed displacement of the falciform process in its frontal portions to the right. Left-sided carotid angiography revealed displacement of the anterior cerebral arteries to the right and compression of the initial portions of the middle cerebral artery to the right and basally. A network of blood vessels was seen to supply an extensive tumor of the left fronto-basal region, compressing both the left frontal and the left temporal lobes.

On the basis of these findings, it was concluded that the patient had a large tumor (possibly a sarcomatous meningioma) located in the postero-fronto-basal region, mainly in the left hemisphere.

On March 20, 1972, an operation was performed at which, after division of adhesions in the left frontal region, a tumor projecting above the cortex over an area of 3 x 3 cm was found in the basal zones of the frontal lobe, compressing the temporal lobe also. The tumor occupied a large part of the anterior cranial fossa and compressed the whole of the

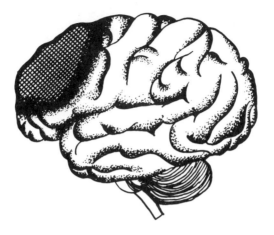

FIG. 21. Position of tumor in patient Sar.

left frontal lobe posteriorly. The tumor was attached to the lateral portion of the wing of the sphenoid zone and to the anterolateral portion of the roof of the left orbit. It consisted of two nodes measuring 5 x 6 x 8 cm and 6 x 5 x 4 cm, respectively (the position of the tumor is shown diagrammatically in Figure 21). Both nodes were removed. Histologically, the tumor was an arachnoidendothelioma.

The detailed neuropsychological investigation of this patient started in the preoperative period and was resumed postoperatively. At the beginning of the investigation, the patient was aspontaneous, confused, and grossly disoriented in place and time. Often he lay wet in bed without responding, but merely stated that he did not know why it had happened. He did not know where he was and did not recognize his surroundings. Nevertheless, he replied talkatively to questions, but it very soon became obvious that his speech was grossly distorted by pathological inertia of established stereotypes and echolalia. A typical extract from a conversation with the patient at this period is given below.

Where are you? "Where am I now?... I am taking part in a pedagogic experiment..." *What sort of an experiment is it?* "That is I... strictly speaking... here we are carrying out... most of the teachers... we are studying the position as regards supplies... how to proceed along the road... health resort... hospital... I am sent for treatment every day..." *And what is this place?* "This is a hospital..." *Where are you?* "In hospital." *Which hospital?* "Korocha hospital..." *Where is that?* "The town of Korocha, near Belgorod..." *And why are you here?* "They sent for me... to Staryi Oskol... where I stayed 2 weeks..." *When did you arrive here?* "Comrade Rakhov, Ivan Trofimovich, was at my house... he now works in the Regional... you know... I had a warrant to receive a larger pension... he trained at my institute..." *Might you be in Moscow?* "No, I am in

Korocha not in Moscow, and this is why: My eldest son has an apartment in Moscow...
he changed his apartment...," etc. (pause). *Where are you now?* "In Belgorod... at the
Ministry... no, at the DOSAF Regional committee... no, not DOSAF... not the DOSAF
Committee... this is a hospital, the Regional hospital... and I came here for a check
up..."

The patient had only a very vague idea of his condition and the nature of
his illness. Sometimes he said he was ill, sometimes he began to doubt this. He
had no active complaints and further questioning showed that he very easily
confused his present experiences with his past impressions.

Are you well or unwell? "I would tell you that I once was very ill..." *Why? What was
the matter?* "Why I was ill... because I had something wrong with my head. I had an
operation... it began in my forehead and then spread to the back... turned to the
left..." *And how is your head now?* "As regards my head, I will tell you this year... I
went to the Crimea... and there in the Crimea... there is a sanitorium where sick people
are usually sent... it is actually in Sochi..." *But surely Sochi is not in the Crimea?* "No I
must be mixing it up..." *What happened to you there?* "To me? I will tell you... in the
first place I wasn't really ill... the reason being... I had been cured... in the past... in
Voronezh... they sent me home... the records were entered into my warrant... and so
they awarded me a personal pension..." *Well then, why are you here?* "That is another
matter..."

Further conversations showed that the patient complained only of blindness
and headache but was aware of no loss of memory, for only occasionally and
after prolonged questioning would he admit that "sometimes I get my examples
mixed up." He had no emotional reactions to his failures or to the prospect of
an operation.

As in the other patients of this group, this patient's praxis was virtually
intact and it was only the pathological inertia in the performance of tasks,
which resulted in an excessive number of elements in the rhythm test and
perseveration of a previous task, that pointed to any serious disturbance of the
dynamics of his motor act. As I have already said, his speech was phonetically
and grammatically intact, but with distinct components of argumentation, and
only occasionally with difficulty in finding the necessary names.

Mnemonic Disorders Before the Operation

Memorizing series of words and sentences. Given a series of 10 isolated
words to memorize he responded without improvement over 8 trials
(4-5-4-4-5-4-4-4). The patient made no effort to memorize new words, but
repeated the second and fifth words of the series and then produced some of
the other words in random order, although having recalled them in one test he
very easily forgot them in the next. Sometimes his performance included
irrelevant associations (e.g., after reproducing the word "cat" he would include
the associated word "dog" in the series).

He was then given a series of 5 pairs of words, which were not linked by any common meaning. To begin with, the patient had to repeat each pair of words, after which he was given the first word of the pair and he had to reproduce the second. The traces of these pairs disappeared gradually as the test was repeated, particularly when the first words of the associated pair were given separately.

To continue the analysis of verbal memory traces, the patient was given isolated words or pairs of words which he had to recall after memorizing a second word or pair of words (homogeneous interference) or after some irrelevant activity, such as mental arithmetic (heterogeneous interference). Although the patient could recall a single word after both types of interference, his ability to recall a pair of words under these conditions was severely disturbed. He either inertly repeated only one of the words (more often taken from the second pair) or he drifted into random associations. Repeating the test usually produced worse, rather than better, results.

Night—needle	*Tooth—bridge*	*?/I*	*?/II*
(1) Correctly	Correctly	Do you make this the quality of the experiment?	And which of you is the physical training instructor?
(2) "	"	Needle. . . night	Tooth. . . I have forgotten. . .
(3) "	"	Bridge. . .	Tooth—bridge. . . I have forgotten.
(4) "	"	Correctly	Night—needle

Presentation of a sentence evoked a pathologically inert system. Although the patient could repeat a sentence more or less immediately, he continued to repeat the same sentence inertly. By the end of the test, he abandoned the task altogether and simply made irrelevant statements instead of the required sentences.

I. *In Tashkent there was a severe earthquake and many houses were destroyed.*	II. *In Tushino there was an air display with parachute jumps.*	*?/I*	*?/II*
(1) In 1947 there were many earthquakes in Tashkent and many houses were destroyed.	In Tushino. . . there was an air display. . . and parachute jumps.	In Tushino there was a display and people came to make parachute jumps.	
(2) In Tashkent there were many houses destroyed during an earthquake.	Something about time. . . I simply can't remember.		

(3) In Tashkent many houses were destroyed. . . in Tashkent very many were severely damaged . . . but it is not stated why.	Correctly	The first was about an air disaster.	And the second about jumps in Tushino
(4) In Tashkent there was much damage and many houses were destroyed.	Correctly	Back home Ivan Ivanovich always gave us examples like this. . .	I have forgotten.

This extract from the records shows that semantic organization did not result in increased stability of the traces. Even though the sentence was correctly recalled initially, it later became complicated by perseveration of either morphological or lexical elements.

Memorizing stories. Attempts to obtain a precise and accurate repetition of a story were not consistently successful. Sometimes the patient grasped the sense of the story but, when repeating it, immediately drifted into irrelevant associations, introducing into his narrative elements of previous conversation or random associations. Sometimes he retained only one theme of the story and forgot the others or replaced them by irrelevant associations. And finally, sometimes the narration of the story consisted entirely of repetition of the same facts over and over again, with the introduction of irrelevant associations. The disturbances described above thus extended to the repetition of complex semantic structures. A few examples are given below.

The patient was warned that a story would be read to him and he would have to repeat it. He answered, "That's fine! I was a teacher myself, I used to tell the class stories. . . that was a long time ago."

"The Hen and the Golden Egg" story was read to him. He said, "I forgot that this was 60 years ago. . ." *But what is the story about?* "There was no gold there, because he had killed her. . ." (The story was read a second time and the patient asked to repeat it.) "A man had. . . 40 children. . . 60 years ago (perseveration of the time mentioned earlier). . . every man had a hen, every hen laid a golden egg. . . these eggs were sold at the shop. . . the children bought fish-hooks there. . ." Contamination of the theme of the story with reminiscences ("I was a teacher. . . that was a long time ago. . . there were so many children in the class") and the introduction of irrelevant associations ("they sold the eggs"—"went to the shop"—"bought fish-hooks") clearly disturbed his repetition of the story.

"The Lion and the Mouse" story was read to him and he was asked to repeat it. He said, "In general, he was set free" (retention of the end of the story only). *No, tell me the beginning as well.* "The mouse finally set the lion free, and they all went for a walk at liberty" (again he told only the end of the story). *How did the story begin?* "If only the dog would catch him. . . but since they could not. . . the lion remained alive. . . we see that the dogs saved the animal and left him at liberty" (possible intrusion of the association "hunter–dogs"; once again, the patient was able to tell only the second part of the story).

The story was read again and the patient asked to tell it in the form of answers to separate questions. *What was the story about?* "About a lion." *And was there something else?* "Against a mouse" (intrusion of a negative attitude toward mice). *What happened in the story?* "From the economic point of view it was about the preservation of life. Since the lion tried to make sure that the mouse would be saved... in the open air... he preserved them... strictly speaking he preserved all mice—that means animals... and he preserved... strictly speaking... preserved mice at liberty. And that of course means that the mice were preserved at liberty..." This time the narrative, given in generalized form, is confined to the first theme of the story, but soon degenerates into the reproduction of stereotyped phrases.

Although sliding into irrelevant associations or inert stereotypes remained the central feature of this syndrome, the primary mnemonic defects were less constant. If tested with shorter stories, consisting of a single semantic theme, sometimes the patient was able to recall it even after having a second story read to him.

Recalling actions. The facts just described above raise the question of whether the disturbance was confined to speech, or whether it might also extend to the performance of movements and actions. Two experiments were carried out. In the first, the patient had to carry out simple movements in response to a spoken instruction. He then had to recall the actions he had just performed. Next, he had to perform conventional actions in response to signals corresponding to the instructions, and later describe in words what he had just done.

The patient had no difficulty in performing simple actions in response to a spoken instruction. He readily switched from one action to another without perseveration, but invariably ran into great difficulty when he tried to state in words what actions he had just performed.

He was given the following instructions: (1) Clap hands three times and (2) comb your hair. After performing both these actions, he was asked what he had just done. He answered this question with difficulty. He was asked what the first action had been. "To-day?... I am afraid I don't remember..." *What was the second action?* "The second—I shaved my beard... I tried to shave..."

Similar but much more severe defects appeared in recalling a second pair of actions. The patient was instructed (1) to place an orange under the pillow and (2) to give a lump of sugar. He carried out both actions easily.

What was the first action? "I gave a lump of sugar." *And the second?* "I put a lump of sugar in my mouth... it was so tasty that I don't know." *No, you have remembered wrongly. Tell me exactly what we did.* "We discussed ordinary daily matters." *What did you do yourself?* "You gave me a lump of sugar" (pseudoreminiscence). *And what did you do?* "I placed this lump of sugar in your mouth..." *And what did you do before this?* "This was one action." *And what was the second?* "I have forgotten." *Did you put something under the pillow?* "I did put something." *What?* "An orange."

Recalling conditioned responses. The difficulty of performing a conditioned response (e.g., if I tap once, raise your right hand; if I tap twice, raise your left hand; if I show my finger, you show your fist; if I show my fist, you show your finger) lies in the conflicting nature of the action required. It assumes that the subject's movement will not be a simple echopraxic repetition of the signal, but that he will use the meaning of the signal given in the instruction. It might be expected that both the direct performance and the recall of conditioned responses would be more difficult for this patient than the performance and recall of simple actions. The patient could perform one conditioned action and could keep it up for a long time. The attempt to express the action he had just performed in words evoked great difficulties. He was almost completely unable to perform two conflicting conditioned actions, and quite unable to repeat in words what he had done.

He was given the instruction: In response to a tap, make a fist with your left hand (for greater clarity, the verbal instruction was supported by a kinesthetic instruction). The patient was able to perform this conditioned response 12 times without mistake. He could do so after a 30 sec empty pause. After a filled pause (mental arithmetic), the instruction first evoked no response, but when the patient's hands were placed in the previous position, he again performed the conditioned response without repetition of the instruction.

He was then given a second instruction: In response to the word "Ivan," raise your right hand. He carried out this conditioned response also, although initially he perseverated elements of the previous response (making a fist with his right hand). He then performed it five times correctly. This conditioned response was maintained after an empty pause of 30 sec, but it disappeared after a similar pause filled with interfering activity (mental arithmetic). In response to the word "Ivan," the patient looked absent-mindedly at the doctor testing him, and when asked "What should you do?", he answered, "raise my fist" (reminiscence from the first test). After reinforcement a second time, this conditioned response became relatively stable and the patient could still perform it after a pause filled with interfering activity.

The situation was completely different when he attempted to recall in words the action he had just carried out. After performing the conditioned response correctly he was asked what he had just done and said: "I raised my fist... In each fist there are five fingers," etc. A second attempt to get him to describe in words what he had done was unsuccessful. *What have you just done?* "I talked to you... there was a knock on the door..." *What should you have done?* "Counted." *What should you have done with your fist?* "I should have struck something." *Are you sure?* "I can't think of anything else."

The patient's ability to retain the practical performance of a conditioned response was thus sharply dissociated from the inability to express in words what he had just done. Similar results were obtained in tests with "conflicting" responses. He was unable to perform an action that conflicted with the instruction (e.g., when I raise my fist, you raise your finger). Instead, he simply gave an echopractic repetition of the examiner's movements, and when asked to express in words what he had done, drifted into irrelevant associations.

There were two special features of the memory disturbance observed in this patient. First, each trace which appeared showed marked inertia and it was very difficult to switch to another system of traces. Second, the suppression of uncontrollable irrelevant associations was sharply disturbed. This was particularly noticeable when he attempted to repeat whole semantic structures. Even though his practical activity was virtually intact, he was unable to recall in words an action he had just carried out. He could not repress irrelevant associatons and confabulation or reminiscences of a previous test.

* * *

The question arises whether the disturbances described above were caused by lesions of the frontal lobes in conjunction with considerable general cerebral components (increased intracranial pressure, dislocation), or whether the lesion of the basal zones of the frontal lobes itself was sufficient to give rise to the whole of the syndrome described.

The operation performed on March 20, 1972 relieved the increased intracranial pressure and dislocation, and led ·to a marked improvement in the patient's general condition.

Mnemonic Disorders in the Postoperative Period

Neuropsychological investigation of the patient in the postoperative period began on the 4th day after the operation and continued throughout the next six weeks. Immediately after the period of postoperative edema (which followed a very mild course in this patient), the change in his general condition was appreciable. His blindness remained unchanged, but his state of general depression disappeared; he became oriented in place and time; his attitude toward his condition became much more critical; he began to complain about his poor eyesight and to be worried that he would be unable to work in that state (how will I be able to look after my garden like this. . .). Nevertheless, there remained some lack of confidence in his estimation of the time, some elements of perseveration, uncertainty about identifying people whom he met, a monosyllabic method of speech with argumentation, and difficulty in repressing irrelevant associations.

Extracts from the records of conversations with this patient on the 4th and 7th days after his operation are given below to illustrate this state of affairs.

Where are you? "In Moscow, in the Institute. . . what do you call it. . . now this. . . surgeon. . . Nikolai Nikolaevich Burdenko." *What month is it?* "April 24 or 25. . . no, March, I was confused. . ." *Have you been with us a long time?* "Yes, I evidently must have. . . they did an operation. . . March 20. . . on my head. . . the surgery lasted a long time and gave results." *What results?* "Well first, when the surgery helped me to think properly, to appreciate correctly what was going on around me. . . I became a citizen again, and this is a splendid thing, even if I only live 1 hour in society, but am able to appreciate the action of this society, that is a wonderful thing."

Who am I? "You are a teacher by profession... you have a habit of behaving like a teacher..." *But this is a hospital; what do I do here?* "I don't know what you have to do here..." *Can I be helpful to you?* "Yes, that is quite right." *Then what am I?* "A doctor." *Then why did you say that I was a teacher?* "Of course, you are nothing like a teacher... we have mutual friends, perhaps... or I was mistaken... it all happened a long time ago... in 1933... or 1932. I was a student at the Technical Institute... I knew the teachers... that is why I thought I recollected your face, I thought we had met there..."

Objective tests also revealed considerable changes in the patient's behavior. He was able to carry out reciprocal coordination tests. He had no difficulty repeating rhythms either from a sample or from a verbal instruction, and gave excessive, uncontrollable taps only when tired. After a short time, even this residual defect disappeared. He could now perform the test requiring a choice reaction, although previously this had been impossible. He correctly repeated the instruction and performed the necessary actions, retained them for a long time, and made only occasional mistakes which he immediately corrected. Elementary calculations (such as 31−7) also were possible, and he had no appreciable difficulty in performing simple problems. He had a good understanding of simple logical relationships (part–whole, genus–species, etc.). The difficulties that did arise, which I shall discuss in detail below, were associated with the appearance of irrepressible irrelevant associations.

Tests of verbal memory. Learning series of 10 words was greatly improved. He was immediately able to repeat six words, and later 8-6-7-9, thus differing only very slightly from normal. The only distinguishing feature was that the patient gave a "commentary" on every word ("house–that's somewhere where you live, cat–that is an animal, table–that's a piece of furniture," etc.).

The process of recalling pairs of words in tests with homogeneous interference (recalling a first pair and then a second pair of isolated words after direct repetition of each pair) still presented difficulties four days after the operation, but disappeared completely 7 to 10 postoperatively. By this time, the patient was able to retain and recall 3-word series, even after interfering activity (mental arithmetic).

Extracts from records of the tests carried out on the 4th day after the operation are given below.

I. *House–forest*	II. *Night–cat*	*?/I*	*?/II*
(1) Correctly	Correctly	House... no, not house, I was confused.	...
(2) "	"	Night–house	Forest... no, I have forgotten.
(3) "	"	Correctly	Cat... and forest... no ... house–forest... but ...

| (4) Correctly | Correctly | Night and cat, no... house—forest... | I have forgotten... |
| (5) " | " | House... forest... and house | Cat... and something else... |

On the 10th day after the operation, after three repetitions, the patient was able to recall two, 3-word series.

On the 4th day after the operation, the patient was able to recall two simple sentences after two repetitions. Recalling more complex sentences was still impaired by the pathological inertia.

I. *The boy hit the dog.*	II. *The girl drinks tea.*	?/I	?/II	?/I	?/II
(1) Correctly	Correctly	Correctly	Correctly	The boy drinks coffee.	There is coffee, but...
(2) "	"	"	"	Correctly	Correctly

I. *Apple trees grew in the garden behind the high fence.*	II. *A hunter killed a wolf on the edge of the forest.*	?/I	?/II
(1) Correctly	Correctly	On the edge of the forest, no, not that ... behind a fence some trees grew. No that isn't quite right.	I have forgotten.
(2) High apple trees grew in the garden behind the high fence.	"	High apple trees grew behind the fence.	Correctly
(3) Correctly	"	On the edge of the forest... no not... high apple trees grew behind the high fence... It interferes with my activity.	A hunter killed a hare on the edge of the forest.
(4) "	"	High apple trees grew behind the high fence.	Correctly

In the early postoperative period, these manifestations of pathological inertia were seen even during the immediate repetition of sentences. By the 10th day after the operation, they had almost completely disappeared; he could not only retain two sentences but actually recall them after interfering activity (calculation).

Similar progress was revealed by tests of remembering stories in the postoperative period. On the 4th day after the operation, the patient could repeat a first and also a second short story, and could then easily recall each in turn. Tests carried out 1 and 2 weeks after the operation gave similar results: He could repeat and recall quite complicated stories. Only two features remained of his previous symptoms. First, repetition was often marked by verbosity, elements of rationalization, and some defects in distinguishing their inner meaning and moral. Second, as soon as interfering activity was introduced, the memorized story was lost, and instead of reproducing it, he sometimes substituted reminiscences of a story read to him previously. In later tests this phenomenon disappeared.

On the 4th day after the operation, two stories were read to the patient: "The Hen and the Golden Egg" and "The Jackdaw and the Pigeons." He repeated each story separately without difficulty, although with the introduction of superfluous words and details. When, after reproducing both stories, he was asked to recall the first story, after a little hesitation he did so as follows: ". . . well now, I will tell you. . . it was to do with. . . a hen. . . a man had a hen which laid golden eggs. . . he thought that if there was gold he could use it for his business. . . he killed. . . and inside. . . there was only its broken heart. . ." The patient recalled the second story just as easily, although with the same lack of precision and the same excess of detail. "This is more difficult. . . a jackdaw had to be trained (a substitution: an attempt to say that the patient himself had to be trained). . . she looked. . . a flock of pigeons was flying in the yard. . . she flew in to join them. . . she forgot that they were different birds. . . she decided to change to crying like a jackdaw. . . the pigeons saw her and chased her away. . . and so she could stay neither with the jackdaws nor with the pigeons. . ."

When asked on the 7th day after the operation what stories had been read to him 3 days ago, the patient immediately (although with the same defects) repeated the theme of the last story, but could not recall the first.

Toward the end of the 4th week after removal of the tumor, the patient no longer had any visible difficulty in recalling complex semantic structures. All that remained of his former defects was verbosity and the introduction of superfluous details, together with slight retroactive inhibition.

These findings showed that the disturbances of mnemonic processes observed in the patient in the preoperative period were due to the general cerebral factors (increased intracranial pressure, dislocation) rather than to the lesion of the fronto-basal cortex.

Further analysis of the regression of the patient's defects showed that the symptoms directly connected with disturbance of the frontal lobes (and, in particular, of the basal zones) do not include disruption of direct memory.

First, we must analyze the course of the patient's intellectual operations, starting with the simplest and going on to the more complex.

Disturbance of arithmetical operations and problem solving. Both in the preoperative and, in particular, in the postoperative period, the patient had no difficulty in carrying out simple calculations (e.g., subtracting a single-figure number from a double-figure number requiring carrying over from the tens column, or even subtracting a double-figure number from another double-figure number). Difficulties arose if, instead of single arithmetical operations, he had to carry out a successive series of these operations, in which the remainder became the minuend, and the subtraction process had to start afresh each time on a different basis. This occurred, for example, during the test "subtract from 100 in 7s" commonly used in clinical practice. In this test, the process of calculation became contaminated by the natural series and the perseveration of previous elements. This disruption of goal-directed activity proved to be one of the central features present in this patient during all the successive stages of regression of the disease. Since this is a fact of decisive importance for our later analysis, I shall examine it in more detail.

On the 4th day after the operation, the patient was instructed to *subtract from 100 in 3s.*
He did so as follows: "100 and more? 99... no, −3, Oh... in 3s... that's another matter... 97, 94, 91... 92... no, 3..."
No, 100−3. "97... 94... 82... No, I can't calculate properly..." *Pay careful attention, 100−3.* "97, 94... 94... 81... No, that is wrong... not 81, something bigger... it won't come again... 89. No, I can't."
This section of the record shows that the required chain of operations was at first replaced by a tendency toward the natural series (100 or more); then the direction "downward" took hold although the tendency toward the natural series still remained (100−1 = 99). The patient then carried out three steps of the program correctly (97 − 94 = 91), but his performance was again disturbed by the natural series (91 − 92). These tendencies distracting the patient could not be overcome by repeating the test.
A similar test (this time subtracting from 100 in 7s) carried out on the 7th day after the operation gave similar results. 100 − 7 = ? "Well, now here we have 1 unit... now we are going upward... but we have to go downward... 100−7 = 93... then −7... 100... Oh, going up again, that would be 100... 107... what can I do... 100 − 7 = 97, no, that isn't right... it can't be 97..."
This result clearly shows that arithmetical operations themselves did not present any particular difficulty; however, the irrepressible tendencies toward the natural direction of the series ("it draws me upward... 100 − 7 = 107") or the perseveration of 1 component (100−7 = 97) were obstacles that the patient could not overcome.
He had even greater difficulty in subtracting from 100 first in 2s and then in 1, and so on. The results of this test were as follows. "100−2−1 = 100... 100−2... I can't take it from the hundred... 100−2 = 98... − 1 = 90... 97... 97−2 = 95... no, that is wrong... 97−2 = 95..."
Try again: "100... 102... I am going up again... and I should go down. Well... 102... that is 92... what can it be?... Not that... 97... No, add 1 more... 98... 97... 95... 94..."

These extracts from the records clearly show that the performance of even a simple consecutive series of actions encountered dynamic difficulties—the uncontrollable, irrelevant established stereotypes or irrepressible perseverations.
Similar irrepressible associations appeared during attempts to solve more difficult problems, activities requiring even greater selectivity of psychological

processes. In this case, the patient showed irrepressible associations that disturbed the organized solution of the problem.

From the 10th day after the operation, the patient was given the problem: *There are 18 books on 2 shelves, but not the same number on each. There are twice as many books on one shelf as on the other. How many books were there on each shelf?* The patient repeated the conditions correctly and started to solve it as follows: "Well now... there is the wall... 2 shelves are fixed to the wall... on these 2 shelves there are books... what we want to know is how many books there were on each shelf..."

Well how many were there? "18." *We know that!* "Yes, of course we know it... we know that books were kept on these 2 shelves... but whose books? The owner's! We know that different numbers of books were on the shelves, twice as many on one as on the other... you ask how many books there were..." *How many were there?* "18... no... you want to know how many were on each shelf... that means... 6 and 12... that is two-thirds of 18."

Clearly, the patient had no difficulty whatever in actually solving the problem. The difficulties were due to irrelevant associations ("2 shelves fixed to the wall...," "the owner") and the stereotyped repetition of the initial condition ("there were 18 books on 2 shelves").

The difficulties were more serious when the patient was given a more difficult problem. *A boy is 5 years old. In 15 years time his father will be 3 times as old as his son. How old is the father now?* The patient started to solve it at once. "How old is the father now... well that is an easy calculation. The 5-year-old lad will be big, he is growing, and he will catch up to his father (irrelevant associations). But after 15 years he will be 20... how much older will the father be than his son? Let's work it out. It is of course a simple calculation... the son is 5 years old... the father... in 15 years time he will be 20! (omission of an essential element of the problem). This problem is solved. How old is the father now?" *Do you mean to say that in 15 years time the father will be 20?* "No, the son... the son will then... now let us calculate... evidently a minimum of 20 years (instead of the logical operation he gives a "rough" guess). Now he is 20... no, that's wrong... (again drifts into the stereotype "the father will be 20"). Everything goes normally but I simply make mistakes in my plan... the son is now 5 years old. The father's age we don't know... when I add 15 years that makes the son 20 years old... presumably the same happens to the father, and so when I start to work it out I see that the minimum for the father is 25 years (instead of the necessary operation 20 times 3, he repeats the stereotyped operation 20 + 5 = 25)... and why not, he could have married at 18 years... he could have done so... but then the position is complicated because he could not have done so under certain conditions of life if he had married later (drifting into associations outside the terms of the problem, and gives random guesses instead of the selective process of solving the problem). But suppose he married later, we then have to consider how old the father was when the son was 5" (returns to the original conditions of the problem). *Well solve it!* "Well, the son is 5 years old... in 15 years time... when 15 years has gone past—the son will be 20... what we want to know is, how much longer will the father have to live when the son is 15 years older... then the father must calculate how many years (projecting his own action of calculation on the action of the father)... how many? 15 years—that's a long time... if the son is 20 years old we have another question, how long can the father calculate in a day... and he might have married at 18 years and at 20 years of age...," etc.

The main obstacle to solving a difficult problem is the ease with which the patient drifts into irrepressible associations and the stereotyped repetition of fragments of previous operations. The difficulties in solving difficult problems persisted one month after removal of the tumor. A more detailed analysis of the patient's other intellectual processes revealed similar facts.

Disturbance of Operations with Logical Relationships

He was asked to find the analogy: automobile—wheel, airplane—...? He replied: "An airplane also has wheels..." *No, I want a complete analogy* (the problem is explained step by step). "... but an airplane flies... and an automobile runs... the difference is tremendous..." (The problem is repeated and explained again.) "Well... I used to be in the air force, so that I know what flying is like, you can say that it is a very interesting job. You do it all, you get ready on the ground, you organize the way the machine will fly, and it takes off into space..." (The problem is repeated and again explained.) "... So... an automobile runs on wheels... if it had no wheels the automobile would not go... an automobile must have wheels because it has an engine, that determines everything necessary for an automobile. You start it up—it begins to work... if I am going to fly an airplane I must get it inside, look to see that the machine is in proper working order... in this case he looked at the machine, decided that everything was alright, that he could start the engine, doesn't matter what sort of engine—but the engine worked during flight..." *But you are supposed to be finding an analogy* (the problem is repeated again). "Well, just a wheel, without a wheel it will not fly..." (The problem is repeated and again explained.) "Now, this is the most important thing. The first is a machine and so is the second: You start it and everything goes normally." The solution is revealed: *automobile—wheel, airplane—wings. Is this correct?* "Maybe it is, maybe it isn't... but there are many other comparisons in this case..."

Despite the fact that the simpler analogies were easy for him, the choice of the proper solution in such a case was quite impossible. The difficulties were greatly aggravated in a second form of the same test in which the patient was instructed to find analogies under conditions requiring the choice between several alternative solutions.

He was asked to choose the proper analogy from the three possible answers given to him: egg—shell, potato—... (garden? soup? peel?). He began his solution as follows: "I must say, I cannot reject the first or the second or the third. If potatoes did not grow in vegetable gardens there would be no potatoes... a potato grew and so it had to be cooked. When it was cooked, the peel had to be thrown away... in Moscow—of course they have other ideas there, but nevertheless it would be thrown into a pit or somewhere..." (The problem was repeated and it was explained to the patient that he had to choose only one of the three possible answers.) *Egg is to shell as potato is—to what?* "Then the more suitable one is 'peel'... because if there is no peel, what sort of a thing would the potato grow into?" *Is the word "vegetable garden" suitable?* "Vegetable garden... that is also suitable... because the potato grows in a vegetable garden. If there were no vegetable gardens there would be no potatoes..." *What about the answer egg—shell, potato—soup?* "Yes, I think that is suitable as well... because you have to cook soup. You must cook the potato first..." *And would that be an analogy?* "It would not be an analogy... I told you... the best would be potato—and peel... that is the best..."

The patient was given a second similar test. Fish—net, fly... (room, hums, spider's web), and it was explained that he must choose one of the three words given to go with the word "fly" in order to make an analogy with the first pair. He began as follows: "All these facts are somehow or other possible for flies, they can hum and do the other things... but the question is—how can I compare by analogy... of course a fly in a room can make a humming noise during flight and make this—that also corresponds to a fly to some degree. But if it falls into a net, the fisherman will take the fish out and use it, cook it for his supper... but if the fly starts to hum, it makes a nuisance of itself. If the fly comes near a person's face, he will chase it away. He knows that it is a nuisance and that he must get rid of it..." *But you must find a complete analogy.* "Of course there is no analogy... yes it must be the room!" *Why?* "Because the fly flies into the room where it can feed, where it can attend to its natural needs... and humming must be connected with it somehow because it is a fly!" *Are you telling me that the complete analogy is fish—net, fly—room? Or humming? Or spider's web?* "Well, a fly will not fly into a spider's web because if it does fly into the spider's web—the spider will soon dispose of it. That puts an end to the problem. Now the second problem is about the humming. It can hum even if not in the room. But in that case, when it comes into the room it can do other things besides humming..."

The patient's difficulty in this fairly difficult test was not that he was deficient in abstract logical operations, but that during the solution of his logical problems he was distracted by irrepressible associations, all equally probable, which prevented him from identifying selectively the connection he sought and rejecting (inhibiting) the other, irrelevant associations. As a result of this disability, his abstract (categorizing) operations fell under the influence of situational associations. This slipping into irrelevant associations increased as the problem was made more difficult, or if a number of ready-made alternative solutions was presented to him.

Repetition of semantic systems with different degrees of fixation. The facts just described, reflecting the clear and irrepressible springing up of irrelevant associations, enable us to return to analysis of this patient's mnemonic activity. There appears to be a dissociation in the patient's mnemonic processes. Well fixed associations of past experience, which have a high probability of recall, are equivalent in value and no special work is required for choosing one of the many alternatives. The patient can do so reasonably accurately. The recall of insufficiently fixed associations, with a low probability of precise and unambiguous repetition requiring active selection from a series of alternatives, caused the patient very great difficulty.

Previously the patient had been a history teacher. Accordingly I gave him a double task: First to recall material well fixed in his previous experience (historical), and then to recall other familiar, but not so well fixed material, a process requiring selective isolation from many irrelevant associations and the inhibition of well fixed stereotypes. The patient performed the first part of the test completely correctly, but the second part was almost impossible and was replaced by the uncontrolable outpouring of well fixed stereotypes.

The patient was asked to talk about ancient Egypt. He did so as follows: "Egypt was one of the largest agricultural states in the East, based on slave labor. The first period of its history began about the 5th millenium, and some people date it at 5600 years ago. This period lasted up to about 2000-3000 years. In this period the soil was tilled in Egypt during the flooding of the Nile, but the Nile is a very powerful river—it floods large areas of country, and the flooded area has pits dug in it. The water enters these pits, so that when the flood water receded, water would be stored in them during the long summers and would irrigate everything connected with the production of food for man. Work at this period was very hard, because animals which could have been of some assistance to man, were in a very poor state. For that reason, the Egyptians would go to war with their neighbors in order to obtain from them animals and also slaves, in the course of their miliary operation. . ." and so on.

He spoke equally well on the subject of "The Reform of Peter the Great," but was unable to recall less well fixed material.

He was asked to tell the story of "Evgenii Onegin," a play he was bound to have read. He did so as follows: "The essence of this play 'Evgenii Onegin' is that Pushkin shows a young man who cannot live in the society in which he is living. He therefore wished to change the composition of society itself, considering that life could be organized better, and by organizing life it would be possible to make better progress. Here he was attracted to Western Europe, and for that reason he tried to leave Moscow and said that Moscow was bad, that Moscow did not satisfy the interests of the ruling class" (he was possibly confusing the theme of Onegin with that of Chatskii in "Gore ot uma").
But what is the theme of Evgenii Onegin? Tell me the details! "There was a ball in Moscow. Evgenii Onegin was invited to this ball. He delighted everybody, he was an excellent dancer, an excellent person in society. . . but at the same time, he was dissatisfied with the existing. . . the existing conditions of life. . . the conditions of this ball. . . perhaps I did not say quite the right thing there. . . and he wanted somehow to leave this ball (back again to Chatskii's theme?), because it did not satisfy the general interests of the ruling class—the nobility, and it did not satisfy the general position of this period, he wanted to give a line of construction. . . no, that is not the right word. . . he wanted to be at the center of movement in this society not only in politics, but also in life, starting from any problem. . . and so this problem led Evgenii Onegin to change the existing order. And what is a change in the existing order? That means we must change the existing order. . . ," and so on.

The repetition of well fixed systems of associations, based on the patient's previous professional knowledge, had the character of a stable and unambiguous logical account, while recalling inadequately fixed, although familiar, material he could not even attempt to distinguish the essentials. The "frontal syndrome," characteristic of this patient, was seen in this test in its full clarity.

Conclusions

In the preoperative period, when a large tumor in the basal zones of the frontal region gave rise to considerable manifestations of increased intracranial pressure and displacement of the brain, the patient showed a massive "frontal syndrome," characterized by inactivity, disorientation, and severe mnemonic disorders. These mnemonic disorders were neither restricted nor modality-specific, and were evidently not connected with two principal factors: Marked pathological inertia of established traces, and inability to restrain irrepressible irrelevant associations. These two factors, not primary disorders of memory, lay at the basis of the patient's disorientation and his active mnemonic disorders.

Removal of the massive tumor (arachnoidendothelioma) of the basal zones of the left frontal region caused a sharp improvement in the patient's general condition, so that the secondary general cerebral manifestations (resulting from increased intracranial pressure and displacement of the brain) and the primary (local) manifestations in the picture of the disease could be distinguished. The depression and disorientation in place and time, conspicuous features in the preoperative period, disappeared completely after the operation. Some improvement of the massive mnemonic defects also occurred. During the last period of observation, he was perfectly able to recall material imprinted previously, and this recalling was almost undisturbed by interfering factors.

These facts indicate that the basal frontal lobes have no direct relationship to the storage and recalling of memory traces.

Although the patient's mnemonic defects underwent definite regression, severe disturbances of his ability to restrain (inhibit) irrelevant associations continued. These disturbances were seen particularly clearly in the course of the patient's intellectual activity, when they led to a phenomenon of talkativeness and pathological argumentation.

We can accordingly draw a conclusion of great importance for the purpose of this book. A lesion of the basal zones of the frontal lobes leads not so much to a disturbance of the direct imprinting and recalling of traces as to a disturbance of the organized course of mnemonic and intellectual activity. The patient's inability to inhibit irrepressible associations is the basic pathological phenomenon arising as a result of a lesion of the basal zones of the frontal lobes. This is not an unexpected conclusion, both in light of data in the literature and my own previous investigations. Its real meaning is revealed by a comparison with the mnemonic disorders observed in patients with deeper lesions of the upper parts of the brain stem and medial zones of the cerebral hemispheres.

Disturbances of Mnemonic Activity in Massive Injuries to the Frontal Lobes

Let us now turn to a case of massive trauma of both frontal lobes, which provided the opportunity for studying all stages of the mnemonic disturbances. Analysis of this case confirms my basic conclusion that a lesion of the frontal lobes leads not so much to primary disorders of memory as to a disturbance of psychological activity connected with pathologically inert stereotypes, on the one hand, and the patient's inability to subordinate his behavior to a precise program, requiring the inhibition of irrelevant associations.

This case is extremely interesting. A young man who has suffered a massive trauma of both frontal lobes has lost the ability to execute organized purposive activity, and has replaced that activity by uncontrollably surfacing associations or inert stereotypes. This basic defect is what caused a very profound disturbance of mnemonic activity of the patient, producing a pattern of mnemonic disturbances that differs from those described earlier.

On January 17, 1969, *patient Kork.* (previously introduced on pp. 100 and 129), a male student of the Institute of Energetics, age 24 years, was struck by a locomotive and received a severe head injury. He was admitted to the Burdenko Institute of Neurosurgery in an unconscious state, with a depressed fracture of the skull in the frontal region, and on January 18 wound toilet was performed. For almost 2 weeks he remained unconscious and his movements were restless; movements were intact, the pupils were dilated and unequal (wider on the right than on the left), they did not respond to light, the corneal reflexes were depressed, a positive Kernig's sign was present, the left angle of the mouth was depressed, and dystonia in the left upper limb was associated with some motor disturbances of the left side. Roentgenograms showed a comminuted fracture of the frontal zone.

Two weeks later the patient began to regain consciousness although his behavior was marked by severe disorientation and aspontaneity. By this time bilateral anosmia, an inconstant tonic nystagmus when looking to either side, and an increased tendency to fatigue have been discovered. The pupils remained dilated (especially on the right), and the reactions of the pupils to light were sharply reduced. Sensation remained intact. Tone was higher in the lower limbs that the upper. Tendon reflexes gradually became brisker, and the biceps reflex was increased on the right and the triceps reflex on the left. Patellar reflexes were increased on the right and elicited over a wider area. The pathological reflexes, so clearly demonstrable in the initial period, gradually became less severe. Deep pathological reflexes—sucking and grasping—persisted although they did eventually diminish.

A pneumoencephalogram (April 10, 1969) revealed a moderately and uniformly hydrocephalic ventricular system. The walls of the ventricles were not deformed and the third ventricle was not displaced. Much air was present at the base of the brain in an open internal hydrocephalus with diffuse adhesions. Arteriography (April 15, 1969) showed straightening of the anterior cerebral arteries accompanied by hydrocephalus of the lateral ventricles.

One month after injury, the EEG showed a marked decrease of the alpha-rhythm with high-amplitude delta- and theta-rhythms in the anterior zones of the hemisphere, combined with a low-amplitude fast rhythm. Ten months after injury, the electrical activity of the brain was still depressed and the alpha-rhythms recorded as groups of low-amplitude waves; regional differences in the amplitude of the alpha-waves were absent and in all parts of the brain there were well-marked asynchronous beta-waves and diffuse delta-waves. The delta-waves and groups of theta-rhythms were recorded mainly in the frontal regions, frequently synchronously, and more especially on the right. These symptoms indicate dysfunction of the diencephalic system and frontal lobes.

By the end of the 5th month of the patient's stay in the Burdenko Institute of Neurosurgery, his neurological state (examination by Prof. Yu. V. Konovalov) was as follows.

The basic symptoms arising from the middle cranial fossa and, in particular, the occulomotor disorders, which were sharply defined in the first period of the disease, have now disappeared, indicating that they were based on hemorrhage at the base of the brain. Olfactory function remains disturbed, and this clearly points to a persistent lesion of the anterior zones of the brain.

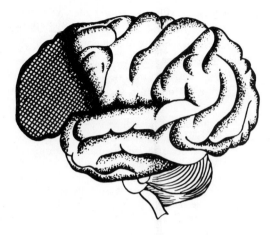

FIG. 22. Position of traumatic brain lesion in patient Kork.

Against this background of slight asymmetry of tone and reflexes, indicating a small lesion of the lateral zones of the hemisphere, residual features of subcortical trauma remain. Clear dissociation in muscle tone and tendon reflexes is found along the long axis of the body between the upper and lower limbs. This indicates the presence of considerable pathological changes in the basal and brain-stem regions of the brain, including damage to the reticular formation, evidently at the diencephalic level. The findings, taken together, suggest a massive pathology of the antero-basal zones of the frontal lobes accompanied by a relatively less severe lesion of the basal zones and brain stem." (See Figure 22.)

The neurological symptoms were relatively slight in degree. The clinical psychological investigation, however, pointed much more clearly to gross pathological changes in the anterobasal zones of the frontal poles.

Let us now examine the psychopathological symptoms that constitute the central symptom-complex in this case and characterize a massive bilateral lesion of the prefrontal (mediobasal) and diencephalic regions.

The tests on this patient began 2 weeks after trauma, i.e., a few days after consciousness has begun to return. In this period, the patient showed signs of disorientation and confusion superimposed on a very severe frontal syndrome with echolalia and perseveration.

He lay in bed unconcerned, with his eyes fixed on one point. Sometimes he moved restlessly, but usually was quite indifferent and akinetic. When he was asked to do a simple movement, such as to lift his hand, he replied, "Why, yes, lift my hand. . . yes. . . I have now lifted my hand. . . ," although in fact he did not move. When he was instructed to shake the physician's hand three times, he

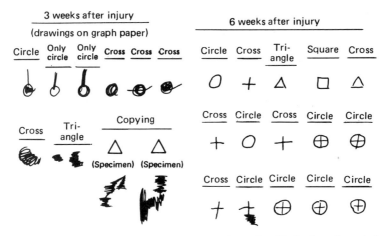

FIG. 23. Motor perseverations in drawings by patient Kork. (in early period after injury).

either took it and held on to it without making any further movement, or he began to squeeze the doctor's hand over and over again.

It was impossible to get the patient to make an imitative movement (of the sort usually used to test postural praxis) or to tap out a rhythmic pattern. He invariably answered, "Yes, yes. . . I have done it already," without making the slightest movement. To get the patient to perform any sort of voluntary movement, his hand had to be placed in the initial position. Even then, however, his movement was extremely inadequate. His responses to drawing tests were frankly perseverative in character (Figure 23).

The defect in the performance of actions described above continued throughout the subsequent weeks. The patient was able to write even difficult words and sentences, but, as before, showed signs of very marked inactivity and perseveration when drawing in response to a spoken instruction or copying from a specimen.

The patient's speech, which returned as soon as he regained consciousness, was much better preserved than his ability to perform movements and actions. This indicated an absence of dysfunction of the speech area in the left hemisphere. Very soon it became clear that the patient's writing also remained intact even when he was unable to perform movements in response to instructions. The integrity of the phonemic, lexical, and grammatical organization of speech by no means implied integrity of the patient's speech activity. Elementary tests carried out in the early period after trauma clearly showed that his use of speech in his activities was affected just as severely as the other forms of his behavior.

The clearest evidence of a disturbance of the patient's speech activity was given by the inert stereotypes which, in the early period of observation, were substituted for adequate verbal communication. These inert stereotypes could be observed in conversation, in his understanding of word meanings, and in his ability to name objects. The patient's primary understanding of word meanings was fully preserved and he had no difficulty whatsoever in naming objects. This primary integrity of the basic speech functions lasted only a very short time, and if the test was continued, instead of pointing correctly to the object named, he began to respond by the inert repetition of the same gesture, or instead of naming the various objects he would repeat the same word in a stereotype manner.

The patient was shown pictures and asked to name them.

Apple	*Knife*	*Cock*	
Apple	Pear	Apple	
Bottle	*Lamp*	*Clock*	*Bottle*
Lemonade	Lemon	20 past 12	20 past 12
Ink stand	*Lamp*	*Cock*	*Kettle*
Ink stand	Triangle	Triangle	Triangle

After the first period of the investigation, inert stereotypes were found only in tests of naming pairs of objects, and even here they disappeared completely after one month.

The pathological repetition of established stereotypes, which increased as the patient became more fatigued, clearly pointed to a massive defect of the frontal systems. In addition, his severe disorientation and memory disturbances, at first glance, suggested a similarity to Korsakov's syndrome.

In the first six weeks after trauma, the patient was unable to say where he was, but said, for example, that he was in Cheboksary, in Kazakhstan, in the operating theater, or in the Institute of Energetics. His assessment of time was also appreciably disturbed. When asked the date, he simply stated any number that came into his head. He was wildly mistaken when assessing the time of day. At 10 a.m., he declared that it was "evidently 4 o'clock in the afternoon." He did not recognize the doctors in the ward, and thought that the physician in charge was his cousin. There were no active confabulations during this period of maximal aspontaneity, but his inadequate judgements were obvious in conversations.

The patient had a poor memory for people around him, he could not retain the names of the doctors in his memory, and although he gradually became aware that he was in the Burdenko Institute, he was quite unable to recall important events of his period in hospital. For instance, 2 or 3 hours after an operation (inspection of the wound) performed 2 months after injury, he was unable to say why his head was bandaged, and suggested that he must have had some sort of accident or that the bandage had been put on so that he would lie more comfortably. He could not recall that he had been transferred to another ward, and knew none of his neighbors. He could not remember the procedures carried out (transfusions, punctures, etc.) only a very short time ago. All he could retain in his memory were a few elements of his own confabulations.

This picture began to change only very gradually. For instance, 6 weeks after injury he could discuss his future more intelligently, and 3 months after injury he knew quite well where he was, although he was still confused in his assessment of the immediate past and in identifying people around him or events in which he had taken part. A few examples of this gradual progress in his state are given below.

Test 18 days after injury: *Where are you now?* "In Cheboksary." *And what are you doing here?* "Nothing. . . I am simply lying. . ." *Are you ill or well?* "Of course I am well." *In that case, why are you lying here?* "I wish I knew why I am lying here, but I don't. . ." *What happened to you to make you ill?* "But nothing has happened to me yet." *Where are you studying?* "In this Institute. . ." *In which Institute?* "This one right here, the Institute. . ." *What is it called?* "The Institute of Energetics." *And what course is it?* "The 3rd." *Which faculty?* "Energetics." *With whom will you work next?* "With a power engineer (energetik)." *And where will you work?* "Wherever it happens to be." *But where do you think?* "Where do I think. . . some sort of thermal power station." *What is the date today?* "The date today. . . the 28th. . ." *And what month is it?* "The month. . . January. . ." *And the year?* "The year. . . 1968. . ." *And what time is it now?* "About 4 o'clock" (in fact, 10 a.m.).

Test 30 days after injury: *Volodya, do you know me?* "Yes, I have seen you somewhere." *Where?* "Here." *Where is here?* "In Cheboksary." *What are you doing here?* "There is nothing wrong with me today, previously I had a toothache." *And what did you do before you were ill?* "I was a student at the Institute of Energetics." *And why are you lying here?* "Well, I had a toothache and lay. . ." *What time is it now?* "2 o'clock in the afternoon" (in fact, 10 a.m.). *What did you have for breakfast?* "For breakfast I had rice pudding" (in fact, macaroni and meat), for lunch I had soup with potatoes" (in fact, he had not had lunch).

Test 40 days after injury: *How are you?* "Nothing much to complain about. . ." *Where are you now?* "In hospital." *In what city?* "In Cheboksary. . ." *What is the matter with you?* "There is nothing the matter with me." *Then why are you being kept in hospital?* "I don't know why. . ." *What is your illness?* "I have no illness." *Then why are you lying here?* "I wish I knew. . . I just lie here all the time. . ." *But have you no idea why?* "I suppose because of toothache." *When did you first meet me?* "At the end of January." *And what month is it now?* "March, 1968." *How did you get here?* "Well, the doctors saw. . ." *What did they see?* "I don't know what they saw there." *Well, what do you think might have happened?* "Something happened to my tooth. . ."

Not until a very long time (about 7 to 8 months) had elapsed after injury were appreciable changes observed in the patient's condition, but even so he remained severely disabled.

By this time, the patient knew quite well that he was in hospital, had had an accident, and that two operations had been performed on him. When speaking about his past, the patient said he was born in the town N., where after finishing school he had worked as a carpenter, and that after that he had gone to the Institute of Energetics, where he was still studying. With some difficulty he was able to state the name of his own doctor, complained that he had not yet been allowed to go home, sometimes displayed features of aggressiveness, and guessed that "his head did not work as it should." The patient still continued to exhibit severe defects of his memory and in the assessment of his surroundings. He was extremely passive and never asked questions of his own accord. Sometimes he got up from his bed and walked aimlessly about the department, speaking to nobody and showing no initiative.

Seven to eight months after his injury, this patient still showed marked aspontaneity, inactivity, and affective changes, sometimes assuming the form of aggressiveness. Most of all, the patient's clinical picture was dominated by an amnesic syndrome, with lack of retention or orientation in current events, but a much higher level of preservation of the traces of his past experience. Despite gradual regression of the syndrome, the severe disorientation and memory disturbances superimposed on the severe aspontaneity continued for some time.

What was the character of these disorders of memory and what was their pathophysiological nature? How do these disorders differ from those observed in patients with massive uncomplicated head injuries or patients with deep tumors situated in the midline?

Mnemonic Disorders

Memorizing series of words. Direct retention of a series of isolated words was not affected seriously enough to account for the massive mnemonic disorders described above. The patient could easily retain a series of 2, 3, 4, 5, or even 6 words, and he began to have difficulty only if the series was made longer still. For instance, he could remember only 5 of a series of 7 words, but when a series of 10 words was given he could remember only 3 or 4. Repeated trials did not lead to any increase in the number retained.

The patient often repeated the same word twice or even three times in succession without noticing that he had said it before. In some cases, he mingled irrelevant associations with the series he was repeating, likewise without being aware of the fact. For instance, when repeating the series of words "pie–brother–bridge," the patient added "... bridge... the brother stood on the bridge..." to them.

Important data shedding light on the mechanisms restricting this patient's ability to memorize could be obtained from an analysis of how his word recall changed in response to an increase in the length of the series. Series consisting of 3 or 4 elements were repeated in order. When asked to repeat a series of 5 words, the "boundary factor" was clearly manifested (he started by repeating the first and last words). When a series of 6 or 7 words was presented, the order of repetition began to be mixed. With a 10-word series, the patient invariably began by repeating the series from the end, with the words he had heard most recently, and he perseverated.

The patient was given groups of 2, 3, or 4 words and his recall tested after a pause of 30 sec, 1 min, 1.5 min, or 2 min. In the first period of the investigation, even a short pause between imprinting and recall was sufficient to cause failure. About 1 to 1.5 months after injury, traces of words presented 1, 2, or 2.5 min earlier could be retained, if the interval was not filled with any form of interfering activity. The following examples will illustrate this situation.

Test carried out 28 days after injury

Clock—night
Correctly

(pause of 30 sec)

(1) Clearly, clearly
(2) What were the words. . . wait a moment. . . now. . .

(pause of 1 min)

(3) It is worse, worse than ever. . .
(4) Not like that. . . night, bed.

Window—pen
(1) Correctly

(pause of 30 sec)

(2) Where is the pen? Put the pen in the window. . . in the room there is a window.
(3) The first, the second. . . I can't even remember.

Even a short pause, compelling the patient to make active efforts to recall, permitted irrelevant associations to creep into his replies, and he could not separate them from the required words. The main disturbance was not so much the rapid decay of established traces, as difficulty in their active recall and the ease with which they were replaced by irrelevant associations. Soon, a short pause no longer had this disturbing effect on recall. Similar results were observed in tests involving recall of sentences, stories, and impressions arising in the patient during his stay in hospital.

If the pause between trace imprinting and recall was filled with interfering activity, however, even a short pause of 30 sec or 1 min prevented recall. Instead, he simply repeated anything that came into his head.

Tone (ton)—course (khod)
Correctly

(pause of 30 sec filled with interfering activity—mental arithmetic)

What were the words? "There were no words."

(pause of 1 min with similar activity)

"Shadow (ten')—hunter (okhotnik)"

(pause of 1 min filled with similar activity)

"Pine—tree"

These disturbances substantially impaired not only the patient's active recall, but also his recognition.

Recognition has generally been regarded as a more elementary form of mnemonic activity that arises long before processes of recall in the ontogeny of memory. This view does not take into account the fact that recognition itself can only result from comparing a new trace with one formed previously. In patients whose mnemonic defects are based on loss of selective activity rather than trace decay, therefore, the process of comparing new and old traces would be substantially disturbed, and the process of recognition might cause the patient considerable difficulty. In the early stages after his injury, this patient was unable to compare newly formed traces with those of earlier stimuli. This is illustrated by the following tests.

Test carried out 20 days after injury: Two words were given to the patient: clock–night. He easily repeated them immediately, but after a pause of 30 sec, when asked what words had been given to him, he looked at the clock (repeating the examiner's action) and said, "Half past 11... 20 past 12..." When next the patient was asked to say whether the words given included words such as "clock," "hand," "pen," "night," etc., he answered "guess" every time, without even attempting to compare each current word with traces of previous words.

We shall meet a similar difficulty in comparing newly presented words with previously imprinted traces later.

The aforementioned facts suggest that this inhibitory effect of interfering activity increased sharply if this activity was homogeneous with the material to be recalled. To confirm this hypothesis, tests were carried out in which the patient was given a group of 2 or 3 words to memorize, being warned that he would have to recall them later. He was then given a second similar series of words, after which he was asked which words were in the first group and which in the second. If he could not answer, the test was repeated, and this was done several times in succession. In the initial period of observation (3 to 4 weeks after injury) if groups of 2 or 3 words were given, he could easily repeat them separately, but then "froze" on one group (usually the last one), which he inertly repeated. Pathological inertia of one group of words, superimposed on the patient's general inactivity, made it impossible for him to switch from one group to the other. The phenomena were observed in later tests in a less severe form, and during the second and third months after injury and the symptoms gradually regressed.

Although traces once imprinted were retained by the patient for a reasonably long time and could be recalled after an empty pause of 1.5 or even 2 min, any interfering activity led to the formation of an inert stereotype that prevented recall. These defects were superimposed on marked inactivity and the absence of critical attitude of the patient toward his defects. The syndrome regressed only gradually, as this inactivity disappeared.

All the aforementioned phenomena were observed during the investigation of audioverbal memory. The next question to decide was if the defect described above also extended to other forms of activity, or was it confined purely to one modality.

Memorizing pictures and movements. Having once named a picture, the patient could retain the traces even after an empty pause of 1 to 1.5 min. He could easily recall the names of a group of 2 or even 3 pictures shown to him upside down, and only in the initial stage after his injury did he sometimes lapse into irrepressible associations. By contrast, the recall of one group of pictures after being shown a second similar group was impossible. Immediately after his injury, the patient could not even recall single pictures, but simply perseverated the name of the last one seen. As the patient's condition improved, this phenomenon was repeated when he was shown pairs of pictures. As regression gradually took place, the simple inert stereotype gave way to "inversion" (the inert naming of the pictures of the second group when asked about the first group, and the delayed naming of the pictures of the first group when asked about the second). Even 7 months after injury, recalling 2 or 3 pictures after a pause filled with interfering activity was still substantially disturbed. Clearly, the defects of mnemonic activity were manifested not only in the audioverbal sphere, but also in the recall of visual images. In fact, the disturbance of the patient's visual memory was more severe than, the disturbances of his word recall, possibly on account of the more complex structure of this activity (naming objects compared with simply repeating words presented).

Similar results were obtained in tests of recall of movements and actions. The defects observed in this sphere continued even longer than those of word or picture recall.

Test 24 days after injury: The patient was instructed to take a picture card and put it under his pillow. He did so. *What have you done?* "I took a picture!" *Where did you put it?* "Behind." *Behind you or behind me?* "Behind you."

He was then asked to perform two actions: (1) take a pen and put it on the blanket on your right and (2) take the towel and put it on the blanket on your left. *What did you do first?* "I took the towel." *And then?* "I did nothing." *Where is my pen?* "In your pocket." *Did you take my pen?* "No." (The pen is shown to him.) *Is this your pen?* "No, yours." *Where did you take it from?* "It was lying here."

(The same test repeated 26 days after injury.) The patient was instructed: (1) Put the towel on the blanket and (2) put a card under the pillow. He did each task correctly. *What did you do first?* "I put the card under the pillow." *And next?* "I simply put it under the pillow." *But before that?* "I put this under the pillow."

He was instructed: (1) Put a towel on the bed and (2) take a card and give it to the examiner. He performed both tasks correctly. *What did you do first?* "I gave you back a card." *And then?* "I reached for the towel." *But what did you do first?* "I gave you back the card." *And then?* "I reached for this affair." *This what?* "The soap and all this. . ."

Only much later (7 months after injury) was the patient at last able to recall the traces of three actions after the introduction of an empty pause, or even a pause filled with interfering activity. Even then, the inhibitory effect of homogeneous activity remained evident in his performance.

Memorizing sentences and stories. Although the patient could recall sentences after an empty pause of 1 to 2 min, any interfering activity prevented recall of the first sentence of a pair. This basic pathology of his mnemonic processes began to regress only gradually. The inert repetition of the last consolidated stereotype yielded at first to contamination of one sentence by another, and to the "inversion" already described. Much later, as his general inactivity diminished, the patient's ability to recall was gradually restored to normal.

Test 30 days after injury

I. *Apple trees grew in the garden behind the high fence.*	II. *A hunter killed a wolf at the edge of the forest.*	*?/I*	*?/II*
Correctly	Correctly	A hunter killed a wolf at the edge of the forest.	A hunter killed a wolf at the edge of the forest.

Do you mean that both sentences were the same? "No, they differed: The pronunciation was different; the stress was not placed where it should be."

(2) Correctly	Correctly	A hunter killed a wolf at the edge of the forest.	A hunter killed a wolf at the edge of the forest.

Do you mean that the two sentences were the same? "Not quite. . ." *What was the difference?* "First, the stress; second, the way the question was asked. . ." *What question?* "Well. . . the final question. . . what was in this sentence. . . a hunter killed a wolf at the edge of the forest. . ." *And was the second sentence?* "A hunter killed a wolf at the edge of the forest. . ." *Then you do mean that the sentences were the same?* "No, there is a difference here. . . the point is that something was killed by a hunter in the first case. . . how many hares were there? Three, what. . .? And in the second case what was killed. . . now I will tell you. . . what am I talking about. . . I think it is like this: one, two, three. . . three hares. . . in the first case. . . one, two three. . . were killed." *Repeat the sentence. . .* "In the first case three hares were killed. . ." *No, repeat the sentence which I read out to you.* "A hunter. . . saw a hare. . . at the edge of the forest. . ."

Semantic structures induced maximal inertia in this patient which continued even after the pathological inertia of groups of isolated words had begun to disappear. The pathological inertia of a previously imprinted sentence could still be observed 7 months after injury.

Similar series of tests were carried out to study memorizing and recall of complete stories. In the first stages after injury, the patient was unable to keep within the bounds of the semantic structure. He continually slipped into uncontrollable associations and incorporated into his narrative more and more fragments of his own, so that at the end of the test the text had absolutely nothing in common with that originally read to him. Pathological inertia was manifested in two ways. First, the patient could not adhere to the text of the story he was recalling and continually drifted into irrepressible associations (in this case, inertia of activity once it had started). Second, the patient showed a tendency to return to the same fragment of the story over and over again (inertia of previously imprinted traces). Let us begin with the results of the tests in the initial period after injury.

Test carried out 30 days after injury: "The Lion and the Mouse" story was read, and the patient instructed to repeat it. "A few days later the mouse saw. . . that the mouse had fallen into a net set by the hunter. . . she ran to. . . (looked at the tape recorder) recognizes the telephone number that she must dial. . . (looks at the bed) so as to put the hunter on the same bed. . . well the mouse recognized this telephone number and chased the hunter away. . ." *Have you finished?* "No, I shall soon. . . it takes a little time. . . the mouse of course thinks, I must be quick and set free. . . the mouse. . . I must set the hunter free quickly. . . from prison. . . and so. . . some time passes. . . he thinks. . . Aha, I must set him free quickly. . . and so. . . some time passes. . . etc., etc."

This account of the test, reflecting the relatively early period of a severe frontal lobe lesion, clearly shows the maximal inertia of the patient's psychological activity. The patient was unable either to stop any activity once it had started or to confine himself to repeating the theme of the story. The phenomenon manifested in the acute period as motor perseveration now very clearly affected his speech system.

Two months after injury, the inability to repeat complete semantic programs described above began to regress. For instance, in the next stage, 2 to 2.5 months after injury, the patient was able to repeat stories immediately after hearing them relatively well. All that remained of the original syndrome was the ease with which certain fragments of the story were replaced by irrelevant associations and by phenomena akin to paramnesia, although only when he had to repeat relatively complex stories. Even in this phase of regression, however, defects in the repetition of stories "from traces" were observed, especially when a second story was read to the patient after the first. Records confirming this statement are given below.

Test 45 days after injury: Two stories were read to the patient, first "The Hen and the Golden Egg," and then "The Jackdaw and the Pigeons." He repeated the stories with the typical defect of this phase. He was then tested to discover whether he could recall the theme of each story in turn. *You have heard two stories. What was the first?* "The first—something about a jackdaw, she met some pigeons, and the second—she did not meet the pigeons and she was forced to fly away. . ." *But surely I told you two stories?* "Yes. . ." *What was the first?* "Well, the first was the one about the jackdaw that met the pigeons. . ." *And the second?* "The second—that was the one about when she didn't meet the pigeons."

The patient could repeat each story separately in a well organized manner, but if he had to recall the first of two stories he began to exhibit the familiar phenomena of inertly repeating the theme of the second story, with a few changes in the actual wording ("the Jackdaw met some pigeons"—"the jackdaw did not meet any pigeons"). This pathological inertia during the repetition of stories continued for a long time, and even 3 months after his injury the patient still had traces of this defect. Not until 4 or 5 months after injury was definite progress at last noticeable. Slipping into irrelevant associations occurred only when he repeated the story after a long interval. The defect disappeared completely only a year after his injury. Traces of the defect could still be detected only if the stories were repeated 2 or 3 days, or even a week after their presentation.

Conclusions

The patient we have studied showed an extremely severe syndrome of aspontaneity and gross disorders of memory, combining symptoms characteristic of a closed head injury with hemorrhage into the brain stem and severe lesions of the frontal lobes. Analysis of this syndrome confirmed the basic proposition regarding the pathology of memory with which I began the second part of this book and which we have seen in other chapters.

The case described confirms the general view that lesions of the frontal lobes lead to pathological inertia of established stereotypes and to increased liability to distraction by irrelevant stimuli. These disturbances lead to pathologically increased inhibitability of traces by interfering factors, rather than to primary disorders of memory. In the earliest stages after injury, the pathological inertia of the patient's nervous processes was manifested in both his movements and his speech. During regression of the syndrome, the movements gradually began to rid themselves of the pathological inertia, but it continued to affect complex forms of mnemonic and intellectual activity, through the period of investigation.

These features distinguished this patient sharply from those with lesions of the back parts of the cerebral cortex, in which the defect of the mnemonic processes was modality-specific in character. They also distinguished him from patients with deep brain lesions in whom the frontal lobes were not affected by any primary lesion but were in a state of dysfunction. This patient did not exhibit the productive confabulations that typify patients with modality-nonspecific lesions.

As already stated, the mechanism of the severe mnemonic disorders observed in this patient was increased inhibitability of traces by interfering factors, rather than trace decay, accompanied by pathological inertia of established stereotypes. In the early phase, this was manifested as total inability to switch from one trace to another. In the later phases of the investigation, this pathological inertia came to light only when the task presented to the patient was made more difficult. It was exhibited clearly during the repetition of stories (especially when the patient had to recall the stories "from traces") and in problem solving. The pathological inertia of established traces, coupled with the patient's marked aspontaneity, made him unable to compare the results of his actions with his original plan, so he began to mix up associations relating to different systems.

The severity of the pathological inertia in this case was such that two forms can be distinguished. Inertia of initiated activity prevented the patient from completing activity in progress. Inertia of associations (or of contents) was manifested as the frequent repetition of the same stereotypes, conventionally described by the term "cycling." Both these phenomena were observed particularly clearly in the early stages of the illness, evidently at a time when the pathological picture was determined by a combination of destruction of the antero-basal zones of the cortex and deep lesions of the brain stem arising after injury.

SUMMATION

We have studied a series of patients in whom various deep brain lesions have led to severe disturbances of memory. In some cases, the lesion was restricted to the region of the third ventricle, in others it involved the hypothalamus and limbic cortex, and in a third group spread to the frontal lobes. The structure of the mnemonic disorders differed in the different groups of patients. The condition described usually as "a general disturbance of memory" conceals different syndromes that depend directly on the location of the lesion, its size, and the presence of concomitant general brain disturbance (increased intracranial pressure, displacement).

The memory disturbances were observed despite the integrity of higher cortical functions, such as gnosis, praxis, and speech. They were modality-nonspecific, and manifested equally at different levels during the recall of verbal, visual, and motor material. The main mechanisms of the memory disturbances were pathologically increased inhibition by interfering factors and equalized excitability, rather than initial weakness of the traces or their spontaneous decay. Reminiscence was also observed, often manifested as the unexpected recall of apparently decayed traces, mixed with the recall of recently given information and disturbing the normal selectivity of mnemonic processes.

We still know very little about the actual pathophysiological mechanisms of the defects just mentioned. Only electrophysiological and, perhaps, biochemical investigations of these mechanisms will reveal the causes of this central symptom of all deep brain lesions which spread to the upper zones of the brain stem, diencephalon, and limbic system. With all the deficiencies of our information, the description of features common to all patients with deep brain lesions is of decisive importance in understanding the function of deep brain structures, as well as in the diagnosis of lesions of certain parts of the brain.

The description of features common to all memory disturbances in patients with deep brain lesions is only one aspect of this problem. Of no less importance is the description of features that distinguish individual forms of memory disturbance and give rise to the unique syndromes of mnemonic disorders associated with lesions situated in "nonspecific" structures in various parts of the brain. These syndromes clearly reveal the wealth and variety of the material concealed behind the ordinary clinical concepts of "disturbance of memory," and demonstrate the importance of differential diagnosis of mnemonic disorders.

The observations presented in this book represent only the first step toward a solution of this important problem. It is still necessary to make a fine analysis of the role played in the formation of these syndromes by pathological factors, such as increased intracranial pressure and displacement of the brain, irritation and prolapse, and the manifestations of reflex systemic shock known in classical neurology as "diaschisis."

The first syndrome of general, modality-nonspecific memory disturbance was observed in cases of pituitary tumor (see Chapter III; Kiyashchenko, 1969, 1973), and in patients with lesions of the third ventricle (Chapter V). Although these syndromes differ in degree, the memory disturbances are primary, i.e., unaccompanied by any disturbance of consciousness. They are associated with general integrity of the patient's whole behavior and his extra-mnemonic activity. Subjectively, these memory disturbances were expressed by the patients in terms such as "my memory is not as good as it was," or "I forget everything," "things will not stick in my mind," "I have to write everything down," etc. Except during a sudden exacerbation of the pathological process, however, all these patients were fully oriented in place, their critical faculties and emotions were reasonably intact, and they experienced a sense of anxiety and confusion. Despite their inactivity and the general lowering of their cortical tone with constant vacillations between sleep and wakefulness, they were adequately aware of their defect.

Rote learning was defective in varied degrees, but recall of recent traces was always inhibited by interfering factors. Instruction to memorize a second group of elements (words, picture cards, movements) or distraction by any form of interfering activity (such as conversation or calculation) prevented recall of the group of elements just inscribed in their memory. The patient either failed completely to recall the material, or confused (contaminated) elements belonging to different groups. In patients with the mildest disorders, these defects could be observed only during the repetition of a series of discrete elements (words, picture cards, movements). The change to memorizing organized structures overcame these difficulties. In patients with more severe disorders, this pathologically increased inhibition could be observed at all levels of organization (words, sentences, or stories). Sometimes the organized material in memory was so unstable that, if read a second story, they immediately forgot the first, or mixed the themes. Despite the introduction of some irrelevant elements, however, when some memory remained the general meaning of the story was also intact. This fact, together with the integrity of consciousness and absence of confusion and confabulation, constituted the essential features of the syndrome.

Two dynamic features were also typical in the psychological activity of these patients. First, because of their increased fatigability, frequent repetition of a test, instead of improving, as a rule usually worsened the results until the patient abandoned the task, stating that he was "all confused." The second characteristic feature was fluctuation of their state. Results of their tests were much better on "good" days than on "bad" days. Sometimes this fluctuation could be observed even in the course of a single test. Special stimulation, mobilizing the patient's attention, could sometimes increase the efficiency of performance for a short time. The primary memory disturbances, then, were dynamic, and intimately connected with the general lowering of cortical tone produced by the pathological process.

The second syndrome of memory disturbance arose in patients with larger pathological lesions (tumors, rupture of aneurysms), involving the diencephalon, segments of the "circle of Papez" (septum pellucidum, mammillary bodies), and the limbic region. The chief distinguishing feature of this syndrome is that it is not restricted to defects of memory, but includes confusion and confabulations or, in brief, disturbances of consciousness.

As a rule, these patients are inadequately oriented in their surroundings. Sometimes they believe they are at home, at work, or in the factory hospital. Sometimes they declare they are staying with neighbors, at the railroad station, etc. Particularly marked defects are observed when they attempt to evaluate events in the immediate past. Many say that a few hours ago they were at their work, they had gone out on an errand, they had come from a distant town, gone shopping, or even that they had gone "potato-picking," or "felling trees." The confabulations characteristic of these patients do not directly result from a disturbance of short-term memory. They are connected with the uncontrollable outpouring of reminiscences which the patients cannot correctly place in time, and about which they are never fully confident. That is why these confabulations are usually associated with a certain general confusion. The patient is never in the state of emotional indifference or euphoria so characteristic of patients with massive frontal lobe lesions.

These disturbances are associated with defects of current "short-term" memory only and, as a rule, they never extend to well-consolidated traces of distant events. Some patients could relate details of their previous work excellently, name their friends and colleagues, and draw a detailed and correct plan of the streets in their home town. In these actions they exhibited no evidence of any disturbance of memory.

Objective investigation of the mnemonic processes of these patients produced results quite similar to those already described, but usually more sharply expressed. In the severest cases, semantic organization no longer compensated for difficulties in retention. Even direct repetition of a story consisting of several semantic themes began to be fragmented and accompanied by inaccuracies, irrelevant details, and contamination. The patients were never confident about their confused, fragmentary repetition of a story, but never replaced the theme of the story read to them by some other complete though irrelevant theme. They could omit complete semantic fragments of the story and replace certain details with irrelevant additions. Once started, however, they never replaced the repetition of a half-forgotten text by other activity. The gross disturbances of memory observed in these patients were not connected with any radical changes of the patient's personality or in his goal-directed activity.

In the third group of patients, the unique disturbances of memory were caused by a pathological process located in the diencephalon but involving the medio-basal zones of the frontal lobe. Careful analysis revealed disturbances of mnemonic activity as a whole, although they are only temporary or transient in character. For that reason I have described the disturbances of memory arising in such patients as "transient." Like the patients of the preceding groups, these patients can retain material in their memory but quickly lose it under the influence of interfering factors. They also show appreciable disturbances in retention and recall not only of discrete material, but also of material organized into semantic systems. They "forget" whole fragments of a meaningful text, or their repetition is fragmentary and contaminated.

What distinguishes these patients is their frequent substitution of irrelevant associations and random details for true mnemonic activity. For instance, when naming a tree they say, "This is a tree, I don't know what sort, whether hard wood or soft wood, ordinary or valuable." When they draw a house, they add: "This is a house, perhaps it needs repairing, it looks a bit tumbledown, some effort should be made to restore it. . . ," etc. When repeating a story, they will not stick to the point but persistently add details and irrelevant associations not included in the original theme. This introduction of irrelevant associations and out-of-context arguments, and their inability to keep to the main theme of the story, form the distinctive syndrome of pathological rationalization, familiar in clinical practice. In this "transient" syndrome of memory disturbance the distractions of irrepressible associations do not take the patient completely away from the required theme. The repetition of organized semantic material produces some "secondary correction" of the disturbed mnemonic processes.

The fourth and last group consists of patients with massive lesions of the frontal lobes, and disturbances in the formation of the stable motives which subordinate human activity to an organized, purposive plan. Many investigators attribute these defects to inhibition of the descending activating reticular formation, which is closely connected with the control of external and internal speech (Luria, 1961, 1962, 1969, 1970; Luria & Khomskaya, 1966, 1972).

Although the memory defects of these patients appear very similar to those described above, their basis is radically different.

In patients with deep lesions the primary memory disturbances were associated with increased inhibition by interfering factors or equalized excitability of different traces. The motives for memorizing material and the connected mnemonic activity remained intact. Mnemonic activity in such cases was therefore affected only in its executive, operational side. In patients with massive lesions of the frontal lobes, however, the motives for memorizing and recalling material become unstable, and easily yield to uncontrollable irrelevant associations, or the influence of existing stereotypes. The patient is unable to revert consciously to a recently imprinted theme. Goal-directed activity is replaced by the recall of irrepressible associations, with no attempt at correction.

The normal person trying to recall the theme of a story rejects all extraneous impressions reaching him during the time that he is performing his task. The theme imprinted earlier is a closed system, and the subject's efforts are directed toward restoring its components. This process is substantially disturbed in patients with massive lesions of the frontal lobes. Impressions reaching such a patient from the external environment, or from his direct experience, are no longer inhibited. They are readily interwoven in the process of repetition. These disturbances of recall can arise despite the primary integrity of the memory, because they result not from pathologically increased inhibition, but from a gross disturbance of conscious activity.

* * *

This analysis has shown that human memory has a very complex structure. It is a grave mistake to regard it as a simple recording, storage, and retrieval of information. Memorizing is a highly complex process of analysis of incoming information, followed by its selection and coding. Recall is an equally complex process of choosing the necessary systems of connections from all the possible alternatives, performed by goal-directed mnemonic activity. Naturally, various systems of the brain participate in this activity and each makes its own particular contribution. Mnemonic activity, therefore, will be disturbed differently depending on the location of the lesion. One of the principal tasks in neuropsychology is to analyze the contribution made by each brain system to human memory.

Research into memory has appreciably intensified in the last few decades. The analysis can be undertaken at the biochemical, molecular, neurophysiological, macrophysiological, and psychological levels. As I have hoped to demonstrate by the investigation described in this book, the neuropsychology of memory occupies an important place in the study of this highly complex problem.

References

Abashev-Konstantinovskii, A. L. The pathology of consciousness. *Zh Nevropatol Psikhiatr im S. S. Korsakova*, 1954, **54**(4).

Abashev-Konstantinovskii, A. L. Psychopathological syndromes of focal significance. *Vopr Neirokhir*, 1961, (5).

Abashev-Konstantinovskii, A. L. Localization problems and clinical psychiatry. *Abstracts of Proceedings of the 4th All-Union Congress of Neuropathologists and Psychiatrists*, Moscow, 1963.

Abramovich, G. B. The pathogenesis of confabulations and other complex statements made by patients with Korsakov's syndrome. *Nevropatol i Psikhiatr*, 1938, **7**(6).

Abramovich, G. B. *Clinical and pathological analysis of Korsakov's syndrome.* Candidate dissertation, Moscow, 1939. (a)

Abramovich, G. B. The psychopathology of Korsakov's syndrome. *Nevropatol i Psikhiatr*, 1939, **8**(2-3). (b)

Abramovich, G. B. Clinical manifestations and mechanisms of retrograde amnesia in Korsakov's syndrome and other pictures. *Proceedings of an All-Union Scientific and Practical Conference to Celebrate the Centenary of the Birth of S. S. Korsakov and Devoted to Current Problems in Psychiatry*, May 20-27, 1954. Moscow–Leningrad: Medgiz Press, 1955.

Abramovich, G. B., & Zakharova, V. V. The mental disturbances in lesions of the mammillary bodies and structures of connected systems. In *Problems of localization and topical diagnosis in neuropathology and psychiatry.*

347

Transactions of the V. M. Bekhterev Psychoneurological Research Institute (Vol. 21). Leningrad, 1961.

Adams, J. A. *Human memory*. New York: McGraw-Hill, 1967.

Adams, R. D. The anatomy of memory mechanisms in the human brain. In G. Talland & N. Waugh (Eds.), *The pathology of memory*. New York: Academic Press, 1969.

Adey, W. R. Organization of the rhinencephalon. In H. Jasper et al. (Eds.), *Reticular formation of the brain*. Boston, Mass.: Little, Brown, 1958.

Adey, W. R. EEG studies of the hippocampal system in learning processes. In *Physiologie de l'hippocampe*. Paris: 1962.

Akbarova, N. A. *Neuropsychological analysis of amnestic disturbances in closed head injuries*. Dissertation for the Degree of Candidate of Medical Sciences, Institute of Neurosurgery, Academy of Medical Sciences of the USSR, Moscow, 1971.

Aleksandrovskaya, M. M., Nevzorova, T. A., & Shpir, E. K. A case of a tumor of the mammillary bodies: Psychopathology and somatic symptoms. *Zh Nevropatol Psikhiatr im S. S. Korsakova*, 1947, (2).

Anokhin, P. K. *Problems in higher nervous activity*. Moscow: Academy of Medical Sciences, SSSR, 1949.

Anokhin, P. K. *Internal inhibition as a problem in physiology*. Moscow: Medgiz Press, 1958. (a)

Anokhin, P. K. *Recent data on interaction between the cortex and subcortical brain formations*. Lecture, I. M. Sechenov First Moscow Medical Institute, Oct. 19, 1958. (b)

Anokhin, P. K. The action acceptor as an afferent apparatus of anticipatory spread of excitation in the conditions reflex. Paper presented at a meeting of the Society of Psychologists, Moscow, 1959.

Anokhin, P. K. *A methodologic analysis of some difficult problems concerned with the conditioned reflex*. Moscow: Institute of Philosophy, Academy of Sciences of the USSR, 1962. (a)

Anokhin, P. K. The problem of aims. *Zh Vyssh Nervn Deyat*, 1962, (1). (b)

Bagshaw, M. H., & Pribram, K. H. Cortical organization in gustation (macaca mulatta). *Journal of Neurophysiology*, **16**, 1953.

Barbizet, J. Etudes cliniques sur la mémoire. *Semaine des Hopitaux*, 1963, **20**, 931-950; **21**, 983-995.

Barbizet, J. *Etudes sur la mémoire*. Série I-II. Paris: E'Expansion Scientifique Francaise, 1964, 1966.

Barbizet, J. *Pathologie de la mémoire*. Paris: Presses Univers. de France, 1970.

Bartlett, F. C. *Remembering*. New York: Cambridge University Press, 1932.

Bassin, F. V. Some unsolved problems in the modern theory of localization of functions. *Zh Nevropatol Psikhiatr im S. S. Korsakova*, 1958, **56**(7).

Beganishvili, B. I. *The psychopathology of Korsakov's syndrome*. Tbilisi, 1968.

Bein, E. S. *The psychological analysis of temporal aphasia.* Candidate dissertation, Moscow, 1947.

Bein, E. S. *Aphasia and ways of overcoming it.* Leningrad: Meditsina, 1964.

Bekhterev, V. M. Essentials of the study of brain functions. *Transactions of the Clinic for Mental and Nervous Diseases.* (No. 6), St. Petersburg, 1907.

Bekhterev, V. M. *The general basis of human reflexology.* Leningrad, 1926.

Belyi, B. I. Disturbance of memory in lesions of the hippocampal circle. *Zh Nevropatol Psikhiatr im S. S. Korsakova,* 1966, **16**(6).

Bergson, H. *Matière et mémoire.* Paris: 1896; St. Petersburg, 1911.

Bernard, P. Essai psycho-pathologique sur le compartement dans le syndrome de Korsakoff. *La Raison,* 1951, **2**, 93–101.

Bernbach, H. A. A multiple copy model in perceptual memory. In D. A. Norman (Ed.), *Models of human memory.* New York: Academic Press, 1970.

Bernshtein, N. A. New lines of development in physiology and their correlation with cybernetics. *Vopr Filos,* 1962, (8).

Bjorn, R. A. Repetition and reversal mechanisms in models for short-term memory. In D. A. Norman (Ed.), *Models of human memory.* New York: Academic Press, 1970.

Blinkov, S. M. The temporal region. *Textbook of neuropathology* (Book 2, Vol. 1). Moscow: Medgiz Press, 1957.

Bondareva, L. V. Disturbance of the complex memory. *Proceedings of a Moscow City Conference of Junior Psychologists,* Moscow, 1969. (a).

Bondareva, L. V. The role of the personality in mnemonic activity. *Abstracts of Proceedings of the 4th All-Union Conference of the Society of Psychologists,* Perm, 1969. (b)

Bonhoeffer, K. *Die akuten Gesiteskrankheiten der Gewohnheitstriker Jena.* Fischer, 1901.

Bonhoeffer, K. Der Korsakowsche Symptomenkomplex in seinen Beziehung zu den verschiedenen Krankheitsformen. *Allg Z Psychiatr,* 1904, **61**, 741–752.

Bonin, C. *Some papers on the cerebral cortex.* Springfield, Ill.: Charles C Thomas, 1960.

Brady, J. The paleocortex and the motivation of behavior. In *Mechanisms of the whole brain* (Russian trans.). Moscow: Foreign Literature Press, 1963.

Bratko, A. A. A structural-functional scheme of conceptual memory. *Proceedings of a Conference on Memory Problems,* Pushchino, 1966.

Brion, S. Korsakoff's syndrome: Clinico-anatomical & physiopathological considerations. In G. Talland & N. Waugh (Eds.), *The pathology of memory.* New York: Academic Press, 1969.

Broadbent, D. E. *Perception & communication.* New York: Pergamon Press, 1958.

Broadbent, D. E. Communication models for memory. In G. Talland & N. Waugh (Eds.), *The pathology of memory.* New York: Academic Press, 1969.

Broadbent, D. E. Recent analyses of short-term memory. In K. H. Pribram & D. E. Broadbent (Eds.), *Biology of memory*. New York: Academic Press, 1970.

Brodmann, K. *Vergleichende Lokalisationslehre der Grosshirnrinde in ihren Prinzipien dargestellt auf Grund des Zellenbaues.* Leipzig: Barth, 1909.

Brown, J. A. Some tests on the decay theory of immediate memory. *Quarterly Journal of Experimental Psychology*, 1958, **10**, 12–21.

Brown, J. A. A comparison of recognition and recall by a multiple response method. *Journal of Verbal Learning and Verbal Behavior*, 1965, **4**, 401–402.

Brown, J. The nature of set to learn and of intraserial interference in immediate memory. *Quarterly Journal of Experimental Psychology*, 1954, **6**, 141–148.

Brown, J. S. Generalization and discrimination. In D. Mostofski (Ed.), *Stimulus generalization*. Stanford, Calif.: Stanford University Press, 1965.

Brown, R., & McNeil, D. The slip of the tongue phenomenon. *Journal of Verbal Learning and Verbal Behavior*, 1966, **5**, 325–337.

Bühler, K. Tatsachen und probleme zu einer psychologie der Denkvorgänge. *Archiv fuer die Gesamte Psychologie*, 1907, **9**, 297–365; 1908, **12**, 1–98.

Burešova, O., & Bureš, J. The physiology of direct memory. *Vopr Psikhol*, 1963 (6).

Butenko, A. A., & Sukhanov, S. A. The diagnosis of Korsakov's psychosis. *Zh Nevrol Psikhiatr im S. S. Korsakova*, 1903, (1–3).

Chaltykyan, G. *The neuropsychological investigation of epilepsy.* Candidate dissertation, Erevan, 1968.

Chlenov, L. G. Inactivity as a manifestation of psychological weakness. *Uch Zap MGU*, 1938, (1).

Claparède, E. Recognition et molité. *Archives de Psychologie*, 1911, **11**, 79–90.

Collins, G. H., Victor, M., & Adams, R. D. A neuropathological study of Wernicke's disease and Korsakoff's psychosis. *Journal of Neuropathology and Experimental Neurology*, 1961, **20**, 289–291.

Conrad, K. Zur Psychopathologie des amnestischen Symptomen-Komplexes. *Deutsche Zeitschrift fuer Nervenheilkunde*, 1953, **190**, 471–502.

Conrad, K., & Ule, G. Ein Fall von Korsakow-Psychose mit anatomischem Befund u. klinischen Betrachtungen. *Deutsche Zeitschrift fuer Nervenheilkunde*, 1951, **165**, 430–445.

Conrad, R. Errors in immediate memory. *British Journal of Psychology*, 1959, **50**, 349–359.

Conrad, R. Serial order instructions in immediate memory. *British Journal of Psychology*, 1960, **51**, 45–48.

Conrad, R., & Hille, B. A. The decay theory of immediate memory and paced recall. *Canadian Journal of Psychology*, 1958, **12**, 1–6.

Corkin, S. Tactually-guided maze-learning in man: Effects of unilateral cortical excisions and bilateral hippocampus lesions. *Neuropsychologia*, 1965, **3**, 339–351.

Corkin, S. Acquisition of motor skill after bilateral medial temporal-lobe excision. *Neuropsychologia*, 1968, **16**, 255–266.

Dekhterev, V. V. The pathological anatomy of alcoholic polyneuritis with Korsakov's symptom-complex. *Zh Nevrol Psikhiatr im S. S. Korsakova*, 1912, (5–6).

Delay, J. *Les dissolutions de la mémoire.* Paris: Presses Universitaires de France, 1942. (a)

Delay, J. *Les maladies de la mémoire.* Paris: Presses Universitaires de France, 1942. (b)

Delay, J., & Brion, S. Syndrome de Korsakoff et corps mamillaires. *Encephale*, 1954, **43**, 193–200.

Delay, J., Brion, S., & Ellisade, B. Corps mamillaires et syndrome de Korsakoff. *Presse Médicale*, 1958, **66**, 1849–1854.

Dobrokhotova, T. A. Amnestic disturbances in tumors of the pituitary and infundibulum. *Vopr Neirokhir*, 1963 (1).

Dobrokhotova, T. A. Mnemonic disorders in brain tumors of different localization. *Proceedings of a Conference on Memory Problems*, Pushchino, 1966.

Doty, R. In *Reticular inhibition of the brain.* Moscow: Medgiz Press, 1962.

Ebbinghaus, H. *Über das Gedächtniss.* Leipzig: Duncker, 1885.

Feigenbaum, E. A. Information processing and memory. In D. A. Norman (Ed.), *Models of human memory.* New York: Academic Press, 1970.

Filimonov, I. P. Localization of functions in the cerebral cortex. *Zh Nevropatol Psikhiatr im S. S. Korsakova*, 1940, **9** (1–2).

Filimonov, I. P. The architectonics and localization of functions in the cerebral cortex. *Textbook of Neurology* (Book 2, Vol. 1). Moscow, 1956.

Gamper, E. Zur Frage der Polyencephalitis haemorrahica der chronischen Alkoholiker. *Deutsche Zeitschrift fuer Nervenheilkunde*, 1928, **102**, 122–129.

Gamper, E. Schlaf-Delirium tremens-Korsakowsches Syndrom. *Zeitschrift für Neurologie und Psychiatr*, 1929, **51**, 236–239.

Geier, T. A. Korsakov's psychosis. *Sovremennaya Psikhologiya*, 1911, Jan–Feb.

Gilyarovskii, V. A. The genesis of memory disorder in Korsakov's symptom-complex. *Sovremennaya Psikhologiya*, 1909.

Gilyarovskii, V. A. The genesis of memory disorder in Korsakov's syndrome-complex. *Obozr Psikhiatr, Nevrol Eksp Psikhol*, 1910 (5).

Gilyarovskii, V. A. On memory disorders in some local brain lesions. *Sovremennaya Psikhologiya*, 1912.

Glees, P. Bilateral destruction of the hippocampus (Cornu Ammonis) in a case of dementia. *Monatsschr Psychiatr Neurol*, 1952.

Golant, R. Ya. *Memory disorders.* Leningrad, 1934.

Golant, R. Ya. Data on tumors of the third ventricle and their psychopathological manifestations, In *Scientific Activity of the V. M. Bekhterev Psychoneurological Institute for 1946*, Leningrad, 1947.

Golant, R. Ya. The clinical picture of third ventricle tumors. *Nevropat i Psikhiatr*, 1950, **19**(3).

Gomulicki, R. The development and present status of trace theory of memory. *British Journal of Psychology Monograph*, 1956 (Suppl. 29).

Grashchenkov, N. I., & Luria, A. R. The principle of localization of functional systems in the cerebral cortex. *Nevropat i Psikhiatr*, 1945, **1**.

Greeno, J. G. How associations are memorized. In D. A. Norman (Ed.), *Models of human memory*. New York: Academic Press, 1970.

Gregor, A. Beiträge zur Psychopathologie des Gedächtnisses. *Monatsschr Psychiatr Neurol*, 1909, **25**, 218; 330-386.

Gregor, A., & Römer, H. *Beiträge zur Kennthiss der Gedächtnisstörung bei der Korsakowschen Psychose.* Zeitschrift für Psychiatr und Neurologie, 1907, **53**.

Grünbaum, A. A. Aphasie und Motorik. *Z Gesamte Neurol Pstr*, 1930.

Grünthal, E. Über das Symptom bes Einstellungstörung bei exogenen Psychosen. *Zeitschrift für Neurologie und Psychiatr*, 1924, **92**, 255-266.

Grünthal, E. Über das klinische Bild nach umschriebenem beiderseitigen Ausfall der Ammonshorn-Rinde. *Monatsschr Psychiatr Neurol*, 1939, **117**, 1-16.

Grünthal, E. Über dem derzeitigen Stand der Frage nach den klinischen Erscheinungen bei Ausfall des Ammonshorn. *Psychiatr Neurol*, 1959, **138**, 145-159.

Grünthal, E., & Störring, G. E. Über das Verhalten umschriebener, völliger Merkufähigkeit. *Monatsschr Psychiatr Neurol*, 1930, **74**, 754-769.

Gudden, H. Klinische und anatomische Beiträge zur Kenntniss der multiplen Alkoholneuritis. *Archiv fuer Psychiatrie und Nervenkrankheiten*, 1966, **28**, 643-744.

Hécaen, H. Clinico-anatomical and neurolinguistic aspects of aphasia. In G. Talland & N. Waugh (Eds.), *The pathology of memory*. New York: Academic Press, 1969.

Hering, K. *Memory as a general function of organic matter.* St. Petersburg, 1877.

Hubel, D. H., & Weisel, T. N. Receptive fields of cells in striate cortex of very unexperienced kittens. *Journal of Neurophysiology*, 1963, **26**.

Ionesescu, V. The problem of temporal epilepsy. *Zh Nevropatol Psikhiatr im S. S. Korsakova*, 1960, **60**(11).

Jacobsen, C. F. A study of cerebral functions in learning. The frontal lobes. *Journal of Comparative Neurology*, 1931, **52**.

Jacobsen, C. F. Function of frontal association area in primates. *Archives of Neurology and Psychiatry*, 1935, **33**.

Jasper, H. H. Functional properties of the thalamic reticular system. In *Brain mechanisms and consciousness.* Oxford, 1954.

Jasper, H. H. Recent advances in our understanding of ascending activities of the reticular system. In H. H. Jasper (Ed.), *Reticular formation of the brain.* London, Churchill, 1957.

Kandel, E. R. Cellular studies of learning. In F. O. Schmitt (Ed.), *The neurosciences.* New York: Rockefeller University Press, 1967.

Kandel, E. R., & Spencer, W. A. Electrophysiological properties of an archicortical neuron in mamillary bodies. *Annals of the New York Academy of Sciences*, 1961, 94-570.

Katarinova, I. V. *Korsakov's syndrome in organic brain diseases.* Candidate dissertation, Kishinev, 1956.

Khomskaya, E. D. Integration in various systems in mentally backward children. *Dok Akad Pedagog Nauk RSFSR*, 1959, 1(5); 1960, 2(1).

Khomskaya, E. D., & Sorkina, E. G. Dynamics of visual perception disturbances in lesions of the parieto-occipital zones of the brain. *Dok Akad Pedagog Nauk RSFSR*, 1960, 2(6).

Khomskaya, E. D. *The brain and activation.* Moscow: Moscow University Press, 1973.

Kimura, D. Right temporal-lobe damage. *Archives of Neurology*, 1963, 8, 264-276.

Kintsch, W. *Learning, memory and conceptual processes.* New York: Wiley, 1970. (a)

Kintsch, W. Models for free recall and recognition. In D. A. Norman (Ed.), *Models of human memory.* New York: Academic Press, 1970. (b)

Kiyashchenko, N. K. *The structure of memory disturbances in local brain lesions.* Dissertation for the Degree of Candidate of Medical Sciences, Moscow University, Moscow, 1969.

Klimkovskii, M. *Disturbances of audioverbal memory in lesions of the left temporal lobe.* Dissertation for the Degree of Candidate of Medical Sciences, Moscow University, Moscow, 1965.

Klimkovskii, M. *Disturbances of audioverbal memory in temporal lobe lesions.* Dissertation for the Degree of Medical Sciences, Moscow, 1966.

Kohnstamm, O. Über das Krankheitsbild der retro- und anterograden Amnesie und die Unterscheidung des spontanen und des lernenden Merkens. *Zeitschrift für Neurologie und Psychiatr*, 1917, **41**.

Konorski, J. Distribution of inhibitary conditioned reflexes after lesion in dogs. In *Brain mechanisms of learning.* Oxford, 1961.

Konorski, J, A new method of physiological investigation of recent memory in animals. *Bulletin de l'Academie Polonaise des Sciences*, 1969, 7, 115-117.

Konorski, J., & Lawicka, W. Analysis of errors by prefrontal animals in the delayed response test. In J. W. Warren & K. Akert (Eds.), *The frontal granular cortex and behavior.* New York: McGraw-Hill, 1964.

Korsakov, S. S. *Alcoholic paralysis.* Dissertation, Moscow, 1887. (a)

Korsakov, S. S. Disorder of mental activity in alcoholic paralysis and its relation to the disorder of the mental sphere in polyneurites of nonalcoholic origin. *Vestn klin i sud psikhiatr i nevrol*, 1887, **2**, 1-10. (b)

Korsakov, S. S. Etude médico-psychologique sur une forme des maladies de mémoire. *Revue Philosophique*, 1889, **28**, 501-530. (a)

Korsakov, S. S. Mental disorder combined with multiple neuritis. *Med obozrenie*, 1889, **32**(13), 3-13. (b)

Korsakov, S. S. Über eine besondere Form psychischen Störungen, combiniert mit multiplen Neuritis. *Archiv fuer Psychiatrie*, 1889, **21**, 669-704. (c)

Korsakov, S. S. Eine psychische Störung combiniert mit multiplen Neuritis. *Allg Z Psychiatr*, 1890, **46**, 475-485. (a)

Korsakov, S. S. *Pathological disorders of memory and their diagnosis.* Moscow, 1890. (b)

Korsakov, S. S. Erinnerungstäuschungen (Pseudoreminiscenzen) bei polyneuritischer Psychose. *Allg Z Psychiatr*, 1892, **47**, 390-410.

Korsakov, S. S. *Selected works.* Moscow: Medgiz Press, 1954.

Korsakov, S. S., & Serbskii, V. A. A case of polyneuritic psychosis with autopsy. In *Collected articles on neuropathology and psychiatry dedicated to Professor A. Ya. Kozhevnikov*, Moscow, 1890.

Kovalev, V. V. *The clinical picture and neurodynamics of Korsakov's Syndrome.* Candidate dissertation, Moscow, 1956.

Kraepelin, E. Über die Merkhfähigkeit. *Monatsschr Psychiatr Neurol*, 1900, **8**, 245-250.

Krasil'shchikova, D. I. Reminiscence in recall. *Uch Zap Leningr Gos Pedagog Inst im A. I. Gertsena*, 1940, **34**.

Krasil'shchikova, D. I. Correlation between memorizing and recall. *Vopr Psikhol*, 1955, (3).

Krol', M. B. *Neuropathological syndromes.* Khar'kov—Kiev, 1933.

Kubie, L. S. The preconscious factors in the process of remembering. In G. Talland & N. Waugh (Eds.), *The pathology of memory*. New York: Academic Press, 1969.

Lashley, K. S. Functional determination of cerebral localization. *Arch Neurol Psychiatr*, 1937, **38**.

Latash, L. P. *The hypothalamus and adaptive EEG activity.* Moscow, 1968.

Latash, L. P., & Popova, L. T. Investigation of short-term memory by Konorski's method in some forms of amnesia. *Proceedings of a Conference on Memory Problems*, Pushchino, 1966.

Leont'ev, A. N. *The development of memory: An experimental investigation of higher psychological functions.* Moscow: Press of the Akad Kommunist Vospit im N. K. Krupskoi, 1930.

Leont'ev, A. N. *Problems in development of the mind.* Moscow: Press of the Akad Ped Nauk RSFSR, 1959.

Leont'ev, A. N. On the social nature of human mental activity. *Vopr Filos*, 1961, (1).

Lindsley, O. B. Higher functions of the nervous system. *Annual Rev of Physiol*, 1955, **17**, 311-338.

Lindsley, O. B. Attention, conscious, sleep and wakefulness. In J. Field (Ed.), *Handbook of physiology.* (Sect. neurophysiol. III, 1553-1593). Washington, Thomas, 1960.

Lobova, L. P., Bragina, N. N., & Dobrokhotova, T. A. Disturbances of memory in tumors of the mediobasal zone of the temporal lobes. *Proceedings of a Conference on Memory Problems*, Pushchino, 1966.

Luk, A. N. Elementary memory disturbances. *Proceedings of a Conference on Memory Problems*, Pushchino, 1966.

Lunev, B. K., Maksukov, G. A., & Nikolaeva, N. F. The disturbance of memory in a disorder of the cerebral circulation in the vertebral-basilar artery. *Zh Nevropatol Psikhiatr im S. S. Korsakov*, 1964, **5**(5).

Lur'e, Z. L., Bein, E. S., & Nikolaeva, N. N. *The amnestic syndrome in a disturbance of the cerebral circulation in the system of the posterior cerebral artery.* Lecture, Society of Neuropathologists and Psychiatrists, Moscow, 1963.

Luria, A. R. *A study of aphasia in the light of brain pathology: Temporal (acoustic) aphasia* (Vol. I), doctoral dissertation, Kiev; *Parietal (semantic) aphasia* (Vol. II). Unpublished investigation, 1940.

Luria, A. R. *Traumatic aphasia.* Moscow: Press of the Akad Ped Nauk RSFSR, 1947.

Luria, A. R. (Ed.). *Problems in the higher nervous activity of the normal and abnormal child* (Vols. I-II). Moscow: Press of the Akad Ped Nauk RSFSR, 1956, 1958.

Luria, A. R. Two types of analytico-synthetic activity of the cerebral cortex. *Trudy Odess Gos Univ*, 1957, **147**.

Luria, A. R. *The mentally backward child.* Moscow: Press of the Akad Ped Nauk RSFSR, 1960.

Luria, A. R. *The role of speech in regulation of normal and abnormal behavior.* London: Pergamon Press, 1961.

Luria, A. R. *Higher cortical functions in man.* Moscow: Moscow University Press, 1962 (1st ed.); 1969 (2nd ed.).

Luria, A. R. *The human brain and psychological processes.* Moscow: Press of the Akad Ped Nauk RSFSR, 1963 (Vol. I); Pedagogika Press, 1970 (Vol. II).

Luria, A. R. The basic forms of memory disturbance in local brain lesions. *Proceedings of a Conference on Memory Problems*, Pushchino, 1966. (a)

Luria, A. R. *Higher cortical functions in man.* New York: Basic Books, 1966. (b)

Luria, A. R. *Human brain and physiological processes.* New York: Harper & Row, 1966. (c)

Luria, A. R. *Traumatic aphasia.* Hague: Mounton, 1970.

Luria, A. R. Memory disturbances in local brain lesions. *Neuropsychologia*, 1971, **9**, 267–375.

Luria, A. R. *Fundamentals of neuropsychology.* Moscow: MGU Press, 1973.

Luria, A. R. *The working brain.* Penguin Psychol. Series, 1973.

Luria, A. R., & Artem'eva, E. Yu. Two ways of ensuring reliability of a psychological investigation. *Vopr Psikhol*, 1970, (3), 105–112.

Luria, A. R., & Karaseva, T. A. Disturbances of auditory-speech memory in focal lesions of the deep regions of the left temporal lobe. *Neuropsychologia*, 1968, **6**, 97–107.

Luria, A. R., & Khomskaya, E. D. (Eds.). *The frontal lobes and regulation of psychological processes.* Moscow: MGU Press, 1966.

Luria, A. R., Khomskaya, E. G., Blinkov, S. M., & Critchley, M. Impairment of selectivity of mental processes in association with lesions of the frontal lobe. *Neuropsychologia*, 1967, **5**.

Luria, A. R., Konovalov, A. N., & Podgornaya, A. Ya. *Disorders of memory in patients with aneurysms of the anterior communicating artery.* Moscow: Moscow University Press, 1970.

Luria, A. R., Podgornaya, A. Ya., & Konovalov, A. N. *Memory disturbances in the clinical picture of aneurysm of the anterior communicating artery.* Moscow: MGU Press, 1969.

Luria, A. R., & Rapoport, M. Yu. Regional symptoms of higher cortical disturbance in intracerebral tumors of the left temporal lobe. *Vopr Neirokhir*, 1962, **67**(5).

Luria, A. R., Sokolov, E. N., & Klimkovskii, M. On some neurodynamic mechanisms of memory. *Zh Vyssh Nerv Deyat im I. P. Pavlova*, 1967, **17**(2). (a)

Luria, A. R., Sokolov, E. N., & Klimkovskii, M. Towards a neurodynamic analysis of memory disturbances with lesions of the left temporal lobe. *Neuropsychologia*, 1967, **5**. (b)

Luria, A. R., & Svetkova, L. S. *The neuropsychological analysis of problem solving.* Moscow: Prosveshchenie, 1966.

Luria, A. R., & Vinogradova, O. S. An objective investigation of the dynamics of semantic systems. *British Journal of Psychology*, 1959, **50**, 89–105.

Magoun, H. W. The ascending reticular activating system. *Res Publ, Assoc Res Nerv Ment Dis*, 1952, **30**.

Magoun, H. W. *The waking brain.* Springfield, Ill.: Charles C Thomas, 1958, 1963.

Malmo, R. B. Interference factors in delayed response in monkeys after removal of the frontal lobes. *Journal of Neurophysiology*, 1942, **5**.

Marston, A. R. Response strength and self-reinforcement. *Journal of Experimental Psychology*, 1964.

Marushevskii, M. Disturbance of the simplest forms of voluntary action in local lesions of the frontal lobes. In A. R. Luria & E. D. Khomskaya (Eds.), *The frontal lobes and regulation of psychological processes.* Moscow, MGU Press, 1966.

Marzaganova, M. A. *Disorders of memory in vascular diseases of the brain in old age.* Dissertation for the Degree of Candidate of Medical Sciences, Moscow, 1971.

Melton, A. W. Implication of short term memory for a general theory of memory. *Journal of Verbal Learning and Verbal Behavior*, 1963, **2**, 1–21.

Melton, A. W. Short term and long term post-perceptual memory. In K. H. Pribram & D. E. Broadbent (Eds.), *Biology of memory*. New York: Academic Press, 1970.

Melton, A. W., & Irwin, I. M. The influence of degree of interpolated learning on retroactive inhibition. *American Journal of Psychology*, 1940, **53**, 175–203.

Melton, A. W., & Lackum, W. J. Retroactive and proactive inhibition in extension. *American Journal of Psychology*, 1941, **54**, 157–171.

Miller, G. The organization of lexical memory. In G. Talland & N. Waugh (Eds.), *The pathology of memory*. New York: Academic Press, 1969.

Milner, B. Psychological defects produced by temporal-lobe excision. *Res Publ, Assoc Res Nerv Ment Dis*, 1958, **36**, 244–257.

Milner, B. Les troubles de la mémoire accompagnant des lesions hippocampiques bilaterales. In *Physiologie de hippocampe*. Paris: 1965.

Milner, B. Amnesia following operations on the temporal lobes. In C. W. M. Witty & O. L. Zangwill (Eds.), *Amnesia*. London: Butterworth, 1966.

Milner, B. Brain mechanisms suggested by studies of temporal lobes. In E. L. Darley (Ed.), *Brain mechanisms underlying speech and language*. New York: Grune & Stratton, 1967.

Milner, B. Visual recognition after right temporal lobe excision in man. *Neuropsychologia*, 1968, **6**, 191–210.

Milner, B. Residual intellectual and memory deficits after head injury. In A. E. Walker et al. (Eds.), *The late effects of head injury*. Springfield, Ill.: Charles C Thomas, 1969.

Milner, B. Memory and mesial temporal regions of the brain. In K. H. Pribram & D. E. Broadbent (Eds.), *Biology of memory*. New York: Academic Press, 1970.

Milner, B., Corkin, S., & Teuber, H. L. Further analysis of the hippocampal amnestic syndrome. *Neurophysiologia*, 1968, **6**, 267–282.

Milner, B., & Teuber, H. L. Alternation of perception and memory in man. In L. Weiskrantz (Ed.), *Analysis of behavioural change*. New York: Harper & Row, 1968.

Mishkin, M., & Pribram, K. H. Analysis of the effect of frontal lesions in monkeys. I-II. *Journal of Comparative Physiology and Psychiatry*, 1955-1956, **48, 49**.

Mishkin, M., & Weiskrantz, L. Effects of delaying rewards on visual discrimination performances in monkey with frontal lesions. *Journal of Comparative Physiology and Psychiatry*, 1958, **51**.

Morton, J. A functional model for memory. In D. A. Norman (Ed.), *Models of human memory*. New York: Academic Press, 1970.

Moruzzi, G., & Magoun, H. W. Brain stem reticular formation and activating of the EEG. Electroenceph. clin. *Neurophysiologia*, 1949, **1**, 455–473.

Müller, G. E. Zur Analyse der Gedächtnisstätigkeit und der Vorstellungsverlaufs. *Z Psychol Ergbd S*, 1913.

Müller, G. E., & Pilzecker, A. Experimentelle Beiträge zur Untersuchung des Gedächtnisses. *Z Psychol*, 1900, **6**, 81–190, 257–339.

Murdock, B. B. Proactive inhibition in short-term memory. *Journal of Experimental Psychology*, 1964, **68**, 184–189.

Murdock, B. B. Recent developments in short-term memory. *British Journal of Psychology*, 1967, **58**, 421–433.

Murdock, B. B. Interpolated recall in short-term memory. *Journal of Experimental Psychology*, 1969, **6**, 526–532.

Murdock, B. B. Short-term memory for association. In D. A. Norman (Ed.), *Models of human memory*. New York: Academic Press, 1970.

Murdock, B. B. Short- and long-term memory for association. In K. H. Pribram & D. E. Broadbent (Eds.), *Biology of memory*. New York: Academic Press, 1970.

Nauta, W. Some connections of the limbic system. In *Mechanisms of the whole brain*. Moscow: Foreign Literature Press, 1963.

Norman, D. A. *Memory and attention*. New York: Wiley, 1969.

Norman, D. A. (Ed.). *Models of human memory*. New York: Academic Press, 1970.

Norman, D. A., & Rumelhart, O. E. A system for perception and memory. In D. A. Norman (Ed.), *Models of human memory*. New York: Academic Press, 1970.

Norman, D. A., & Wickelgren, W. A. Short-term recognition memory for style digits and pairs of digits. *Journal of Experimental Psychology*, 1965, **70**, 479–489.

Nutzubidza, N. A. The role of the hippocampus in higher nervous activity. *Zh Vyssh Nerv Deyat im I. P. Pavlova*, 1964, **14**(1).

Ojeman, R. G. Correlation between specific human brain disease and memory changes. *Neurosciences Research Program*, 1964, Bull. No. 2.

Ombrédane, A. *L'aphasie et'elaboration de la pensée explicite*. Paris: Presses Universitaires de France, 1951.

Pavlov, I. P., *Twenty years experience in the objective study of higher nervous activity (behavior) of animals*. Moscow–Leningrad: Gosizdat, 1938.

Penfield, W., & Jasper, H. *Epilepsy and the functional anatomy of the human brain* (Russian trans.). Moscow: Medgiz, 1958.

Penfield, W., & Milner, B. Memory deficit produced by bilateral lesions of hippocampal zone. *Archives of Neurology and Psychiatry*, 1958, **74**.

Petersen, L. P., & Petersen, D. Short-term retention of individual items. *Journal of Experimental Psychology*, 1962, **58**, 193–198.

Pham Minh Hac. *Types of memory disturbances in lesions of the lateral zones of the left cerebral hemisphere*. Dissertation for the Degree of Candidate of Medical Sciences, Moscow, 1971.

Pick, A. *Die agrammatische Sprachstörungen*. Berlin: Springer, 1913.

Popova, L. T. *Disturbances of mnemic processes in the clinical picture of some local brain lesions*. Candidate dissertation, Moscow, 1964.

Popova, L. T. *Memory and its disturbance in local brain lesions*. Moscow: Meditsina, 1972.

Popova, L. T. *Memory disturbance in local brain lesions.* Moscow: Medgiz, 1973.

Popova, L. T. & Latash, L. P. Role of rhinencephalo-diencephalic structures of the human brain in memory processes on the basis of the results of neuropsychological and clinical-physiological investigation. *Proceedings of a Conference on Memory Problems,* Pushchino, 1966.

Postman, L. Extra-experimental interference and the retention of words. *Journal of Experimental Psychology,* 1961, **61**, 97–110.

Postman, L. Short-term memory and incidental learning. In A. W. Melton (Ed.), *Categories of human learning.* New York: Academic Press, 1964.

Postman, L. Unlearning under conditions of successive interpolation. *Journal of Experimental Psychology,* 1965, **70**.

Postman, L. Mechanisms of interfering in forgetting. In G. Talland & N. Waugh (Eds.), *The pathology of memory.* New York: Academic Press, 1969.

Pozner, M. I. Representational systems for storing information in memory. In G. Talland & N. Waugh (Eds.), *The pathology of memory.* New York: Academic Press, 1969.

Pribram, K. H. Towards a science of neuropsychology. In R. A. Patton (Ed.), *Current trends in psychology and the biological sciences.* Pittsburgh University Press, 1954.

Pribram, K. H. Comparative neurology and evolution of behavior. In *Behavior and evolution.* New Haven: Yale University Press, 1958.

Pribram, K. H. A further analysis of the behavior deficit that follows injury to the primate frontal cortex. *Journal of Experimental Neurology,* 1961, **3**. (a)

Pribram, K. H. A theory of physiological psychology. *Vopr Psikhol,* 1961, (2). (b)

Pribram, K. H. The new neurology: Memory, novelty, thought and change. In G. H. Glaser (Ed.), *EEG and behavior.* New York: Basic Books, 1963.

Pribram, K. H. The amnestic syndromes. Disturbances in coding. In G. Talland & N. Waugh (Eds.), *The pathology of memory.* New York: Academic Press, 1969. (a)

Pribram, K. H. The neurobiology of remembering. *Scientific American,* 1969, **220**, 73–88. (b)

Pribram, K. H., & Broadbent, D. E. (Eds.). *Biology of memory.* New York: Academic Press, 1970.

Pribram, K. H., & Weiskrantz, L. A. A comparison of the effect of medial and lateral cerebral resections on conditioned avoidance behavior or monkeys. *Journal of Comparative Physiology and Psychology,* 1957, **50**.

Prisco, L. Short-term memory in focal cerebral damage. 1963 [cit. by B. Milner, 1970].

Ramon-y-Cajal, S. *Histologie du système nerveux de l'homme et des vĕrtebrés.* Madrid: Institut Ramon-y-Cajal, 1909-1911.

Ranschburg, P. *Das kranke Gedächtniss.* Leipzig: Barth, 1911.

Razran, G. Semantic, syntactic and phonophonetographic generalization of verbal conditioning. *Journal of Experimental Psychology,* 1949, **39**, 642–652. (a)

Razran, G. Stimulus generalization of conditioned responses. *Psychological Bulletin*, 1949, **46**, 377–385. (b)

Reitman, W. What does it take to remember? In D. A. Norman (Ed.), *Models of human memory*. New York: Academic Press, 1970.

Ribeau, T. *Memory in its normal and pathological state*. St. Petersburg: 1912.

Riess, B. F. Semantic conditioning involving the galvanic skin reflex. *Journal of Experimental Psychology*, 1940, **26**, 238–240.

Rozhdestvenskaya, M. V. The psychopathological symptoms of tumors of the third ventricle. In *Problems in mental disorders in tumors of the third ventricle*. Ordzhonikidze: 1960.

Rubinshtein, S. L. *Being and consciousness*. Moscow: Press of the Akad Nauk SSSR, 1957.

Scoville, W. B. The limbic system in man. *Journal of Neurosurgery*, 1954, II.

Scoville, B., & Milner, B. Loss of recent memory after bilateral hippocampal lesions. *Journal of Neurology, Neurosurgery and Psychiatry*, 1957, **20**, 11–21.

Sechenov, I. M. *Selected works* (Vol. 1). Moscow: 1952.

Sereiskii, M. Ya. Korsakov's psychosis in the light of modern clinical medicine. In *Fifty years of the S. S. Korsakov Psychiatric Clinic*. Moscow: Press of the Akad Med Nauk SSSR, 1940.

Shiffrin, E. M. Memory search. In D. A. Norman (Ed.), *Models of human memory*. New York: Academic Press, 1970.

Shmar'yan, A. S. *Brain pathology and psychiatry*. Moscow: Medgiz, 1949. (a)

Shmar'yan, A. S. General principles of brain stem pathology. *Transactions of the Central Institute of Psychiatry* (Vol. 4). Moscow, 1949. (b)

Shumilina, N. I. The functional role of the frontal regions of the brain in conditioned-reflex activity of dogs. In A. R. Luria & E. D. Khomskaya (Eds.), *The frontal lobes and regulation of psychological processes*. Moscow: MGU Press, 1966.

Smirnov, A. A. Intellectual processes during memorizing. *Izv Akad Pedagog Nauk RSFSR*, 1945, (1).

Smirnov, A. A. *The psychology of memorizing*, Moscow–Leningrad: Press of the Akad Ped Nauk RSFSR, 1948.

Smirnov, A. A. *Problems in the psychology of memory*. Moscow: Prosvescheniya, 1966.

Sokolov, E. N. A nervous model of the stimulus and the orienting reflex. *Vopr Psikhol*, 1966, (4).

Sokolov, E. N. *Mechanisms of memory*. Moscow: MGU Press, 1969.

Solov'ev, I. M. *The psychology of investigative activity of normal and abnormal children*. Moscow: Press of the Akad Ped Nauk RSFSR, 1959.

Sperling, G. The information available in brief visual presentation. *Psychological Monographs*, 1960, No. 498.

Sperling, W. A model for visual memory tasks. *Human Factors*, 1963, **5**, 19–30.

Sperling, W. Phonemic model for short-term auditory memory. *Proceedings of the American Psychological Association*, 1968, **4**, 68-69.

Sperling, W., & Speelman, R. Acoustic similarity and auditory short-term memory: Experiments and a model. In D. A. Norman (Ed.), *Models of human memory*. New York: Academic Press, 1970.

Sukhanov, S. A. Korsakov's psychosis. In *Semiotics and diagnosis of mental diseases*, Moscow, 1905.

Talland, G. A. Psychological studies of Korsakov's psychosis. *Journal of Nervous and Mental Disease*, 1958, **127**, 197-219; 1959, **128**, 214-226.

Talland, G. A. *Deranged memory*. New York: Academic Press, 1965.

Talland, G., & Waugh, N. (Eds.). *The pathology of memory*. New York: Academic Press, 1969.

Tsao Ping. *Integration of systems of connections as a method of studying the neurodynamics of normal and abnormal children*. Candidate dissertation, Moscow, 1960.

Tsvetkova, L. S. *Retraining of patients with local brain lesions.* Moscow: Pedagogika, 1972.

Tulving, E. Short- and long-term memory: Different retrieval mechanisms. In K. H. Pribram & D. E. Broadbent (Eds.), *Biology of memory*. New York: Academic Press, 1970.

Ule, G. Pathologisch-anatomische Befunde bei Korsakov-Psychosen und ihre Bedeutung für die Lokalisationslehre in der Psychiatrie. *Aerztl Wochenschr*, 1958, **13**, 6-13.

Underwood, J. B. The effect of successive interpolations on retroactive and proactive inhibition. *Psychological Monographs*, 1945, **59** (No. 3).

Underwood, J. B. Interference and forgetting. *Psychological Review*, 1957, **64**, 49-60.

Underwood, J. B., & Postman, L. Extra-experimental sources of interference in forgetting. *Psychological Review*, 1960, **67**, 73-95.

Uznadze, D. N. Experimental basis of the psychology of set. In *Experimental investigations in the psychology of set*. Tbilisi: 1958.

Uznadze, D. N. *The experimental basis of the psychology of set.* Tbilisi: 1961.

Uznadze, D. N. *Experimental psychological investigations.* Moscow: Nauka, 1966.

Van der Horst, L. Über die Psychologie des Korsakowsyndrom. *Monatschs. Psychiat. Neurol.*, 1932, **83**, 65-84.

Vardanya, L. S. The visual element in retroactive inhibition. *Proceedings of the 18th International Psychological Congress*, Moscow, 1966.

Victor, M., & Adams, R. D. The effect of alcohol on the nervous system. *Proceedings of the Association for Research in Nervous and Mental Disease*, 1953, **32**, 526-573.

Victor, M., Talland, G., & Adams, R. D. Psychological studies in Korsakoff's psychosis. *Journal of Nervous and Mental Disease*, 1959, **128**, 528-537.

Victor, M., & Yakovlev, P. I. S. S. Korsakoff's psychic disorder. *Neurology*, 1955, **5**, 394–407.

Vinogradova, O. S. A dynamic classification of responses of hippocampal neurons to sensory stimuli. *Zh Vyssh Nervn Deyat*, 1965, **15**.

Vinogradova, O. S. Neuronal correlations of orienting reflex extinction in various brain structures. *Vopr Psikhol*, 1969, No. 1.

Vinogradova, O. S. The hippocampus and orienting reflex. In *Neuronal mechanisms of the orienting reflex*. Moscow: MGU Press, 1970. (a)

Vinogradova, O. S. Registration of information and the limbic system. In G. Horn & R. A. Hinde (Eds.), *Short-term changes in neural activity and behavior*. New York: Cambridge University Press, 1970. (b)

Vinogradova, O. S., Semyonova, T. P., & Konovalov, V. Ph. Trace phenomena in single neuron of hippocampus and mamillar bodies. In K. H. Pribram & D. E. Broadbent (Eds.), *Biology of memory*. New York: Academic Press, 1970.

Vygotskii, L. S. *Selected psychological investigations*. Moscow: Press of the Akad Ped Nauk RSFSR, 1956.

Vygotskii, L. S. *The development of higher psychological functions*. Moscow: Press of the Akad Ped Nauk RSFSR, 1960.

Warrington, E., & James, M. Disorders of visual perception in patients with localized brain lesions. *Neuropsychologia*, 1967, **5**.

Warrington, E. K., & Weiskrantz, L. A study of learning and retention in amnestic patients. *Neuropsychologia*, 1968, **6**, 783.

Waugh, N. C. Serial position and memory span. *American Journal of Psychology*, 1960, **73**, 65–79.

Waugh, N. C. Primary and secondary memory in short-term retention. In K. H. Pribram & D. E. Broadbent (Eds.), *Biology of memory*. New York: Academic Press, 1970.

Waugh, N. C., & Norman, D. A. Primary memory. *Psychological Review*, 1965, **72**, 89–104.

Waugh, N. C., & Norman, D. A. The measure of interference in primary memory. *Journal of Verbal Learning and Verbal Behavior*, 1968, **5**.

Weiskrantz, L. Behavior changes associated with ablation of amygdaloid complex in monkeys. *Journal of Comparative Physiology and Psychology*, 1956, **49**.

Weiskrantz, L. Impaired learning and retention following experimental temporal lobe lesions. In M. Brazier (Ed.), *RNA and brain function*. Berkeley: University of California Press, 1964.

Weiskrantz, L. Experimental studies in amnesia. In C. W. M. Witty & O. L. Zangwill (Eds.), *Amnesia*. London: Butterworth, 1966.

Weiskrantz, L. (Ed.). *Analysis of behavioral change*. New York: Harper & Row, 1968.

Wickelgren, W. A. Multitrace strength theory. In D. A. Norman (Ed.), *Models of human memory*. New York: Academic Press, 1970.

Williams, M., & Pennybecker, I. Memory disturbances in third ventricle tumors. *Journals of Neurology, Neurosurgery and Psychiatry*, 1954, **17**, 115-124.

Williams, M., & Smith, H. Mental disturbances in tuberculous meningitis. *Journal of Neurology, Neurosurgery and Psychiatry*, 1954, **17**.

Williams, M., & Zangwill, O. L. Disorders of temporal judgment in amnestic states. *Journal of Mental Soc.*, 1950, **94**, 484-493.

Witty, C. W. M., & Zangwill, O. L. (Eds.). *Amnesia.* London: Butterworth, 1966.

Woodworth, P. *Experimental psychology* (Russian trans.), Moscow: Foreign Literature Press, 1950.

Zalmonson, A. N., & Erdman, Yu. N. The structure of Korsakov's syndrome. In *Transactions of the Psychiatric Clinic, Moscow State University* (No. 5), 1934.

Zangwill, O. L. Neuropsychological models of memory. In G. Talland & N. Waugh (Eds.), *The pathology of memory*. New York: Academic Press, 1969.

Zankov, L. V. *Memory of the schoolchild.* Moscow: Uchpedgiz, 1944.

Zankov, L. V. *Memory.* Moscow: Uchpedgiz, 1949.

Zinchenko, P. I. Problems in the psychology of memory. In *Psychological science in the USSR* (Vol. 1). Moscow: Press of the Akad Ped Nauk RSFSR, 1959.

Zinchenko, P. I. *Involuntary memorizing.* Moscow: Press of the Akad Ped Nauk RSFSR, 1961.

Zinov'ev, P. M. The structure of the clinical picture of some forms of Korsakov's psychosis. In *Transactions of the Psychiatric Clinic of Moscow State University* (No. 5), 1934.

AUTHOR INDEX

364

INDEX OF
PATIENT CASE HISTORIES

TABLES AND ILLUSTRATIONS

Note:—Tables 6–10, 13, 14, 16–18, 21–24, 27, and 28 adapted from N. K. Kiyashchenko. Tables 11, 12, 19, 25, and 26 adapted from Pham Minh Hac. Table 20 adapted from M. K. Klimkovskii.